The
Economic History
of India, 1857–2010

The Economic History of India, 1857–2010

Fourth Edition

Tirthankar Roy

OXFORD
UNIVERSITY PRESS

OXFORD
UNIVERSITY PRESS

Oxford University Press is a department of the University of Oxford.
It furthers the University's objective of excellence in research, scholarship,
and education by publishing worldwide. Oxford is a registered trademark of
Oxford University Press in the UK and in certain other countries.

Published in India by
Oxford University Press
22 Workspace, 2nd Floor, 1/22 Asaf Ali Road, New Delhi 110 002, India

©Oxford University Press 2020

The moral rights of the author have been asserted.

First Edition published in 2000
Second Edition published in 2006
Third Edition published in 2011
Fourth Edition published in 2020
Fifth impression 2024

ISBN-13 (print edition): 978-0-19-012829-6
ISBN-10 (print edition): 0-19-012829-1

ISBN-13 (eBook): 978-0-19-099203-3
ISBN-10 (eBook): 0-19-099203-4

Typeset in Arno Pro 11.5/13.5
by The Graphics Solution, New Delhi 110 092
Printed in India at Nutech Print Services - India

To
Sharmila and Kalyan Majumdar

Contents

Preface to the Fourth Edition   ix

List of Tables, Figures, and Maps   xi

List of Abbreviations   xvii

Exchange Rate, 1800–1947   xix

1. Introduction: What Are the Questions?   1

2. Transition to Colonialism: 1707–1857   17

3. The Pattern of Economic Growth: 1857–1947   66

4. Agriculture   99

5. Small-Scale Industry   139

6. Large-Scale Industry   161

7. Plantations, Mines, Banking   189

8. Infrastructure   212

9. How the Government Worked   241

10. Population   258

11. The Economy and the Environment   277

12. **The Princely States**   301

13. **Indian Economy after Independence**   317

14. **Conclusion**   343

Primary Sources   346

Further Readings   350

Index   365

Preface to the Fourth Edition

The previous edition of this textbook was published almost 10 years ago. The preface to that edition said that one of the benefits of a detailed regional history was that it could inform debates and discourses on world history. The big debate in world history in recent times was the debate about the emergence of world inequality, answering the question why some countries grew rich and others stayed poor since modern economic growth began in the early nineteenth century. There is a risk involved in conducting such debates at a high level of aggregation. The risk is homogenization, wherein one country gets identified with one experience defined artificially as the opposite of another country's experience. No matter how elegant the explanatory models are, that procedure should lead to a wrong explanation of the history of most world regions, and therefore, of world inequality. In the years since the previous edition appeared, I have grown ever more convinced of the need to underline that message.

That need motivated, partly, this revision. Chapters 1 and 3 go further than before to make the general argument that economic change in colonial India was a composite of different experiences, and the task for an economic history of India is to show, not why India fell behind the world due to the actions of external and internal factors but why the same factors could generate differences within India. Chapter 13 shows how these lessons from history help us understand the present times better, when again economic growth has caused divergence and inequality within India.

Beyond sharpening the focus of the study, the revision has covered new research and scholarship, new thinking on old topics, and new questions asked recently. It has added a fresh chapter on the princely states and an almost new chapter on the environment. The years between the previous two editions of the book (2006–11) were far more dormant by comparison with 2011–18, when many studies on India appeared. The outburst is mainly due to a revival of interest in India in the economics schools of the world, matched by the response from journal editors and book publishers. The revision incorporates these developments in an area that seems to be waking up from a long sleep. The facility to cite many contemporary works made the book much shorter than the previous edition.

Tirthankar Roy
London

Tables, Figures, and Maps

TABLES

1.1 Major provinces in 1881, with approximate dates of
    annexation   4
1.2 Growth rates of real national income   5
1.3 Agriculture and non-agriculture: Shares in income
    and employment (percentage)   7

3.1 Regimes of growth and stagnation (per cent change
    between two years)   68
3.2 Further data on regimes of growth and stagnation
    (per cent change between two years)   69
3.3 Sector-shares in national income (percentage)   71
3.4 Sector-shares in workforce (percentage)   71
3.5 Women in industrial work 1901–31 (colonial India)
    and 1961–91 (Indian Union)   73
3.6 Labour force and occupational structure, the Indian
    Union, 1881–1951   74
3.7 Agricultural growth 1865–1940 (1865=100)   75
3.8 Terms of trade   76
3.9 Composition of trade, 1850–1935 (percentages of
    total export or total import)   79
3.10 Direction of foreign trade, 1850–1940 (percentages
    of total export or import)   80
3.11 Real wages   82

3.12 Food availability   83
3.13 Net investment in agriculture and private
      non-agriculture   86
3.14 Estimates of investment, 1901–46   87
3.15 Estimates of saving, 1901–46   88
3.16 Receipts and payments on the government account,
      1901–46   91
3.17 Balance of payments, 1921–39   93
3.18 Structure of balance of payments, early and late
      colonialism (Rs million, annual average)   93
3.19 Composition of factor payments (percentage of
      total net payment), 1860–1939   94

4.1   Growth rates of net domestic product (NDP), total
      and in agriculture, 1868–9 to 1946–7 (trend growth
      rates, percentage annual)   100
4.2   Area cropped (square miles), British India   101
4.3   Trend growth rates of crop output, acreage, and yield
      (percentage annual for British India), 1891–1946   102
4.4   Area irrigated, 1885–1938 (million acres,
      excluding Burma)   103
4.5   Irrigated area as a proportion of cultivated area in
      major provinces, 1885–1938 (percentages,
      'British India' excludes Burma)   104
4.6   Wage labourers in agricultural workforce
      (percentage), 1901–31   121
4.7   Interest rate (per cent per year)   125
4.8   Agricultural wages, average annual in Rs, 1785–1968   129

5.1   Employment in industry 1911–45 (millions)   141
5.2   GDP in industry, 1900–46 (1938–9 prices)   142
5.3   Productivity in handloom weaving, 1901–39   142
5.4   Industrial composition, 1931 (percentage share in
      total industrial employment)   143
5.5   Production of cloth by origin, 1795–1940
      (million yards)   146

5.6 Regional clusters of factories other than large
    mills, 1939   159

6.1 Employment in factories, 1891–1938   162
6.2 Industrial composition, 1921 (percentage of total
    employment)   162
6.3 Average real wage in large-scale industry, 1900–44
    (annual average)   178

7.1 Production of major minerals, 1891–1938   201
7.2 Growth of deposits (in Rs billion)   205

8.1 Selected railway statistics, 1860–1940   220
8.2 Average transportation charges (per maund mile)   224
8.3 Selected statistics of the posts and telegraph,
    1858–1938   230

9.1 Composition of government revenue and
    expenditure, 1858, 1900, and the 1920s   244
9.2 Gross public investment as a proportion of public
    expenditure, 1898–1938 (percentage)   246
9.3 Public debt and debt–GDP ratio   248
9.4 Shares of the centre and the provinces in gross public
    investment, 1920–37 (percentage)   249

10.1 Population of colonial India and the Indian Union,
     1881–1951   260
10.2 Crude death and birth rates, 1881–1951   262
10.3 Mean age at female marriage   263
10.4 Major channels of internal migration, 1901–31   268

12.1 British India and the states, 1905   304

13.1 Average annual growth rates of GDP by sector
     of origin, 1865–2018   335
13.2 Investment ratio and size of government (proportion
     of GDP, percentages), 1900–2016   336

13.3 Size of the external sector (proportion of current GDP, percentages)   336

FIGURES

1.1 Structural change: Business growth and agricultural stagnation   6
1.2 Population transition   8

2.1 East India Company sale room, 1808–9   29

3.1 Components of GDP 1900–46 (billion Rs in 1938–9 prices)   70
3.2 Goods handled by railways (million tonnes)   77

7.1 Workers cleaning and sorting coffee, South India   195

8.1 Construction of the Bengal–Nagpur railway, 1890   222

10.1 A team of men dusting both banks of a small stream with insecticide to prevent malaria, c. 1929   267

11.1 Environment and economy interactions   278
11.2 Santal village, c. 1890   290

12.1 Maharana and the British agent at the hunt, c. 1878   310

13.1 Soviet experts in Bhilai steel plant, 1962   327

MAPS

1.1 British India and the princely states, around 1900   3

2.1 Geographical zones (showing major railways) around 1900   18
2.2 Types of settlement, c. 1858   37

4.1 Areas of rice cultivation   107

4.2 Areas of wheat cultivation   108
4.3 Cotton, groundnut, jute, tobacco, tea   109
4.4 Rainfall (annual)   137

5.1 Clusters of small-scale Industry   155

10.1 Major channels of internal migration   269

Abbreviations

CEHI	*Cambridge Economic History of India*
EHR	*Economic History Review*
EPW	*Economic and Political Weekly*
GDP	Gross domestic product
IESHR	*Indian Economic and Social History Review*
IMS	Indian Medical Service
JAS	*Journal of Asian Studies*
JEH	*Journal of Economic History*
MAS	*Modern Asian Studies*
NDP	Net Domestic Product
RMMS	Rashtriya Mill Mazdoor Sangh
UP	United Provinces (before 1947) and Uttar Pradesh (after 1947)

Note on spelling convention: Many Indian place names have changed since the end of colonial rule in the region. However, to maintain consistency between the sources and the text, I retain the old names. Thus, Mumbai is written as Bombay, and so on. If the difference between the old and the new names is marginal, the text uses the new name.

Exchange Rate, 1800–1947

(pence per rupee and rupees per pound)

1800–70	24 d. and Rs 10
1871–5	22 d. and Rs 11
1876–80	20 d. (average) and Rs 12
1881–9	18 d. (average) and Rs 13.3
1890–8	14 d. (average) and Rs 17.2
1899–1917	16 d. and Rs 14.9
1918	18 d. and Rs 13.3
1919	23 d. and Rs 10.4
1920	*January–September*: 26 d. and Rs 9.2;
	October–December: 19 d. and Rs 12.6
1921	16.2 d. (average) and Rs 14.8
1922–6	16 d. and Rs 14.9
1927–47	18 d. and Rs 13.3

1

Introduction

What Are the Questions?

INDIA, 1857–1947: COLONIALISM AND GLOBALIZATION[1]

From the end of the eighteenth century, South Asia began to experience two overlapping processes of change that transformed patterns of production and consumption in the region. These were the rise of colonial rule and the integration of the region in the emerging world markets for commodities, capital, and labour, 'globalization' for short.[2] By 1947, the larger nations of South Asia presented a paradoxical mix of acute rural poverty and robust industrialization. The book describes the changes in the structure of the

---

[1] By 'India', I mean undivided India or mainland South Asia or the combined territory of the three larger nations, India, Pakistan, and Bangladesh. Only the last chapter, Chapter 13, is about the Indian Union. For general accounts of the emergence of colonial rule in South Asia, see Crispin Bates, *Subalterns and Raj: South Asia since 1600* (Abingdon: Routledge, 2007).

[2] On the various definitions of globalization in economic history, see Pim de Zwart and Jan Luiten van Zanden, *The Origins of Globalization: World Trade in the Making of the Global Economy, 1500–1800* (Cambridge: Cambridge University Press, 2018).

economy initiated by this dual process and asks how we should explain the paradox of extraordinary achievements amidst poverty and stagnation.

The first process, the transition to colonialism, was underway for almost exactly a century, 1757–1856. During this period, the British East India Company annexed the Indian territories that came to constitute British India. After the Battle of Plassey or Palashi in 1757, and especially after the grant by the Mughal emperor of the taxation rights of Bengal, Bihar, and Orissa to the Company in 1765, the Company established a power-sharing arrangement with the nawab, or the Mughal governor, of Bengal. The partnership was an unequal one and soon tilted towards absolute control by the Company over the administration of Bengal. In 1799, the Company defeated its principal southern rival, Mysore, and in 1803–4 and 1817–18, overcame its major adversary in the north and the west, the Marathas. In 1856, after Awadh was annexed, the British territorial campaign came to a stop.

At the end of the mutiny that took place in 1857, India became a colony of the British Crown. About 60 per cent of the land area in present India, Pakistan, and Bangladesh belonged then to British India (Table 1.1 and Map 1.1). Outside British India, there were more than 500 princely states in South Asia, nominally independent but militarily dependent on the British. They had, by then, come to terms with British hegemony, in a one-sided relationship the like of which no previous imperial power in the region could claim to have enjoyed. This relationship is sometimes called 'indirect rule', though it was qualitatively a different arrangement from the indirect rule that the European colonists developed later in Africa.

The second process, integration of the region with the world financial and commercial system, had been active from the eighteenth century, but its impact earlier had been greater in some coastal regions and weaker in the interior. The industrial and transportation revolution of the mid-nineteenth century changed that. The seaboard now emerged as transportation hubs, and these hubs moved a lot of the agricultural produce coming from the interior. The two worlds became firmly integrated, just as the Indian economy became integrated with the world economy. The ratio of foreign trade to

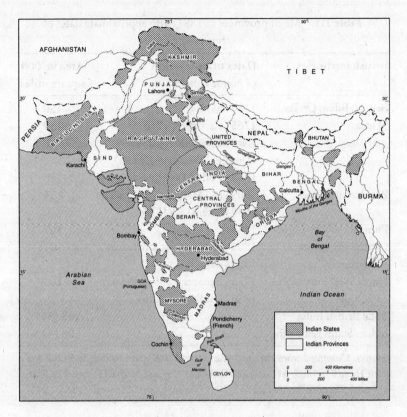

Map 1.1. British India and the princely states, around 1900.

Source: Author

domestic product increased from possibly 1–2 per cent in 1800 to a little less than 10 per cent in the 1860s and to 20 per cent by 1914. International flows of income, capital, and labour were larger in the colonial period than before or after.

British colonial rule was not just another government; it was a qualitatively different kind of government from past regimes and indigenous ones. The new rulers did not arise from the established ruling classes. They were strangers. The British were a mercantile population turning industrial by the end of the eighteenth century, whereas India was overwhelmingly agricultural. Set up by outsiders and merchants, the new regime could initiate policies and follow

Table 1.1   Major provinces in 1881, with approximate dates of
annexation

British territories	Dates of annexation of major constituents	Area in '000 square miles
Bengal, Bihar, Orissa	1757–65	150
Madras	1765 (Carnatic), 1766 (Northern Circars), 1792–9 (Dindigul, Malabar, Canara), 1801 (Ceded Districts)	139
Bombay and Sind	1803–18 (Maratha territories), 1848 (Satara), 1843 (Sind)	124
Punjab	1849	107
Central Provinces and Berar	1803–18 (Maratha territories), 1853 (Berar)	101
North West Provinces and Oudh	1775 (Benares), 1853 (Jhansi), 1856 (Oudh or Awadh)	106
Total British India		868 (58%)
Indian States remaining		509 (42%)

Sources: Compiled from data in India, *Statistical Abstract relating to British India from 1876/7 to 1885/6* (London: HMSO, 1887); and Michael Fisher, *The Politics of British Annexation of India 1757–1857* (Delhi: Oxford University Press, 1993).

principles of governance that upset the established (agrarian) order as never before. Like any other Indian regime in the past, the new rule was dependent on the taxation of landed wealth. However, it was also committed to protecting trade and private investment in the region, which was beginning to play a major supporting role in Britain's engagement with the world economy. India was crucial to Britain and the British Empire as a market for its manufactures, chiefly textiles, machinery, and metals, and as a source of food, migrant labour, industrial raw materials, and manufactured goods intensive in labour and natural resources. Through commodity and factor market transactions, close ties developed between India and Britain and, via Britain, between India and the rest of the world.

Colonialism strengthened globalization also by setting up institutions and infrastructure necessary for a market economy to smoothly function, including uniform weights and measures, contract law, unified currency, the railways, the telegraph, a redefinition of private property as ownership right, and a commitment to protect it via a new set of courts of law. There is no doubt that the trading opportunities, the institutional changes, and the transportation and communications infrastructure encouraged peasant production for the market, in place of production for consumption or local exchange, and encouraged business growth.

These were big changes, no doubt. But did they make the average Indian better off? We should start with the national income.

ECONOMIC PERFORMANCE: THE FACTS TO BE EXPLAINED

Official estimates of national income for colonial India do not exist. Although some contemporary estimates exist, not until the 1960s did reliable historical national income statistics become available. There are differences amongst these later research works. S. Sivasubramonian's series is perhaps the most detailed and reliable. His estimates begin from 1900. For the quarter century before that date, we have somewhat less detailed estimates from various sources, especially research done by Alan Heston and Moni Mukherjee. Table 1.2 draws these estimates together to report on growth rates of real national income.

Table 1.2 Growth rates of real national income

	National income	Population	Per capita Income
1860–85[a]	1.76	0.53	1.23
1885–1900[b]	1.01	0.55	0.46
1900–14[c]	1.45	0.45	1.00
1914–47[c]	1.14	1.08	0.06

Sources: a. M. Mukherjee, National Income of India (Calcutta: Firma KLM, 1965); b. A. Heston, 'National Income,' in Cambridge Economic History of India (CEHI) 2, eds Dharma Kumar and Meghnad Desai (Cambridge: Cambridge University Press, 1983), 376–462; c. S. Sivasubramonian, National Income of India in the Twentieth Century (New Delhi: Oxford University Press, 2000).

Between 1860 and 1914, the growth rates of total income and average income were positive and attained quite respectable levels by international comparison. Between 1914 and 1947, however, national income grew at approximately 1 per cent per year. When adjusted for population growth rate, which was beginning to rise, the growth rate of average income was near zero.

Should we conclude that the fundamental lesson from national income statistics is that the Indian economy stagnated during the colonial period? Should the task be to explain why globalization and colonialism at best did not deliver gains and, at worst, acted as obstacles to economic growth? To draw such lessons from the incomes data would be a mistake. National income per capita is only an average. There was no such thing as an average Indian. For a more realistic picture of how conditions of living changed, we should investigate the major components of income.

Figure 1.1 divides national income (excluding government and rural rent) in the first half of the twentieth century into two parts: agriculture, and industry and services. The graph on the left tracks the total income and the graph on the right tracks income per worker, both at constant prices. The figure does not tell us that the

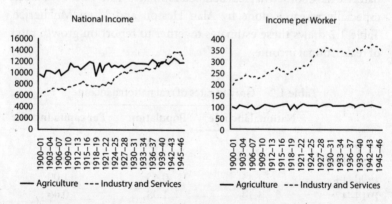

Figure 1.1   Structural change: Business growth and agricultural stagnation

National income (million Rs, left) and income per worker (Rs per head, right) by activity, 1938–9 prices.

Source: Sivasubramonian, *National Income*, Tables 6.2 and 2.11.

economy under colonial rule was stagnating. It shows that industry and services, much of it being private business enterprise or linked with it, forged ahead, whereas agriculture stagnated. In fact, when we break down agricultural income by regions, we might see that Punjab forged ahead and Bengal fell behind since the end of the nineteenth century (Chapter 4). The task before the book, then, is to answer the question: Why did colonialism and globalization generate inequality within the economy? Why did businesses make good use of these forces of change, but peasants in many regions could not?

Could the peasants migrate to the cities and find better-paying work? Table 1.3 shows, predictably, that industry and services increased their share of the national income during these years. That is, these activities generated more income than did agriculture. But the table also shows that the employment shares of these activities did not increase at all, suggesting that these activities did not generate many jobs. Looking at this from the other end, few people trapped in low-income activities like agriculture had the opportunity to migrate to the higher-income ones. Of course, people did leave the village to work in the cities all the time, but few did permanently; men moved more frequently than did women; and the numbers were relatively small. It was never an easy move. In the end, agricultural growth in the twentieth century left the huge population directly or indirectly dependent on land with no more output per head than in the past. Whether the limited movements of workers between low-paying jobs and high-paying ones derived from lack of education, barriers to acquiring skills, the weight of the caste system that frowned upon change of occupation, or there were not enough good jobs,

Table 1.3   Agriculture and non-agriculture: Shares in income and employment (percentage)

	Income-shares		Employment-shares		
	1900	1946	1875	1900	1946
Agriculture	51	40	74	75	75
Non-agriculture	49	60	26	25	25

Source: Sivasubramonian, National Income.

we cannot say for sure. Limited labour mobility, in any case, adds a
second question to the one asked above. Who could migrate, under
what conditions, and with what effect?

That is not all. One of the reasons why the average income grew
little in the early twentieth century was that population was growing
at a faster pace than before. The population transition was a revolutionary change compared with the past pattern of population growth
(Figure 1.2). In a region where famines had occurred frequently,
famines began to become rare after 1900, resulting in a permanent
fall in mortality rates. Almost the entire natural increase in population in the last quarter of the nineteenth century was removed due
to the three great famines of 1876, 1896, and 1898. But after that,
episodes of food scarcity did not lead to mass deaths on the scale
they did in the past. The smooth fitted line shows that the inflec-
tion occurred around 1915, and there was no significant population
shock after that (the 1921 drop was due to the influenza epidemic, a

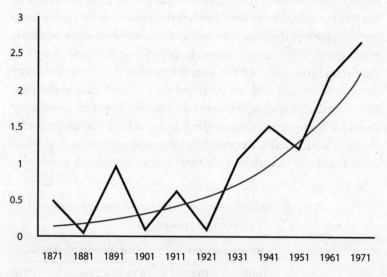

Figure 1.2   Population transition

Source: India, Censuses of India, various rounds.
Note: Average population growth rate (percentage per year per decade) with a
trend line added.

one-off event). The last of the great famines the regions witnessed, the Bengal Famine of 1943, did not reverse the trend. A humanitarian disaster caused by World War II, it was not a great population shock and did not affect average longevity.

I can now add a third set of questions to the two asked before on inequality and labour mobility. Why did famines happen? Why did they disappear from around 1900? What were the other factors involved in causing a population transition in the early twentieth century? What role, if any, did colonialism and globalization play in the transition?

So far, the government has been marginal to this discussion on income, employment, and population. There is a reason for this. The British Indian government was a small one, compared with the governments we find today. Its revenue–gross domestic product (GDP) ratio rarely exceeded 6–7 per cent. It was not a militarily weak government because it did spend adequate amount of money on maintaining an army. It had little left over to do other things. In many respects, British India set up a more modern form of government than previous Indian regimes. It had a more diversified revenue base than the Mughal Empire did or the states succeeding the Mughals did. It spent less on luxuries and more on the genuine duties of the state, such as defence, welfare, infrastructure, and institutions. Yet, it spent far too little on those heads that would make a real difference to the poorest earners. These neglected heads included healthcare and education, where India's record was generally poor. The government did little to help raise agricultural productivity.

Why was the government so small? Why did it not grow bigger and perform more welfare and developmental duties? Did ideology hold it back? Did the poverty of agriculture, which delivered a lot of the taxes, hold it back? Or did the colonial structure hold it back? If the answer is colonialism, then we have an easy way to test whether the answer is right. Consider the princely states. Were they doing a lot better than British India because they were not under colonial rule? I have now added a fourth question (why the government was poor) and a fifth one (were the princely states different) to the three asked before on inequality, labour mobility, and population growth.

There is yet a sixth set of questions that can be added to this list. If colonialism and globalization were, on balance, adverse forces of change, we would expect the Indian economy after 1947 to achieve an economic revolution because colonialism had ended and the new regime removed and regulated many of the past links India had developed with the world economy via trade, investment, and migration. The reality is much more complex. There were areas of success, no doubt. Agriculture experienced a Green Revolution, for example. But there were also many areas, including business growth and social welfare, where the outcome was not revolutionary. What went right and what went wrong with managed economic development in postcolonial India? The return to market liberalism since the 1990s and the revival of economic growth in India would tell us that perhaps the country had gone too far in rejecting globalization along with rejecting colonial ties. Is that conjecture correct?

And finally, there is the issue of the environment. Worldwide, environmental concerns have risen and so has the scholarship studying how the natural world around us is changing. The scholarship recognizes that the history of accelerated degradation of the environment, as well as conservation efforts, goes back to the early days of colonial rule in Asia and Africa. Colonialism and globalization caused environmental degradation as well as increased awareness of environmental degradation. Why did colonialism and globalization have such a contradictory effect on the environment?

This book attempts to answer seven main questions and a few others that derive from these seven. The seven main questions are:

1. Why did colonialism and globalization generate inequality? Why did these forces promote industry and services and fail to transform agriculture sufficiently (Chapters 3–8)?
2. Why did poor people not move to better jobs on a large scale (Chapter 10)?
3. Why did the population begin to grow at a faster pace from the 1910s (Chapter 10)?
4. Why was the government so small and limited in its effects (Chapters 8, 9)?

5. What was the performance record of the princely states (Chapter 12)?
6. How did the state and the markets impact the environment (Chapter 11)?
7. What went right and what went wrong with the development effort of the state after colonialism ended (Chapter 13)?

One would expect that the existing theories of economic history will answer these seven questions. They do not. This book is needed because they do not. That claim needs an explanation.

INDIA AND THE THEORIES OF ECONOMIC HISTORY

Economic history began as a field in the nineteenth century, mainly to answer the question: Why did the Western Europeans and the Americans grow rich quickly? The answer then was that they had discovered 'capitalism', a system of economic organization that promoted market exchange, including markets in labour services and capital.

Competitive markets free from government regulation and political interference created the incentive to work harder for personal gains and delivered productivity growth. The three classical theorists of capitalism—Adam Smith, Karl Marx, and Max Weber—stressed different aspects of capitalism, but all agreed that capitalism distinguished the modern West from the rest of the world and raised the productive power of the economy. In the 1980s, a modern version of classical economic history—known as new institutional economic history—added that markets could fail to generate such incentives when information was scarce and uncertainty large. The government was still needed to set up rules, called institutions, which could mitigate the effects of poor information and high uncertainty. Beyond that qualification, the modern version stayed close to the classics, in suggesting that the main task for economic history is to explain why the Europeans and the Americans got richer.

Where were the poorer countries in this story? The classical theory implied that the societies of India and China somehow could not discover the right kind of capitalism. But that was no more than an inference. The quality of evidence-based research on Asia and Africa in the classical tradition was too weak to support any claim.

In the 1960s, the Marxists shifted the focus to the poorer countries. The average income data across countries showed that while Western Europe and North America forged ahead (from early 1800s), countries like India stagnated and fell behind. These hundred-odd years also saw the spread of capitalism worldwide through an enormous rise in trade, cross-country capital flows, and labour migration, as well as the spread of European colonial rule in Asia and Africa. The Marxist historians said that these two forces—colonialism and globalization—jointly made the third world poor. Using their political and military power, the Europeans forcibly extracted money and goods from the poorer regions to sustain economic growth in Europe. They offered a story. Capitalism worked, as Marx had shown, because capitalists exploited labour efficiently. Capitalism as a worldwide force caused growth as well as poverty because it was based on exploitation of poor countries that supplied labour by rich ones that had more capital. When colonialism joined capitalism, the result was increasing poverty and underdevelopment for the countries of Asia and Africa.

Many regional nationalist movements fighting for the end of colonial rule since the 1940s had already made a similar claim. One of the more influential versions of the claim emerged in India. Around 1900, two writers, Dadabhai Naoroji (1825–1917) and Romesh Chunder Dutt (1848–1909) said that British rule was making ordinary Indians of their time poorer. Dutt suggested that trade with Britain destroyed the Indian handicrafts, which led to poverty.[3] Naoroji argued that payments abroad as business profits, salaries, and pensions of government officers and interest on public debt were a form of drain of savings and made Indians poor. Their target was not only colonial rule but also the open economy that the rule wanted to maintain. These writers were almost forgotten in the mid-twentieth century when Marxist historians rediscovered them and used India

[3] R.C. Dutt, *The Economic History of India in the Victorian Age* (London: Kegan Paul, 1906).

as examples in their history of the whole world. Together, these two traditions enriched the story that colonialism and globalization made India poor, a story that I have called in an earlier edition of this book the Left-nationalist theory of Indian economic history.

In academic scholarship, the Left-nationalist version flourished until the 1980s, but then declined. The Marxists had failed to explain why countries that were never colonized—like China—had stayed poor as well. Few professional historians using Indian data believe that the two propositions that Dutt and Naoroji made can stand up to serious evidence. Even many nationalist leaders who followed these intellectuals did not accept the Dutt–Naoroji view that colonialism had done more harm than good to India.[4]

In the last 20 odd years, the economic emergence of countries like India and China revived interest in their economic history. There were two strands in this research. One of these applies the classical economics ideas, suggesting that the poorer countries were institutionally different from Western Europe, that is, had a weaker version of capitalism and, therefore, fell behind.[5] A second strand suggests that India and China were not institutionally very different from Europe but had fewer natural resources to generate an industrial revolution.[6] Both these propositions enabled comparing a colonized country like India and an independent country like China better than in Marxist history, and both were, like the classical theory, upbeat on capitalism.

This book does not use either the modified version of world economic history or the Left-nationalist version of Indian history as

---

[4] B.R. Ambedkar, for example, believed that India's caste system was the main obstacle to welfare and development, and that the colonial rulers came with the promise of destroying it, though they did not live up to it.

[5] Daron Acemoglu, Simon Johnson, and James A. Robinson, 'The Colonial Origins of Comparative Development: An Empirical Investigation', *American Economic Review* 91, no 5 (2001): 1369–401.

[6] Kenneth Pomeranz, *The Great Divergence: China, Europe, and the Making of the Modern World Economy* (Princeton, NJ: Princeton University Press, 2000); Prasannan Parthasarathi, *Why Europe Grew Rich and Asia Did Not: Global Economic Divergence* (Cambridge: Cambridge University Press, 2011).

frameworks of analysis. It does not use these 'theories' of economic history for a simple reason—these theories do not enable asking the seven questions that I believe describe the broad pattern of economic change in colonial and postcolonial India.

Moreover, these theories are too preoccupied with explaining inequality between nations to notice inequality within India, which is this book's main concern. They obscure the broad pattern of economic change in India. For example, in the cross-country data set that economists use to discuss world inequality, every country is represented by exactly one attribute, average income. Every country's history is represented by one number. By considering only average income, the rise in international inequality becomes the only fact that there is to explain. This project is untenable if the averages hide growing diversity and inequality inside every country. A good reason to do economic histories of regions is that we can abandon the fixation with averages and uncover the diversity of experiences that these numbers hide, bring the attention back to the diversity, and ask why globalization and colonialism had a differential impact on the Indian economy.

On a similar ground, I do not think that the Left-nationalist version of world economic history is useful either. Although the idea that British rule made the Indians poor lives on in internet blogs, popular history, and nationalistic discourses, evidence-based history has long found it inadequate and untestable. The nationalist version is out of touch with the advancement in world economic history that has produced a more complex view of European colonialism than that of a grand machine of exploitation. It is too caught up in providing a justification for nationalism to ask questions like the ones I have identified in the previous section.

What, then, should be the aim of an economic history of India?

THE BOOK

This book has a message. The central message is that colonialism and globalization produced different outcomes for different livelihoods and regions. To see why, and what these regions and livelihoods were, we need to study the economic history of India.

Several of the questions that I have listed earlier concern the operation of inequality between castes, gender, agricultural regions, agriculture and industry, countryside and the port city. Inequality and diversity were fundamental conditions of Indian history. Colonialism and globalization created opportunities for some people, were oppressive to some other people, and never either uniformly good or uniformly bad for all people.

Consider some examples to show how this argument works. Inequality derives from a variety of factors, both environmental and social in origin. India, being a tropical region, contains a huge mass of arid lands. It is harder for arid zones to experience income growth than it is for temperate zones or seaboards because the arid lands do not have enough water. The monsoon did supply a lot of water for agriculture, but the monsoon occurring in just three months did not provide work throughout the year. Modern economic growth was owed to overseas trade, which favoured the seaboard, and to an agricultural revolution, which favoured the regions that could access water cheaply.

A few such regions emerged in colonial India or had existed from before. In a few regions, like Punjab, the water problem found a solution. The business of the big cities was never seriously depressed during the timespan of the book. The volume of long-distance trade in India grew from roughly 1–5 million tonnes in 1840 to 150–160 million in 1940.[7] As profits in trade were reinvested, colonial India led the contemporary developing world in two leading industries of the industrial revolution: cotton textiles and iron and steel.[8] At the

---

[7] Tirthankar Roy, *India in the World Economy from Antiquity to the Present* (Cambridge: Cambridge University Press, 2012); India, *Statistical Abstracts for British India* (London: HMSO, 1942), 652–70, 712.

[8] In 1928, 48 per cent of the cotton spindles installed outside Europe, North America, and Japan were in India. Robert Dunn and Jack Hardy, *Labor and Textiles. A Study of Cotton and Wool Manufacturing* (New York: International Publishers, 1931). In 1935, 50 per cent of the steel produced outside Europe, North America, and Japan was produced in India. BKS, 'The European Steel Industry: Production Trends and the World Market', *The World Today* 6 (1950): 265–74.

time of Independence in 1947, the port cities were home to some of the best schools, colleges, hospitals, universities, banks, insurance companies, and learned societies available outside the Western world. A big part of that infrastructure had been created by the Indian merchants and industrialists, in collaboration with foreigners.

When new jobs opened in these areas of expansion, be it the port city or the prosperous agricultural area, people from poorer areas would migrate there in search of better work or more work. Such movements happened. But there were barriers to such moves too. Education was not accessible to all. Skills were learnt at home rather than in schools. Caste became a barrier to learning a new skill. Women, being married at a very early age in India, could not easily migrate in search of jobs. Men took more of the good jobs available, again causing inequality to rise. At every step, the book reveals gainers and losers from processes of change.

The narrative journey starts in the eighteenth century. The eighteenth-century economy of the subcontinent was already a very uneven one. On the one hand, there were present a rich indigenous commercial tradition, territorial states that respected private property in land and trade because their sustenance depended on the peasants and the merchants, a literate elite running the fiscal administration, and rich cities that were home to highly skilled artisans. But much of that wealth was confined to the riparian, deltaic, and seaboard territories. The greater part of peninsular India consisted of drylands, poor peasants, few roads, slow traffic, few towns, forests, waterless uplands, and uninhabited deserts. With such divergent initial conditions, the onset of globalization and the emergence of British power led to a variety of trajectories, as the next chapter will show.

2

Transition to Colonialism
1707–1857

During the 150 years covered in this chapter, one empire fell and another emerged. Warriors and landlords ran the Mughal Empire. Merchants foreign to the land created the new empire. India had not seen a merchant-ruled state before. Being set up by outsiders and merchants, the new state could introduce a type of government the region did not have before. This chapter is about that unique legacy.

Why did trade lead to an empire? How different was a merchant state from the indigenous agrarian ones? What was its legacy? The chapter will answer these questions. First, let us discuss conditions immediately before the establishment of the State.

ECONOMIC CONDITIONS IN THE MID-1700S

The Indian subcontinent has five major geographical regions: the mountains and foothills, the western desert and savanna, the floodplains of the two great Himalayan river systems (the Ganges and the Indus) or the Indo–Gangetic basin, the peninsular uplands, and the seaboard (see Map 2.1). At the beginning of the eighteenth century, the Himalayan foothills had been largely forested, and the desert and the savanna sustained only pastoralist groups. The history of the rise

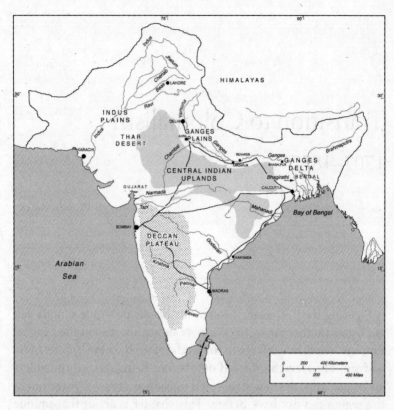

Map 2.1.   Geographical zones (showing major railways) around 1900.

Source: Author

and fall of states concentrates on the other three regions: the Indo-Gangetic basin, the Deccan Plateau, and the seaboard.

Owing to fertile alluvial soil, access to the waters of the peren-nial Himalayan rivers, flat terrain, and easier transportation, the Indo-Gangetic basin had powerful imperial states that lived on taxation of land, a lot of overland trade, and flourishing towns. By contrast, the Deccan Plateau, which dominated the peninsular, was an agriculturally poorer zone, growing locally consumed millets, participating in distant markets to a limited extent, and exposed to the threat of harvest failure and famines. It did have segments of rich black soil that sustained prosperous communities, but in general, the plateau was water-scarce, resource-poor, and less urbanized.

The seaboard was always engaged in maritime trade and drew its livelihood from trade. Parts of it—such as the western Bengal delta, Krishna–Godavari delta, coastal Gujarat, and Malabar—were more involved in maritime trade than the interior, were ruled by smaller states, and had long received foreign settlers. The power of the great Mughal Empire was weak on the seaboard. It was not much interested in maritime trade nor had much naval power. But the autonomy of the seaboard states was not always backed up by military might, leaving them vulnerable to conquest. In one such zone, in the lower Bengal delta, European colonization began in the middle of the eighteenth century.

The Fall of the Mughal Empire

From early in the eighteenth century, shortly after the death of Aurangzeb (1707), the last of the great Mughals, the Mughal Empire that had ruled over the floodplains since 1526 started breaking up. The Mughal Empire broke up for many reasons: fiscal crisis, constant wars, and Aurangzeb's religious intolerance.[1] Its attempt to capture the Deccan Plateau did not succeed because the Mughal army, consisting of a large cavalry, was not suited for battles in the dry and hilly terrains of the south.

In Bengal, Hyderabad, and Awadh, former provincial governors established independent rules. In Deccan, eastern Rajasthan, and north-western India, landlords and warlords rebelled. In 1739, the shah of Iran, Nader Shah, invaded Delhi, sacked the capital, drained the treasury, and humiliated the Mughal king Mohammad Shah. Several new states emerged, militarily the most powerful being the dominion of the Marathas.

In the second half of the eighteenth century, the political balance of power shifted again. In 1761, the main Maratha army lost a major

[1] J.F. Richards, *The Mughal Empire* (Cambridge: Cambridge University Press, 1995).

battle to the Afghans in the wake of a contest for supremacy over northern India (the Third Battle of Panipat). In 1765, the British East India Company received the taxation rights of Bengal, Bihar and Orissa from the Mughal emperor. After the Third Anglo-Maratha War of 1818, the Company was the main political and military force in India.

Did the fall of the empire and the rise of new states frequently at war with each other affect economic conditions? In one view, the collapse of the empire led to tax farming and local conflicts. Merchants and bankers connected with imperial finance, and luxury manufacture in the towns suffered decline.[2] Another view holds that the rise of new states on the ashes of the empire stimulated economic activity. Some of the new states used the old administrative order intact, even improved it. Bengal, under Murshid Quli Khan, could devise 'efficient tax gathering procedures', encourage 'rural investments', and foster 'a more prosperous agriculture'.[3] In the Indo-Gangetic basin, the weakening hold of the empire encouraged trade and encouraged the feudal landholders to forge partnerships with merchants and bankers. Many taxation rights were being contracted away by these states so that merchants and bankers gained by using such rights.

The foundation of the state were the landholders. Who were they?

Landed Property and Land Revenue

In Mughal India, the common tax was a land tax that amounted to between one-third and one-fourth of the gross produce of land.[4]

---

[2] Irfan Habib, 'The Eighteenth Century in Indian Economic History', in *The Eighteenth Century in Indian History: Evolution or Revolution?*, ed. P.J. Marshall (New Delhi: Oxford University Press, 2003), 100–19; M. Athar Ali, 'Recent Theories of Eighteenth Century India', in Marshall, *The Eighteenth Century*, 90–9.

[3] Burton Stein, 'A Decade of Historical Efflorescence', *South Asia Research* 10, no. 2 (1990): 125–38.

[4] N.A. Siddiqui, 'Land Revenue Demand under the Mughals', *Indian Economic and Social History Review (IESHR)* 2, no. 4 (1965): 373–80.

Among the successors, the Marathas and in South India, rates like 50 per cent of gross produce off irrigated land and one-third off dry land seem to have been usual. The actual collection from the peasant was less than the stated rate. The revenue system had a history of remissions and rescheduling in times of stress. Since land productivity was not very high, the burden of taxation on the cultivators was a heavy one.

The process of payment, collection, and delivery of taxes sustained a complicated and hierarchical system of property rights. The Indo-Gangetic basin had three tiers of rights to agricultural land. These were: the right to cultivate the soil, the right to collect taxes from the cultivators, and the right to grant taxation rights. The peasants enjoyed the first type of right, the village landlord or zamindar in North India the second, and the kings, the warlords, and military commanders the third. The picture differed slightly in the drier zones of South India. The middle tier of a landlord or zamindar located in the village was less common in the south. The top layer was also a little different. Military commanders, who often lived in isolated forts, asserted the right to reward themselves with land tax, but they did not form parts of an imperial court as in the north.

What kinds of rights were these? They were rights to enjoy the products of the soil in return for service. They were not technically ownership rights and would not sell easily. In practice, sales did happen, but they were not common. The income of tax officers and that of the peasants were interdependent, which would mean that the former had a say in land sales. This situation also discouraged private investment in the land. Agricultural growth took the form of bringing new land under cultivation. The ruler would offer tax-free grants to a community of migrant peasants to induce it to clear forests and wastes. The lands were expected to add to the resources of the state when, a few years later, they could be taxed.

There were four types of cultivators. These were: individuals holding a share in jointly owned village land; holders of offices who held revenue-free or lowly assessed land; chieftains of forested zones populated by indigenous people, who usually paid lumpsum tributes rather than taxes on assessed lands; and tenants. Individual proprietors appeared everywhere. In the fertile regions such as the eastern

Gangetic plains, they came from the upper castes. In regions around Delhi, the usual proprietary body was not an individual but a collective of kin who managed the administrative and economic affairs of a village. Some of these 'village republics', as the British called them later, arose from pastoral groups acquiring land in the eighteenth century. In western and southern India, in general, the proprietary right was expressed as a share in total village land. Such shareholders were called *mirasdars*. In western and southern India, officers of the state lived in or near the village. Two officers were universal, village head (the so-called headman) and accountant. Mirasdars performed such offices in Tamil villages. Their duties included revenue collection and construction of irrigation systems.

The hierarchical system changed somewhat in the eighteenth century. Of these rights—to cultivate, to collect tax, and to grant taxation power—the right to collect tax began to be sold more often from the seventeenth century onwards.[5] These were technically not hereditary ownership rights. The king had the power to take back land grants if the holder did not supply the required service. The collapse of the empire and the rise of smaller states with insecure administrative and financial resources led to a change. Anyone promising to collect tax and send a part of it to the treasury could join an auction of such rights and take a contract. As wars became more frequent in the eighteenth century, the rulers were forced to offer terms that made the revenue rights more marketable and, in effect, hereditary.[6]

The process is sometimes called 'gentrification'. The landlords enhanced their social power and took over many of the governance functions of the state. In northern India, the zamindars and the *talukdars*; in eastern Rajasthan, the *bhomias*; in deltaic southern India, the mirasdars—all commanded more land than before. Merchants

[5] Tapan Raychaudhuri, 'The State and the Economy: The Mughal Empire', in *CEHI*, Vol. 1, eds I. Habib and T. Raychaudhuri (Cambridge: Cambridge University Press, 1983), 172–93.

[6] Burton Stein, 'Eighteenth Century India: Another View', in Marshall, *The Eighteenth Century*, 62–89.

and bankers participated in the eighteenth-century land market as contractors or tax farmers. With growing commodity trade in grain, cotton, indigo, and opium, peasant property rights were sold and resold more often.[7]

The village did not just cultivate land.

Industry

Rural industry included basic textiles, pottery, agricultural implements, sugar, leather, and oil and was widely dispersed. But its consumption, technology, and organization were simple. With a lot of the surplus grains taken away from the village, the village was ordinarily not a site for the consumption and production of high-quality goods. Families and households worked in rural industry with simple, locally fabricated tools for the subsistence consumption of villagers. Only a few products, such as raw silk, salt, saltpetre, and indigo, were produced in the villages by part-time peasants but were traded more widely.

The urban industry was a very different matter. The revenue delivered to the central treasury maintained public administration and consumption by those connected with the state. Those connected with the state were, on average, wealthy. Their consumption power was high and provided a sustained demand for high-quality crafts and services. The trade in high-quality and intricately crafted goods was well developed. Urban industries included finer textiles, carpets and shawls, decorative metalware and pottery, wood and ivory carving, and manufacture of arms and musical instruments. Both family units and factories existed in this sphere. Some of these crafts were produced inside *karkhanas* (literally factories) that the courts and the aristocrats owned.

Production processes were well developed in urban crafts. Their superior skill was evident not so much in technology as in the use of costly materials, such as gold thread or pashmina, and in industrial

[7] Sumit Guha, 'The Land Market in Upland Maharashtra', *IESHR* 24, no. 2 (1987): 117–44.

organization. Division of labour, specialization, and master-appren-
tice hierarchy were more advanced in these industries. There were
many merchants engaged in these trades, for these goods sometimes
sold as exports and used imported raw material.

The collapse of the Mughal Empire dispersed the skilled urban
crafts earlier concentrated in a few cities in the Indo-Gangetic
basin such as Lahore, Agra, Delhi, and Multan, to towns located
in or near the new states such as Benares, Farrukhabad, Lucknow,
Moradabad, Jhansi, Gwalior, Bijapur, Ahmadnagar, Aurangabad,
and Warangal. Overland trade in these goods may have suffered
due to the eighteenth-century conflicts. But overseas trade was
another matter.

Foreign Trade

For centuries, India was a major link in the maritime trade between
Asia and Europe. A coastline 4,600 miles long, easy access from both
West and East Asia, local availability of textiles and other goods in
demand worldwide, a well-developed shipbuilding industry, and a
strong mercantile tradition contributed to India's strategic position
in the Indian Ocean trade. Ocean-going traders operating on the
Indian coasts had many divisions and types. Some of the more important groups lived in Gujarat, Malabar, Coromandel, and Bengal. The
Arabian Sea trade conducted between Gujarat and Malabar at the
Indian end and the Persian Gulf and Red Sea ports at the West Asia
end was of great antiquity. Shipbuilding was an established tradition
in both these regions, and the best timber for such industry came
from the Western Ghats in modern Kerala. Indian ships called on
the ports of the Red Sea and the Persian Gulf. The market of the
hajj, wherein converged caravan trade from a large area, was one
of the principal conduits through which Indian goods, chiefly textiles and spices, found their way to European markets. In the East,
Javanese shipping carried Indian textiles to the Spice Islands in eastern Indonesia in exchange for spices. The linking of sea routes and
land routes, or the port cities with the interior, was as yet weak. In
turn, the territorial powers did little to create and sustain port towns.
These were rather the creation of the Indian Ocean.

Two new variables emerged in the sixteenth century. One of these was the rise of continental monarchies—the Mughal, the Safavid, and the Ottoman empires in the western part of the Ocean. And the other was the rise of Portuguese power after Vasco da Gama arrived in Kerala in 1498.[8] These empires transacted in a lot of goods amongst themselves, protected overland trade routes, and gave business to city bankers. But on the seaboard, they had limited powers to control. Here, the Europeans were changing the world of trade.

Portuguese Arrival

The Portuguese voyages in the fifteenth century marked the beginning of serious European interest in Asian trade and politics. The motivations behind these early voyages remain a mystery. The varied attractions included the lucrative trade in spices, Christianity and the crusading impulse, access to food and gold in North Africa, and an accidental set of circumstances that gave the Portuguese court access to Italian and Spanish sponsorship. Portugal was the home of superior navigation skills. But it was also one of Europe's poorest regions. High mortality and impoverishment of the nobility may have made the nobles desperate to seek resources and fame outside.

The Portuguese quickly established a foothold in India and tried to monopolize the sea route between Europe and Asia by issuing licenses to merchant marines belonging to other ethnic groups. In short, they tried to establish a state on the waters. Seen in a long-term perspective, these attempts failed. Partly, the Portuguese did not have enough resources for the task, and partly, they lost interest in these manoeuvres in the western Indian Ocean as they began to expand towards Japan and China. In the end, they were left with a small and rather impoverished colony in Goa and a motley collection of adventurers in Bengal.

[8] On Portuguese enterprise in South Asia, see M.N. Pearson, *The Portuguese in India* (Cambridge: Cambridge University Press, 1987); Sanjay Subrahmanyam, *The Portuguese Empire in Asia, 1500–1700. A Political and Economic History* (London and New York: Longman, 1993).

Historians debate the reasons for the relative lack of success of the Portuguese enterprise. In one view, it was too 'redistributive' and 'pre-capitalist'; that is, it lived off profits of others rather than making its own actions profitable and being driven by commercial profits. In another view, the Portuguese empire ended due to external factors, including the resistance of territorial states, such as the Mughals, Ottomans, Japanese, and the Persians. In the time of the later European actors in India, especially the Dutch and the English, some of these territorial states had begun to weaken.

The Mughal imperial court sometimes checked Portuguese inroads into India (for example, an attack on their settlement in Hooghly in 1632). But already, the Dutch and the English traders had started to compete with the Portuguese for control over the seas.

Western Europeans

The formation of the English East India Company in 1600 (from 1708, formally, United Company of Merchants of England Trading to the East Indies) under a royal charter and the merger of several firms trading in the East Indies into the Dutch East India Company (Vereenigde Oost-Indische Compagnie) in 1602 started a new era in trade. These merchants had an interest in buying spices from the Indonesian archipelago and found Indian cotton textiles a convenient means of payment. But, by the late 1600s, Europe was a bigger market for Indian cotton textiles than was Asia.

Although nobles and rulers of the land connected with the Mughal Empire or regional states often participated in trade and sometimes tried to restrain the trade carried on by Europeans, these attempts did not pose a serious threat to the Europeans. The Mughals and the local nobles were powerful on land but weak in the sea. It was this naval weakness that allowed the Europeans to bargain and carve out a commercial-cum-political space for themselves in the seaboard.

The principal commodities in trade in the seventeenth and eighteenth centuries were foodgrains such as rice, cotton textiles, horses, and silver. Rice was a crop of monsoon Asia. In India, along the coasts and in the deltas of major rivers, rice is grown. Bengal was a prominent surplus producer. Orissa, the Godavari delta, and the

Cauvery delta were the other supplier regions. As trade between South Asia and Europe grew from the seventeenth century, grain trade grew too. The availability of larger and sturdier ships helped. New trade settlements and warfare also stimulated grain trade.[9] Central and West Asian horses were a principal item of import into India. The horses were instruments of warfare and transport. In the eighteenth century, the pattern of warfare began to change. The increasing importance of the artillery and infantry meant a decreasing role for the cavalry and horses.

Textiles and silver involved the Europeans more closely than did rice and horses. In the seventeenth century, Indian textiles paid for Indonesian spices. Later, Indian cotton textiles started to shape fashions in clothing in the British markets. Cotton textiles exports to Europe came in five main types: muslins (cloths made of fine cotton yarn), fine calicoes (cloths made of medium-to-fine yarn), ordinary cotton calicoes (cloths made of coarse-medium yarn), silk cloths, and silk-cotton mixed fabrics. The term 'calico' referred to plain-weave cotton fabric, either bleached or unbleached. Calico derived its name from Calicut on the Kerala coast, from where the first consignmesnts of Indian textiles went to Europe. A part of the calico exports consisted of 'chintz', that is, painted or printed cloth. These brightly coloured fabrics with Indian patterns generated so much interest in Europe that manufacturers in the Midlands and Yorkshire and France began producing them.

The trade depended on a plentiful supply of precious metals from Spanish America. Silver came from the Bolivian mines into the Spanish imperial fiscal system, was procured by western Europeans or their agents, and shipped to India and China to pay for cotton and silk cloth. The British Company tried to sell English goods in India, such as woollen clothing and metals. They succeeded late in the eighteenth century in iron goods. From soon after the Battle of Plassey in 1757 until about 1785, territorial revenues of Bengal were also partly used to finance exports. That transaction meant making

---

[9] S. Arasaratnam, 'The Rice Trade in Eastern India 1650–1740', *Modern Asian Studies (MAS)* 22, no. 3 (1988): 531–49.

the peasant subsidize the Company's business enterprise. Historians, however, often exaggerate the significance of the transaction. These years saw a fall in Company's trade, as the greater part of the revenues was spent on fighting wars within India rather than on trade. In any case, the import of British iron goods, especially guns and cannons, made silver unnecessary as a means of exchange.

The Indian Ocean trade was quite important for the economies of Bengal, coastal Gujarat, and Coromandel. But seaborne trade was not vital for the inland economies and the subcontinent as a whole. The most generous estimates suggest that at the end of the eighteenth century, the proportion of export in national income was between 1 and 2 per cent, which was rather small. But although small in scale, the political significance of the sea was great. The sea was the site of rising political power, something the region had not seen before.

Commercial success aided political power. By the end of the eighteenth century, Europeans dominated the routes and the markets for Indian goods. Indian shipping was not a small-scale enterprise. At its peak, the Gujarati merchant marine based in Surat consisted of about one hundred vessels of 200–400 tonnes each. Many owners of ocean-going ships were politically powerful. Still, Indian shipowners and traders never became transcontinental explorers in the way the Europeans did.

There were several factors that made the Europeans more successful in dominating world seaborne trade. Naval superiority, based on a partnership between the parent state and the merchant firms, was one of these. The fortified settlements backed by strong fleets, which the Europeans built, not only kept the sea routes open but also kept the territorial powers in check. By contrast, Indian states rarely backed Indian seagoing merchants. Second, there were differences in technology and business organization. Although Indian ships charged lower freight rates, European ships were, on average, bigger, sturdier, and better defended. The volume of cargo carried, as well as the number of guns carried, made the larger size necessary. European trade was organized around large joint-stock companies, whereas Indian firms developed around families or individuals. The stability of such a firm was too dependent on the resources

Figure 2.1   East India Company sale room, 1808–9.

Source: From a book of engravings published in 1808–10 called *Microcosm of London*. © Alamy Stock Photos

and talents available in the family. The Company not only brought many wealthy persons and stakeholders to work together but also possessed an identity independent of persons, which gave it more stability and power (Figure 2.1).

By 1800, the Company was also a formidable political actor in India. How did this happen?

THE RISE OF THE EAST INDIA COMPANY STATE

The Process of Territorial Expansion

Until 1740, the Europeans did not actively join Indian politics. But they had the resources necessary to join military campaigns on a small scale. Since its foundation in 1600, the East India Company had not only accumulated great power and wealth in London but also owned ports, docks, warehouses, and overseas settlements.[10] All European firms trading in India in the 1600s and 1700s wanted to create their own secure spots on the coast to conduct business. There were several advantages to doing that: defending their assets from attacks by European rivals and, increasingly, attracting Indian artisans and merchants closer to these territories. In India, the Company had managed to establish three ports—Bombay, Calcutta, and Madras—where it functioned as landlords. Of these three ports, Calcutta, located in Bengal, was rapidly growing in population in the 1740s, thanks to the migration of wealthy Bengali merchants from the western borders of the state where they were targets of attacks by the Maratha force stationed in Central India. These towns, and especially Calcutta and Madras, would prove to be a great naval and military asset when the British Company ran into trouble with the local rulers and the French East India Company.

These firms were part-political entities from the beginning, becoming fully engaged in politics in the eighteenth century. The British Company operated under a royal charter that granted it a monopoly of trade, but the monopoly was not always enforceable. Private merchants defied it and could get away because policing power was vested with the local kings who did not see it as their duty to defend an order of the English king. Besides, private traders sometimes formed clandestine business partnerships with Company employees. The London directors knew this but, beyond occasional penalties, could do little to curb conflicts of interest. In the backdrop of these developments, rivalries with the French East India Company broke out in the wake of the War of the Austrian Succession (1740–8) and the Seven Years War (1756–63). The rivals joined opposite camps in a power struggle in Carnatic, a small kingdom near British Madras and French Pondicherry. In Bengal, Anglo-French rivalry was again present but played an indirect role in the rise of the British. There, the Company ran into a dispute with the local ruler (nawab) and allied with Indian merchants and bankers to overthrow the regime. After initial reverses

---

[10] Om Prakash, *European Commercial Enterprise in Pre-colonial India* (Cambridge: Cambridge University Press, 1998).

against the French in the south and the nawab of Bengal in the east, the Company established itself as the ruler of Bengal (1757–65) and a de-facto ruler of the Carnatic (1760).

The next major territorial acquisitions occurred in the south. The Nizams of Hyderabad were Mughal governors who established a virtually independent rule by the third decade of the eighteenth century. Having suffered Maratha raids and entered a series of inconclusive engagements with the Marathas, the Nizam allied with the French. When the French became friendly with the two rival powers, Mysore and Marathas, the ruler Nizam Ali Khan allied with the English (1766), handing over the 'Northern Circars', a large chunk of coastal Coromandel, to the Company, to enable the English to pay for their troops. In 1803, districts in the west and south of the state, including the fertile Raichur Doab, were also handed over.[11]

These two modes of acquisition set the pattern of territorial acquisition by the Company in India.[12] It could bully weak states into delivering power over territories, and it could take sides in local rivalries and gain from military victories. Between 1775 and 1818, the Rohilla Afghans, the Marathas, and Mysore had to give up lands to the British. The Sikh wars in 1846 in a similar fashion delivered Punjab to British control. These conflicts worried the Indian princes. The worry increased in 1848–56, when British India asserted its right to annex a princely state if the ruling prince seemed to be governing badly and, worse, if he died without a male heir ('the doctrine of lapse'). The acquisition of Awadh by diktat (1856) followed in this way.

By 1856, the map of British India had settled. Sixty per cent of the land area and a somewhat higher percentage of the population belonged in the British-ruled territory (see Map 1.1). The British controlled the coastline, possessed all important ports, and the coastal trade routes. Several hundred large and small principalities governed the remaining 40 per cent of the area. With some of these,

---

[11] Doab, the tract between two confluent rivers.

[12] Tirthankar Roy, *An Economic History of Early Modern India* (London: Routledge, 2013).

the British had drawn up non-aggression treaties. The others were too small to matter, or so the British rulers thought.

Why Did Trade Lead to an Empire?

The Company was a political entity. It operated under a royal charter, maintained a small-scale military infrastructure, and sought the help of the Royal Navy in the late eighteenth century. Philip Stern has shown that the Company saw itself as a political intermediary between Britain and India long before the conquest of Bengal.[13] But having the power to protect profits and using power for territorial acquisition are different things.

Why did the empire happen? One answer to the question is that the Company was not a firm like most firms today. It was a firm with two personalities. The London directors were rich merchants and bankers and would want to avoid wars if possible. Small traders, soldiers, and sailors managed the distant branches. These people came from a different class of British society from the London businesspeople. The local actors were closer to those Indians on whom the firm's activities depended and negotiated with the latter all the time. They understood local politics and threats better than the directors. The disintegration of the Mughal Empire and warfare in Europe affected the decisions of these people. The British Empire emerged from the limited ability of the directors to stop their employees from joining local politics for personal gain.[14]

This explanation stresses the political element too much. In fact, acquisition of power could help the Company's commerce too. It could avoid having to import silver. The trade that the outstation officers managed could not do without the help of a large number of Indian bankers, subcontractors, transporters, and wage

---

[13] Philip Stern, *The Company–State: Corporate Sovereignty and the Early Modern Foundations of the British Empire in India* (Oxford: Oxford University Press, 2011).

[14] Holden Furber, 'Review of A. Mervyn Davies, *Clive of Plassey: A Biography*, New York: Charles Scribner's Sons, 1939', *American Historical Review* 45, no. 3 (1940): 635–7.

workers. These relationships broke down often. These problems compounded for the European private traders who obtained goods like silk or indigo from the interior of the country and thus took more risk. At a time when territorial powers were weaker than before, any trader would want to take a share in power to protect trade.[15]

A puzzle remains: Why did the Company succeed on the battle-field? The Company was a strong power in the seas. But the battles that left the Company in possession of an empire were fought on land, with resources raised from land. On land, the Company played the strategic game of creating a militarily strong state better than its rivals. The successor states had too little time and too few resources to get their tax systems in shape, which pushed them into making unreliable alliances and adopting extortionate tactics. The battles that followed further eroded their fiscal capacity. The Company followed another strategy. Most Indian states relied on military-cum-feudal lords for both taxation and the supply of soldiers. Such loyalty often failed. The British raised an army of paid soldiers. They did it while reforming the land tax system, which reform turned the village landlords from military agents into landowners. In the process of this gradual transfer of power from the warlords to the state, the Company created a state that could collect more tax per head and operated a more powerful military machine.[16] Further, after the Parliament started to share the rule of India (1784 Pitt's India Act, see later), its Indian partners saw the Company as a more credible ally, leading to stronger military alliances.[17]

The Conversion of the Company from Merchant Power to a State

The Company's empire in India raised two problems for the British State. Who was the real ruler of the Indian territories, the king, the

---

[15] Tirthankar Roy, *East India Company: The World's Most Powerful Corporation* (New Delhi: Allen Lane, 2012).

[16] Roy, *Economic History of Early Modern India*.

[17] M. Oak and A.V. Swamy, 'Myopia or Strategic Behavior? Indian Regimes and the East India Company in Late Eighteenth Century India', *Explorations in Economic History* 49, no. 3 (2012): 352–66.

Parliament, or a trading firm? How could a merchant firm rule in the name of the king, and rule in a manner that sometimes brought disrepute to the king? For example, the fact that it used the taxpayers' money to fund trade supplied ammunition to the view in London that a coterie of merchants had created a corrupt rule in Bengal and was running it in the name of the Crown. Responding to these criticisms, in 1784, Parliament created the body (Board of Control) that would establish parliamentary oversight upon the Company's rule in India.

Its role as a state showed up in a series of reforms in landed property rights.

NEW PROPERTY RIGHTS IN LAND

The Mughals were an agrarian empire, a state that depended on land taxes. The British formed a maritime empire, one that emerged from the Indian Ocean trade and financed its military enterprise initially by commercial income. As the Company acquired territorial states, it needed to change itself from a maritime into an agrarian state. British India followed a distinct pathway from its rival or partner Indian princely states. It created a standing army financed by the central treasury, as opposed to armies contributed by feudal land grantees. This move made it militarily more powerful than its neighbours. But to achieve this end, the Company brought land taxation under closer central control and intervened in landed property rights. Landlords and warlords either lost their hold on land or had to reinvent themselves as demilitarized landowners.

After receiving the taxation rights of Bengal (and soon, territories in southern and western India), the East India Company set out to reform the land taxation system. These reforms did not happen from a sense that landed property had been insecure before. Indian rulers were keen enough to protect peasant property rights. The reforms were done to make land more saleable instead. The earlier system was to create two interests in every plot of land, that of the cultivator and that of the tax collector. This entanglement created two situations that the British did not like. First, it made the tax-collecting landlord a powerful and militaristic actor. Second, it had made land poorly marketable. If land became more saleable, land price would rise, moneyed people would buy land, and the zamindars would either leave the village or transform into propertied people rather than warlords. Through market exchange, property should pass on to the most efficient producer and make both the state and the owner better off. The solution was to define only one right above all, that of ownership.

Contemporary economic thinking influenced the choice of a system of property rights based on ownership. The thinking said two things: That private property created an incentive to work harder, and that rent was an effect of scarcity and could be taxed without reducing the incentive to work hard. In 1818, James Mill (1773–1836), utilitarian philosopher and economist, received an appointment with the Board of Control of the East India Company. Mill had already established his reputation as the author of the *History of British India* (1817). In the same year, David Ricardo (1772–1823) had published his *Principles of Political Economy*. Mill knew Ricardo well and endorsed his theory of rent. The theory stated that rent arose due to scarcity of land relative to labour. As population growth drove expansion of cultivation into less fertile land, landowners captured the difference in fertility between the better and worse quality land as rent. The theory implied that rent was an 'unearned' income that could be taxed without affecting production. The theory also implied that tax should be levied on the net produce of land, which was the amount to be obtained from land solely attributable to fertility rather than capital and labour. These points made the zamindar a fit target of taxation, against which they would receive full ownership over the property they had so far controlled.

A legal paper of ownership was created. Whose name would be written on that paper?

Permanent Settlement or Zamindari Tenure

Under the zamindari tenure or Permanent Settlement (1793), property rights went to the former tax-collecting landlords or zamindars in exchange for a tax amount fixed forever (hence permanent).

After the Company took control of Bengal, revenue farming continued out of necessity, with the change that auctions became more open and the terms of the lease shorter. The highest prices at the auction were frequently too high relative to the area's ability to pay. The winner of the bid either defaulted or tried to collect exorbitant rents from their tenants, who fled from their land. Revenue farming, therefore, was both unpopular and inefficient. The Permanent Settlement was the final result of this process. It gave the zamindars ownership and security, provided they paid their tax. The Permanent Settlement extended in the 1800s to coastal Madras and North-Western Provinces (eastern UP [United Provinces before 1947 and Uttar Pradesh after 1947]). In these years, the Company had too little information and local influence to upset the rural magnates and contract with the peasant-cultivators directly. It contracted with the formerly tax-collecting landlords instead.

The first 15 years of the Permanent Settlement saw a burst of auctions of zamindari estates in greater Bengal, induced by sharply raised effective revenue collection and the inefficiency of many zamindars.[18] The auction sales tended to break up large estates into smaller lots. In Bengali, the word *laat* referred to resold bits of large estates, and 'going to laat' meant going bankrupt.

The zamindari settlement turned the peasants into the zamindars' tenants, liable for rent payment. The government left open the freedom of the zamindar to raise the rent. The administrators thought that the zamindars, 'grateful for the benefits secured to them, would in turn foster their tenants'.[19] In practice, the zamindars tried to exploit the tenants and sometimes joined with dominant tenants to exploit weaker ones. After Company rule ended, a series of tenancy acts (1859–1928) strengthened the occupancy rights of tenants and protected their rent.

[18] B. Chaudhuri, 'Agrarian Relations: Eastern India', in *CEHI* 2, eds Dharma Kumar and Meghnad Desai (Cambridge: Cambridge University Press, 1983), 94.

[19] B.H. Baden-Powell, 'The Origin of Zamindari Estates in Bengal', *Quarterly Journal of Economics* 11, no. 1 (1896): 36–69.

Ryotwari and Variations

Under all other arrangements, ownership property rights were exchanged for a commitment to pay a revenue that was subject to revision, approximately every 30 years (Map 2.2). When the Company acquired territories in the rest of India in the early nineteenth century, property rights reforms were done in a state of greater information and confidence. These were regions where the counterparts of the zamindars were weak and rare. Therefore, it was easier to consider peasant proprietorship in these regions. The arrangement where cultivators received proprietorship was known as ryotwari. In

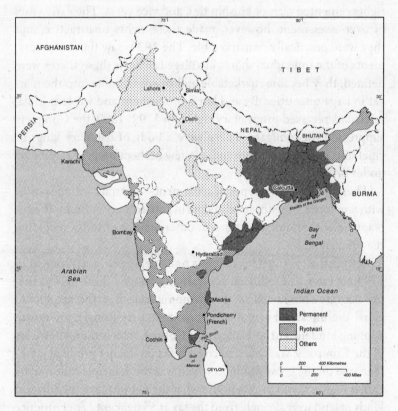

Map 2.2   Types of Settlement, c.1858

Source: Author

southern and western India, the ryotwari settlement was the common form. By the time ryotwari was established (around 1820), the mind of the major reformers had turned against zamindari from a sense that the zamindars were more intermediaries than cultivators. Ryotwari was, in principle, a direct contract between the ryot, or the cultivator, and the state. It meant a tax contract that remained valid for some time and was renegotiated after that.

In the upper Doab and Rohilkhand (present-day western UP and Haryana), the military power of the talukdars came down. Sometimes, the village republics or dominant kin groups became recognized as the proprietary body. The joint landlords of village lands were collectively responsible for the revenue. Therefore, joint rights cemented clan or kinship ties, and vice versa. The early years of over-assessment, however, made these rights unattractive, and they were practically unmarketable. The 1830s saw the first assessments of the individual shares in village lands. As these shares were defined, they became marketable and began to come into the market in large quantities. By and large, in southern and western India, mirasdars received proprietary rights. In 1799–1800, the Company suppressed the 'poligars'. These were a body of tributary kings or chieftains peculiar to South India. A few of them became zamindars under British rule.

These three general types of settlement—contract with peasants, with landlords, or with shareholders in coparcenary communities—reappear with minor variations in other regions of India, including the princely states.

Setting the ryotwari tax rate was not an easy process. Whereas in 1793 tax rates had followed convention, the new thinking was that the tax rate should follow the economic rule that the tax should equal the unearned rental component. Robert Pringle, an award-winning student at the Haileybury College, which trained officers of the Company, was asked to create a tax on the net produce rather than one on the gross produce, which was the principle followed by earlier regimes, and to determine what the net produce on different kinds of land were. Pringle fixed the tax at 55 per cent of net produce and carried out an extensive exercise classifying soil and cost of cultivation. Massive information problems rendered the entire exercise a failure and the high rate set was a disaster for the peasants.[20] The first 20 odd years of ryotwari saw an agricultural depression.[21]

Towards the middle of the 1840s, a new assessment was under way. The architects of the new system were George Wingate, an engineer with the Company, and H.E. Goldsmid, a revenue officer. They were as doctrinaire as Pringle on the infallibility of Ricardo but created a more detailed information system on the relative fertility of plots of land and combined it with climate and market access. The information demands on that process were still enormous and beyond the capacity of the officers in charge. Wingate and Goldsmid ingeniously argued that the historically established rent should be the benchmark for the absolute level, provided it had allowed culti-vation to expand. For that would be a sign that the tax was less than the true economic rent. In effect, the rate came down. From early in the second half of the nineteenth century, conditions improved. But whether the reversal was due to the effects of rising prices and expanding world market or the success of the Wingate–Goldsmid settlement, it is not known.

While reforming the tax system, the Company took away some of the customary privileges of the local magnates, for example, the authority of the local officials to punish the defaulting tax collec-tor or peasant. Suppression of this right made it possible for land to change hands faster and more easily when defaults occurred. The Company made the public sale of ownership mandatory when tax defaults occurred. At a broader level, recognition of ownership rights meant devaluation of customary tenancy rights; recognition of peasants' rights meant de-recognition of the customary rights of the pastoralists, and poor legal protection of the village commons encouraged enclosures.

[20] Neeraj Hatekar, 'Pringle's Ricardian Experiment in the Nineteenth Century Deccan Countryside', *IESHR* 33, no. 4 (1996): 437–57.

[21] H. Fukazawa, 'Western India', in Kumar and Desai, *CEHI 2*. An older discussion can be found in P.J. Thomas and B. Natarajan, 'Economic Depression in the Madras Presidency (1825–54)', *Economic History Review (EHR)* 7, no. 1 (1936): 67–75.

Gainers and Losers from Institutional Reforms

Who gained and who lost through these processes? The answer varied by region.

In zamindari areas, the older elite initially gained. But some of this gain faded away as the nineteenth century wore on. Many zamindars did not live in the village. In one view, big tenant farmers, often called *jotedars*, took advantage of the zamindars' distance from the land and unstable economic conditions to acquire wealth and power. The Permanent Settlement, 'long regarded as the propelling force behind a revolution in Bengali rural society, would appear to have effected a less fundamental change than is usually supposed'.[22] In a different interpretation, except in a few districts, the small peasant dominated Bengal agriculture.[23] Such peasants became more dependent on creditors as they became more dependent on buying and selling in volatile markets, and the market power of merchants and bankers increased. Both these accounts suggest that the zamindars did not dominate the countryside, at least, not for long. After 1870, groups of rich farmers consolidated their economic power by producing for a rising market, whereas the zamindars' power to share that gain by raising rents reduced because of tenancy acts that regulated rents. Elsewhere, members of the older elite, that is, groups with access to land but unwilling or unable to cultivate it, were more likely to sell land, leave the village, take a degree, and join urban services. At the same time, groups more likely to buy land were cultivators and labourers. In short, the long-term picture of the landlord areas was that of a slow attrition of the landlord's economic and political power.

In the countryside, the pattern of land transfers should suggest who was rising in power and who lost. Property rights reforms did stimulate land market transactions. But there is little direct

---

[22] Ratnalekha Ray, *Change in Bengal Agrarian Society c1760–1850* (Delhi: Manohar, 1979), 284.

[23] Rajat Datta, 'Agricultural Production, Social Participation and Domination in Late Eighteenth Century Bengal: Towards an Alternative Explanation', *Journal of Peasant Studies* 17, no. 1 (1989): 68–113.

evidence on just how big a change this was, that is, how often land rights changed hands. As we have seen, soon after the Permanent Settlement, zamindari titles changed hands a lot. In ryotwari areas, land transfers did increase somewhat. However, the extent of transfer was not very significant, as data collected for a later period shows (see Chapter 4).

The zamindari and ryotwari areas differed in the pattern of their subsequent development. Their ability to spend money on public goods was one of the potential differences. In zamindari areas, the government left the responsibility for making investments to the zamindars. In the ryotwari areas, the government implicitly assumed responsibility. Taxes being fixed forever in the zamindari areas, the government could not hope to recover returns to investment in the form of taxes. Nor could the zamindar raise rent after 1859, because new laws regulated rent. So the zamindar could not hope to recover returns on investment. In ryotwari areas, both these roads remained open. In all regions, however, agricultural productivity was low because cultivation depended on the monsoons and short seasons when agriculture was possible. The low yield limited local capacity to spend money as well.

In agriculture, the main source of change was the State. In the non-agricultural occupations, the change came from markets.

FOREIGN TRADE

At the close of the Napoleonic wars, the market for Indian textiles fell owing to tariffs on Indian goods in England, which increased between 1797 and 1814. Almost simultaneously, technological change in weaving, such as Horrocks' power loom, reduced the difference in cost of production. The Company's commercial monopoly in India ended with the Charter Act of 1813 (the monopoly in China trade continued until 1833). Already, the Company had become more of a state than a merchant. Its power centre, however, was in the port cities, where trade was booming.

Three features of this boom stand out. First, the importance of foreign trade in the economy increased. An approximate measure of the importance is the ratio of trade to national income. The average annual growth rate of trade was 4–5 per cent during 1834–1913. The rate at which national income at current prices was growing over 1868–1913 was about 1.5 per cent. According to the best estimates, the rate of growth of national income was still smaller between 1821 and 1871.[24] It follows that the ratio of trade to income was rising for much of the nineteenth century. Second, while India lost its textile export market from the early 1800s, the overall scale of trade increased, no matter how we measure the change.

Third, the composition of trade changed. Textiles (in export) and bullion (in import) had dominated the eighteenth-century trade. Between 1800 and 1850, imported goods paid for exports. The demand for precious metals was still large, but it was not a means of paying for export. The export of cotton cloth also dropped sharply after 1800. Textiles began to be replaced by new exportable articles such as indigo, opium, silk, tobacco, and cotton, and to a more limited extent, salt, sugar, and saltpetre. In 1811, the principal export from India was cloth (33 per cent of export value). Next in importance were opium (24), indigo (19), raw silk (8), raw cotton (5), and sugar (5). By 1850, the major exports were opium (30 per cent of value), raw cotton (19), indigo (11), sugar (10), and foodgrains (4). The composition of imports was simpler. Textiles and metals accounted for nearly 60 per cent of the import value in 1850.

Indigo and opium were both available in the hinterland of the ports.[25] Indigo was a dye used in cotton textiles. The world trade in indigo began to rise after the establishment of a machine textile industry in England. At first, supplies came from the West Indies. But this source became uncertain during the Napoleonic wars. Since Bengal had conditions suitable for its cultivation, European capitalists

---

[24] GDP at current prices increased by about 25 per cent between 1821 and 1871, based on Stephen Broadberry, Johann Custodis, and Bishnupriya Gupta, 'India and the Great Divergence: An Anglo-Indian Comparison of GDP per capita, 1600–1871', *Explorations in Economic History* 55, no. 1 (2015): 58–75.

[25] B.B. Chowdhury, *Growth of Commercial Agriculture in Bengal, 1757–1900* (Calcutta: Quality Printers, 1964); John F. Richards, 'The Opium Industry in British India', *IESHR* 39, no. 2–3 (2002): 149–80.

invested in indigo production in the Bengal countryside. European firms based in Calcutta funded them and handled marketing and shipment. They were known as agency houses.[26] The European producers of processed indigo were called 'planters', misleadingly because they did not own plantations. The planters advanced money to peasants and made them sign contracts that specified the extent of land to be sown with indigo but left prices and quantities of leaves delivered to be fixed by tradition. The business was profitable to the peasants, as long as relative prices between competing crops did not change. In the 1850s, the price of rice increased much faster than indigo, and in 1859–60, the peasants turned unwilling to sow indigo. Since many of the same peasants had already taken advances, the planters took the contracts to the courts, seeking punishments for the defaulters. Some of them used more brutal methods to make the peasants fulfil their bargain. The resultant chaos was known as the blue mutiny. The administration refused to bail out the planters but designed a contract law instead.[27]

Opium was an old crop in Benares, Bihar, and central India. Private traders and Company officers were aware of the huge potential market for the product in China, and the administration was keen to control the trade to capture more revenue from it. The Company devised a monopoly procurement of opium through granting the license to cultivate and trade to contractors. But it never quite trusted the contractors to give either the Company or the peasants a fair deal, and between 1775 and 1797, a state monopsony emerged. The contractor system ended in favour of a state–peasant contract, and progressively, the infrastructure necessary for regulation of production and quality was set up.

In the late 1700s, European merchants on the southern China coast, who had seen the popularity of opium shops in the coastal towns, tried to control an existing but only loosely organized trade

[26] Called agency houses because they served their own business and also sometimes did business on behalf of others, as agents. The system called managing agency (Chapter 6) evolved from this tradition.

[27] Tirthankar Roy and Anand V. Swamy, *Law and the Economy in Colonial India* (Chicago: University of Chicago Press, 2016).

in opium. Threatened by the agents of the state in the harbours of Whampoa and Macau, the opium traders withdrew to Canton. Ships plied between Calcutta and Canton. Opium exchanged for silver, which made opium a coveted target for sea pirates. The foreign-owned 'opium runners' usually travelled in a group, to deliver the goods to armed vessels waiting in the harbours; many of these were also foreign-owned. These floating depots of opium sold some of the goods locally and delivered the bulk to Chinese junks that journeyed up the rivers to sell retail to opium shops and agents conducting overland trade.

The trade was regulated in China and made illegal in 1796. But a weak Chinese State found itself powerless to suppress it. Opium shops multiplied in the maritime towns. The tension between the State and the foreign merchants broke out in the Opium War of 1839–40 when large quantities of opium were seized and destroyed by the authorities, inviting retaliatory strikes by the Company's navy. The war ended with the Treaty of Nanking (1842). Under the terms of the treaty, foreign traders would enjoy concessions and immunity from local law. The treaty also led to the transfer of Hong Kong to Britain, which provided a more secure site for trade.

Opium stabilized the British Empire. Between 1780 and 1833, the Company, and after that, the private traders, invested on average more than a million pounds sterling each year in buying tea in Canton. At first, imported silver was needed to buy tea. But the opium sale supplied another means to purchase tea. The resultant international exchange of stimulants—tea for opium—contributed to the balancing of trades of three countries: India, Britain, and China.[28]

Opium trade helped Indian business. The ships that conducted the Bengal–China trade, the Parsis of Bombay and Calcutta, and the Marwari merchants involved in the inland trade in Malwa opium made great profits from the business. Merchants of Hong Kong had

[28] Michael Greenberg, *British Trade and the Opening of China, 1800–42* (Cambridge: Cambridge University Press, 1969); Tan Chung, 'The Britain-China-India Trade Triangle (1771–1840)', *IESHR* 11, no. 4 (1974): 411–31.

a stake in the trade. In this way, the empire consolidated Asian capital, which in turn contributed to other forms of enterprise. Leading Parsi business houses, for example, accumulated capital in opium before moving into cotton mills. Opium profits shored up government income, and via the exchequer, flowed back into canals and railway construction in India.

After indigo and opium, raw cotton was a big item of export. Descriptions of the Arabian Sea trade before European entry sometimes recorded trade in Indian cotton. Little is known as to how large or how systematic the trade was. It is safe to assume that cotton did not involve a specialized trading system. This obscurity was to end in the nineteenth century. Cotton export to Europe began from the second half of the eighteenth century in response to growth of cotton spinning in Britain. Cotton was not an indigenous crop in Britain, but a certain quantity was imported mainly for use as candlewick. Clothing manufacture using cotton yarn, rather using a mixture between cotton and linen, nevertheless did develop in the eighteenth century mainly in response to the importation of Indian cotton yarn. In the 1760s, the domestic production of cotton goods expanded very rapidly. Between 1767 and 1785, patents were taken by James Hargreaves for the spinning jenny and Richard Arkwright for the spinning frame. These inventions and the wider adoption of the steam engine in factories increased the demand for raw cotton greatly. Between the year when the spinning jenny began and 1801, annual cotton imports into Britain increased from 2000 to 280,000 tonnes. Nearly 90 per cent of this quantity came from the United States, where a dramatic growth of cotton cultivation followed the invention of Eli Whitney's saw gin (1793). The trade in Gujarat cotton, which was, in fact, an older trade, expanded at the same time from less than 100 in the 1780s to about 2000 tonnes at the end of the century.

The Company noted the prospect of selling raw cotton instead of textiles. It sponsored surveys in the 1790s about production, quality, and internal trade. The experience of selling Indian cotton in Britain was, nevertheless, disappointing. Partly because of the poor quality of ginning and partly internal transport costs, Indian cotton did not sell well in London. A large part of Gujarat cotton went to Bengal overland, and the prices offered did not succeed in diverting it to export trade. The situation changed during the Napoleonic wars. Trade with the United States became uncertain, and trade with Asian sources became more attractive than before. After 1800, for the next three decades, a series of partnerships between the administration and private entrepreneurs attempted to reproduce American cotton in India, lower the cost of transport, and make use of Whitney's gin to address the most serious problem of Indian cotton, the heavy admixture of seeds and dirt. Partly through these efforts, but mainly because of investments made by Indian traders and farmers, the cotton export trade steadily expanded. However, it was not before the beginning of railway construction (1850s) and the American Civil War (1861–5) that Indian cotton truly established itself as the fibre of choice in Britain.

DOMESTIC TRADE

At the time of Aurangzeb's death (1707), the Ganges and the Indus provided the main arteries for domestic trade in bulk commodities in North India. The two major arteries met in the Punjab, where caravans that crossed the Himalayas to connect India with Afghanistan, Iran, and Central Asia, also joined. Apart from grain, the overland traders carried salt, cloth, spices, and horses. In the Deccan peninsula, where neither navigable rivers nor wheeled traffic could penetrate far into the interior, the main mode of overland carriage of goods was the pack bullock. Bullock trains of enormous size, managed by the *Banjaras*, connected northern India with southern India and connected the coasts with the capital cities in the Deccan. Coast-to-coast shipping conducted by maritime communities supplemented this overland traffic.

In the eighteenth century, frequent warfare took a toll on trading. The decline of the Mughal fiscal system upset those channels of grain trade that were linked to taxation. But the emergence of specialized clusters of textile production in the coastal areas stimulated the movement of cotton and grain from the interior towards these zones. The presence of the Europeans, who sometimes lent their idle shipping capacity, stimulated coast-to-coast trade. In regions located near the river Ganges, there was little disturbance. Cities such as Benares, Patna, Murshidabad, or Dhaka seemed to do well commercially.

The rise of British power in the eastern Gangetic plains stimulated domestic trade in grain, even as it adversely affected the fortunes of the older capitals such as Murshidabad and Dhaka, and with it, some of the older banking and merchant firms that depended on the custom of the Nawabi regime. Anand Yang shows that a late eighteenth-century boom in Patna based on revenue farming, banking, and manufacturing came to an end around the middle decades of the nineteenth century with decay of artisanal production. But after that shock, trade and finance revived again in the city, now based on agricultural trade and finance.[29] Another study suggests a rise in the market power of the 'non-resident' grain merchant in late eighteenth-century Bengal.[30] Demand for grain in growing cities like Calcutta was, of course, buoyant. In the western Gangetic, some regions specialized in the production of indigo and cotton and purchased grain from areas situated further away.[31]

What do we know about the merchants? Who conducted the trade?

MERCHANTS AND BANKERS

The major activities, in which large-scale private capital was engaged in the eighteenth century, were trades in cotton, grain, cloth, and opium; tax farming; lending to the State; money changing; and internal remittances. Weak and warring states needed the bankers.

[29] Anand A. Yang, *Bazaar India: Markets, Society and the Colonial State in Bihar* (Berkeley: University of California Press, 1998), chapter 5.

[30] Rajat Datta, 'Merchants and Peasants: A Study of the Structure of Local Trade in Grain in Late Eighteenth Century Bengal', *IESHR* 23, no. 4 (1986): 379–402. On Bihar merchants and bankers, see Kumkum Chaterjee, *Merchants, Politics and Society in Early Modern India Bihar: 1733–1820* (Leiden: E.J. Brill, 1996).

[31] Asiya Siddiqi, *Agrarian Change in a Northern Indian State: Uttar Pradesh 1819–1833* (Oxford: The Clarendon Press, 1973).

Money changers flourished because of the existence of many local currencies. The remittance business grew because of the emergence of new zones in which political power was weak. The Company needed the bankers to move large sums of money between its ports.

Some Indian firms were big. The big firms frequently combined trade with banking. There were also specialized banking houses or *pedhis*. These firms performed money changing or converting one currency to another, provided and cashed bills of exchange or hundis, lent to governments, and occasionally took up revenue contracts. Such activities brought business firms and rulers closer to each other. Professional traders and bankers did invest in industry in the case of exportable goods such as textiles, but not crafts in general. Commercial and financial capital, thus, found relatively little use outside agricultural commodity trades. A large part of the profits went into the purchase of gold jewellery and into spiritual assets, such as building temples, construction of ghats in Kashi, or charity and relief during famines.

In the early 1800s, the *Khatris*, the *Lohanas*, and *Bhatias* were the trading communities prominent in Delhi, Agra, Punjab, Rajasthan, and Sind. Their counterparts among the Muslims were the *Khojas* and the *Parachas*, said to have been converted Khatris. They were engaged in the overland trade with Central Asia and Afghanistan and occasionally took part in the local administration. Marwaris of western Rajasthan were mainly bankers and moneylenders, who also took part in trade. None of these groups played a significant role in maritime trade. Agents of North Indian merchant-banking firms conducted business in other parts of Asia. They did not become marginal even after the emergence of European dominance in the Indian Ocean but continued to operate in commercial centres connected by overland trade routes.

Some historians draw attention to overland trade and argue that a preoccupation with maritime traders leads to a neglect of this form of enterprise.[32] Stephen Dale, for example, studies Multan merchants

---

[32] Sushil Chaudhury, *From Prosperity to Decline: Eighteenth-Century Bengal* (Delhi: Manohar, 1995).

based in Astrakhan, a port city on the Caspian Sea.[33] Scott Levi and Claude Markovits have worked on similar groups in other parts of Asia.[34]

In the Arabian Sea trade, Indian maritime traders remained prominent long after the rise of European trade in the region. Hindu and Muslim trading communities in Gujarat and Saurashtra conducted some inland trade and a lot of maritime trade between the Gujarat coast of India and the Persian Gulf, Arabia, Africa, and Malabar. The seafaring merchants of Kachchh, who were major players in the Arabian Sea trade, had well-developed institutions of commerce and banking; knowledge of the seas, shipping, and shipbuilding; a history of collaborating with political actors; and access to both maritime and overland trade routes.[35] In South India, the Telugu-speaking *Komatis* and the Tamil-speaking *Chettis* were the two prominent trading communities. In eastern India, according to medieval Bengali ballads and European travel accounts of the seventeenth century, members of the Bengali trading castes took part in the Bay of Bengal trade. Members of the *Subarna Banik* caste group joined Indo-European trade in the early nineteenth century, made a lot of money, and invested that money into education, real estate, and zamindari estates. In the early eighteenth century, North Indian traders became prominent in silk trade and high finance. A steady stream of merchants and bankers migrating from western and northern India also began from this time. The Marwari firm of the Jagatseth in Bengal, who had exclusive control of the mint, commanded much wealth and reputation.

The rise of the Company regime ended the career of some of the older firms. Businesses dependent on near-bankrupt regional states

---

[33] Stephen F. Dale, *Indian Merchants and Eurasian Trade, 1600–1750* (Cambrdige: Cambridge University Press, 1994).

[34] Scott C. Levi, *The Indian Diaspora in Central Asia and its Trade, 1550–1900* (Leiden: E.J. Brill, 2002).For example, Claude Markovits, 'Indian Merchant Networks Outside India in the Nineteenth and Twentieth Centuries: A Preliminary Survey', *MAS* 33, no. 4 (1999): 883–911.

[35] Chhaya Goswami, *The Call of the Sea: Kachchhi Traders in Muscat and Zanzibar, c. 1800–1880* (Hyderabad: Orient Black Swan, 2011).

found that their days were numbered. Others had to adapt and seek new avenues. A famous example of decline was the Jagatseth. The Jagatseth sided with the English in the palace revolution that saw the Company begin to control Bengal. The Seths declined later because the Company did not need them anymore as an ally in politics or the mint business. The last Jagatseth, Gobindchand, died in obscurity as a poor state pensioner in 1864.

On the other hand, many of the communities engaged in trade and banking found new ways of earning profit. For example, the firm of Trawdi Shri Krishna Arjunji Nathji of Surat saw continued prosperity in return for loans that it made available for British campaigns against Holkar.[36] Indian 'brokers' and partners of Indo-European trading firms made money too. The Bengali Subarna Baniks succeeded dramatically. In Western India, Parsis were the counterparts. Parsis were traditionally not traders or financiers, but artisans, carpenters, weavers, and shipbuilders. Their entry into trade was a result of their contact with the Europeans as brokers.

By the end of the eighteenth century, European merchants and former employees of the Company were setting up firms in Calcutta. These were called agency, because they needed to take a license from the Company. They were agency in another sense too; they often handled other people's money in trade and finance. The agency houses traded in opium, indigo, silk, foreign textiles, and sugar. They were also engaged in a limited way in banking and insurance. Until about 1834, they received deposits of Company officials attracted by high interest rates and the exchange rates on remittances. The demand and price of indigo were notoriously unstable. A violent crash in the early 1830s drove many of these firms to the wall. After that, deposits of Company officials dried up. The agency houses began to rely more on Indian partners for capital and management. These firms entered banking, insurance, coal mining, silk filatures, and shipbuilding, along with indigo, opium, and sugar.

Several Indian individuals became millionaires during this time. Notable examples were Dwarkanath Tagore (1794–1846),

[36] Lakshmi Subramanian, *Three Merchants of Bombay: Business Pioneers of the Nineteenth Century* (New Delhi: Allen Lane, 2012).

Rustomjee Cowasjee, Motilal Seal (1792–1854), and the Prawnkissen Law family. Seal and Law were Subarna Baniks. The firm Carr Tagore was the largest in scale and had the most diversified interests. Using his official connections with the government and friendships with British entrepreneurs, Tagore was able to develop a major financial and commercial house. His interests included colliery, tea, salt, steamboats, indigo, and a major bank. His zamindari estate grew indigo. His own bank, the Union Bank, dominated the financing of the indigo trade.

Some of these partnerships ended in 1846–7 when the Union Bank collapsed due to fraud. After this date, Bengali moneyed people tended to invest in zamindari. Historians sometimes see this shift as a failure of Bengali enterprise and the outcome of a get-rich-quick mentality. The weakness of these firms had a more basic cause. Money was expensive. These firms traded a lot but could not rely on a strong banking system. The Company was reluctant to give banking licenses; there was little regulation of banks; many trading firms did banking on the side; and the banking business was too dependent on lending to one or two commodity trades. Furthermore, many wealthy Bengalis turned towards educating their children in the new colleges and universities located in their cities. So did the Parsis in Bombay. Both communities lost interest in staying purely commercial.

Already, some of these firms had diversified from trade to industry.

INDUSTRY

The early nineteenth century saw a fall in the scale of production and export of Indian cotton textiles because of the decline both in European demand and in demand from the impoverished Indian aristocracy. Import of machine-made cloth and yarn shrunk India's position as a supplier of cloth to the world. The resultant process of unemployment of artisanal workers is called 'deindustrialization'.

Much of the research available on the subject tested how big the decline was rather than what effect it had on the rest of the economy. Early historical works on regional economies that commented on industrial decline used impressionistic data and discussed particular places and industries.[37] A.K. Bagchi and Michael Twomey estimated the overall scale of the decline using indirect measures such as actual or potential job loss.[38] Another work supplies a more directly measured and, therefore, more reliable figure for job loss in Bengal textiles in the early nineteenth century.[39] What do these numbers mean?

The significance of the job loss depends on two things: the size of the labour force and the productivity of the labour force. The size of the labour force cannot be known for certain. The extent of the loss in Bengal, estimated at 4 per cent of the initial workforce spread over several decades, was large but cannot be called catastrophic. As for productivity, hand-spinners were mainly domestic workers who performed spinning in their spare time. The low opportunity cost of their labour meant that they were willing to perform spinning for a small payment. Their income loss, therefore, should be smaller than the employment loss. On the other hand, the massive fall in yarn and cloth prices that brought it about also enabled the poor to buy more cloth and the handloom weavers to buy yarn more cheaply than before, enhancing their productivity. Overall, the effect of the Industrial Revolution on Indian artisans was uncertain.

[37] Romesh Chunder Dutt, *The Economic History of India in the Victorian Age* (London: Kegan Paul, 1906); R.D. Choksey, *Economic History of Bombay–Deccan and Karnatak (1818–1868)* (Poona: Gokhale Institute of Politics and Economics, 1945); A. Sarada Raju, *Economic Conditions of the Madras Presidency 1800–1850* (Madras: University of Madras,1941); H.R. Ghosal, *Economic Transition in the Bengal Presidency (1793–1833)* (Calcutta: Firma K.L. Mukhopadhyay, 1966); and A.V. Raman Rao, *The Economic Development of Andhra Pradesh 1766–1957* (Bombay: Popular, 1958).

[38] A.K. Bagchi, 'Deindustrialization in India in the Nineteenth Century: Some Theoretical Implications', *Journal of Development Studies* 12, no. 2 (1976): 135–64; Michael J. Twomey, 'Employment in Nineteenth Century Indian Textiles,' *Explorations in Economic History* 20, no. 1 (1983): 37–57.

[39] Indrajit Ray, 'Identifying the Woes of the Cotton Textile Industry in Bengal: Tales of the Nineteenth Century', *EHR* 62, no. 4 (2009): 857–92.

The iron and steel industry is sometimes cited as another example of deindustrialization. The evidence again is uncertain. The import of iron goods did increase from the late eighteenth century. Much of this demand was for cannons, guns, cutlery, or construction material, which the Indian iron smelter and blacksmith did not make on a large scale.

Overall, there may not have been a shock at all. Many new types of innovative enterprises were developing in the port towns in the early 1800s. Several of them involved European capital, technology, and artisanal skills. The general growth of Indo-European business after the end of the Company's monopoly over Indian trade in 1813 encouraged private investment in India. In the nineteenth century, artisan-entrepreneurs having some connection with the East India Company tried to erect iron shops after the English model. The migration of European artisans to India had begun in the eighteenth century. Many more travelled to India to make a career after the end of the Company's charter in 1813.

A Scottish ironmaster, Andrew Duncan, for example, set up a charcoal-using smelting factory in the Birbhum District of Bengal in about 1810. The factory failed a few years after. In Bengal, South India, and Kumaon, several other ventures in iron smelting began. The most famous one was established in the river port Porto Novo by the ironmaster Josiah Marshall Heath in 1825. This enterprise produced good quality of iron, and the Company thought it was worth supporting. It never made much money. The Company officers puzzled over why it was going bankrupt. Recent research suggests a common problem that the charcoal-burning iron industry was beginning to face in the early nineteenth century—the high cost of wood fuel as forests receded. Besides, the factories usually located near the supply of ores, which were often remote places. Transportation from longer distances proved prohibitively expensive in the absence of good roads and railways.[40]

---

[40] Tirthankar Roy, 'Did Globalization Aid Industrial Development in Colonial India? A Study of Knowledge Transfer in the Iron Industry', *IESHR* 46, no. 4 (2009): 579–613.

Because the transportation problem was not serious there, a more secure foundation for industrialization was emerging in the port cities, Bombay, Madras, and Calcutta. The European population in these cities had encouraged the manufacture of many types of consumer goods patterned after goods in use in Europe. Contemporary reports mentioned horse carriages and furniture, watches, clocks, shoes, and glassware. Some of the artisan-proprietors of the firms set up large workshops producing intermediate goods. On the western bank of the river Hooghly near Calcutta, shipbuilding yards started. Here, one William Jones set up a canvas manufacturing unit, and the Company's large salt warehouse created a small European settlement. Much of the factory enterprise remained concentrated around the cities. In this way, though still on a very small scale, British capital, institutions like partnership, and certain artisanal skills moved into the port cities. These links paid off in the late nineteenth-century industrialization of these cities.

THE STATE AND PUBLIC GOODS

One of the striking features of Company rule was a rise in government revenue. Revenue figures over time are slightly misleading since the territory was expanding in area and population. Adjustments for these changes would still show a significant rise in government income. For example, in Bengal, revenue per square mile increased from Rs 236 in 1763, to 520 in 1817, and further to 724 in 1853.[41] This rise was very large in real terms. It was achieved via institutional change in land rights, which eliminated a variety of intermediary earners between the peasant and the state. That was not all. The government was determined to make trade pay more. Salt, for example, was made to yield an income through an inland duty where manufacture was in private hands, from profits where the government monopolized procurement, and from customs duty on imported salt. The government exercised a monopoly on salt production and trade in lower Bengal. Similarly, opium also paid well.

[41] Roy, *Economic History of Early Modern India*.

How was money being spent? In the century of consolidation of colonial rule (1757–1857), the government left a mark in external and internal security, currency, irrigation, law and justice, education, and embankment construction. After the army, the bureaucracy, and war-related expenditure were taken out, there was little money left for investment in infrastructure and public goods. Nevertheless, by 1857, a beginning was made in setting up a postal system, a railway network indirectly financed by the budget, and the telegraphs. Their effects were fully felt in the second half of the nineteenth century, and will, therefore, be taken up in later chapters.

The source of the Company's military power was a standing army. The standing army originated in the troops raised and maintained in Bengal, Bombay, and Madras, known as the Presidency armies. From the mid-eighteenth century, British regiments were sent to fight in India. Until 1784, the expense of British regiments in India was paid from British revenues; thereafter, the Board of Control (a body appointed by the Parliament to manage the governance of India) could hire British regiments and pay the cost with Indian revenue. Limits were set on the numbers hired from Britain. From the early nineteenth century, the cost of the army was paid mainly from the Indian revenue.[42]

From some time towards the end of the eighteenth century and until the 1830s, 'dacoits', river pirates, and gang robbers formed a major preoccupation of the Company administration. In the mainly forested districts in central India that had belonged to the semi-independent Maratha chiefs or their vassals, and through which major pilgrim and trade traffic passed on their way from the west coast to Ujjain, Benares, Mirzapur, and Mathura, mini cavalry armies called pindaries raided victims in the 1810s and 1820s. In roughly the same region, groups of people who had perfected the art of strangling, called thuggees, robbed travellers. Another region where gang

---

[42] T.A. Heathcote, *The Military in British India: The Development of British Land Forces in South Asia, 1600–1947* (Manchester: Manchester University Press, 1995).

robbers caused difficulty was lower Bengal, where the numerous rivers supplied both easy victims and easy escape routes.

The administrators were fascinated by the organization behind these activities and saw the perpetrators, with some justification, as it would any other professional caste. They had strong team spirit, shared a religious bonding, and received tacit patronage of powerful individuals. Local princes patronized these activities from a variety of motives. Some of the gang leaders had earlier formed the irregular soldiery of their armies. Some of these princes doubted the strength of British rule and wanted to retain links with soldiers in case the tide turned. And of course, they took a cut on the income if possible.

Overall, the crime wave owed to a larger problem, which was economic: the demilitarization of soldiers on a very large scale as warfare came to an end in central and northern India. The former soldiers who lost jobs and needed to change occupations numbered in the hundreds of thousands. So far, little research has been done on how the shrinking and fragmentation of old armies and camp followers affected the regions and communities from which the soldiers came. Surely, many amongst the disbanded soldiery went back to land. But a sufficiently large number were unwilling or unable to change profession and still bore arms.

A full history of predatory gangs and their impact on society in this period of Indian history is not available. The problem occupied a lot of public resources and energy, but we cannot say if the administration over-reacted and dramatized the threat or that the threat was serious enough. Recent scholarship suggests that important clauses of law, concepts of criminality and society, and measures to streamline systems of police and justice took shape through the process of dealing with these groups.[43]

In 1799, the Company first considered the introduction of a uniform currency for territories under its control. At that time, major currencies in circulation included the Bengal silver rupee, the Arcot

[43] Radhika Singha, *A Despotism of Law: Crime and Justice in Early Colonial India* (Delhi: Oxford University Press, 1998); Kim Wagner, 'Thuggee and Social Banditry Reconsidered', *The Historical Journal* 50, no. 2 (2007): 353–76.

silver rupee, and the Madras gold pagoda.[44] Apart from these, many states issued their currencies, and local transactions took place in copper coins or cowries, both accepted media of exchange for a long time. Multiple currencies affected trade and taxation. Bankers earned a commission that the state could easily pocket itself had there been a unified currency system. A unified system made sense.

The Company wanted to have the Bengal *sicca* rupee replace all others. However, since the gold-silver price ratio varied between Madras and Bengal, the plan did not seem feasible in 1799, and multiple currencies continued, including several that the Company itself coined. In 1835, a Company silver rupee of uniform weight came into circulation throughout the region. One long-term effect of this reform was a gradual devaluation and eventual disappearance of many local means of exchange, such as cowries, since increasingly the rupee became the acceptable basis for revenue payments. The announced exchange rate between the rupee and the pound sterling was 15:1.

From early in its rule, the engineers employed in the Company's army campaigned for investment in irrigation, to raise peasant incomes and state incomes together. The idea was not a new one. When the Company took control of the upper Gangetic plains, the engineers found a network of irrigation channels in the western part of the plains. It was clear that water management had engaged all medieval regimes. In the older cities, there was evidence of sophisticated systems of lifting and channelling water to supply the palace complex and sometimes ordinary residents (Fatehpur Sikri and Vijayanagar, for example), construction of large tanks (Hauz Khas in Delhi, tanks in Vijayanagar), and construction of canals (in or near Delhi constructed in the fourteenth century, and in Gaud, the sixteenth-century capital of Bengal).[45] In South India, the 'grand

[44] Amiya Kumar Bagchi, 'Transition from Indian to British Indian Systems of Money and Banking 1800–1850', *MAS* 19, no. 3 (1985): 501–19.

[45] I.H. Siddiqui, 'Water Works and Irrigation System in India during Pre-Mughal Times', *Journal of the Economic and Social History of the Orient* 29, no. 1 (1986): 52–77.

anicut' on the Cauvery, attributed to the Chola rulers, was another large pre-British system.

These ancient canals were in a state of disrepair decades before the Company's rule began. The Company administration, by and large, appreciated the importance of these systems and restored some of them. The restored works appeared on the Jamuna (1817–1840s), the deltas of the Cauvery (1830s and 1840s), and Godavari and Krishna (1840s and 1850s). An accent on large riparian projects meant that some of the other local systems of storage, like tanks in the Tamil Nadu region, were neglected.[46]

Law was one field in which the state spent a lot of energy. Institutional economic history suggests that the economic rise of the Western world owed to institutions. One example would be laws that ensured security of property and contract. By implication, the non-Western regions should have begun with a weaker system of indigenous law, which the European colonists should have reformed and improved upon. Against this prediction, historians of colonial India maintain that there was nothing wrong with property rights before the British started their rule. The British colonialists did not say that they wanted to reform laws because the Indian laws did not protect property. In fact, they wanted and tried to preserve the indigenous tradition of rights and laws, because they thought Indian legal theory was well developed, and that persistence with customary law would keep the population happy. The officers found in Sanskrit and Persian-Arabic codebooks a good enough structure of the common law.[47] The first governor general of the Indian territories, Warren Hastings (in office 1774–85) was a firm believer in the theory that India should be governed by Indian laws. He took steps to train and educate officers in Indian classical texts by opening institutions in Calcutta and Benares.

The state, however, persisted with tradition only in property law, especially land ownership, succession, and inheritance. Commercial law, such as contract or negotiable instruments or companies' law, was

[46] Prasannan Parthasarathi, 'Water and Agriculture in Nineteenth-century Tamilnad', *MAS* 51, no. 2 (2017): 485–510.

[47] Roy and Swamy, *Law and the Economy in Colonial India*.

less burdened by tradition, because tradition here was embedded in mercantile practice rather than coded by the states. The legislators freely imported British and Western models in this sphere. Disputes between European traders and Indian merchants and weavers were quite frequent. At times, the Company officers and private European merchants felt powerless to enforce contracts in the absence of a judiciary and laws that could admit commercial disputes of such nature.[48] Indian merchants and artisans settled some of their disputes informally. But many other new business groups, such as the Europeans, were not part of these communities. In Indo-European trade, attempts to protect capitalist interests usually involved striking deals with the Indian village heads and brokers and leaving the enforcement of the contract to the social or political authority that these agents commanded over the producers. These informal means were criticized on the point that traditional institutions did not secure large-scale business of an impersonal nature well enough. The outcome was a series of commercial laws (contract, negotiable instruments, companies, and procedures) instituted soon after Crown rule began in 1858.

At the same time, persistence with tradition in property law did not help in reducing disputes but created new problems. The pre-colonial system of courts had left few documents and archives to show what traditional law was in practical terms. The British rulers followed religious scriptures to guess what it was. Religious texts did not speak in one voice, and therefore, judgments based on these texts were open to disputation. Further, religious law upheld the sanctity of caste, community, and joint family as owner of property, while undervaluing the rights of women, rights of individuals, testamentary rights, and the right to divide property. The judges did not always accept this.

---

[48] R.E. Kranton and A.V. Swamy, 'Contracts, Hold-up, and Exports: Textiles and Opium in Colonial India', *American Economic Review* 98, no. 3 (2008): 967–89; Bishnupriya Gupta, 'Competition and Control in the Market for Textiles: Indian Weavers and the English East India Company in the Eighteenth Century', in *How India Clothed the World: The World of South Asian Textiles, 1500–1850*, eds Giorgio Riello and Tirthankar Roy, 281–308 (Leiden: Brill, 2009).

While laws often encouraged divisions in society, there was uniformity in the judicial infrastructure and procedures. The Royal Charter of 1726 expressly sanctioned the principle that anyone living in the territories under the control of the Company and seeking redress under English law would be allowed to do so. The charter also allowed three courts to be established in the three major residencies of the Company. Known as Mayor's Courts, these tried cases involving European residents. The Royal Charters became progressively more detailed from then on. The 1774 one not only allowed a Supreme Court to be established in Calcutta but also empowered it to try cases of violation of contracts.

In Hastings' time, a multi-tier legal system existed, consisting of the nawab's courts that tried criminal cases, the local civil court using a mix of Anglo-Indian law, and the Supreme Court that tried Europeans. After 1823, a two-tier courts system came to be established. The major port cities or the so-called Presidency towns were governed by Acts of Parliament, royal patent and charters, and judges appointed on the principles laid down in England. At the apex of the Presidency system was a Supreme Court, where the judges were all Crown appointees and recruited from England, Ireland, and Scotland. The jurisdiction of the Court was local for the Presidency towns and personal over all British-born residents of India. The law in force was Indian religious law where both the disputants were Indians and came from a single religion.

In the provinces, the system was different. The provinces were governed only by local legislation and Indian legal authority. Here, many of the judges were Indians, known as *amin* and *munsiff*. The judiciary in the first half of the nineteenth century suffered from corruption. Many European administrators and merchants thought that Indians usually approached the lower courts of law with the assumption that the judges could be bribed. Partly, this sentiment was a defensive gesture of the Europeans settled in the interior to avoid being tried by the Indian judges. But the charge of bribery was raised by the Indians as well.

In the early 1800s, emphasis on indigenous tradition meant that the legal professionals would have to be trained in Hindu law in Benares or Muslim law in the Calcutta Madrassa. The language of the local courts was Persian rather than English. But the quality of education in Benares and Calcutta was not held in respect, and knowledge of English and English law was becoming an advantage. The profession needed literacy with English laws. A new breed of Indians educated in the Hindu College in Calcutta entered the field. Later in the nineteenth century, the Elphinstone College in Bombay began to perform a similar role. By the 1840s, the lobby fighting for traditional language and education was much weaker than in Warren Hastings' time of rule (1774–85).

Mass education contributes to economic growth directly because education improves the capability and productivity of human beings, and thus adds to resource endowment, and indirectly by increasing the choice of occupations, making it more likely that the person with the right aptitude for a line of work would learn and perform that work. To fulfil such promises, education must be open to all and offer scholars a choice about how they wish to use education, that is, offer a choice about what skills they wish to develop. The second condition demands a standardized curriculum as opposed to a content that is tailored to produce specific skills. It also demands removal of barriers to entry that often function along the lines of caste, class, or gender. On all of these points, the Company state produced a system that was very different from its predecessor. Whereas education was earlier a private or community good, it became, in principle, an open-access public good. And whereas the curricular content was earlier too tied to particular professions, and therefore, widely variable, it now became standardized. In the second quarter of the nineteenth century, this model started taking shape.

The best source on the state of indigenous education in early colonial Bengal and Bihar is a report prepared by William Adam and commissioned by William Bentinck, the governor general.[49] His findings showed that literacy levels were very low even in the most advanced districts, and the teachers in privately maintained schools

---

[49] William Adam, *Third Report on the State of Education in Bengal; including Some Account of the State of Education in Behar, and a Consideration of the Means Adapted to the Improvement and Extension of Public Instruction in Both Provinces* (Calcutta: Bengal Military Orphan Press, 1838).

received a small salary. The Scottish missionary, Alexander Duff, described indigenous education in Bengal in the early nineteenth century as consisting of small one-teacher schools organized collectively by a few families of Brahmins and upper castes and meant for their children.[50] The curriculum was literary and oriented to Bengali and Sanskrit. Admission was gender- and caste-biased. Girls stayed away from school.

There were exceptions to the situation. Sanskrit schools located in Nadia, Benares, or Mithila received greater zamindari sponsorship and tended to specialize according to the targeted literate profession, the broad division being that between medical and theological instruction. These communities, especially Brahmins, could alone take admission into these schools. It was still exclusively male education. In the rest of India, the state of schooling was even more dismal than in the most developed districts of Bengal. According to surveys by Francis Buchanan Hamilton in Bihar (c. 1820), the number of persons who taught, those who could 'keep common account', those who could 'sign their names', and those who could 'understand common poetry' added up to 1.3 per cent of the population.

Why was schooling so abysmal in precolonial India? A possible answer is the demand for schooling. In principle, the more strictly parental occupation determines the children's occupational choices (as in a pure type of caste system), the less would be the incentive for parents to teach their children anything other than the family profession. Merchants and priests needed education to perform their profession. But few people expected to follow a craft that demanded literacy. English education and the introduction of science and practical learning in government schools turned the situation around. Schooling now became a training ground for a whole range of new jobs—like government service, law, medicine, teaching, and employment in commercial firms—where recruitment did not mind caste or social background. Almost all these jobs were unconnected with hereditary training and hereditary craft. The expected return from

[50] D.H. Emmott, 'Alexander Duff and the Foundation of Modern Education in India', *British Journal of Educational Studies* 13, no. 2 (1965): 160–9.

schooling increased for a larger population. As the landlords began
to shift their children and their patronage from their schools to the
state-aided formal sector, rural schools declined.

Another factor that suppressed demand for education was the
very limited diffusion of printed books. Indigenous elementary education did not use printed books. The 'learned' forms of education
used manuscripts meant for limited circulation. The literate population had limited access to books as late as 1800. A printed book
industry was virtually non-existent. In precolonial India, printed
books might well have been discouraged, or at least not encouraged,
by the political elite, as some authors have generalized for Islamic
Asia as a whole.[51] Europeans introduced printing technology into
India on a large scale.

In the decades before Crown rule started, moral-religious learning
yielded to secular and scientific learning in formal schools. Thomas
Macaulay (1800–1859), historian, poet, politician, and advisor to
the Government of India on matters of law, wrote a 'minute' setting
out the reasons why the government should sponsor only a western-
ized curriculum. The minute became infamous because Macaulay
dismissed Indian learning as worthless despite being ignorant of
the subject. However, his accent on Western secular and scientific
knowledge had numerous Indian supporters. Most wealthy and
influential Indians wanted such a change and believed that the
new educational ideology enunciated by Macaulay would give better preparation for working in the modern economy. Government
spending on education increased, but private sponsorship to the
new system was crucial too.

Along with law, education, and canals, flood control was one area
of public investment and policy. Monsoon floods, storm waves, and
inundation occurred in the Bengal delta with predictable regular-
ity. Construction of embankments along river banks and seafronts
had been carried out from a long time ago in Bengal. Considerable
attention went to this form of investment in the early nineteenth
century, but the State lost interest when the officers realized that

[51] Lynn White, Jr., 'Technology Assessment from the Stance of a
Medieval Historian', *American Historical Review* 79, no. 1 (1974): 1–13.

the embankments often occurred inside zamindari estates and the zamindars did not cooperate very well.

While the Company State established itself as a government, its legitimacy came under attack.

THE MUTINY AND ITS AFTERMATH

British power faced its worst crisis in the summer of 1857. The Mutiny broke out in May 1857 in isolated military camps, and before being suppressed in the monsoon months of 1858, had developed into a civilian resistance to the Company's rule over Indian territories. The rebellion was fought by professional soldiers of the Indian infantry regiments. Civilian rebellion was sporadic. Merchants and bankers rarely joined the rebellion; most appeared to dislike it and subvert it. The affected regions were located in northern and central India, whereas the port cities remained largely passive or actively helped the British move soldiers, materiel, and money.

Because of these differences, a single theory of the rise and fall of the rebellion cannot work. There was dissatisfaction within the army. Until the final Maratha wars, the distance between the Indian soldiers and the European commanders in the Company army had been relatively small. In the 30 years of peace that followed, the hierarchy hardened. The doctrine of lapse (the British would take over a kingdom without a male heir) fed resentment towards the British and made the revolt especially violent in the newly acquired territories like Awadh and Jhansi. On the other side, many Indian merchants and bankers did not feel compelled to help the feudal lords and jeopardize their economic ties with European merchants and the port cities.[52]

The rebellion led to major shifts in governance and policy.[53] The government announced a halt to further territorial acquisition. Some historians say that the government also turned more conservative,

[52] Tirthankar Roy, 'The Mutiny and the Merchant', *The Historical Journal* 59, no. 2 (2016): 393–416.

[53] I. Klein, 'Materialism, Mutiny and Modernization in British India', *MAS* 34, no. 3 (2000): 545–80.

especially in the matter of changing institutions. That proposition is not true. After 1858, the state intervened heavily in law and justice; it centralized the legislation process and passed a huge number of new laws protecting commercial and peasant property, including major tenancy and debt laws. A correct assessment would be that the new laws reflected caution about avoiding transfer of property in the countryside while encouraging contractual exchange in commerce and industry.[54]

***

During 1757–1857, the Mughal Empire ended and the British Empire began. Why did the new state emerge from maritime trade? The traders had reason to be worried about the profits in a time of conflict, and local employees of the Company often served private interests by joining politics. But why was the Company politically and militarily more successful? The chapter shows that the answer lies in property rights reforms, a standing army, and greater credibility as an ally of the contending Indian powers.

Was the time between the two empires a time of decline or growth? In one view, it was a time of decline because the fall of the Mughal Empire meant weakening of state power and of merchants who depended on the state. In another view, it was a time of growth because the successor states gave merchants business. The contrast between these two scenarios is overdrawn because economic and business growth needs *both* strong states and free enterprise. Successor states may have given merchants more room to grow, but they were not fiscally strong and stable enough to create integrated markets in their domain. The Company ports solved this problem; they were well protected and became magnets for migrant Indian merchants.

With this foundation, direct British rule of India began. The rest of the book is about that rule and its legacy, and it starts with a statistical description of the economy during the next 90 years.

[54] Roy and Swamy, *Law and the Economy in Colonial India.*

3

The Pattern of Economic Growth
1857–1947

Economic change in colonial India followed a definite pattern. This chapter describes the pattern with statistical data. The chapter shows that the average rate of growth of national income per capita was low, but that the average picture is misleading since the experiences of agriculture on the one hand and industry and services on the other differed greatly. Agricultural income grew in the late nineteenth century when there was market expansion driven by world demand for Indian commodities and utilization of surplus land. After 1900, agriculture was almost stagnant. Private enterprise in trade, industry, transport, and finance, on the other hand, saw continuous expansion and take-off in the early twentieth century.

The presence of these two dissimilar trajectories complicates the task of explaining the pattern of change. Most explanations of the performance of the economy place too much weight on per capita or the average income. Using such a measure, the nationalists might conclude that British colonial policy left India poor; but that would amount to overlooking the substantial business growth. Similarly, a business-oriented account cannot explain why agriculture performed poorly.

The chapter suggests that the open economy helped businesses grow, whereas scarcity of water and good soil left agriculture stagnant. The state needed to do more for agricultural development. It did invest in irrigation canals in the nineteenth century but ran out of money in the twentieth. Its small financial resources meant that it spent too little also on healthcare and education.

This account leads us to ask four questions: What are the lessons from national income statistics? Why did business grow? Why was agriculture stagnant? What factors constrained the state from earning more money and spending more money? Fuller answers to these questions will follow in subsequent chapters. This chapter will set the stage. The next section looks at rates of economic growth. The following sections consider, in that order, trends in agriculture, trends in non-agricultural enterprise, poverty and inequality, saving and investment, government finance, and the external sector. The concluding section returns to the problem of defining and explaining the general pattern of growth.

NATIONAL INCOME

What economic historians observe as India's national income in the period 1900–47 is the expression

GDP + net factor income from abroad + taxes

This expression is national income inclusive of taxes. For periods before 1900, the measures vary. Table 1.2 discussed growth rates of national income for sub-periods. Different authors produced these estimates using slightly different methods. But the basic conclusion is not too sensitive to the variations.

Between 1866 and 1914, the growth rates of total income and average income were positive and attained respectable levels by international comparison. Between 1914 and 1947, national income grew at approximately 1 per cent per year, which rate, when adjusted for rising population growth, yielded a near-zero rate of growth of average income. From now on, the two sub-periods will be referred to as 'pre-war' and 'interwar', respectively. By contrast with income, growth rates of employment did not change between these two regimes. The average annual rate of growth of employment was 0.5 per cent between 1875 and 1900, and 0.5 per cent between 1900 and 1946. This rate would mean that average productivity of labour grew in the pre-war period and fell in the interwar period.

Thus, a pre-war phase of expansion came to an end around World War I, coinciding with an upward turn in the population growth curve. Several indices relating to commerce, infrastructure, mining, and agriculture confirm that the trajectory did shift around then (Tables 3.1 and 3.2). A closer look at Table 3.1 will tell us that the

Table 3.1 Regimes of growth and stagnation (average annual percentage change)

	1891–1920	1921–38
National Income:		
Total	1.4	1.5
Per head	0.9	0.1
Agriculture	1.6	0.0
Industry	n.a.	4.4
Acreage irrigated	3.1	1.4
Railway mileage per capita	3.2	0.6
Postal articles handled per capita	9.0	−1.8
Real value of telegraphs sent per capita	2.7	0.2
Factory employment	10.0	2.2
Total employment	0.6–0.8	0.3–0.6
Real value of export	1.1	−0.2
Real value of import	1.3	−0.3
The real value of bank deposits	8.2	4.9
Cultivated land (m acres)	2.6	0.2
Production of coal (m tonnes)	27.0	3.3
Population	0.3	1.5

Sources: Estimated from various sources, including India, *Statistical Abstracts for British India* (London: HMSO and Calcutta: Government Press, various years). *Note*: n.a. stands for not applicable.

Table 3.2   Further data on regimes of growth and stagnation
(percentage change between two years)

	1900–25	1925–50
Industrial production	141	143
Mining activities	222	98
Commercial activities	185	54
Government services	33	29
Railway and communications	129	25
Agricultural production	8	3

Source: K.M. Mukerji's estimates, cited in M. Mukherjee, *National Income of India* (Calcutta: Firma KLM, 1965), 67.

slowdown was uneven across activities. Financial services and industry did not stagnate. The negative trade growth reflected the effects of the Great Depression. The slowdown was intense in agriculture and related activities.

The inequality between activities shows up better if we divide the national income in a slightly different way than the conventional one. Economists conventionally analyse national income through the threefold division, primary, secondary, and tertiary sectors. The division is not necessarily useful since the tertiary sector includes two very dissimilar entities—public administration and private trade. The separation of industry and services also overstates the difference between manufacturing and trade, which were highly interdependent activities in colonial India. I follow a different division. Agriculture remains a class by itself, as it should be since it is subject to the influence of geography more than the other livelihoods. The rest of the economy is divided into government and private. Between 1900 and 1946, private enterprise (including trade, transportation, financial services, manufacturing, and small-scale industry) doubled in size (Figure 3.1), whereas agricultural production was relatively stagnant. The government remained small.

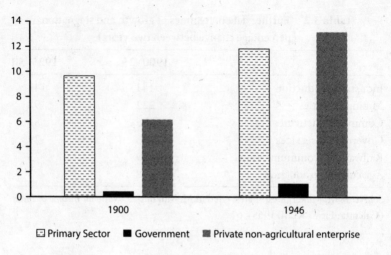

Figure 3.1   Components of GDP 1900–46 (billion Rs in 1938–9 prices)

Source: Based on Sivasubramonian, *National Income of India in the Twentieth Century*.

EMPLOYMENT AND LABOUR FORCE

Census data on employment by occupation is available from 1881. However, the early censuses, especially 1881, 1891, and 1901, involved several problems of definition. The works of Daniel and Alice Thorner and J. Krishnamurty made adjustments on this account. After these adjustments, two conclusions stand out. First, participation rate fell in the long run. Second, there was no major change in occupational structure in the long run (Tables 3.4 and 3.6).

If we observe employment shares, the numbers may tell us that there was growing unemployment in industry and services, which pushed people into cultivation. This was how some economic historians read employment data.[1] But when we combine income and employment shares, we see that there was no crisis in industry and

---

[1] For example, Surendra J. Patel, *Agricultural Labourers in Modern India and Pakistan* (Bombay: Current Book House, 1952).

services (Table 3.3). Between 1900 and 1946, agriculture's share in income declined from 51 to 40 per cent, industry's share increased from 11 to 17 per cent, and services' share increased from 37 to 43 per cent. There was a corresponding divergence in per worker output or productivity (Figure 1.1). Industry and services did not need many more people because productivity of labour was growing there.

It was agriculture that was stagnating. We should, then, expect peasants and agricultural labourers to leave land and enter industry or services. The stability of employment shares suggests *very limited*

Table 3.3   Sector-shares in national income (percentage)

	1900	1925	1946
Primary sector	51	42	40
Industry	11.5	13	17
Modern	2.5	5	11
Small-scale	9	8	6
Others	37.5	45	43
Total including other sources	100	100	100

Source: Based on S. Sivasubramonian, *National Income of India in the Twentieth Century* (New Delhi: Oxford University Press, 2000).

Table 3.4   Sector-shares in workforce (percentage)

	1875	1900	1925	1946
Agriculture	73.4	74.9	76.5	74.8
Industry	13.6	10.6	9.0	9.6
Modern	0.2	0.5	1.2	1.8
Small-scale	13.4	10.1	7.8	7.8
Others	13.0	14.5	14.5	15.6
Workforce (%)	100.0	100.0	100.0	100.0
Workforce: millions	117.7	131.3	138.3	158.2

Source: A. Heston, 'National Income,' in *CEHI 2*, eds Dharma Kumar and Meghnad Desai, (Cambridge: Cambridge University Press, 1983) for 1875; Sivasubramonian, *National Income*, for the other years.

population transfer between these two types of livelihood. Thus, relatively few people left agriculture for other higher paying jobs. The few who did, worked longer hours from before, which meant an improved earning capacity than in agriculture, which provided work for part of the year.

A big surprise is the low (possibly falling) women's participation rate in the early twentieth century. If indeed agriculture was unable to provide jobs to all, why did more women not come out of home and land to work? Analysts of employment data like Daniel Thorner tended to dismiss the women's data as unreliable. Women did commercial work only as members of the family unit and worked part-time. They were wrongly called 'workers' in the earlier censuses. But this is probably not the correct view or the whole picture.[2]

The correct picture is that it was much harder for women to join industry and services, because these activities were concentrated in the towns and cities. This problem was universal and did not appear only in India. Men and women faced differential chances of a move into the wage labour market. The difference arose from the need, in the case of women, to accommodate wage work into the domestic routine, in which the care of small children was the most crucial task. Before modern industrialization began, mainly households performed industrial work. The family itself was the unit of work, and the balancing of domestic with commercial work did not pose a problem. But it did become a problem as work began to shift outside the home. To continue working, women needed to leave home and children for some time during the day, which was not easy.

In many traditional societies, this difficulty shows up in the shape of two tendencies. First, women's participation in urban industrial labour fell for many years, and then, as childcare and home duties became easier to manage, it started rising. In the course of industrialization, women's presence in the urban industrial labour market followed a U-shape. Secondly, age-wise, women's participation rate peaked for a group in which adult unmarried girls formed a majority, for example, 15–24 years; the rate then fell in a group in which the

[2] Alice Thorner, 'Women's Work in Colonial India, 1881–1931' (paper, School of Oriental and African Studies, London, 1984).

majority were married with small children, and the rate rose again when many among the married women returned to work. If the over-time rate follows a U shape, the across-age rate follows an M shape.[3]

In India, the problem appeared with exceptional force. In India, marriage customs posed the most difficult obstacle (see Table 10.3 on average age at marriage). The low age at marriage meant that few young adults joined the workforce (or the absence of an M shape), and consequently, the majority of potential workers found it diffi-cult to leave home and enter the factory as work shifted from home to factory (a pronounced U shape, Table 3.5). We find both these predictions to be correct in census data. In short, the fall in women's participation rate was an effect of two things working in combina-tion—non-agricultural work moving further away from home and the low average age at marriage that kept women tied to the home. Women withdrew from paid work in industry and services and crowded into agricultural work, because here work was available nearer home. When they could move, women might still face other

Table 3.5   Women in industrial work 1901–31 (colonial India) and 1961–91 (Indian Union)

	Women Workers as Percentage of Industrial Workforce	Women Industrial Workers as Percentage of Women Workers
1901	34.3	17.3
1911	34.3	12.7
1921	32.1	11
1931	24.1	11.7
1961	25.8	9.6
1971	12.4	7.7
1981	14.1	9.1
1991	15	8

Source: India, *Census of India,* various rounds, statistics on occupations.

[3] Tirthankar Roy, *Rethinking Economic Change in India: Labour and Livelihood* (London: Routledge, 2005), chapter 7.

Table 3.6 Labour force and occupational structure, the Indian Union, 1881–1951

	1881	1901	1911	1921	1931	1951
Population (million)	213.2	238.1	251.9	251.2	278.7	356.6
Workforce (million)	100.8	115.7	121.0	117.7	119.4	139.5
Participation rate (%)	47	49	48	47	43	39
Participation rate for men (%)	63	63	62	60	58	54
Participation rate for women (%)	31	33	34	33	27	23
Occupational structure (% of workforce):						
Primary sector[a]	74	75	76	77	76	76
Secondary and tertiary sectors	26	25	24	22	22	24
Industry and trade[b,c]	20	16	16	15	15	–
Industry[b]	–	–	10	9	9	10
Trade and transportation	–	–	7	7	7	7
Other services	–	–	7	6	6	7

Sources: Alice Thorner, 'The Secular Trend in the Indian Economy, 1881–1951', *Economic and Political Weekly (EPW)* 14, no. 28–30 (1962): 1156–65; Daniel Thorner, '"De-industrialization" in India, 1881–1931,' in *Land and Labour in India*, eds Daniel and Alice Thorner (New York: Asia Publishing House, 1962).

Notes: a. Includes animal husbandry, forestry, hunting, fishing, and 'general labour'. b. Includes mining, construction. c. For all of British India, including Burma.

obstacles in the city labour markets, for example, legislation that made employers less willing to hire women.

TRENDS IN AGRICULTURE

Real agricultural income increased by 33 per cent between 1870 and 1914. In the next 30 years, the growth was approximately 3 per cent (Table 3.7). The earlier expansion was due to several factors. On the demand side, rising world demand drove the expansion in the late

Table 3.7   Agricultural growth 1865–1940

	Agricultural Export (m Rs)	Agricultural Export (m Rs at 1873 prices)	NDP in Agriculture (b Rs)	Net Sown Acreage (m acres)	Agricultural Export/ Total Export (%)
1865	590	513	15.5	n.a.	87
1880	526	438	17.6	<120	79
1895	783	631	18.9	170	72
1910	843	570	25.4	209	69
1925	2400	854	22.8	207	64
1940	789	537	24.7	209	48

Source: India, *Statistical Abstract relating to British India* (London: HMSO and Calcutta: Government Press, various years).
Note: n.a. stands for not applicable.

nineteenth century. After 1875, world agricultural prices started rising relative to other prices, a trend that continued for almost the next 50 years. The price of wheat in 1925 was three times what it had been in 1875. Further, thanks to the Industrial Revolution, terms of trade between export, consisting mainly of what the peasants sold abroad, and import, consisting mainly of mass consumption goods like cotton cloth, was increasing, which meant that by selling a constant basket of goods, the peasant could access an expanding basket of consumption goods. The ratio of agricultural price to import price rose even more (Table 3.8). The expansion of the world economy, greater overseas demand for primary commodities, and productivity growth in manufacturing jointly created this trend. The devaluation of the rupee between 1873 and 1893 due to global depreciation in silver (the rupee was a silver coin and could be freely minted until 1893) also stimulated export, if temporarily. On the supply side, the government made considerable investment in artificial irrigation systems, which made an expansion of cultivation into the drier areas possible.

From the mid-1920s, agricultural prices began to fall. Worldwide, there was an overproduction of agricultural goods. By 1910–20, good land ran out in India. Rents started rising. The government, facing strained finances, reduced investment in irrigation. Thus, the

Table 3.8   Terms of trade (1873 = 100)

	Export–import	Agriculture–non-agriculture	Agriculture-import
1861–5	84.3	101.0	86.6
1871–5	105.3	110.4	105.8
1881–5	117.6	110.4	126.3
1891–5	127.9	135.8	146.2
1901–5	120.3	140.2	140.5
1911–5	123.6	147.4	156.7
1921–5	110.8	126.4	128.3
1931–5	95.8	116.8	104.2
1941–5		136.0	

Source: M. McAlpin, 'Price Movements and Economic Fluctuations,' in Kumar and Desai, *CEHI 2*, 878–905.
Note: Five-year averages.

pattern of agricultural growth that had begun in the nineteenth century came to a stop. The rural crisis took a serious turn in the years immediately after the Depression. The Depression raised debt and rent burden on the peasants and forced liquidation of their assets.

No such crisis was in evidence outside agriculture.

TRENDS IN NON-AGRICULTURAL ACTIVITIES

Industry in this time processed a lot of agricultural material, whereas trade and finance mainly dealt with the production and sale of agricultural commodities. Because agriculture, industry, and services were closely interdependent, the interwar slowdown in agriculture could not leave industry and services unaffected (see Table 3.1 figures). But there were other drivers, such as urban consumption and export trades, that sustained industry and services.

Colonial India was a trading economy. Trade sustained banking. Most banks and moneylenders mainly financed agricultural production and trade. Trade also sustained a large part of industrial investment. Given the limited capacity of the domestic financial institutions to fund long-term investment, most Indian industrialists resourced long-term capital from trading profits. Trade grew. The growth rate was impressive. In 1840, shipping tonnage in the three principal ports was about one million.[4] In 1939, shipping tonnage in eight principal ports in India was 39 million, and the railways carried 121 million tonnes of goods.[5] These figures suggest an extraordinary rise in trading volumes.

The major part of the growth occurred in goods carried by the railways (Figure 3.2). The railways drew some business away from older systems like boats, carts, and caravans. But the difference in efficiency between the railways and these other systems was so large that it is likely that the new system enabled a lot more trade than before. Although the ports were a minor carrier of goods in weight, in terms of value, the ports were a significant trading point. Railways

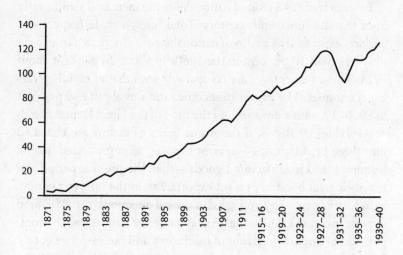

Figure 3.2   Goods handled by railways (million tonnes)

Source: India, *Statistical Abstract relating to British India* (London: HMSO and Calcutta: Government Press, various years).

[4] Tirthankar Roy, *India in the World Economy from Antiquity to the Present* (Cambridge: Cambridge University Press, 2012).
[5] India, *Statistical Abstract for British India 1930–31 to 1939–40* (London: HMSO, 1942–3), 658–70, 712.

carried raw agricultural products like grain and cotton. The ports carried high-valued textiles or tea, in addition to grain or cotton.

Keeping trade routes open was a political priority for the colonial rulers. The British Empire that ruled over half the world functioned as a huge free trade zone. No single country in the empire could raise tariffs, not until the interwar period. India had little option to change the rules on its own. Assumption of political power by the British Crown (1858) and the opening of the Suez Canal (1869) integrated India closely with the British and the world economy. Ocean freight rates on bulk goods from India in 1893 were a third of what they were in 1873. By 1893, more than two-thirds of export from India passed through Suez. Between 1880 and 1925, the real volume of trade to and from India doubled. More than half of Indian exports consisted of agricultural goods such as grains, seeds, raw cotton, and raw jute.

Foreign trade as a ratio of national income increased significantly from the late nineteenth century. Total foreign trade (export and import) expressed as a ratio of national income increased from possibly less than 10 per cent in the 1860s to about 20 per cent about 1914. These percentages are comparable with that of rapidly growing economies. The export-to-income ratio was about 8–9 per cent in 1900–39, with a drop around the time of the Great Depression.[6]

As Table 3.9 shows, if the major items of export are classified into three broad groups—peasant exports, semi-processed natural resources, and manufactured goods—then the pre-war period saw mainly a great burst of peasant exports. But in the interwar period, as industrial capability improved in several directions, manufactured exports increased. The same general tendency also altered the composition of imports in favour of machinery and intermediate goods. Limited tariff protection had been present from the mid-1920s. Import substitution strengthened in the interwar period. The most important sector receiving protection was cotton textiles.

In the direction of trade, dependence on the Chinese and British markets was initially large—an inheritance from the early

[6] The ratio declined from this range in post-Independence India, to become about 3–4 per cent in 1980. Thereafter, trade liberalization saw the ratio rise again.

Table 3.9 Composition of trade, 1850–1935 (percentages of total export or total import)

	1850–1	1910–11	1935–6
Export			
Agricultural (raw cotton, raw jute, foodgrains, seeds)	26.2	55.0	29.5
Semi-processed goods (indigo, opium, hides, and skins)	42.8	12.5	neg.
Manufactured goods (tea, jute, cotton textiles)	4.8	19.3	28.1
Import			
Cotton textiles	40.5	33.5	15.3
Machinery	neg.	3.7	11.1
Intermediate goods (mineral oil, metals)	16.8	13.8	13.3

Source: K.N. Chaudhuri, 'Foreign Trade and Balance of Payments' in Kumar and Desai, CEHI 2, 804–77.

nineteenth century. But the dependence declined in the pre-war period (Table 3.10). India's dependence on Britain as a source of imports was almost total in the mid-nineteenth century and changed relatively little until World War I. In the interwar period, there was a drop in Britain's share and increase in those of Japan, the United States of America, Germany, and Italy. The interwar period, in short, was one of diversification both in India's capability and in its trade partners. In the early twentieth century, intra-Asian trade expanded while Europe's dominance in Asian trade reduced. The intra-Asian trade followed from the emergence of big trading firms and the modern cotton textile industry in Japan. A three-way cotton-oriented trade and division of labour between India, China, and Japan emerged as a result. In turn, intra-Asian trade stimulated primary goods exports from China and South East Asia.[7] The importance of

[7] See Kaoru Sugihara, 'Patterns of Asia's Integration into the World Economy, 1880–1913,' in The Integration of the World Economy, 1850–1914, ed. C. Knick Harley, vol. 2 (Cheltenham: Edward Elgar, 1996).

Table 3.10   The direction of foreign trade, 1850–1940 (percentages of total export or import)

	1850–1	1910–11	1940–1
Export from India to			
Britain	44.6	24.9	34.7
China	35.0	9.2	5.3
Japan	neg.	6.4	4.8
United States of America	neg.	6.4	13.9
Import of India from			
Britain	72.1	62.2	22.9
China	8.6	1.8	1.8
Japan	neg.	2.5	13.7
United States of America	neg.	2.6	17.2

Source: K.N. Chaudhuri, 'Foreign Trade and Balance of Payments', 804–77.

Britain as a destination of Indian goods increased somewhat in the interwar period, mainly due to preferential tariffs under the Imperial Preference treaty (1921).

Trade acted as the foundation for industrial and financial development, for trading profits were an important source of industrial investment and much of the banking sector funded commodity trade. As far as we can measure, the index of industrial production in the modern factories was increasing at a comfortable pace both before and after World War I. There were two types of industry: large-scale industry and small-scale industry. Large-scale industry consisted of mills employing wage labour and machinery. The small-scale industry consisted of artisan households and small factories. GDP in the larger factories increased at rates of over 4 per cent per year between 1900 and 1947. Small-scale industry grew at less than 1 per cent. Although total income grew slowly in this sector, labour productivity increased, as it did inside large-scale industry as well.

If peasant agriculture did badly, business did well, and not many could move from the former to the latter, we should expect inequality and poverty to increase. What is the evidence on these dimensions of economic change?

INEQUALITY AND POVERTY

Around 1800, the rich included owners of assets like land and capital, and top-level European officers working for the government or the army. The poor included agricultural labourers and tenants. Some of these classes experienced a change of fortunes in colonial times. One general interpretation claims that British policy 'enormously increased the economic power of the landlord, the trader and the moneylender over the primary producer ... [peasant, artisan, landless labourers]'.[8] This is not quite the correct picture. A paper compiles the evidence on wages, incomes, and income classes to examine this thesis and finds the picture on inequality to be a more complex one.[9] The landlords, like the zamindars, did not get richer in the long run and formed a tiny proportion of the population anyway. Top European officers who earned very high salaries were also too few to make a difference. Low and stagnant land productivity, along with barriers to mobility between occupations, ensured that while agriculture expanded in scale, it did not deliver significantly more income to landlords, peasants, tenants, and labourers. But occupations directly or indirectly dependent on trading could escape the land-yield constraint. These rising classes included what we would call the middle class today, mainly service workers such as traders, bankers, doctors, skilled artisans, factory workers, and engineers working in the factories. To sum up, there was the emergence of a middle class that gained from the open trading economy. This was an effect of globalization and not colonial rule, directly.

What about poverty? Agricultural labourers formed the poorest occupation class in colonial India. Their average real earnings can be estimated from wages data, adding assumptions about work intensity and the number of earners in the family. While real wages did

[8] A.K. Bagchi, *The Political Economy of Underdevelopment* (Cambridge: Cambridge University Press, 1982), 20.

[9] Tirthankar Roy, 'Inequality in Colonial India' (Economic History Working Paper No. 286, London School of Economics and Political Science, London, 2018).

occasionally rise in some regions where agricultural expansion took place (Punjab in the late nineteenth century for example), the long-run trend was stagnation. If we apply the World Bank's benchmark of a poverty line for 1973 to colonial era, the distance between average income and a poverty line did not change significantly in colonial India, or the poorest did not become poorer. But more people joined their ranks.

There can be three explanations for stagnant real wages. First, demand for labour was depressed, say because of the destruction of the artisan industry. But as we have seen, industry and services did grow, so this explanation is not convincing. If indeed the wage stagnation resulted from unemployed artisans crowding rural jobs, and if artisan wages were higher than agricultural wages, we should expect artisan wages and agricultural wages to converge. But we do not see such a convergence (Table 3.11). Second, wages were set by custom and, therefore, changed little. However, there is evidence to suggest that the force of custom in the labour market weakened. For example, many types of farm servant arrangements were in decline from 1900. Third, labour supply increased. Of course, population did grow rapidly, but not until 1921.

Table 3.11   Real wages (1900=100)

	Urban Artisans[a]	Agricultural Labourers	Mill Workers[b]
1875	114.2	136.3	
1895	108.9	128.8	
1900	100.0	100.0	100.0
1916	103.7	107.1	114.7
1920	103.2	74.1	130.1
1925	181.3	129.7	180.6
1937	157.6	107.1	237.4

Source: See the three papers by K. Mukerji (1959, 1960, and 1961) under 'income and wage data' in the Further Readings section at the end of the book.
Notes: a. These wages usually refer to the average daily earnings of three categories of general-purpose artisans: blacksmiths, carpenters, and masons. b. Bombay cotton mill workers average monthly wage.

Table 3.12 Food availability

	Net Food Production (million tonnes)	Net Import (million tonnes)	Population (millions)	Per Capita Availability (oz. per day)
1900–4	55.6	−1.1	289	18.6
1910–14	61.9	−2.0	314	18.8
1920–4	58.4	0.8	312	18.6
1930–4	57.7	1.2	348	16.6
1940–4	57.6	0.5	397	14.4

Source: India, *Statistical Abstract relating to British India* (London: HMSO and Calcutta: Government Press, various years).

In the long run, there was another factor that aided labour supply growth. A great deal of agricultural work was seasonal. Most people who cultivated land were idle for several months in a year. From the late nineteenth century, more of such people sent a few members of their families (usually the male members) to work outside agriculture, in the cities and industries. This reallocation of time within agricultural households did not happen on a large enough scale to make people distinctly better off, but it did happen.

With agriculture in stagnation, population rising, and the number of poor people rising too, food availability per head fell in the twentieth century (see Table 3.12). This crisis was acute in overpopulated and land-scarce Bengal and formed the backdrop to a famine in 1943 (Chapter 10).

The regions that saw more growth overall and the ones that saw more stagnation were different.

REGIONAL INEQUALITY

Regions were indeed dissimilar in resource endowments and accessibility. The water-scarce Deccan or Rajasthan was different from the water-rich but densely populated Bengal and Bihar; and the agricultural interior was different from the commercially developed port cities and the seaboard more generally. Surely, their economic growth prospects should differ too. Regional domestic product before 1950 is unavailable. The attempt to construct regional incomes is somewhat promising for the British Indian provinces.[10] For the princely states, many of which did not collect production data, the attempt is futile.

There are, however, a few works that measure inequality across regions and then try to explain it. One set of works attempts to explain present-day inequality with causes that appeared in earlier times. One article shows that in those districts of British India where the colonial rulers had delivered property rights to non-cultivating landlords or zamindars (in 1793), rather than to the cultivating peasant, investments were lower in the post-Independence period.[11] The explanation is that in the landlord areas, conflicts and lack of cooperation between the elite and the peasants became more likely and made lobbying for resources in the post-Independence period less successful. Another study following a similar method finds that the directly ruled colonial regions ended up worse off than the princely states in the supply of public goods.[12] The new scholarship has spawned several attempts at extensions and one criticism of the data set used.[13]

[10] See P. Caruana-Galizia, 'Indian Regional Income Inequality: Estimates of Provincial GDP, 1875–1911', *Economic History of Developing Regions* 28, no. 1 (2013): 1–27, for an innovative reconstruction.

[11] A. Banerjee and L. Iyer, 'History, Institutions, and Economic Performance: The Legacy of Colonial Land Tenure Systems in India', *American Economic Review* 95, no. 4 (2005): 1190–213.

[12] L. Iyer, 'Direct versus Indirect Colonial Rule in India: Long-term Consequences', *Review of Economics and Statistics* 92 (2010): 693–713.

[13] S. Kapur and S. Kim, 'British Colonial Institutions and Economic Development in India' (NBER Working Paper No. 12613, National Bureau of Economic Research, Cambridge Mass., 2006); Latika Chaudhary, 'Land Revenues, Schools and Literacy: A Historical Examination of Public and Private Funding of Education', *IESHR* 47, no. 2 (2010): 179–204; V. Iversen, R. Palmer-Jones, and K. Sen, 'On the Colonial Origins of Agricultural Development in India: A Re-examination of Banerjee and Iyer, "History, Institutions and Economic Performance"', *Journal of Development Studies* 49, no. 12 (2013): 1631–46.

The empirical methodology involves regressing present-day 'outcomes' upon historical causes that were active centuries before. Historians do not usually accept the validity of this way of explaining the past. The method asks the reader to believe that ancient causes produced present outcomes. There is no certainty that they did. A different cause may have produced the outcome instead, one that emerged and disappeared in the intervening time. Another paper on regional inequality that looks at the contemporary levels of inequality suggests that the colonial pattern of growth, which favoured commodity trade based in the port cities, also favoured regions (like Bengal) with more world market access. However, after the Great Depression and the rise of protectionist policies in independent India, trade became weak as a driver of economic change, leading to a decline of commercial regions like Bengal. The fact that Bengal had a different set of agrarian institutions is incidental to the story of regional differentiation; trade and industry are more central.[14]

Growth and inequality trends should follow trends in investment and savings. What does the data show?

SAVING AND INVESTMENT

A low rate of investment caused the slow average growth of income in the economy. A difference in the rates caused the inequality between agriculture and non-agricultural enterprise (Table 3.13). The reason for the difference in rates was that in industry and services, trading profits and foreign capital were available. In agriculture, neither the peasants nor the landlords had sufficient access to financial capital.

The contribution of trading profits is hard to measure. Examples of the measurable forms of savings include domestic savings in bank deposits and securities and foreign investment inflow. Deposits and securities were not the only forms of assets in which Indians saved. A substantial part of savings consisted of gold and silver, and a smaller part of savings went as investments abroad and as purchases of

[14] Tirthankar Roy, 'Geography or Politics? Regional Inequality in Colonial India', *European Review of Economic History* 18, no. 3 (2014): 306–23.

Table 3.13 Net investment in agriculture and private non-agriculture

	Agriculture		Private Non-agricultural Enterprise	
	% of National Income	% of Sector Income	% of National Income	% of Sector Income
1901–13	0.9	1.2	3.1	6.7
1930–9	0.8	2.0	2.0	3.4
1940–6	0.5	1.4	0.7	1.2

Source: It is not possible to read off agriculture's share in overall saving and investment precisely. Since roughly a third of public investment went into agriculture, and less than a tenth of private investment went into agriculture, applying these proportions, net investment in agriculture as a percentage of national income can be estimated (Based on works cited under Table 3.14).

government bonds in India. Except gold and silver, all other forms of saving could convert into investment through the intermediation of banks. These other forms were more common among the urban classes and urban institutions.

Net capital formation and savings were 2–4 per cent of national income in the first half of the twentieth century (Table 3.14).[15] The proportion of investment in machinery, the percentage of investment in agriculture, and the share of the government in aggregate investment were all relatively small and, in some cases, in decline. A curious feature of the data is the rather high proportion of depreciation or replacement expenditure (note the difference between gross and net capital formation). Net foreign private investment was small, at around 1 per cent of national income.

Table 3.15 presents data on savings. The proportion of income going to the purchase of gold and silver deserves special attention. In the normal course, and any good agricultural year, Indians purchased gold and silver in large quantities. Among the few exceptions to this

[15] In the same period, the ratio increased from about 8 to 18 per cent of income in Japan. In some industrialized countries such as the United States, it fell to levels that were still larger than India's.

Table 3.14 Estimates of investment, 1901–46

	1901–13	1930–9	1940–6
Per cent of gross capital formation[a]			
Gross capital formation	100.0	100.0	100.0
Construction	61.2	67.5	70.2
Machinery	29.8	29.2	28.5
Agriculture	2.0	3.5	4.6[b]
Other	27.8	25.7	23.9
Inventory	9.0	3.3	1.4
Public sector	32.7	22.2	18.0
Private Sector	67.3	71.8	82.0
Per cent of national income[d]			
Gross capital formation	6.93	9.35	7.30
Net capital formation[c]	4.00	2.84	2.12
Public investment	2.23	2.08[d]	1.32

Source: Raymond W. Goldsmith, *The Financial development of India, 1860–1977* (New Haven and London: Yale University Press, 1983), Tables 1–10 (p. 20) and 2–9 (p. 80).

Notes: a. This is defined as domestic investment plus foreign investment inflow. The 1901–13 figures relate to 'total' capital formation, whereas the ones between 1940–6 relate to 'domestic' capital formation. However, by this time, the inflow of foreign capital had become small. b. 'Rural' in the source. c. Net capital formation is gross minus depreciation. d. The national income (Gross National Product) figures used are different from Table 3.1 earlier. But the resultant differences in the ratios are small, usually less than 0.5 per cent. e. A study by M.J.K. Thavaraj estimates a slightly lower percentage for all three periods. The differences are small, and its source is not immediately clear. The difference can be due to (*a*) deliberate exclusion of transfer of assets between private and public sectors in Thavaraj's estimates, or (*b*) due to the national income figures used. The rather crude income figures generally included the Indian states, whereas the public investment figure did not. See his 'Capital Formation in the Public Sector in India: A Historical Study, 1898–1938', in *Papers on National Income and Allied Topics*, ed. V.K.R.V. Rao (Delhi: Allied Publishers, 1962).

normal behaviour were the years of the Great Depression and the two World Wars (also the depression of the 1830s, see Chapter 2). During the wars, gold import was restricted legally. During the

Table 3.15   Estimates of saving, 1901–46

	1896–1913	1930–9	1940–6
Per cent of national income			
Financial saving[a]	2–3	3.2	3.3
Net accumulation of gold and silver	1.5	−1.5	0.00

Source: Goldsmith, *Financial Development*, 20–21, and 80.
Note: Financial saving consists of deposits and securities with the private sector, foreign investment outflow, and purchase of government bonds in India.

Depression, there was net export. Administrators often complained that when the harvest was good, the peasant spent lavishly on a daughter's marriage and gold jewellery. In bad times, the peasant had to mortgage land at high interest rates. Others understood that buying gold or silver was a rational response to climatic risks like the prospect of a deficient rainfall. In the absence of insurance markets, precious metals were the best available store of value. Because these metals traded globally, their prices varied in a narrower band than the prices of nearly everything that sold in the villages. In other words, climatic and price risks depressed expected incomes from investment projects and, thus, reduced the demand for productive investment and raised the demand for gold instead.

All other forms of saving could eventually end up with investors. But gold ornaments did not, except to a limited extent when the peasants mortgaged precious metals against loans. Thus, metal was a form of 'leakage' from funds available for productive investment. Net gold and silver transactions took a toll of at least 2 per cent from the potential aggregate investment/income ratio. A smaller proportion of financial saving was also hoarded in the form of notes and coins and had the same effect.

Why were investment rates low in agriculture? The obvious answer to this question is that average incomes were small. And income was small because the yield of land was small. Some colonial administrators believed, as do some present-day historians, that the structure of the capital market in rural areas was to blame for the high cost of loans. The village moneylender had a lot of financial power and exploited the debtors by charging high interest rates. These accounts believed that the British Indian laws of contract had strengthened the hands of the moneylender in enforcing unfair debt contracts. Not discounting that such a possibility did exist, money-lender power should not be overstated. After all, the creditor was just as exposed to climatic risk as was the client. When the rains failed in an arid region, landowners and lenders both suffered. The interest rates should reflect that risk.

Credit for industry and services was expensive because the main economic activity, agriculture, drew in nearly all of the short-term finance every year. The tropical monsoon climate created a short cultivation season and a long dry or slack season. Extreme seasonal fluctuations in demand for money meant that loans needed to be advanced to a vast army of local merchants suddenly, for short periods, among clients who were too far away from banks and discounting facilities and who could not read documents. Most loans were unsecured, cash-based, and entailed high risk. For all these reasons, interest rates rose to high levels during the busy season (November to March usually), and since money was hoarded during the slack months in readiness for the next busy season, little was available for long-term non-agricultural uses.[16]

Potentially, the government could, by subsidizing inputs or making direct investments, break the jam in agriculture. What did it do?

SIZE OF GOVERNMENT

The State is necessary to make investments in public goods, including infrastructure and education. Private enterprise can also help the creation of such assets, and in fact, the philanthropic activities of Indian merchants and industrialists led to the creation of many colleges, schools, charities, and hospitals. But such activities were confined to the big cities and port cities. Peasants and rural labourers were more deprived and State-dependent. In the tropical climate,

---

[16] Tirthankar Roy, 'Monsoon and the Market for Money in Late Colonial India', *Enterprise and Society* 17, no. 2 (2016): 324–57.

the State was also needed to make investments in irrigation systems, which were sometimes too large-scale for private investment to manage.

A puzzling feature of British India was the consistently small size of the State, even as the trend in the rest of the world (for example, Japan, Russia, and Britain itself) was for States to grow bigger. Tax per head in British India was among the smallest in the world and small within the empire.[17] The State earned too little money because it relied on the land tax, and land yielded little. This dependence on an archaic tax was reducing over time but not quickly enough. The State was militarily strong because it spent enough money to maintain a large army. By this means, British India kept the princely states pacified and the internal and external borders open to trade, migration, and investment. But the State never had much money left over from military expenditure to spend on public good or agricultural development.

Subject to the small revenues and the burden of funding the army, what did the State do? There were two main types of government expenditure in British India: expenditure in India and expenditure abroad. Expenditure in India included defence, administration, and infrastructure. The two common types of government expenditure abroad were pensions paid in sterling to retired employees and interest on public debt raised in London. The key resources needed for the State to function—skilled labour and capital—were sourced from Britain until the early twentieth century. The government could finance its expenditure by three means. The first was current revenues. Of current revenues, 70–80 per cent came from taxes. The second was borrowings from abroad, and the third borrowings at home.

Chapter 9 goes into these items in greater detail. Table 3.16 describes the general pattern of public finance in the first half of the twentieth century. A few points are noteworthy. The government earned so little that it had to borrow heavily to finance its

---

[17] Ewout Frankema, 'Raising Revenue in the British Empire, 1870–1940: How Extractive were Colonial Taxes?', *Journal of Global History* 5, no. 3 (2010): 447–77.

Table 3.16 Receipts and payments on the government account, 1901–46

	1901–13	1930–9	1940–6
Percentage of national income			
Current revenue	5.39	3.50	4.26
Net capital receipts			
Net issue of rupee debt	0.22	0.49	3.48
Net issue of sterling debt	0.30	−0.19	−0.96
Expenditure[a]	5.91	3.80	6.78
Investment	2.21	2.08	1.32

Source: Based on Goldsmith, Financial Development, Tables 1–21, 1–22 (39–40), 2–29, 2–31 (112–15).
Note : a. Calculated by summing items on the receipt side.

expenditures, in London and India. These borrowings peaked at the time of the World Wars. There were two types of securities sold by the government. One was denominated in sterling and the other denominated in rupees. In the nineteenth century, Europeans were the main buyers of both. For example, the expatriates living in India held a lot of rupee securities. But over time, the proportion of Indian banks and Indians increased among the buyers of rupee securities. The London borrowings as a proportion of national income peaked in the last quarter of the nineteenth century. The loans financed wars and railway construction. By 1900–13, military compulsions were weaker and railway investment was beginning to decline. After the Great Depression, net borrowings in London steadily declined. But the government's debt in the form of rupee securities increased.

The three main heads of investment were railways, irrigation, and roads and buildings. Of these three items, the first was the largest. But its share in gross investment fell from 51 per cent in 1898–1913 to 27 in 1930–8. Irrigation was a small item of expenditure (11–16 per cent in this period). The share of roads and buildings increased from 31 to 46 per cent. The share of investment in government expenditure and the ratio of public investment in national income both fell in the interwar years. Given the limited capacity of the government to raise taxes, the capacity to invest depended on its administrative expenditure commitment and the capacity to borrow abroad.

In short, the government was small, had limited means for investment, was losing this means, was dependent on debt, and relied on foreign markets for hiring its personnel and raising capital. Its limited capacity for investment became controversial. More controversial still was its dependence on foreign factor markets and the expenditures in Britain that this entailed. We need to understand how openness made a difference to the government and the economy.

OPENNESS

Openness in colonial India meant not only openness to trade (that is, low levels of tariffs and other barriers to trade), but also openness to factor movements, that is, the facility to borrow or hire abroad at relative ease. The government did this, as I have shown. To some extent, private enterprise also did the same thing, that is, they hired managers and engineers abroad and borrowed abroad.

Good estimates exist only for the interwar period (Tables 3.17–3.19). In the 1920s, there were two major types of net inflow: Net export of goods and the net inflow of foreign investment. These two together formed about 4.4 per cent of national income. Three types of net outflow balanced these: private remittances (2.7 per cent of national income), government remittance (0.4), and net purchase of gold and silver (1.3). Estimates available for the middle of the nineteenth century suggest that the pattern was not fundamentally different around the beginning of Crown rule (1858). The five items above were even then the principal items in the external account and, in most years, carried the same signs as these did later.

Tables 3.18 and 3.19 show that India was a net exporter of goods and a net importer of services around 1900.[18] In 1900, India had a shortage of skilled labour services and capital and got these from abroad. Foreign capital and foreign workers ran the State and ran industrial, banking, and trading firms. Capitalist businesses needed

[18]   These patterns reflect different modes of integration with the world economy. For example, India was a net importer of goods and a net exporter of services in 2000.

Table 3.17 Balance of payments, 1921–39

	1921–9	1930–9
Per cent of national income		
Net export of goods	3.2	1.4
Net export of treasure	2.4	1.1
Net private remittances into India	−2.9	−2.7
Net government remittances into India	−1.0	−1.2
Net capital movements[a]	1.7	1.4
Balance of payments	0.0	0.0

Sources: A.K. Banerji, *India's Balance of Payments* (Bombay: Asia Publishing House, 1962), Tables V, XXVI, and XXXVII; and national income figures from Sivasubramonian, *National Income*.

Notes: Defined as net foreign investment inflow plus purchase of government bonds by foreigners. In this table, this item is estimated as a residual balancing item. This item requires some explanation on the database. In external transactions, the most reliable data is available for commodity and treasure. Discharge of public debt in sterling is also reasonably correct. Banerji has estimated, within some margin of error, the factor payments. There is no reliable estimate available for net investment by the private sector, and therefore, no reliable estimate available for net capital movements. In this table, net capital movements are calculated by simply adding the other four items (all the five items together should add to zero). But this figure is subject to the margin of error that applies to Banerji's series on factor payments.

Table 3.18 Structure of balance of payments, early and late colonialism
(Rs million, annual average)

	1866–76	1930–9
Net export of goods	221	318
Net export of treasure	−87	314
Net private remittances into India[a]	−66	−609
Net government remittances into India	−130	−269
Net capital movements[b]	61	2463
Balance of payments	0	0

Sources: A.K. Banerji, *Aspects of Indo-British Economic Relations, 1858-1898* (Bombay: Oxford University Press, 1982), 157, and Banerji, *India's Balance of Payments*, Tables V, XXVI, and XXXVII.

Notes: a. Both factor payments and private foreign investment for 1866–76 consists of only factor payments for 1930–9. b. Only net change in government debt for 1866–76, both private foreign investment and government debt for 1930–9. 3. Derived as a residual.

Table 3.19 Composition of factor payments (percentage of total net payment), 1860–1939

	1860–1	1921–2	1938–9
Main payment items:			
Freight, insurance, etc., on import	n.a.	26	12
Net railway dividend	9	0	0
Remittance by the government	43[a]	31[b]	28
Interest and dividend on private investment	18	38	37
Total net payment for services and non-commercial transaction	100	100	100

Source: Banerji, *Aspects of Indo-British Economic Relations*, Table 34,168–9; and Banerji.

Notes: a. 'Home charges' as defined by Banerji. b. Consists of interest on public debt and pension payments only.

to get these resources from abroad, because capital was scarce and expensive in India, and many types of skilled labour were unavailable too.

Some contemporary writers on the economic system, however, saw these foreign transactions as a symbol of India's colonial status and as damaging.

DRAIN THEORY

Every year, the government paid to Britain a sum of money in sterling informally called the 'home charges'. About half of the home charges in the pre-war years consisted of debt service. The second most important item was payment for maintenance of an army and marine force. A third component was pension payments for officials who had served India and retired to Britain. India Office expenses and stores purchased were the other items of expenditure.

These payments, Indian nationalists argued, reduced the capacity of the domestic economy to generate savings and investment, an argument that became known as the drain theory. The main campaigner for the theory, Dadabhai Naoroji, claimed that the interest on public debt raised in London was a form of a drain of resources. So were guaranteed profits of railway companies. Indian nationalists also alleged that the charge on account of the British Indian army or the marine fleet was unproductive because it was sometimes deployed for purposes other than the defence of India.

In principle, the drain implies a payment against which the country did not gain any value. Did these payments create value or not? This point is impossible to test. Repatriated profits came from business firms that created jobs and incomes inside India. Public debt went to finance the railways, irrigation, roads, and buildings in the nineteenth century. Canals, roads, and railways raised incomes and created jobs in India. Railway guarantees were paid to firms that might not have invested in the railways without the guarantees. Was military expenditure wasteful? For many Indian businesses, who had migrated as far away as Natal, Aden, Hong Kong, or Malaya, defence of India and the Indians did not just mean protecting a land border. If India paid for the cost of the army, the British paid for the cost of the navy.

Thus, many of the specific claims the drain theorists made were superficial, besides being impossible to test. These claims overlooked the fact that in the nineteenth century, both the government and private enterprise needed to buy services from the United Kingdom, which India could not deliver on its own. After all, the two countries were worlds apart in their technical-scientific and managerial capabilities. It was not just the government that purchased services abroad. In 1900, skilled labour services and capital from abroad went into modern industry, banks, colleges and universities, medical and engineering fields, and trading firms. Businesses and institutions needed to get these resources from abroad, because capital was scarce and expensive in India, and many types of skilled labour were unavailable.

Not all such transfers could be justified this way. One exception was the salaries paid to top British officers serving in India. These salaries formed a higher ratio of per capita income than salaries of top officers today would do, and the positions at the very top were blocked to Indian candidates. Could the government save money on this account by hiring Indians? It possibly could. Whereas some of these jobs that employed Europeans on high salary (university teachers, engineers, doctors, scientists) required special skills unavailable in the country, not all did. Did that over-spending affect government investment? That is hard to believe, for the officers on such pay formed a tiny fraction of the government workforce.

Government payment abroad reduced the government's capacity to follow a stabilization policy independent of British economic interests. This effect was in evidence whenever the Indian currency was under pressure, for example, during the Great Depression (see also Chapter 9, 'The monetary system'). The close link between the budget and the balance of payments was maintained by India's export surplus and the government's capacity to raise sterling loans in London. Late in the interwar period, the system broke down. Net export, affected by the Depression, declined. Sterling loans were not easy to raise. And yet, the government's remittance commitment had not changed. The casualty was the investment–income ratio.[19]

FOREIGN INVESTMENT

India received several types of capital. The usual short-term flows, which the annual accounts do not show clearly, went to meet the seasonal demands of trade. The India Office sold bills in London (called council bills) redeemable in India, which went to meet export transactions that peaked in the harvest seasons. Interest rates in India varied greatly by season, and high rates attracted these capital flows in the busy season. In the 1920s, there were other kinds of inflow of short-term foreign capital for investment

[19] By contrast with the colonial pattern, after Independence in 1947, restrictions on gold import brought the share of gold transactions close to zero. The government account showed a net receipt due to foreign aid, but the shares of trade, foreign investment, and private remittance declined. Balance of trade turned negative, owing to large imports of capital goods, oil, and sometimes food. Later in the 1970s, private remittance from expatriate workers in the Gulf increased. The shares of trade and investment increased again from the 1980s.

in the Government of India's rupee debt, but as the Depression began, the flow reversed.

Long-term capital came as net private foreign investment and net increase in public debt. Private foreign investment remains the weakest link in the balance of payments database. Based on what data is available, it seems that net foreign investment was usually positive, but a small item (about 1 per cent of national income). Railways dominated private investment in the third quarter of the nineteenth century, but that changed towards the century's end, with the formation of tea, jute, and mining companies. Such investment was initially in the form of shares sold in London by companies based in India.

In the interwar period, the pattern changed into direct investment in subsidiaries of foreign firms. At least some of these multinational firms were attracted by the higher import tariffs introduced from the 1920s. At Independence, foreign capital accounted for about a quarter to a third of the capital stock in the private corporate sector, according to different estimates. Plantations, jute textiles, and engineering had more than two-thirds of the capital stock foreign-owned. British companies owned 77 per cent of foreign capital. Much of this capital had come in as portfolio investment. Of the remaining amount, the major part came from the United States of America, all of it as direct investment.

***

This chapter extracted from macroeconomic statistics a few significant facts about the economic performance of colonial India. One of these is that industry and services did well, whereas agriculture did poorly in comparison. And another is that a pre-war period of expansion led to a slowdown in the interwar period. A variety of regional conditions—government poverty, land and water scarcity, openness, and preference for gold—together shaped the pattern of growth we observe in the macroeconomic data.

The divergence between rural and urban India had a human side. Few people trapped in low-productivity agricultural work could move into urban jobs easily. Agricultural labourers possibly faced skill-related barriers. Women faced serious difficulty leaving the household. Even as commercialization encouraged work participation and occupational mobility for men, it discouraged participation and occupational mobility among women. Better value for men was associated with a devaluation of women. The long-term stability in occupational structure and the retreat of women from the workforce reflected that new valuation to some extent.

No single theory of how colonial rule or world markets damaged India or benefited India can explain all these facts. Instead of seeking such grand theories, we should go deeper into the working of agriculture, industry, services, population growth, and the government to explain these facts. Subsequent chapters will do that.

Central to the whole story is the condition of agriculture. Chapter 4 shows why agricultural growth happened, why it slowed, why it did not always generate prosperity, and why the pattern of agricultural change varied a lot regionally.

4

Agriculture

Throughout the colonial period, agriculture provided a livelihood to more than two-thirds of the employed population in
India. If the artisans lost export markets in the nineteenth century,
peasants and merchants gained export markets. And yet, agricultural
productivity stayed small and stagnant, and growth rates in agriculture were low (Table 4.1). Regional inequality increased, as some
regions took part in the export-driven growth more successfully than
did the others. The pattern of inequality that took shape during the
colonial period turned out to be long-lasting. Pockets of rural poverty in later times had already emerged as pockets of rural poverty in
the past. Areas that experienced the 'Green Revolution' in the 1970s
and 1980s had started on the road to prosperity during British rule.

Why was growth so uneven? Why was growth low overall? Why
did regions differ so much? This chapter will describe agrarian change
over the period 1858–1947 and return to these questions at the end.
The chapter has eight parts: trends, resources and techniques, commodity market expansion, regional experience, factor markets, effects
of commercialization, explaining slow growth, and conclusions.

MEASURING AGRICULTURAL CHANGE

Data to measure agricultural change in the nineteenth century is
limited. Official statistics started collecting land use data seriously

Table 4.1   Growth rates of net domestic product (NDP), total and in agriculture, 1868–9 to 1946–7 (trend growth rates, percentage annual)

	Agriculture	NDP	Population	Per capita NDP
1868–98	1.01	0.99	0.40	0.59
1882–98	1.08	1.29	0.51	0.78
1900–46	0.31	0.86	0.87	−0.01

Sources: A. Heston, 'National Income,' in *CEHI* 2, eds Dharma Kumar and Meghnad Desai, (Cambridge: Cambridge University Press, 1983), Table 4.3A, for 1868–98; Sivasubramonian, *National Income of India*.
Notes: '1898' stands for an average of three years, 1896–7, 1897–8, and 1898–9. '1900' and '1946' are similarly averages of three years.

from the late nineteenth century. However, the statistical abstracts for 1870 do report some figures for the extent of cultivated area. The data looks patchy and incomplete, so that the total figure must be an underestimation. Still, making generous allowances for the problem, the data suggests a very large increase in cultivated area between 1870 and 1939 (Table 4.2). Adjusted for multiple cropping, which canals in some areas enabled, the growth would be larger. The main gainers from this expansion were the food crops, wheat, rice, and pulses, and the industrial crops, cotton, jute, sugarcane, oilseeds, and groundnuts. We cannot exactly measure how much land these crops gained in the late nineteenth century, but we know that these crops gained from shifts in crop choice in the regions that received railways and canals. By comparison, millets (jowar, bajra, and ragi) did not gain much land.

For the period after 1890, crop output data improves. These are still difficult to use. Three scholars have tried to make the statistics more usable. They are: George Blyn on area and output in British India (territories of present-day India, Pakistan, and Bangladesh excluding princely states), S. Sivasubramonian on real national income in agriculture in undivided India (territories of present-day India, Pakistan, and Bangladesh, including former princely states), and Takashi Kurosaki on area, production, productivity, and income in India, Pakistan, and Bangladesh between 1900 and

Table 4.2   Area cropped (square miles), British India

	Area in square miles			Percentage of total area		
	1870	1890	1939	1870	1890	1939
Cultivated area including current fallow	237,249	281,690	401,368	31	30	49
Forests		80,639	106,255		8	13
Available for cultivation	182,069	169,683	15,663	24	18	2
Not available for cultivation		195,038	125,290		20	15
Total area	749,118	954,258	812,124	100	100	100

Source: India, *Statistical Abstract relating to British India* (London: HMSO and Calcutta: Government Press, various years)

Note: Bengal data is unavailable for 1870 and 1890. I apply the same land area for Bengal in 1939 to 1870 and 1890, and apply the ratios of land use for the rest of India to Bengal for 1870 and 1890. The area 'available' is reported as 'culturable waste' in 1939.

2001.[1] Each work has its strength, but they do not suggest significantly different results for the colonial period. I will, therefore, use mainly Blyn in the tables later.

Between 1891 and 1946, the dynamism described earlier was over. The average growth rate of crop output was only 0.4 per cent. Non-food and commercial crops did significantly better than food crops, but the overall growth rate was still very low. These depressing results raise the question: Why was there stagnation in agriculture

[1] George Blyn, *Agricultural Trends in India* (Philadelphia: University of Pennsylvania, 1967); S. Sivasubramonian, *National Income of India in the Twentieth Century* (New Delhi: Oxford University Press, 2000); Takashi Kurosaki, *Comparative Economic Development in India, Pakistan, and Bangladesh: Agriculture in the Twentieth Century* (Tokyo: Maruzen Publishing House, 2017).

Table 4.3 Trend growth rates of crop output, acreage, and yield (percentage annual for British India), 1891–1946

	Output	Acreage	Yield per acre	Periods of growth and stagnation in yield per acre		
				1891–1916	1916–21	1921–46
All crops	0.37	0.40	0.01	0.47	−0.36	−0.02
Foodgrains	0.11	0.31	−0.18	0.29	−0.63	−0.44
Non-foodgrains	1.31	0.42	0.67	0.81	0.34	1.16

Source: Blyn, *Agricultural Trends in India*, Appendix Table 5A.
Note: The trend rates are the average of 10 rates, each relating to a five-year period. Blyn divided the entire period into 10 such divisions.

despite growth in exports and trade? One possible answer is that production conditions in agriculture limited growth.

PRODUCTION CONDITIONS

In a tropical monsoon region, the rainy season can make producing one crop fairly easy, but the long dry and hot rest of the year makes growing anything else very difficult. That would limit the prospect of growth unless irrigation in winter or summer allows the production of winter and summer crops. Besides, much of the Indian subcontinent does not have nutrient-rich loamy soil. In the Indo-Gangetic plains, both soil and water generally offered favourable conditions. But in peninsular India, both soil and water were deficient in quantity or quality, except in the presence of alluvial deposits or the black cotton soil. Economists and agricultural scientists discovered in the early twentieth century that the Indian yields were significantly smaller than yields of similar crops in East Asia, Europe, and North America. The reasons for this difference were not clear. One thing was certain that almost any available organic methods to raise yield, such as the application of manure, would need water, and India was deficient in water.

Most waters for agriculture came from the monsoon rains. The monsoon season did not last for more than three months. During the rest of the year, extreme heat and aridity would dry up a lot of the surface water. Except for a few regions, like the Bengal delta, seasonal dryness was universal in India. Because of high evaporation of surface water, irrigation would need either mobilizing water over long distances or accessing water from underground. Both were expensive options.

The two most common modes of irrigation were canals and wells. Canals could not be constructed with private money because they had to be large in scale, and wells were very costly to build in the Deccan Plateau. Given such costs, the fact that land irrigated as a percentage of cropped area increased from 12 to 22 between 1885 and 1938 (Tables 4.4 and 4.5) is quite significant. But this expansion was not enough to transform agriculture throughout the country. Both canals and wells came up in a few regions that had access to perennial sources of water. Four regions were important: Punjab, deltaic Madras, western UP, and Sind. Except for deltaic Madras, all the other areas were in the Ganges or Indus basins. In the Indo-Gangetic basin, the Himalayan rivers fed by snowmelt as opposed to monsoon rains carried more water throughout the year to support canals. The alluvial soil and easy access to underground water supported wells

Table 4.4   Area irrigated, 1885–1938 (million acres, excluding Burma)

	1885–6	1938–9
Canals		
Government	6.90	24.41
Private	0.94	3.53
Tanks	4.38	5.87
Wells	8.74	13.21
Total irrigated	23.09	53.73
Total cultivated	185.09	243.58
Irrigated/cultivated area (%)	12.4	22.1

Source: India, *Statistical Abstract relating to British India* (London: HMSO, and Calcutta: Government Press, various years)

Table 4.5 Irrigated area as a proportion of cultivated area in major provinces, 1885–1938 (percentages, 'British India' excludes Burma)

	1885–6	1938–9	% increase in irrigated area due to	
			Government canals	Wells
Punjab	29.3	57.4	95.5	9.3
Madras	24.1	23.5	49.6	18.6
UP	19.3	26.6	57.0	37.2
Rest of British India	6.0	12.5	31.3	10.7

Source: India, *Statistical Abstract relating to British India* (London: HMSO, and Calcutta: Government Press, various years)
Note: The last two columns may add to greater than 100 if acreage under other systems shrinks.

as well. In the drylands of the Deccan Plateau, canals could not be constructed easily because perennial sources of water were limited.

Despite agriculture being so constrained, the opportunity to sell grain and cotton in world markets and distant markets stimulated agricultural growth. Because productivity would not easily change, the growth of markets brought gains to a few regions and to areas where surplus land was available.

COMMERCIALIZATION

As the railways and port cities brought down costs of trading and made distant markets more accessible, domestic and foreign trades in agricultural commodities grew. Trade in agricultural goods existed in organized forms and on a large scale in the precolonial period. But the market expansion in the nineteenth century was different.

There were three differences. First, before colonial rule, product markets were mainly local; weights and measures varied from place to place; and transportation systems like bullock caravans or riverboats were not suitable to carry goods in bulk everywhere. The railways weakened these constraints, integrated markets, and helped marking systems converge. Second, agricultural trade integrated India with the world economy. From the time of the Industrial Revolution, a new demand arose for agricultural commodities, both as food and as raw materials. At the same time, technological modernization kept industrial goods cheap. The relative price of agricultural goods worldwide started to rise from the 1860s, or the terms of trade between agriculture and industry started to rise. The rise continued until the Great Depression of 1929. And third, the growth of trade induced changes in factor markets, that is, stimulated movements of capital and labour. Commercialization of agriculture means the combination of these three processes.

Export in value increased by 500 per cent between 1870 and 1914. Non-manufactured goods accounted for 70–80 per cent of the exports. The trend in agricultural prices moved consistently upward in a way that was thought to be without precedent by contemporary writers and administrators.[2] With a doubling of prices between 1870 and 1914, the real revenue burden on the farmers fell by 100 per cent. Price levels in 1928 were about three times what they were in 1875. The area cropped increased in most regions in the period 1870–1920, usually led by marketable crops such as wheat, cotton, oilseeds, sugarcane, and tobacco. Rents and prices of land increased. The scale of credit transactions increased too. So did the scale of land transfers. Circulation of agricultural labourers in and out of agriculture increased. And last, indices of transportation and rural trade, such as the number of carts at work, show a significant rise where such data are available.

After 1925, and in some regions from before that date, conditions began to turn adverse. By the early 1920s, world agricultural markets had begun to face persistent oversupply and price depression. In India, major cash crops faced stagnant or falling prices, though cotton was temporarily free of crisis. The agricultural depression was one factor among many that led to the Great Depression in 1929–32. The Depression upset product markets and rural credit markets. Already in the 1920s, good-quality arable land was beginning to become scarce (Table 4.2).

[2] K. Mukerji, 'Price Movements in India between 1823 and 1871', *Artha Vijnana* 5, no. 4 (December 1963).

Which crops led commercialization? Opium and indigo had led an earlier wave of commercialization (Chapter 2). These were no longer lucrative trades after 1860. Chapter 2 showed that the export trade in raw cotton had begun before 1800 and grew in scale between 1800 and 1850. The users of Indian cotton changed from domestic spinners, towards spinners in Britain and China, before shifting back to cotton mills in India. Bombay's business as a port began to grow rapidly.[3] Initially, Indian cotton was of a quality unsuitable for mills in Lancashire. When the American Civil War broke out in 1861, supplies of cotton from the American South to the Lancashire cotton mills stopped abruptly. India now emerged as a major supplier, and mills abroad found ways of mixing Indian cotton with other varieties to make it usable. Cotton export and prices crashed during the latter half of the decade as American supplies resumed. From the 1860s, mills in Bombay were the major new market for raw cotton. This boom reached a peak during and after World War I. By then, Japan, which had become one of the world's largest textile exporters, also purchased Indian cotton.[4] Cotton for export came from a few regions that specialized in the crop, mainly Khandesh, south Gujarat, southern Bombay-Deccan, Madras-Deccan, and Punjab.

In the 1870s, Indian wheat exports to Europe began to grow. Indian wheat accounted for 14 per cent of the total British import of wheat in 1883. Fall in transportation costs and repeal of an export duty on wheat sold from India encouraged the trade. Wheat went from Punjab, UP, and Bombay-Deccan. In the former two regions, wheat was a staple consumption good. In Bombay-Deccan, where the staple food crops were millets, wheat mainly went to the export market.

In the second half of the nineteenth century, Bengal, Burma, and South East Asia emerged as the world's main sources of rice. In South East Asia and Burma, rice accounted for over half of total export. In India, rice occupied from a quarter to a third of total export in a

---

[3] Amalendu Guha, 'Raw Cotton of Western India: Output, Transport and Marketing, 1750-1850,' *IESHR* 9, no. 1 (1972): 1–41.

[4] The Indo-Japan trade continued until the 1980s.

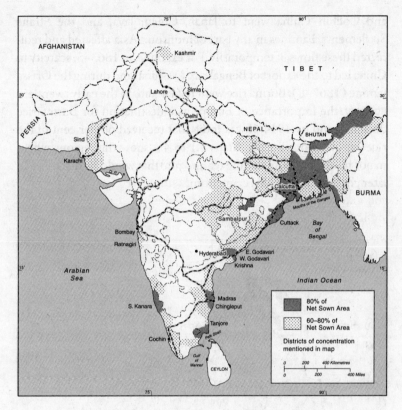

Map 4.1   Areas of rice cultivation

Source: Author

normal year. Bengal rice continued to reach other Indian provinces, as well as settlements of immigrant Indian workers in the empire. They preferred Bengal rice to the locally grown ones. Ceylon, owing to its plantations, was a destination for Bengal rice. Burma rice, on the other hand, went to Europe, was re-exported from Britain, and used for the manufacture of starch and spirits. Thanks to the use of the telegraph, rice and wheat markets were integrated to the extent that these grains were often substitutes.[5] Rice from Siam

[5] S. Arasaratnam, 'The Rice Trade in Eastern India 1650–1740,' *MAS* 22, no. 3 (1988): 531–49; A.J.H. Latham and Larry Neal, 'The International Market in Rice and Wheat, 1868–1914,' *EHR* 36, no. 2 (1983): 260–80.

and Cochin–China went to Japan, China, Java, and the Straits
Settlements. Famines in any part of monsoon Asia affected and redirected these flows, if temporarily. For example, in 1863–5, scarcity in
China led to the export of Bengal rice to China, and during the Orissa
famine (1867–8), Burma rice went to Ganjam. In the early twentieth
century, the importance of Europe as a destination for Burma rice
declined, and by 1914, it was India that received 60 per cent of the
rice exports from Burma. Maps 4.1 to 4.3 show the regions where
major traded crops, including tea and jute that would be discussed in
later chapters more fully, came from.

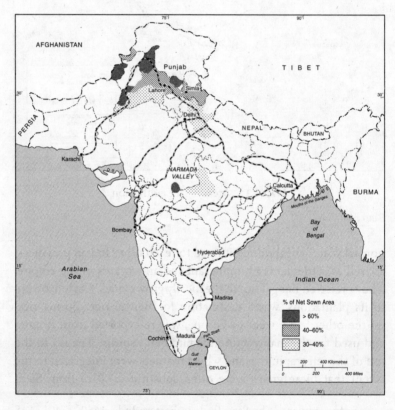

Map 4.2   Areas of wheat cultivation

Source: Author

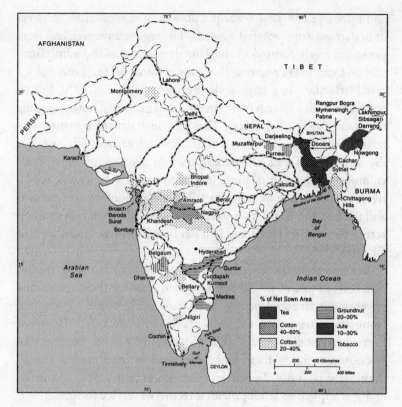

Map 4.3   Cotton, Groundnut, Jute, Tobacco, Tea

Source: Author

The maps suggest that the pattern of agricultural growth differed between regions. How did they differ, why, and when did the pattern shown emerge?

AGRICULTURE IN MAJOR REGIONS

The North

Before the mid-nineteenth century, Punjab was mainly a dry area consisting of vast wastes that supported pastoralism but little cultivation. Monsoon rains died away in the western part of the region, and intensive cultivation was possible only in areas close to rivers or in narrow strips watered by wells. The region, however, had large perennial rivers formed in the Himalayas, and as the administrators and engineers realized, this river system had the potential for canal irrigation on a large scale. Between 1870 and 1920, British engineers built a system of inundation and perennial canals, tapping the waters of the five rivers. This new infrastructure turned vast tracts in the doabs (interfluvial tracts), which earlier sustained only the most basic forms of pastoralism, into arable land. Nine 'canal colonies' created out of these irrigation projects appeared, collectively irrigating five million acres. The earliest colony was Sidhnai and the last Nili Bar. The largest were Lower Chenab (two million acres), Lower Bari Doab, and Nili Bar (a million acres each, see also Chapter 8).

In these colonies, the greater part of the available land went to claimants in lots of 14–50 acres each. In allotting these grants, the government favoured people of peasant background. Agricultural labourers, artisans, or village servants were excluded. However, former pastoralist groups did occasionally receive land grants. Recruitment from Hindu and Sikh peasants from central Punjab dominated land distribution and settlement policy. Special considerations applied to families with a record of service to British rule, including service in the army; this policy saw Punjab emerge as a major recruiting ground for the army. The grant deed stipulated various conditions the grantees needed to meet regarding the maintenance and improvement of the land. These conditions could appear to the peasants as undue interference. Until 1912, the land grantees were technically tenants of the state, a situation they accepted reluctantly. The Colonization of Government Lands (Punjab) Act 1912 allowed them to become proprietors. If one of the motivations behind the entire colonization scheme was to seek the loyalty of the peasants to British rule, it succeeded in that aim. Punjab peasants were, by and large, loyal to the rule in the interwar period when peasants elsewhere became restless and started participating in the nationalist movement.

Between 1867 and 1921, Punjab saw an infrastructure revolution. The length of canals expanded from less than 2,000 miles to more than 15,000 miles, road length nearly doubled, and railway mileage grew fourfold. Between 1891 and 1920, agricultural production increased significantly, and the main source of output growth was an expansion in area cropped. In that respect, Punjab was not different from the rest of India in the late nineteenth century. The difference was that, in Punjab, uncultivable wastes had become arable, whereas, in the rest of India, cultivable wastes came under the plough in the nineteenth century. The canals raised output, cultivated area, trade, and revenue.

After 1921, the conversion of wastes reached its limits. By then, Punjab agriculture had also benefited from successful plant breeding experiments in wheat and cotton, so that productivity continued to increase. Lyallpur was one of the sites where superior strains developed. Private merchants popularized these inputs.[6]

In present-day western UP and Haryana, a dense network of canals came up in the nineteenth century. In UP, canal mileage increased from 4,751 in 1871 to 16,136 in 1921. Unlike Punjab, UP was not initially water-scarce. Here, the availability of extra and cheaper water encouraged the cultivation of water-intensive cash crops such as sugarcane. On the other hand, railways encouraged the cultivation of grains and oilseeds, which were cheaper now to transport than before. Consequently, a broad regional specialization emerged in UP, with the canal belts in the Western Doab taking up wheat and sugarcane, while areas on the periphery, in Bundelkhand and the submontane districts, shifted to other grains and oilseeds. Other crops to have benefited from canal irrigation were barley and maize. Indigo and sugarcane were cultivated over smaller areas. But they were significant for the regional economy. From the 1870s, foodgrain export became an important trade. Agents of European grain-exporting companies settled in the major trading-cum-financial towns that also became connecting points of railways and road or river routes.

---

[6] On the role of seeds (and canals) on Punjab's agricultural growth, see Carl E. Pray, 'Accuracy of Official Agricultural Statistics and the Sources of Growth in the Punjab, 1907–47', *IESHR* 21, no. 3 (1984): 313–33.

The West and the South

Outside the Deccan Plateau, western India consisted of a high-rainfall coastal region, the Konkan, and a low-rainfall coastal region, South Gujarat. Konkan grew paddy. Poor communications and the absence of railways left the rice-based Konkan out of the new commercial network and turned it mainly into a labour exporter to Bombay city. Railways and the cotton famine stimulated agricultural prospects in the Charotar region of South Gujarat. Nadiad town, a market for tobacco, became easily accessible from both Bombay and Ahmedabad in 1863. Land devoted to tobacco possibly more than doubled between 1870 and 1900. Tobacco being a capital-intensive crop, its cultivation increased inequality while offering profit opportunities to the richer class of farmers. The number of irrigation wells doubled. In the early twentieth century, large cultivators here also took an interest in dairying, which encouraged processing industries on a small scale. The number of milch cattle doubled between 1900 and 1915, while the number of plough cattle increased only 10–20 per cent in the same period.

Much of peninsular India is on the Deccan Plateau, a region bounded on the north by the Vindhya and Satpura ranges, in the west by the Western Ghats, and in the east by the Eastern Ghats. Poor soil and unreliable rainfall had made most of the Deccan a millet-growing region oriented to subsistence agriculture. However, the black soil zones were suitable for the cultivation of cotton. Cotton cultivation and trade had been growing slowly in this region through the first half of the nineteenth century. In the second half of the nineteenth century, two developments facilitated the process. By connecting Bombay with the cotton-growing regions in the interior, the railways stimulated cotton cultivation and trade. Second, a network of canals came up in the Nira River valley south of Poona as a famine protection measure. The canals attracted migrant farmers from outside the region, who had the knowledge and the capital necessary to induce a successful switch from millets to sugarcane. The Nira River area later became a major concentration of sugar manufacturing.

Cultivated areas increased by 67 per cent between 1843 and 1873 in Bombay–Deccan. Cotton led the increase, but there was no decline in foodgrain area or availability. It is hard to discern if there was any significant acreage expansion anywhere in the Deccan Plateau after that. Cotton and oilseeds acreage grew relative to millets, implying a positive impact on peasant incomes of the new export market prospects. In smaller pockets where the government irrigation schemes reduced the cost of expanding acreage, the effects on both acreage and crop composition were positive.

In Madras–Deccan, too, overall acreage trends remain uncertain, but there was significant growth in cotton and groundnuts in the early twentieth century after the railways connected the region with Bombay. There were shifts in cropping patterns and the direction of trade. There was some switching from millets to cotton, oilseeds, and fodder crops. Between 1871 and 1921, prices, acreage, road mileage, and the number of carts for transportation expanded in Bellary District, and there were signs of greater price integration between regions.[7]

Canal irrigation expanded in the delta districts, Godavari and Krishna, between 1847 and 1852. The high tax burden, transport bottlenecks, and other problems initially restrained the commercial potentials of paddy, the main crop. As these constraints eased, long-distance trade in paddy began to expand. The canals encouraged diversification into oilseeds, sugarcane, tobacco, turmeric, chillies, and plantains. The cultivated area increased significantly in the second half of the nineteenth century. The agrarian expansion stimulated grain trade and credit markets. These activities were concentrated in towns that rapidly grew in population and economic importance. They included Vijayawada, Eluru, Rajahmundry, and Vizagapatam. Markets and transportation systems also enabled regions within coastal Andhra to specialize. An example of extreme specialization was the Guntur District, where the bulk of India's tobacco crop came from.

[7] Bruce L. Robert, 'Economic Change and Agrarian Organization in "Dry" South India 1890–1940: A Reinterpretation', *MAS* 17, no. 1 (1983): 59–78; David Washbrook, 'The Commercialization of Agriculture in Colonial India: Production, Subsistence and Reproduction in the "Dry" South', c. 1870–1930', *MAS* 28, no. 1 (1994): 129–64.

The territory of what is now the Tamil Nadu state consisted of several agro-ecological regions. In the coastal 'wet' districts (mainly Tanjore and Chingleput), paddy was of overwhelming importance.[8] This region resembled deltaic Bengal and coastal Andhra in cropping patterns. In the drier interior districts of Salem, Coimbatore, and Trichinopoly located on the edge of the Deccan Plateau and similar to Madras–Deccan, coarse rice and millets were initially the major crops. In the first half of the nineteenth century, large canal irrigation projects were built on some of the major rivers and extensive road-building also occurred. The canal water was mainly concentrated in Tanjore, which was situated on the Cauvery delta and was a rice-growing district. On this foundation, inter-regional trade expanded in traditional commodities such as rice and garden crops.

The dry regions of Tamil Nadu included tracts with black soil suited for cotton. The demand for raw cotton produced in Tamil Nadu (mainly in Coimbatore, Ramnad, Madurai, and Tirunelveli Districts) increased from the 1830s and rose quickly after the 1860s. Raw cotton trade introduced new marketing and financial systems. It was a major source of livelihood in small towns where cotton was processed and packed for export. In the interwar period, cotton improved its position as a cash crop because of the growth of a mill textile industry in Madras and Coimbatore. The second most important cash crop was groundnut, grown extensively in North and South Arcot. The export market for groundnut grew with the expansion of the modern food processing industry in Europe. Commercial expansion and rising prices reduced the real burden of taxation. When added to the increased profits from cotton exports, this factor encouraged private investment in the form of irrigation wells. Wells became the main irrigation system in Coimbatore and Madurai districts and played a key role in the post-Independence green revolution in Tamil Nadu.

[8] 'Wet lands' generally mean lands that have assured manmade irrigation, whereas 'dry lands' mean rain-fed cultivation.

The East

Eastern India was a geographically diverse territory. The province of Bengal alone included at least four zones sharply distinct, one from the other, with respect to settlement pattern, transport and communication, resource endowments, and historical experience. One of these four sub-regions, the submontane, was only a small strip of land. The other major regions were the fertile alluvial floodplains of the Ganges, the semi-arid laterite zone bordering Chota Nagpur, which was an outer extension of the Deccan uplands, and the fertile but remote southern seaboard. The alluvial flats spanned the floodplains of the Ganges river system and were by far the largest of the three zones. Much of this land is now in Bangladesh. Within this region, the existence of all-weather waterways made the river banks stand out as the commercial and political centres, whereas the further an area was from the river, the smaller its commercial potential until the railways came in. The uplands were made up of the eastern projection of the central Indian plateau, spanning Bengal and Bihar. In cultural and economic terms, these territories combined features of the alluvial and the upland zones but had less of good soil and water.

The Bengal seaboard was not a great hub of agricultural commerce. The huge rivers running through the sea-facing areas were not easily navigable. A large part of the seaboard consisted of forests. There were few industrial and commercial settlements, and while there was trade in grain, dried fish, and salt in the lower delta, the scale of these trades was not very large. From at least the eighteenth century, if not earlier, the seaboard regions saw immigration and settlement of groups of peasants. However, even in 1900, vast areas of the mangrove forests called the Sundarbans remained quite remote, commercially speaking.

Unlike Punjab or western India, the alluvial plains in Bengal did not see major changes in cropping patterns. It remained paddy-based. There were only marginal shifts, such as the decline of indigo and the rise of jute and sugarcane. Economists and historians tend to see the effects of this commercialization in a negative light. Between 1860 and 1940, the population of Bengal increased and so did the pressure on land. Many historians consider that the peasants of Bengal were progressively squeezed from two sides—land shortage and increasingly harsher forms of exploitation, first by landlords and later by moneylenders or some combination of the two classes.[9] Conditions of the peasants were depressed in the course of commercialization, and the Great Depression made them poorer. Indirect evidence for this pessimistic view comes from production and yield data that shows regression in interwar Bengal and rice crops. But that negative view may be overdrawn. There was consolidation and stability among occupancy tenants, partly owing to commercialization and partly to new laws protecting tenancy.[10]

The main railway lines that connected the interior agricultural districts with the ports or market towns appeared between 1854 and 1885. The pre-railway transportation system consisted of overland or river-borne trade. Overland traffic was expensive and slow, especially because of the large number of rivers. Water transport was impossible for almost eight months of the year because of the low water level or poor navigability of many of the major rivers. These eight months included the harvest seasons. The railways quickly drew trade away from the rivers and increased the volume of trade. The extent of commercial production and the direction of trade changed between 1860 and 1900. The period saw an increase in the size of new population clusters based on non-agricultural activity. These included Calcutta itself, the Raniganj mining-industrial area, Serampore industrial area, and north Bengal and Assam plantations. These towns were points of demand for rice. In the eastern districts, from the 1850s, demand from the newly established jute mills near Calcutta and demand for raw jute from jute mills elsewhere in the world stimulated jute cultivation.

[9] Sugata Bose, *Peasant Labour and Colonial Capital: Rural Bengal since 1770* (Cambridge: Cambridge University Press, 1993).

[10] Sumit Guha, 'Agrarian Bengal, 1850–1947: Issues and Problems', *Studies in History* 11, no. 1 (1995): 119–42.

Assam experienced a different path of agrarian development. The infrastructure revolution did not leave the region untouched. Four hundred miles of railway track came up in the last quarter of the nineteenth century. Dense river traffic already connected lower Bengal with Assam. However, the multiplier effect of these developments on the regional agrarian economy was small, according to most economic historians of Assam. Much of this development was meant to serve the tea plantations sector, which expanded significantly. Because so much of the new infrastructure suited the plantations in the foothills, the plains were still relatively underpopulated, and Assam in 1901 was one of the few land-abundant regions left in South Asia. In the early twentieth century, this open land frontier received a steady stream of immigrants, peasants from eastern Bengal in search of farmland. The cropped area increased. Foodgrain production in these new frontiers remained mainly subsistence-oriented.

These developments affected the pattern of urbanization. For example, the importance of Gauhati had earlier been more political than economic. Between 1870 and 1940, it emerged as a port of transit. The town became a commodity trade station, exporting cotton, silk, lac, mustard seeds, and forest produce while importing salt, textiles, and foodgrains. Nearly the whole of this business was in the hands of Marwari merchants—recent immigrants in the region—some of whom set up grain mills, cotton ginning units, and oil presses late in the interwar period.

Central India

Different parts of central India specialized in wheat and cotton. In turn, expansion in these crops saw some contraction in locally grown sugarcane and left millet acreage more or less stagnant. The key driver in this story of commercialization was the railways rather than new systems of irrigation.

The black soil of the northern districts of the Central Provinces and Berar and the Narmada Valley was ideally suited for wheat cultivation. The main wheat zone in central India spread over Saugor, Damoh, Jubbulpore, Mandla, Seoni, Narsinghpur, Hoshangabad,

Nimar, and Betul Districts. Over half of the cropped area in these districts grew wheat and these regions emerged as the main wheat-exporting ones outside Punjab and western UP. The conditions of irrigation were different here. Rainwater was trapped on the land by constructing banks to increase the moisture of the soil in the drier months. In some cases, a rice crop grew in this water just before the wheat-sowing season. Such special systems of irrigation, however, depended on cooperation between neighbours and also depended for their effectiveness on the heaviness of the soil.

Major railway lines connecting the Central Provinces and Berar with Bombay, Calcutta, and northern India became ready between 1860 and 1880. The railway link between Jubbulpore and Bombay opened in 1870. Within the next five years, wheat export from Narmada Valley almost doubled. The peak was reached in 1888–91 when wheat exports accounted for nearly half of all exports from the Central Provinces and Berar. In these 20-odd years, acreage cropped in the whole province increased from 3.5 million to 4.2 million. After that, a series of bad harvests and competition from Argentina reduced the scale of wheat cultivation in central India, and there was diversion of crop area to pulses and other grain crops. However, the growth impetus did not immediately slacken, for by then the region was beginning to see some industrialization.

Cotton cultivation in Wardha and Nagpur and several other districts to the west was stimulated initially by the cotton famine. But Lancashire's interest in Berar cotton waned afterward. A revival occurred at the turn of the century when government experimental farms tried to encourage cotton cultivation in the region. The farmers rejected attempts to promote the long-staple cotton preferred by Lancashire but did expand the hardier short-staple varieties that found a market in Japan and Europe. Between 1900 and 1920, cotton acreage in the province increased from 0.9 to 1.4 million. The area, by then, was beginning to develop as a centre of mill industry, and the countryside had developed many cotton gins. Berar emerged as the destination of one of the largest streams of internal migration—farm labourers from Chhattisgarh.

The railways had a similar effect, if on a smaller scale, on rice and oilseeds export from Chhattisgarh. Chhattisgarh, otherwise with poor access to ports and railways, found an outlet for its products from 1883 when a rail link opened between Nagpur and Rajnandgaon. But in the main, Chhattisgarh supplied labourers to expanding agrarian regions.

FACTOR MARKETS: LAND, LABOUR, AND CREDIT

Land Market

Chapter 2 has shown that new laws made land more marketable in theory. The previous sections showed that land was producing more. These tendencies should encourage more purchase and sale of land. Did that happen?

There was some sale, no doubt. In Bengal, for 30 or 40 years after the zamindari settlement began, a lot of lands came into the auction market. In the ryotwari areas, peasants mortgaged their land more frequently than before and often had to sell if they were unable to repay loans. In northern and southern India, former military and priestly groups, who owned land but did not cultivate with their own hands, sometimes sold land on joining other professions. The withdrawal of the non-cultivating elites and the consolidation of the peasants left asset inequality broadly unchanged.[11] The general character of land transfers, in other words, was not only from the poor to the rich but also from the rich to the poor.

Even though the land was more easily marketable now than before, land sold to a very limited extent; usually, 1–2 per cent of landholding changed hands over several decades. Several factors contributed to reducing activity in the land market. The conditions of commercial expansion were limited to a few areas. Peasants held on to land for the insurance or status value of the land. Colonial law created private property rights but founded inheritance and succession laws upon uncoded local custom and obsolete religious codes, which put the rights of the family or kinship groups before that of

[11] On a measure of asset inequality, see Dharma Kumar, 'Land Ownership and Inequality in the Madras Presidency: 1853–54 to 1946–47', *IESHR* 12, no. 3 (1975): 229–61.

the individual. Because a sale under such conditions would need agreement from a whole group, the members of which have different interests, selling land became very difficult.

Tenancy

Peasants sometimes leased land from others. The scale of tenancy increased in the colonial period. In the zamindari areas, all peasants were technically tenants without ownership rights. And yet tenancy was not subject to laws protecting tenant rights until much later. This imbalance empowered the zamindar. Some zamindars used their power to exploit the weaker peasants, usually with the help of dominant peasant clans. A series of tenancy acts (1859–1928) recognized and strengthened the occupancy rights or the so-called 'raiyati' rights of peasants settled on a piece of land for many generations. In other regions too, tenancy protection was a general trend at this time.

Such moves could have ambiguous effects on the land market. On the one hand, by strengthening cultivator rights, it could encourage mortgage and, eventually, more transactions in such rights. On the other hand, with the superior tenant receiving legal protection, it could make the tenant something like a small-scale landlord and encourage the sublease market. In practice, tenancy regulation did encourage subleases. Demand for lease shifted continuously outward. Tenancy regulation tried to keep up with this trend, but never quite managed to do so. In effect, many of these leases were unregulated. Outside Bengal, protection of superior tenants had a similar effect on the land market, that is, push in the market into lease rather than ownership rights. This is a process that contemporary sources called 'subinfeudation'.[12]

The average rents that the tenant paid to the owner, or the superior right-holder, increased from the late nineteenth century. Nominal rents increased manifold between the early twentieth century and mid-twentieth century in North India and a few other regions. In

---

[12] Government of Bengal, *Report of the Land Revenue Commission Bengal*, Vol. I (Calcutta: Government Press, 1940), 34, for example.

Bengal, tenancy laws had some effect in checking official rent rates but may have encouraged sub-tenancy and empowered the richer tenants in the process.

Labourers

The extent of wage labour and migrant labour employment increased in colonial India (Table 4.6). In one view, this was evidence of widespread distress. New property rights in land, decline of handicrafts, high risks of cultivation, and peasant indebtedness pushed small peasants to lose land and become wage labourers.[13] A different reading of the data says that landlessness did not increase in rural India, but older forms of landlessness associated with caste gave way to a new form associated with wage work.[14] The census occupational surveys, which were better able to observe wage earners than customary service, exaggerated the change.

Moreover, scrutiny of the census data found that more women than men workers became wage-dependent.[15] How do we explain

Table 4.6   Wage labourers in agricultural workforce (percentage), 1901–31

	Total	By Gender	
		Men	Women
1901	19.5	14.3	30.2
1931	36.3	19.5	43.8

Sources: Patel, *Agricultural Labourers in Modern India and Pakistan*; Krishnamurty, 'The Growth of Agricultural Labour in India', 327–32.

[13] Surendra J. Patel, *Agricultural Labourers in Modern India and Pakistan* (Bombay: Current Book House, 1952).

[14] Dharma Kumar, *Land and Caste in South India: Agricultural Labour in Madras Presidency in the Nineteenth Century* (Cambridge: Cambridge University Press, 1965).

[15] Alice Thorner, 'The Secular Trend in the Indian Economy, 1881–1951', *EPW* 14, no 28–30 (1962): 1156–65; Daniel Thorner, '"Deindustrialization" in India, 1881–1931', *Land and labour in India*, eds

that more women than men became wage-dependent? Earlier works dismissed the finding, assuming that the data on women's work was unreliable. A recent work assumes it was real and explains it.[16] Because women married early in India (Chapter 10), migrants were predominantly men. Many families cultivating land or employed in the handicrafts sent a few members to the urban industry or services. These members were men. The women stayed behind because they had children to look after. For a variety of reasons, but mainly because most women did not work full-time but all could find some seasonal farming work, more of them reported themselves to the census as agricultural workers.

In the colonial times, many agricultural labourers moved out of permanent contracts and moved into temporary or casual contracts. Slavery and serfdom were rare in precolonial India. The closest equivalent of serfdom was a caste-based obligation to perform labour and restrictions on ownership of land. In some situations, such as precolonial Malabar, individuals so tied to land were, in effect, sold when the land sold.[17] But a more prevalent form of labour-tying was the farm servant contract whereby the male head of a family pledged his labour, sometimes his family's labour, for one, two, or three years, to a specific employer. While caste sometimes cemented these relationships, there was an insurance motive behind the arrangement. The timing of rainfall was a life and death matter for peasants in monsoon agriculture. For many employers, it was well worth paying subsistence to a person throughout the year against an assured supply of effort on the few days when sowing and harvesting must necessarily take place. The average duration of employment contracts, however, was in decline in rural India from the late nineteenth century. The percentage of farm servants in agricultural labour households was

D. Thorner and A. Thorner (New York: Asia Publishing House, 1962); J. Krishnamurty, 'The Growth of Agricultural Labour in India', *IESHR* 9, no. 4 (1972): 327–32.

[16] Tirthankar Roy, *Rethinking Economic Change in India: Labour and Livelihood* (London: Routledge, 2005).

[17] Kumar, *Land and Caste.*

falling everywhere. In Madras, where farm servant contracts were particularly prevalent, the fall was dramatic.

An increasing supply of migrants reduced the employers' need for labour hoarding. From the late nineteenth century, certain poverty-stricken areas provided a seasonal agricultural workforce. Large numbers migrated every season from the uplands of Godavari, Krishna, Guntur, and Vizagapatam Districts to the Krishna–Godavari delta for farm work. Many from Chhattisgarh went every cotton season to Berar cotton fields and gins. The wheat field of Narmada Valley, that is, Jubbulpore, Saugor, and Damoh, received migrants from UP in the north and Rewa, whence the Gonds descended the hills during harvests. Bihar workers migrated to Bengal in the jute harvest season. Azamgarh workers were recruited for large-scale earthwork in Bengal. From Ratnagiri, many went to work in the cotton fields of Broach. Punjab canal colonies received migrants from Rajputana. Agricultural labourers also went to the plantations, urban services, railways, and other public works, and more rarely, to the mills. Such migration broke up traditional employment contracts.

With labour becoming more mobile than before, wage rates should converge across markets. A test conducted for the nineteenth century finds that the tendency was weak.[18] This result is not surprising because the migration of people in this region of many castes and languages always occurred along specific channels. One group did not necessarily offer itself in areas where another group was working. That does not mean that mobility was limited. Historians call this situation 'segmented' labour market.

Credit

Official banking enquiries conducted late in the interwar period estimated a large growth in rural credit, a development that caused more worry than celebration in administrative circles. Commercialization

[18] W.J. Collins, 'Labor Mobility, Market Integration and Wage Convergence in Late 19th Century India', *Explorations in Economic History* 36, no. 3 (1999): 246–77.

increased peasant dependence upon working capital credit. For example, the decision to produce non-food crops meant that the peasant had to buy food from the market, which could lead them to borrow. The monetization of rent and tax, combined with the disparity between seasons of tax collection and harvests, required money advances. Cash crops like wheat or cotton needed finance because, being traded over long distances under prior contracts, these involved more investments. Commercialization increased the demand for relatively high-cost inputs. Sugarcane, cotton, and tobacco require water and nutrients. Therefore, they needed greater investment in land preparation (levelling, ploughing, cattle, and implements), irrigation (more and deeper wells, more buckets), and fertilizers. Cotton crops on black soil needed heavy ploughs and many bullocks. These crops demanded more investment in money and time. They remained on the field longer than most foodgrains and thus required a longer waiting period between investment and sale of crops.

On the supply side, the creation of property rights in land and investment in water enhanced the mortgage value of land. The railways, growth of market towns, and new profit opportunities increased the mobility, migration, settlement, and enterprise of persons of trader–moneylender castes. Legislation concerning credit contracts gave the creditors more power to recover loans.

Why, then, was rural credit controversial? For one thing, no matter the growth in the supply of credit, interest rates remained high (Table 4.7). For another, the new relationship between the debtor and the creditor in the Indian village became controversial because of a feeling that the peasants were taking loans by mortgaging their property to the moneylender and were at risk of losing land. In Poona and Ahmednagar Districts in the summer of 1875, peasants rioted.[19] Almost no lives were lost. In a few dozen houses belonging to Gujarati

[19] Ravinder Kumar, *Western India in the Nineteenth Century: A Study in the Social History of Maharashtra* (London: Routledge and Kegan Paul, 1968); Neil Charlesworth, 'Myth of the Deccan Riots of 1875', *MAS* 6, no. 4 (1972): 401–21; I.J. Catanach, *Rural Credit in Western India 1875–1930* (Berkeley and Los Angeles: University of California Press, 1970),

Table 4.7 Interest rate (per cent per year)

Type of loan	1772	1812	1857–8	1880	1905–10	1930–5
Peasant loan	30–40	24–36	36–50	50		10–37
Land mortgage 1			12	18–24	12–24	
Land mortgage 2					9–12	

Source: For full details, see Tirthankar Roy, 'Factor Markets and the Narrative of Economic Change in India 1750-1950', *Continuity and Change* 24, no. 1 (2009): 137–67.
Notes: The data in this table were constructed by using a variety of sources. The two 1905–10 numbers refer to rural North India (1) and Bihar indigo planters (2).

and Marwari moneylenders, the peasant mobs burnt their property and the account books. With the memory of the mutiny still fresh in their minds, officials panicked and ended up designing the Deccan Agriculturists Relief Act (1879), which greatly restrained money-lender activity, land transactions, and the credit market.

A second region where the growth of credit caused much alarm was Punjab. Here, the canal colonies had given a big push to land prices and land market transactions, as well as the mortgage market. Officials felt that the control of professional moneylenders over rural assets was increasing to the detriment of the peasants. The Punjab Land Alienation Act (1900–1) followed, to again restrain mortgage and transfers. The Punjab act did not completely succeed because some lenders and debtors started to use benami mortgages or mort-gages in someone else's name.[20] The long-term effect, however, was restrictive upon the lender.

The British officers disliked the moneylenders for a political reason. They believed in an ideology that had grown roots since

Chapter I; Eric Stokes, *The Peasant and the Raj: Studies in Agrarian Society and Peasant Rebellion in Colonial India* (Cambridge: Cambridge University Press, 1978), cited by Sugata Bose, ed., *Credit, Markets and the Agrarian Economy* (Delhi: Oxford University Press, 1994), 11.

[20] M.M. Islam, 'The Punjab Land Alienation Act and the Professional Moneylenders', *MAS* 29, no. 2 (1995): 271–91.

the Mutiny, which told them that British rule served the peasants and worked against feudal interests in the countryside. Why, then, were peasants generally poor and why did they depend on high-cost credit? These officers blamed the exploitative tactics adopted by the moneylender. No doubt, the moneylender had unusual power in the countryside. They had more knowledge of accounts, of law, and the courts of law. But the high cost of loans did not reflect only this power. They took a high risk because most loans were not, in fact, mortgage-backed, but unsecured. The risk of harvest failure was unusually high in the tropical monsoon agriculture. Similarly, peasant borrowings did not everywhere indicate that peasants were poor and weak. In the 1920s in Punjab, peasants borrowed because they were making money in an agricultural boom and borrowed to buy land.[21]

If rural indebtedness was not always a symbol of exploitation, then what was the problem with it? Why was it expensive to borrow? Why was there not a larger flow of credit? On questions like these, a new scholarship sheds light. The older scholarship on rural credit in India offered a mainly political account of the debtor–creditor relationship, one in which moneylenders with monopolistic power, reinforced by colonial contract law, exploited poor peasants. By contrast, the emerging scholarship considers more fully creditor risk. Creditor risk stems from the high risk of crop failure, the difficulty of insuring against climatic risk, and the fact that most peasants were too poor to have liquid assets and collaterals. In principle, creditor risk can be mitigated with a contract law and strong enforcement of contracts. In British India, a contract law was passed in 1872. But the administrators thought that the law went too far, especially when the contract allowed for transfer of landownership from the debtor to the creditor, and that the debtors needed protection from ruin when a contract was enforced. Therefore, a sentiment developed against mortgage-backed credit, land for mortgage was withdrawn from supply, and lenders supplied less credit from before.[22]

[21] Malcolm Darling, 'Prosperity and Debt,' in Bose, *Credit, Markets*, 29–56.

[22] Latika Chaudhary and Anand Swamy, 'A Policy of Credit Disruption: The Punjab Land Alienation Act of 1900', *Economic History Review* 73, no.

Transfers of ownership from the peasant to the professional lender happened on a limited scale, not only because of legal intervention. There were substantial barriers to the entry of non-agricultural classes into agriculture. Merchants and moneylenders, in general, were willing to lend short-term. Many new purchases of land in different regions did use borrowed money in the twentieth century. But even if buying new land had become easier than before, taking possession of the land was never easy for an outsider, partly because of the unhelpful land laws. A great number of land transactions, therefore, were internal to the peasant economy, even internal to kin, clan, and caste.

For these reasons and because of the anti-moneylending laws like those in Punjab and Deccan, the rural credit business came into the hands of the rich peasant rather than the professional lender. The rich and middle peasants commanded the credit market and tied credit transactions with sale transactions (that is, collected an implicit interest from commodity prices, something a moneylender could not do). Even where a moneylender class could still be distinguished, their power to influence the terms of transaction were often limited.[23]

WHO GAINED FROM COMMERCIALIZATION?

Earnings of Peasants and Workers

Real GDP in agriculture increased at the approximate rate of 1–2 per cent per head in the late nineteenth century (Chapter 3). It increased somewhat faster than did real wages. The average income of the peasants, however, was still quite small, which should explain

---

1 (2020): 134–58; Latika Chaudhary and Anand Swamy, 'Protecting the Borrower: An Experiment in Colonial India', *Explorations in Economic History* 65, no. 3 (2017): 36–54.

[23] Neeladri Bhattacharya, 'Lenders and Debtors: Punjab Countryside, 1880–1940', *Studies in History* 1, no 2 (1985) 305–42; Sumit Guha, 'Weak States and Strong Markets in South Asian Development, c. 1700–1970', *IESHR* 36, no 3 (1999): 335–53.

why they willingly migrated to off-season urban work. Because of the seasonality of monsoon agriculture, there was seasonal unemployment in the countryside. Agriculture rarely offered full-time work for more than 220–240 days in a year and much less than that in the dry regions. Even though average earnings in the factories of the nineteenth century were only marginally higher than what a peasant expected to earn in agriculture, there was work available in mills, mines, and plantations. Even the relatively well-off agricultural families could afford to send their adult males off to non-agricultural wage work, recalling them to meet the peak season tasks.

Average real wage, as far as we can measure, changed very little either way from the beginning of British colonial rule to its end (Table 4.8). These numbers derive from wage rates converted into annual earning, assuming a work intensity. In a highly seasonal agricultural condition, the reliability of these numbers depends on how we measure or assume work intensity (number of days of work in a year) and changes therein. As of now, that data does not exist. There remain few examples of wage labour communities getting significantly better off. So, the image of a long stability in earnings may be valid.

I should add two qualifications to this stability argument. First, there was little stability in the institutional arrangements in which workers worked. In the mid-nineteenth century, many labourers worked under annual contracts for fixed wages. By 1900, such long-term contracts were in decline everywhere, as mentioned before, and money wages became more negotiable and fluctuating as a result.

Second, the regional picture varied. In the peak period of agricultural export, there were reports of a rise in real wages from many regions. Labourers experienced an improvement in the cash crop–growing areas of South India or the Upper Doab.[24] Signs of material prosperity for the rural population, in general, can be seen in Punjab too. In coastal Andhra, real wages in the 1920s were higher than

[24] Peter Mayer, 'Trends of Real Income in Tiruchirapalli and the Upper Kaveri Delta, 1819–1980: A Footnote in Honour of Dharma Kumar', *IESHR* 43, no. 3 (2006): 349–64; Ian Stone, *Canal Irrigation in British India* (Cambridge: Cambridge University Press, 1984).

Table 4.8   Agricultural wages, average annual in Rs, 1785–1968

	Money wage	Real wage at 1873 prices
1784–8	14	27
1810	18	35
1830	24	32
1857	24	29
1870–5	35	35
1882–5	38	27
1899–1900	48	37
1920	73	29
1929	100–10	47
1931	59	38
1936	53	28
1941	41	15–18
1946	205	31
1951	241	48
1960		42
1968		42

Note: The data in this table were constructed by using a variety of sources. For details, see Roy, 'Factor Markets'; and Tirthankar Roy, 'Globalisation, Factor Prices and Poverty in Colonial India', *Australian Economic History Review* 47, no. 1 (2007): 73–94. Some of the numbers in this table were revised after these publications. A brief description is in order. Most wages relate to eastern and southern India until the 1870s and to all-India averages thereafter. The former data set is collated from British Parliamentary Papers and a number of contemporary published surveys. The data set for the 1870s–1920s was gathered from two official and all-Indian sources: that relating to the interwar period from a range of published or unpublished provincial surveys; and the post-1950s from published research, especially Moni Mukherjee, *Selected Papers on National Income* (Calcutta: Firma KLM, 1995), and A.V. Jose, 'Agricultural wages in India', *EPW* 23, no. 26 (1988): A46–A58. Typically, the eighteenth- and nineteenth-century numbers are available in the sources in the form of annual or monthly wages, whereas the later numbers are reported as daily wages. I convert all numbers into annual, where given by any other unit of time, assuming a year of 220 working days. For the eighteenth and nineteenth centuries, the deflator used is the price of rice in Bengal, available in the Global Price and Income History Group website, http://gpih.ucdavis.edu/, accessed on 29 April 2020. For the later periods, weighted commodity prices index or the agricultural GDP deflator were used. The wartime prices and wages are not entirely reliable because of fluctuations within the year.

those in the 1900s.[25] In districts (especially in Madras) where commercialization combined with large net emigration, there was a rise in wages.[26] For Bengal, data compiled by the K.L. Datta committee on prices suggested a rise in real wage between 1891 and 1911. On the other hand, for the Deccan regions, real wages do not seem to have changed very much in the early twentieth century. Even where an increase did take place, the extent was small and sometimes short-lived. After all, agricultural workers mainly moved between unskilled rural occupations rather than out of them.

The long-term stability of the real wage of agricultural workers did not, however, impart a similar stability among urban wages. After about 1925, urban real wages rose significantly thanks to industrialization and factory trade unions, thus widening the urban-rural gap in standards of living. The divergence suggests that agricultural labourers did not ordinarily join those labour markets.

While wages did not rise, and much higher-paying jobs were out of their reach, the number of wage-dependent households started to rise. Land area grew very slowly since the second decade of the twentieth century. The old land was already under occupation. Therefore, any additional population must live either by dividing old plots, which would push them towards tenancy, or labour. Thus, demographic transition in a land-scarce region increased the ratio of labourers in the agricultural population. But demography would not explain the immobility of the average wage. Consistent with the economic theory of wages, real wage in agriculture followed trends in labour productivity quite closely; this we can see whenever it is possible to measure both. The landowners gained from commercialization when they had enough good quality or adequately watered land. But the landless gained to a small extent and frequently lost out quickly any real-wage gains they made during periods of low prices. In the interwar period, population growth and fixed land combined

[25] K. Atchi Reddy, 'Wages Data from the Private Agricultural Accounts, Nellore District, 1893–1974', *IESHR* 16, no. 3 (1979): 301–21.

[26] Dharma Kumar, 'Agrarian Relations: South India', in Kumar and Desai, *CEHI* 2, 238–9.

to create conditions where food was becoming scarce (Table 3.12). Agricultural labourers were the group most vulnerable to the buildup of a famine-like condition.

Social status sometimes added its weight to suppress wages. In precolonial India, landless labourers came from those castes whose primary duty was to perform agricultural labour. Access to land continued to be caste-biased. With some exceptions, the wealthier sections in the countryside came from the middle castes, who had long been engaged in cultivation, whereas the poor tended to come from castes that had performed labour for generations. The so-called upper castes by ritual status generally moved out of land and into the services. Commercialization, in that case, tended to strengthen the social and political position of middle castes and weaken those of the oppressed castes. In Peter Robb's expression, economics 'reinforce[d] subservience'.[27]

While in some areas, rise in peasant power might reinforce caste oppression, overall, obligatory labour and serfdom declined in colonial times. From the early twentieth century, there was an improvement in the social status of the depressed castes. The element of compulsion and force in their employment became weaker. Various forms of social oppression, such as enforced dress codes and codes of conduct towards the upper castes, became weaker too.[28] The length of the working day came down substantially. Migration within and outside agriculture increased. The possibility of migrating to the cities and other British colonies made occupational choice more diverse. The decline of attached labour owed to the widespread exit of these castes from agricultural labour. They entered plantations, mines, urban services, public works, and government utilities. Many emigrated to other tropical colonies and into similar types of work.

[27] Peter Robb, 'Peasants' Choices? Indian Agriculture and the Limits of Commercialization in Nineteenth Century Bihar', EHR 45, no. 1 (1992): 97–119.
[28] See Haruka Yanagisawa, A Century of Change: Caste and Irrigated Lands in Tamil Nadu 1860s–1970s (Delhi: Manohar, 1996).

Who among the Peasants Gained? And Who Lost?

In the richer agricultural regions, peasants with enough land gained in income and political power. In the ryotwari areas, they owned land. In zamindari regions, the zamindars made friends with tenants commanding big holdings. Dominant tenant groups organized themselves in caste collectives, using caste as a bargaining platform and as a means to 'combine powerfully against the zamindar'.[29] Local administrations usually supported the peasant community in matters of dispute. The big tenants owned or controlled land, credit, water, implements, and animals. Real work in the village, therefore, was impossible without the consent and cooperation of the big tenants.

Such groups reaped the gains from commercialization when market conditions turned in their favour. The Jat peasants in Punjab and Upper Doab, the *Vellalas* in Tamil Nadu, the *jotedars* or large tenants with superior rights in western and northern Bengal, the *Kanbi Patidars* of south Gujarat, the rich *Reddy* farmers in Madras–Deccan, the Maratha peasants and *Saswad Malis* in the Maharashtra sugarcane belt, and counterparts of these groups from various other regions illustrate that process. The process was not a smooth one. Famines and the Great Depression caused reversals. But these were temporary reversals and did not upset the trend. After Independence, this class of relatively wealthy peasant communities made successful attempts to control and shape local and national politics. In studies on the political economy of independent India, they have been variously called 'commercial peasants' (Donald Attwood), 'rich farmers' (Pranab Bardhan), and 'bullock capitalists' (Lloyd and Susan Rudolph).[30]

---

[29] Peter Robb, 'Hierarchy and Resources: Peasant Stratification in Late Nineteenth Century Bihar', *MAS* 13, no. 1 (1979): 97–126.

[30] See Donald W. Attwood, *Raising Cane: The Political Economy of Sugar in Western India* (Abingdon: Routledge, 1992), Chapter 1, for a discussion; Pranab Bardhan, *The Political Economy of Development in India* (Delhi: Oxford University Press, 1984), Lloyd and Susanne Rudolph, *In Pursuit of Lakshmi: The Political Economy of the Indian State* (Chicago: University of Chicago Press, 1987).

At the lower end of the scale, opportunities for improvement were limited. Those with small holdings suffered a lot during famines and slumps. The famines impoverished them and reduced the supply of working males.[31] They had to live with the insecurity of tenancy, high risks of cultivation, limited capital resources, and the collapse of the world market.

Does this uneven picture suggest a definite increase in inequality? That conjecture is hard to test, because there is not enough data to measure inequality among the agricultural population. It is more plausible that the depression in agricultural yield reduced the chances of significant improvements in conditions of living for every class that depended on land, rich and poor alike. The Bengal zamindars were in decline for a long time.

Let me now return to the big question the chapter started from: Why was income from agriculture relatively stagnant even as markets grew?

EXPLAINING STAGNATION

Institutional Explanations

Most economists prefer to read history through the lens of institutions, often making their explanations more complicated than they need to be. The accent in institutional explanations falls on property rights. The property-right based explanations come in two forms: One blames land rights and the other blames credit. When the landlord lends money on the side, the two join together.

New property rights went to groups like the Bengal zamindars that did not cultivate the land. Tenants did not own the land and had no incentive to invest and improve the quality of the land. Peasants in the ryotwari regions did have property rights, but being unable to deal with price fluctuations or being pushed by the government tax pressures, they went to the moneylenders, mortgaged their land, and

[31] See, for example, D. Rajasekhar, 'Famines and Peasant Mobility: Changing Agrarian Structure in Kurnool District of Andhra, 1870–1900', *IESHR*, 28, no. 2, (1991): 121–50.

borrowed money. Moneylenders would either gain ownership of the land or gain interest income at the expense of the peasant. In any case, as a class, they were either unable or unwilling to invest in land improvement. Why make the effort, if making money by exploiting the poor farmers was easy enough?[32]

These theories suggest that there was underinvestment in agriculture because most money ended up with the landlord or the lender who did not want to invest; and that for the peasants, commercialization was forced, that is, against their best interests. They joined a market that did not give them good return and enough incentives to sell their output.[33] Indian nationalists at the turn of the twentieth century made the first statement of the forced commercialization argument. Their target was the land tax. After 1860, the real tax burden fell everywhere and the profit motive for market participation strengthened. In the 1970s, a different version of forced commerce appeared, one that blamed lenders and landholders.

[32] One economist gives this causal link between indebtedness and technological backwardness a theoretical form. The moneylender was also the owner of the land, which was tilled by a landless peasant. The moneylender, thus, earned income from two sources, interest on consumption loan and crop share. If he or she invested in land, crop share increased, but the need for consumption loan and interest income would fall. Fearing this loss, the moneylender would not make productive investments. Amit Bhaduri, 'A Study in Agricultural Backwardness under Semi-Feudalism', *Economic Journal* 83, no. 329 (1973): 120–37. For an application of the argument, see Amit Bhaduri, 'The Evolution of Land Relations in Eastern India under British Rule', *IESHR* 13, no. 1 (1976): 45–53.

[33] For statements of different versions of the argument, see Irfan Habib, 'Colonialization of the Indian Economy, 1757–1900', *Social Scientist* 3, no. 8 (1975): 23–53; Sumit Sarkar, *Modern India: 1885-1947* (Delhi: Macmillan, 1983), 24–42; A.K. Bagchi, 'Markets, Market Failures, and Transformation of Authority, Property and Bondage in Colonial India', in *Institutions and Economic Change in South Asia*, eds Burton Stein and Sanjay Subrahmanyam (Delhi: Oxford University Press, 1996), 48–70; Patel, *Agricultural Labourers*, 48–63; Utsa Patnaik, 'On the Evolution of the Class of Agricultural Labourers in India', *Social Scientist* 11, no. 7 (1983): 3–24.

The evidence rejects most of these predictions and claims. Research on national income shows that the average rural incomes increased in the 50 years before World War I. Regional evidence shows that the peasants almost always gained in money and power when irrigated land in sufficient quantity was available (zones like Punjab, coastal Andhra, or western UP). A simple test to see if the peasants were forced to sell would be to see if more sales from the farm-gate happened when prices were low or when prices were high. If the former, we would infer that such sales were not in the best interests of the seller and forced in a sense. If the latter, we would infer that price incentive, rather than diktats from landlords or lenders, influenced sales. Data on the sale of crops at the farm-gate are unavailable. An indirect measure would be if the farmers cropped more area under a crop that gave them a better price in the previous year, thus shifting resources away from other uses. If they did, we should again read the result to mean that price incentive, rather than compulsion, shaped peasants' choices. Statistical tests show that the cropping decisions reacted positively to price incentives, and that the peasants were ordinarily capable of capturing gains and avoiding losses.[34] They had choice in the matter and exercised choice. Landlords and lenders could not take away that choice.

B.B. Chaudhuri says that the notion of the peasants doing something because they were forced by debt is simplistic. Debt was not universally a burden nor of similar scale everywhere, and the practice of treating debts uniformly as evil confuses routine unsecured trade credit with occasional mortgage-backed credit (because there was a marriage in the family or a decision to buy more land).[35]

[34] Dharm Narain, *The Impact of Price Movements on Areas under Selected Crops in India 1900–1939* (Cambridge: Cambridge University Press, 1965); Omkar Goswami and Aseem Shrivastava, 'Commercialisation of Indian Agriculture: What Do Supply Response Functions Say?', *IESHR* 28, no. 3 (1991): 229–60;

[35] B.B. Chaudhuri, 'The Process of Agricultural Commercialisation in Eastern India During British Rule: A Reconsideration of the Notions of "Forced Commercialisation" and "Dependent Peasants"', in *Meanings of Agriculture*, ed. Peter Robb (Delhi: Oxford University Press, 1996).

Rural people often took mortgage-backed loans not because they were poor but they thought they were rich enough to be able to pay back. For example, the peasants who joined in the Deccan riots of the 1870s had become indebted during a time when cotton trade and prices were rising. Debts, in this case, reflected creditworthiness rather than distress.

These institutional models of under-investment implicitly believe that it was technically easy to make investments in land and improve productivity. If the moneyed people in the village did not do this, they must be unwilling to invest. There is a simpler alternative explanation for under-investment. Gainful investment was not technically possible. For example, however rich I am, I may never be rich enough to get water where water is deep underground. Or, if I am a farmer with a tiny holding, I must pay a high interest on borrowings, because the lender knows I am a risky client with little asset to fall back on. This possibility leads me to an alternative explanation, one that says that the cause of under-investment was that the landholding was either too small for farmers to command low-cost credit or land was of poor quality.

Resource Endowment

Zones of acute rural poverty consisted of two broad types: relatively high-rainfall rice-growing regions with low land-person ratio (eastern India) and the low-rainfall regions in peninsular India. Land was scarce in one of these areas and water in another. Because of these two types of scarcity, gains from commercialization were limited, not sustained (when, say, the supply of good land ran out), and investment rates were low.

In the former situation, the land produced a lot, but the average landholding was too small. In Bengal, Bihar, or eastern UP, income from rice was divided between too many people dependent on land. The land yield was above the Indian average, but the number of households dependent on wages and insecure tenancy was growing. Fragmentation of peasant holdings made the individual peasant an unreliable debtor and, therefore, subject to control by the rich trader-cum-creditor, who was also often the holder of superior tenancy rights. Further, parts of the rice regions were so overexploited about 1901 that population growth had led to the cultivation of inferior land. In Bengal, acreage cropped per head was among the lowest in the world in 1891 and fell by 80 per cent between 1891 and 1941. Degradation of land made land improvement more expensive and uncertain than before.

In the drylands (Map 4.4), there was a different obstacle to investment: Expected earnings from investment in land were low because of the high cost of ensuring a secure supply of water in the dry seasons and the high risk of harvest failure. In the arid Deccan Plateau,

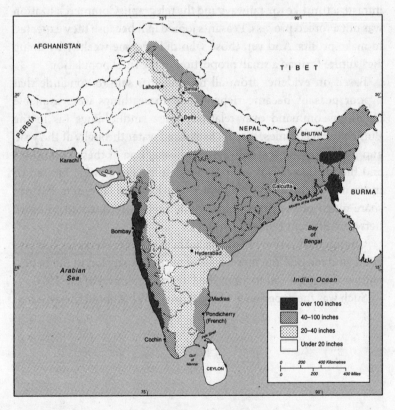

Map 4.4   Rainfall

Source: Author

sinking wells was the only reliable way to ensure two or three good crops in a year. The low water table in the uplands, the thin topsoil, the scarcity of perennial rivers, and the basaltic rock underneath made digging wells or constructing canals prohibitively expensive. The main grains in these areas were a locally consumed arid crop, millets, which yielded a small profit in the best of seasons.[36]

***

All parts of colonial India experienced growth of agricultural trade in 1860–1920 and a slowdown in trade after that. The increased demand was met by expanding the cultivated area and with improved infrastructure like the railways and the telegraph. Commercialization was not a forced process. Peasants joined in it because they expected to make profits. And yet, those who did become wealthy by doing agriculture formed a small proportion of the rural population.

Based on evidence from all regions, it is safe to conclude that a poor peasant became richer when three things were available together: command over relatively large landholdings (as in the Punjab canal colonies), access to assured water throughout the year, and easy access to the railways. Take away one of these conditions and the profits from producing agricultural goods were limited or more of it went to the merchants. Agricultural labourers did not share much of the gains, but they did get more freedom to move between different types of contract.

Commercialization ran out of steam in the interwar years, because good land ran out. Further bursts of output expansion in the better-endowed regions had to await the Green Revolution of the 1970s.

Such was the experience of the farmers. What about the artisans?

[36] Tirthankar Roy, 'A Delayed Revolution: Environment and Agrarian Change in India', *Oxford Review of Economic Policy* 23, no. 2 (2007): 239–50.

5

Small-Scale Industry

In 1900, the majority of India's industrial workers were in industries that did not use either machinery or large factories. This chapter describes their experience. Traditional handicrafts formed a large part of this set, but the share of modern small-scale industry, which used some machines and hired some labour, was rising.

According to a popular interpretation, the handicrafts declined owing to competition from machine-made goods imported from Britain. Recent scholarship revises that interpretation. Imports did not damage all crafts. The producers of simple goods used as raw materials in other industries—goods like metals, cotton yarn, dyes, wool, jute goods, and silk—were more likely to become unemployed. Mechanized and mass production systems produced these goods much more cheaply. Industries using manual skills and decorative techniques, and serving urban consumers, survived on a large scale. For example, even as indigenous iron smelting disappeared, traditional blacksmiths continued to produce household utensils. Similarly, as cotton spinning disappeared, cotton handloom weaving continued to sell apparel that carried distinctive designs or were made in certain styles.

Such skill-intensive crafts benefited from foreign trade by accessing cheaper raw materials and tools. The decline in one kind of craft and survival in another did not mean that unemployed workers could shift to new jobs. There were many barriers. For example, amongst those who lost jobs in spinning were rural women with limited options about learning a new skill or working away from home.

Overall, small industries showed increasing differentiation and inequality. Before I get to that topic, it is necessary to discuss more fully what kind of industry the chapter will describe.

TYPES OF INDUSTRY

Standard histories of Indian industrialization deal mainly with 'modern industry' or 'large-scale industry', defined by three features: use of machinery and steam-powered technology; large factories and large-scale employment of wage labour; and legal identity, such as being subject to the factory act or the company act. The next chapter will discuss such industrial units. This chapter deals with units where these features were either absent or present in a partial way. In short, the chapter deals with units that employed labour-intensive technologies, were situated in households or small wage-based workshops, and had no legal form.

Some of these firms used technologies that pre-dated the colonial period. Major examples of such 'traditional' small-scale industry or handicrafts were handloom weaving, leather manufacture, furniture, metal utensils, carpets, and pottery. There were, however, a few small-scale firms that were modern in origin; these used some machinery and machine tools and had a larger scale than the family or the workshop. Examples include foundries, cotton gins, jute presses, edible oil extractors, rice mills, bricks and tiles manufacture, and flour mills.

The dividing line between traditional and modern, and between large and small, was not a sharp one. Most types of modern small-scale industry, in fact, supplied old products. Thus, grain milled by machinery and that milled by hand both supplied the same consumers, but by different technologies. Sometimes, however, new technology led to a new product altogether. For example, buyers of rice often saw the machine-milled rice as a distinct product from hand-pounded varieties. Sometimes, the modern represented a form of technological adaptation of the traditional form. For example, handloom weavers set up small factories equipped with power-driven looms. Large-scale industry supplied raw materials to small-scale industry. Workers often moved between the two. Workers and entrepreneurs in small-scale industry sometimes learnt their skills and acquired new ideas by working in large-scale industry. For example, former workers in cotton mills bought discarded power looms, reconditioned these, and started small weaving factories.

LONG-TERM PATTERN OF INDUSTRIALIZATION

The statistics on industrial employment are available from two main sources: the census, which gives total employment in industry, and publication on officially registered factories, which gives employment for legally registered factories. Occupational statistics began to be collected and reported from 1881, but the level of detail and the definition of work and workers changed so much between the early censuses that it is not easy to create reliable series by using the censuses before 1911. The following tables given next rely on the census data processed and readied for use by S. Sivasubramonian.

Tables 5.1 and 5.2 suggest together that small-scale industry experienced a fall in employment and a rise in output, that is, a rise in productivity. Data on production in the largest of the handicrafts, the handloom textiles, confirms the productivity increase (Table 5.3). Handloom textiles accounted for a quarter to a third of employment in small-scale industry. Evidence of productivity increase is present

Table 5.1   Employment in industry 1900–45 (millions)

	1900	1935	1945
Industry	13.9	13.3	15.0
Large-scale industry	0.6	1.8	3.1
Small-scale industry	13.3	11.5	11.9
Total workforce	131	143	156
Small-scale as per cent of workforce	10.2	8.0	7.6
Large-scale as per cent of workforce	0.4	1.2	2.0

Source: S. Sivasubramonian, *National Income of India in the Twentieth Century* (Delhi: Oxford University Press, 2000).

Table 5.2   GDP in industry, 1900–45 (1938–9 prices)

	1900	1935	1945
GDP per worker			
Large-scale industry	510	732	881
Small-scale industry	105	181	149
Per cent of national income			
Large-scale industry	1.8	5.3	9.9
Small-scale industry	8.6	8.6	6.4

Source: Sivasubramonian, *National Income of India*.

Note: World War II was a reversal for the artisans because it made imported materials dearer.

Table 5.3   Productivity in handloom weaving, 1901–39

	Looms (million)	Workers in handloom industry (million)	Cotton cloth output (in million lbs of yarn equivalent)	Output per loom (Index)	Output per worker (Index)
1901	2.2	3.3	207	100	100
1921	2.0	2.4	235	125	156
1932	2.0	2.1	379	202	288
1939	2.0	n.a.	426	227	n.a.

Source: Tirthankar Roy, 'Acceptance of Innovations in Early Twentieth Century Indian Weaving', *EHR* 55, no. 3 (2002): 507–32.

Notes: Output is average of two adjacent years. Looms and workers exclude Burma. For 1901, there is available a total figure of 2.7 million looms including Burma, which probably accounted for about half a million looms. A handloom census in 1921 found 1.5 million looms excluding Burma, but the census had poor coverage. The correct figure should be around two million. Looms and workers include cotton as well as non-cotton fibres. Cotton accounts for over 70 per cent of the looms. The percentage was higher for the earlier years.

also in tanning and metalwork. The productivity increase owed, as we shall see, to both technological change and a shift of work from households to wage workshops, increasing the average hours contributed per worker. If we assume that the trend began in the first half of the twentieth century and that the rise in real income per worker in small-scale industry derived only from rising hours per worker, the estimated hours per worker increased in small-scale industry by 34 per cent between 1900 and 1947.

These facts suggest that there was a change in industrial organization. An indirect sign of organizational change is women's participation in industrial work. Women were more numerous in household industry, where work was part-time, and they were rare in wage-based industrial work, where work was full-time. Women were leaving industrial work from the early twentieth century, suggesting a fall in household units and rise in the wage-based units. That change implied a rise in average hours per worker.[1]

Small-scale industry concentrated in the interior—mainly UP, Punjab, and Madras—whereas large-scale industry concentrated in the port cities. This pattern appeared because large-scale industry depended on overseas trade, ports, and banks. The small-scale industry depended more on local markets, materials, and skills available locally. Textile production dominated both (Table 5.4). Next in importance were food processing, metals, wood products, and hides and skins. In short, industries intensive either in natural

Table 5.4   Industrial composition, 1931
(percentage share in total industrial employment)

Textiles	26.2
Food, drink, tobacco	9.4
Hides and skins	2.0
Metals and machinery	11.1
Chemicals	3.9
Wood, stone, glass	10.4
Total including others	100.0

Source: Sivasubramonian, National Income of India.

[1] Post-Independence census data in the Indian Union shows a steady fall in the share of household industry. The fall had almost certainly begun earlier.

resources (cotton, metals, minerals, animal substances) or labour dominated the composition of both.

This discussion suggests that the crafts saw a change in industrial organization and a rise in work intensity and productivity. How well do analytical models that fit in the craft experience in modern economic history explain these facts? There are two options available and neither performs this task well.

TWO MODELS OF TRANSITION IN HANDICRAFTS

The first analytical model is deindustrialization. Until recently, historians of Indian industrialization believed that the artisan tradition in the region suffered a catastrophic shock in the nineteenth century after imported European manufactured goods began to flood Indian markets. The process is known as deindustrialization. Scholars such as Amiya Bagchi, Michael Twomey, and Amalendu Guha have measured the extent of the decline, found it of significant order, and read that fact as confirmation of a similar hypothesis advanced by the Indian nationalists at the turn of the nineteenth century.[2] Census data shows that between 1881 and 1931, employment in industry fell from about 20 million to 13–15 million, while at the same time, employment in agriculture increased from 71 to 100 million.

Arguing against the claim of a deindustrialization, Morris D. Morris said that since a large number of artisans survived the shock and continued to work in the twentieth century, historians should explain not only why decline happened but also

---

[2] A.K. Bagchi, 'Deindustrialization in India in the Nineteenth Century: Some Theoretical Implications', *Journal of Development Studies* 22 (1976): 135–64; Michael J. Twomey, 'Employment in Nineteenth Century Indian Textiles', *Explorations in Economic History* 20, no. 1 (1983): 37–57; Amalendu Guha, *The Decline of India's Cotton Handicrafts: 1800–1905, A Quantitative Macro-Study* (Calcutta: Centre for Studies in Social Sciences, 1989). Bagchi's calculations have invited some controversy. See Marika Vicziany, 'The De-industrialisation of India in the Nineteenth Century: A Methodological Critique of Amiya Kumar Bagchi', *IESHR* 16, no. 2 (1979): 105–46.

why survival happened.[3] Later scholarship pointed out two other anomalies. The fall in census employment seemed to affect women more than men. Why should a general decline affect women more? Finally, productivity increased in small industry (Table 5.2), which should not happen in an industry that is rapidly becoming obsolete.[4]

The second analytical model is proto-industrialization. Economic historians of Europe and Japan offer a model of the expansion of the handicrafts in modern times. Variously called 'proto-industrialization', 'labour-intensive industrialization', and 'industrious revolution', these models suggest that cheap surplus labour inside family units, combined with growing desire for consumer goods, could lead to a continued expansion of the crafts in the eighteenth and nineteenth century.[5] Proto-industrialization is not very useful to explain the Indian case. The model does explain why work intensity and productivity might increase inside the household but does not explain why, in India, women left industry. Besides, many Indian artisans who continued to the present times did not do so because their labour was cheap, but they possessed specific skills that machines could not compete with.

From the 1990s, a new scholarship emerged to offer a third view of the handicrafts. Whereas the deindustrialization model in India sees all the crafts as weak and vulnerable to competition of mechanized industry, the revision suggests that the crafts were diverse, that some quality and skills machines could not reproduce, and consumers were willing to pay for that quality. While not disputing that mechanized production had an adverse effect on the handicrafts, as indeed it did all over the world, the new writings suggest that the adverse effect was more severe in the production of low-skill goods

[3] Morris D. Morris, 'Towards a Reinterpretation of Nineteenth Century Indian Economic History', *JEH* 23, no. 4 (1963): 607–18.

[4] Tirthankar Roy, *Crafts and Capitalism: Handloom Weaving in Colonial India* (New Delhi and London: Routledge, 2020).

[5] Gareth Austin and Kaoru Sugihara, eds, *Labour-intensive Industrialization in Global History* (Abingdon and New York: Routledge, 2013); Akira Hayami, *Japan's Industrious Revolution: Economic and Social Transformations in the Early Modern Period* (Tokyo and London: Springer, 2015).

rather than high-skill consumer goods; that surviving artisans gained from the same processes—free trade and industrialization—which threw their colleagues into unemployment. They could gain from foreign trade by obtaining access to imported raw materials, distant markets, and from the transfer of useful knowledge. Some artisans made money in the process and invested that money in larger workshops. Sometimes, their decision to adapt the technology worked better in a larger unit than the family. The shift towards wage-based workshops entailed a decline in the share of women workers because these workshops employed migrants and men dominated the migrant labour pools in India.

Handloom weaving is the most important traditional industry and an important test case for these generalizations.

HANDLOOM WEAVING

Between 1860 and 1900 (significantly, a period of railway expansion), hand spinning collapsed and hand weaving suffered a decline. But conditions of hand weaving improved after that (Table 5.5). Their markets were changing. Agricultural growth improved the purchasing power of peasants in some regions. Spinning mills began to appear in cotton-growing regions in western and southern India,

Table 5.5 Production of cloth by origin, 1795–1940 (million yards)

	Handloom cloth	Indian mill cloth	Imported cloth
1795	1102–437	0	0
1820	1065	0	26
1840	1026	0	199
1860	1035	0	825
1880	677	122	1334
1900	646	421	2005
1920	931	1563	1511
1940	1945	3905	579

Source: Tirthankar Roy, 'Consumption of Cotton Cloth in India, 1795–1940', *Australian Economic History Review* 52, no. 1 (2012): 61–84.

and handloom weavers were among their clientele. This growth greatly cheapened their raw material. Weavers relocated their businesses to these clusters.

At the end of World War I, two and a half million handloom weavers were in business. The total employment in industries connected with hand weaving was possibly about three million or more. This figure represented 20 per cent of industrial employment. Handloom weaving was, by far, the largest industry. The total production of cotton cloth expanded about 30 per cent between 1900 and 1939. The estimated number of looms at work did not change at all, but the estimated number of workers fell somewhat. Rising production and constant loom count suggest that the productivity and the capacity of the looms increased (Table 5.3). Information on technology confirms the point.

The power-driven loom was, on average, six to eight times faster than the hand-driven loom. Why, in the presence of such a wide productivity gap, did the handloom survive at all? We should approach the question by dealing with, in that order, markets, organization, and technology.

Competition between machinery and crafts was limited to certain products. In the mid-nineteenth century, two types of cloth faced keen competition from foreign or Indian mill-made cloth: 'coarse-medium' cotton cloth and printed and bleached cotton cloth. By contrast, cloths that used very coarse or fine cotton yarn or complex designs woven on the loom or non-cotton yarn came from the handloom. An example of a designed garment was the sari. The sari allowed for particular types of border design that only the handloom could effect. The handloom survived partly because that type of sari continued to be in demand. These designs or products were either so labour-intensive that the mills did not enter them by choice or used non-cotton fibres (silk and synthetics) that the cotton mills did not want to handle because they did not make yarn from those fibres. Thus, in cloths made of silk and other fibres, handlooms dominated.

The growing purchasing power of a section of the peasants and workers sustained the demand for handloom cloth. Although agriculture was generally stagnant in the early twentieth century, some forms of rural income were growing. Real wages in large-scale industry increased 85 per cent between 1900–4 and 1935–9. Within agriculture, foodgrain production was stagnant, but non-foodgrains, which included major industrial raw materials, expanded. In some regions, agrarian expansion continued. In South India generally, agriculture was doing well and so was weaving. In Bengal, agriculture was stagnant and weaving was in decline.

The usual organization in the nineteenth century was the household. Women and girls of weaving families were engaged in warping the yarn and winding the thread onto bobbins for use as weft yarn. They shared with men the task of sizing, that is, applying starch paste on the warp thread to make it strong enough to withstand the tension of the loom. Weavers, as a rule, were men, sometimes assisted by young adults. About one in ten women in weaver families knew how to weave. Usually, they learnt to weave half-heartedly and from observation rather than via systematic apprenticeship such as the boys went through. In fields allied to textiles, such as sericulture, women performed vital tasks in the manufacturing process. Wherever men's and women's work were connected in this way, women's work participation tended to be higher, and so did the extent of household industry. Thus, women formed 40 per cent of the textile workforce in 1931 and a similar percentage in household industries.

The situation changed in the twentieth century. The household was in decline in handloom weaving. In the interwar period, a significant number of handloom factories appeared in the textile towns of the cotton regions of western India. These factories employed migrant male labourers and were started by rich weavers and merchants who had made money in the relatively new trades in cloth, yarn, dyes, gold thread, and silk. They generally used improved tools. On the other hand, wherever the household survived, women took on more work in these units, often as weavers. In the 1950s, women weaving on looms was a common picture in the South Indian towns. It is now almost the standard practice.

Because depression and dynamism coexisted, capital and labour had become increasingly mobile. There was migration from rural regions towards new points of trade and towards the railways and spinning mills. One example of such a flow is migration into textile towns in western India, such as Sholapur, Malegaon, Bhiwandi,

Burhanpur, and Surat. The workers, as well as the capitalists, were handloom weavers who came from depressed and overpopulated regions like eastern UP and the Hyderabad state. Today, in many towns of western India, the older quarters house settlements of handloom weaver communities. Some of them continue to work in the textile business, though rarely in handlooms.

The early twentieth century saw an increasing adoption of several new types of tools and processes. Three things helped: a campaign by provincial governments, capital accumulation, and examples set by leading weavers or master weavers. The increasing wealth of capitalist weavers and the increased stability of their markets made them more willing to try new tools. It is in this activity that foreign contact contributed in the most positive ways.

Nearly all of the tools and processes adopted by the weavers in late colonial India, such as the fly-shuttle slay, the frame-mounted loom, the jacquard, dobby, drop box, and synthetic dyes, had been invented in Europe and came to India embodied in imported equipment. The older vintage of loom was the throw-shuttle type, set up in a pit dug in the living room of a weaver's home. From this system, there was a change towards the fly-shuttle loom or a loom mounted on a wooden frame. The frame loom took up less space, could weave longer lengths of yarn, and thus, became popular with the handloom factories. Warp preparation changed from systems whereby the warp was stretched out towards the use of a warp beam such that longer lengths of thread could be woven. Warp preparation was previously a side activity of women in weaving localities. The warping mill replaced this form of collective labour. Another type of technical change was the synthetic dyestuff in place of vegetable and animal substances, with the result that dyeing became less specialized and integrated into textile production. Through these changes and the handloom factory, weaving and processing separated as tasks, and thus specialization and division of labour increased by comparison with household-based weaving.

Based on the data that we now have, inequality increased within handloom weaving in the early twentieth century. Inequality increased because the transition in the industry increased returns to capital and skill, and it benefited capital and skilled labour more than it did generic labour. Capitalists gained because there were new avenues for making money, but these avenues required more capital. For example, cotton yarn, earlier made locally by hand, was now either imported or manufactured in mill towns and distributed in handloom towns and villages by merchants specializing in long-distance trades. Weavers bought dyes, gold thread, and silk yarn from local and foreign markets. Merchant profit as a category and merchants themselves became more noticeable in sources on weaving from the interwar period.

Among producers, at the top were groups of producers that manufactured silk or cotton cloths involving complicated designs, who often used elaborate looms, were urban, took part in long-distance trade, and were in some way involved in a business network. At the other end were the rural artisans who supplied simple routine articles to their peasant neighbours. Rarely were these articles traded beyond the immediate neighbourhood. In the nineteenth century, famines and economic distress induced migrations of artisans like these. Generally speaking, the weaver handling silk or fine cotton cloth had an income between three and five times that of a weaver making 'coarse' or 'ordinary' cloth.

The traditional handloom set up in a pit in the handloom weaver's living room was a very different machine from the power-driven loom. But the automatic handloom mounted on a frame inside the factory and the power-driven loom looked similar and worked on the same principle, but for the source of energy. In the interwar period, many power-driven looms were discarded at scrap rates by the mills. Buying such a loom and reconditioning it to fit the weaver's factory shed was not an expensive proposition. Relatively well-off weavers started to replace handlooms by power-driven looms in products where such a switch was possible. The first such looms appeared in handloom towns in about 1900 and ran with fuel oil. From the 1930s, the power looms spread much faster when many interior towns with handloom industries received electricity. The ground was ready for what was to become India's largest industry at the end of the century.

The handloom–power loom clusters occurred in small towns in western and southern India, which developed a business ecosystem that differed in fundamental respects from those associated with the factory industry and traditional business communities in the big cities. A recently published book tries to understand this form of capitalism, based on small-scale textile production and trade in smaller towns. The book questions the common belief that the handicrafts were destined to collapse when competing against machine-made goods and stresses the importance of local and regional resources in sustaining craft-based urban enterprises.[6]

THE IRON INDUSTRY

In precolonial India, iron ore and charcoal were available along the fringes of the Deccan Plateau and in some Himalayan regions. However, most such sources of supply were located far away from the cities and the ports, and far away from the potential consumers of complex metal products. Artisan communities producing semi-finished iron tended to be located near the ores and worked on a scale and level of capability adapted to meeting local rural demand for iron. The singular feature of the industry was that the knowledge of ironmaking remained confined to communities living near the ores. The indigenous smelting industry was almost universally a local craft pursued by semi-nomadic tribes. The knowledge of smelting did not travel far from the hills and forests where the ore deposits were. These groups were quite often miners, smelters, and smiths at the same time.

The method of production was simple. A band of a dozen or so men mined on the surface of a small area, set up a furnace, and when the wood fuel was exhausted in that area, moved away to a different location. The whole process occurred on a small scale by European standards. The typical output of one round of smelting in a forest furnace was about five kgs crude iron. The best estimate of annual output per furnace would not perhaps exceed 1–2 tonnes. Due to the small scale, production costs were high, compared with the

[6] Douglas E. Haynes, *Small Town Capitalism in Western India. Artisans, Merchants, and the Making of the Informal Economy, 1870–1960* (Cambridge: Cambridge University Press, 2012).

much larger smelting workshops in Western Europe. But the industry was protected by high transport cost. At the same time, transport costs limited trade, average scale of production, and interregional knowledge exchange. The range of iron goods was limited to agricultural implements. A much smaller but wealthier urban tradition manufactured a diverse range of consumer goods but usually utilized recycled material rather than ores.

When European iron began to come into India on a large scale from the early nineteenth century, the local industry quickly became obsolete. Throughout the 1800s, iron and hardware were the main imports after cotton textiles and railway materials. The railways reduced transportation costs and brought markets within easy access to the cheaper imported pig iron and steel. Wood fuel began to become scarce, as forests were reserved. Alternative demands for wood in construction, shipbuilding, and railways grew. In some regions, wood even ran out. Given its dependence on rural markets, artisanal smelting could not expand its scale, economize, and thus absorb costs.

European artisans in India tried the larger-scale and horizontally integrated factory. The physical distance between their targeted market, which was the government, and the origin of ores again posed a transport problem. The one hypothetical advantage they had was cheap labour. But Indian labour was located near the ores, usually found working within traditional institutions such as the household and used to operating small-scale units. On the other hand, skilled labourers imported from Britain were few, expensive, and often unreliable and inefficient. Moreover, in common with indigenous smelting, European smelting had to contend with the rising scarcity of wood fuel.

But even as there was loss of an extensive smelting industry, the net effect of imported iron was not negative. It stimulated consumption and indirectly helped the blacksmith. In the nineteenth century, Indians consumed iron in greater quantity and variety than before. According to one estimate, the average consumption of iron increased from 0.9 kgs/capita in 1788 to 3.2 kgs/capita in 1914. While the proportion of imports in total consumption increased (from 30 to 78 per cent), imports did not only replace domestic production but also stimulated it.[7] For example, cutlery, which had been a semi-specialized urban branch of the smithy, quickly switched over to Swedish and Sheffield steels, substituted imported cutlery, and strengthened its craft skills, while cutting off ties with indigenous smelting.

The main beneficiary of imported iron was the blacksmith serving urban markets. The skilled blacksmith experienced a steady increase in real wages, and more village blacksmiths joined the urban found-ries and forges. In contrast with the smelters, many of the special-ist blacksmiths had belonged to urban communities, were located closer to consumer markets rather than ore supplies, and were, therefore, less susceptible to the adverse effects of narrow markets. In this sphere, globalization had a more adaptive effect. The only complementary factor necessary to make good use of imported tools and ideas was craft skills, already available in abundance. Retraining needs were not always great and retraining prospects were better in the towns. Much knowledge was embodied in small tools, partly imported and partly substituted with refashioned local tools. There were small economies of scale in the smithy; consequently, capital cost was of little consequence. The city, the ports, the barracks, and the public works allowed a convergence of knowledge to develop between European and Indian artisans. Blacksmiths benefited from the unconventional communication opportunities provided by these new sites while adapting new knowledge in their way.

LEATHERWORKERS, POTTERS, CARPENTERS

Tanning of hides and skins became a major export item. From the 1870s until the Great Depression, it remained a major export. After that, the export of tanned hides and skins fell, but increasingly local leather manufactures used tanned hides and the export of such manufactures began to increase. Today, leather is one of South Asia's principal manufactured exports. Much of the industry built upon a foundation of skills, expertise, and capital accumulated during the colonial period.

[7] Tirthankar Roy, 'Knowledge and Divergence from the Perspective of Early Modern India', *Journal of Global History* 3, no. 3 (2008): 361–87.

Tanning was originally a rural craft. It occupied groups of people who were also part-time agricultural labourers. They were placed lowly in the caste hierarchy and had little bargaining power in dealing with their main customers, the peasants. In most places, hides were bartered for grain. But the terms of the barter were adverse for the suppliers. The usual organization in rural tanning was either a single household or a collective. The tanning locality was a little apart from the main village where the village was a large one. In this locality, men, women, and children worked together in jointly owned pits.

The export market concentrated hide trade in Kanpur (Cawnpore), Madras, Bombay, and Calcutta. And the superior quality demanded by foreign consumers of Indian hides encouraged the hide merchants to establish factories in these cities. These developments, first of all, weakened the rural barter system. Anyone who had access to hides now wanted to sell it to an exporter. It also encouraged leather artisans to migrate to the cities in large numbers. They were re-employed as factory labourers in the merchant-owned urban tanyard. In the course of this change, flaying, tanning, and leather manufacture, which had formerly been performed by the same person, separated. Division of labour and specialization increased thereby. The old customs did not completely vanish, but the factory was a freer system of work.

The North Indian potters also performed rural labour on the side. The growing demand for metal utensils, the rather poor quality of their pottery, and the difficulty of long-distance trade in the average earthenware articles adversely affected them. The vessels of mass consumption were flimsily made, given the force of a custom that frowned upon re-usage of earthenware. The only segment where superior skills existed was the objects of art made by specialist groups. Their industry (such as the one in Khurja town in North India) needed more expensive kilns. Towards the end of the period of study, this sector diversified into ceramic tools and components, which is now one of its major outputs.

The major occupation of carpenters in the colonial period was the supply and repair of agricultural implements. As a result, carpenters and smiths often belonged to the same caste but different sub-castes. Usually, they were found nearby. Like the blacksmiths, a bifurcation of demand occurred in the case of the carpenters as well.

The furniture industry as we know it today developed from the colonial period. The very nature of interior decoration and furnishing, which urban Indians consider standard today, was a product of the cultural contact with the British. The industry developed initially by drawing in artisans who were engaged in supplying traditional rural demand. It concentrated in towns and cities that had a large number of people willing to buy new types of furniture and was mainly factory-based. Thus, in the course of adapting to new demand, there occurred increasing specialization, urban migration, and changes in organization in favour of larger city-based workshops (see Map 5.1 for clusters of major forms of small-scale industry).

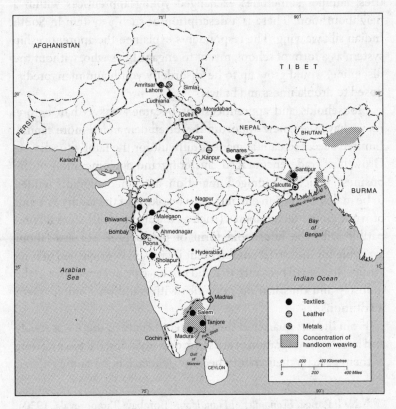

Map 5.1   Clusters of small-scale industry

Source: Author

LABOUR AND CAPITAL

The family firm and the master–apprenticeship system were the two general pre-factory systems of production that survived the colonial period. These institutions performed the important function of industrial training before technical schools started. These two systems were not completely distinct. There were hybrids too. For example, neighbourhood women often worked together inside someone's home or common spaces. North Indian embroidery, especially Lucknow chikan, is an example of this. Warping of thread before it went into the handloom was performed by women and girls in a common area shaded by trees inside the weavers' village. Another hybrid was inter-family hiring. In big hubs of craft industries, families sometimes exchanged young apprentices within a neighbourhood. There is a description of such a system in South Indian silk weaving. The respondents explained the apprenticeship system as a form of school, meant to engage boys who, without the discipline, would grow up to be 'disorderly youth and men, predisposed to drunkenness and brawls'.[8]

Households and apprenticeships became weaker than before. As we have seen, new opportunities often demanded more capital. Limited access to capital made it difficult for the family to survive. Growth of trade encouraged clustering and agglomeration of the business, which encouraged migration, and since migrants tended to be males, migration encouraged a break-up of the family as a unit of work. Some technologies (such as a warping mill) were incompatible with the household form of production. Surplus labour available for industrial employment increasingly originated among groups, like small peasants, that did not have prior experience in the industry and thus had no prior ties with traditional employment institutions.

From the last quarter of the nineteenth century, there was steady and large-scale migration of artisan groups to industrial towns. Some of them gave up their craft to become general labour. Some entered

[8] N.G. Ranga, *Economics of Handloom* (Bombay: Taraporevala, 1930), 110.

the mills. Still others only relocated their craft near sources of manufactured or imported raw material and market points. Employment
was typically in factories in these towns. In almost all cases, the relo-
cation of work from the countryside and households towards the
urban factory attracted more men than women (see Chapter 10).
The conditions of employment of children must have changed too,
but we know too little about that process. The masters of the old
master–apprentice systems would not see themselves as teachers of
a craft, but increasingly, just as employers.

Small-scale industry, in general, had little or no contact with the
formal banking sector. It had little contact even with the informal
money and capital markets. The main form of working capital
finance was trade credit and personal saving. It was probably easier
to raise fixed capital loans in certain towns than in others. Surat, a
major textile centre, was an example where employers and traders
in the *jari* (gold thread) industry routinely gave loans to the artisans
engaged on contract for purchase of machinery. This was not a common system, however.

In industries such as handloom weaving, the capitalists came from
artisan communities. On the other hand, in tanning, capitalists came
from merchant communities. In the former, weaving skill was the
main form of capital. Those who possessed such capital could often
control the trade because they could guarantee quality. Weavers
often knew their markets very well or were in touch with the consumers, which knowledge helped them keep control of the industry.
In an exportable craft like leather, the larger scale of trade and the
non-traditional market made working capital and information both
scarce resources. In this case, the merchant firms had greater control
over production.

Community resources mattered too. Silk weavers had been
urban elites and had well-developed, collective associations and
guilds, which could be used in a market context to diffuse the ill
effects of growing inequality, keep control over scarce capital and
knowledge, and channel community resources to the benefit of the
members. Caste and community associations among the skilled
artisans developed or were revived, to take care of some of these
roles.

MODERN SMALL-SCALE INDUSTRY

Modern small-scale industry is an under-researched field. What we do know on the subject can be organized into four points. First, factories with little machinery and less than a hundred workers were almost unknown before 1900 but quite common in the 1930s. Second, modern small-scale industry concentrated in textiles, food-drink-tobacco, wood, and ceramics. Many factories were seasonal. Third, a segment among them, such as the power loom factories, operated in old products. They represented advanced forms of the handicrafts. Others were of new origin and had no such prehistory. Fourth, the growth of modern small-scale industry dispersed factories beyond the main mill towns such as Calcutta or Bombay. Modern small-scale industry clusters were located all over India. Generally, they were located near raw material sources. But there were exceptions. Some of these clusters formed near big cities. An example was tanning in Dharavi, which later became a part of Bombay. Another example was engineering and metal-working firms such as foundries in Howrah, near Calcutta. One reason that industries like these clustered was the availability of cheap electric power. Power was not yet widely diffused in the 1930s.

Further, these new firms usually sold products via urban marketing networks. Leather was exported and, therefore, benefited from being close to a port. Sometimes their markets were concentrated. For example, the engineering firms supplied cast iron tools, parts, and consumer goods to urban users, including the government and the mills. Cotton gins did business with the Bombay mills. Finally, nearly every small firm used the railways and many used the telegraph. In short, while modern small-scale industry was more dispersed than large-scale industry, it retained an urban, sometimes a big-city, bias.

Rich farmers invested in agricultural processing factories in the canal colonies in the Punjab, Coastal Andhra, Upper Doab, Tamil Nadu, and the sugarcane belt on the Nira canal system in Bombay. In Tamil Nadu, rich peasants started factories. In Punjab, coastal Andhra, Tamil Nadu, Nira Valley, and Khandesh, prosperity based on rice, wheat, sugarcane, and cotton induced many farmers to set

Table 5.6   Regional clusters of factories other than large mills, 1939

Industry	Districts of major concentration
Gins and presses	Towns all over Khandesh and Bombay–Deccan[a], Berar, Broach–Baroda, Bellary, Coimbatore
Rice and oil mills	Krishna–Guntur–East Godavari, Coimbatore, Madurai, Tanjore
Bidi	Singhbhum, North Arcot, Malabar, Nasik–Ahmadnagar, Guntur
Handloom[b]	Sholapur, Malabar
Silk mills	Surat, Bangalore
Saw mills	Nagpur, Jabalpur (Jubbulpore), Malabar
Tannery	North Arcot, Bombay suburbs
Shellac	Manbhum (Purulia)
Tiles, kiln	Malabar–Quilon–South Kanara, Barnala–Bhatinda–Patiala
Glass	Agra–Firozabad
Cashew and coir	Quilon, Alleppey
Brass and aluminium	East Godavari
Engineering workshops	Krishna, Ludhiana–Jullundur, Kanpur–Lucknow–Meerut, Howrah

Source: Reproduced from T. Roy, 'The Pattern of Industrial Growth in Interwar India', *Journal of Indian School of Political Economy*, 1994.
Notes: a. Includes the cotton-growing districts of the southern part of the Bombay Presidency, notably, Bijapur, Dharwar, Belgaum, Sholapur, and Ahmadnagar. b. Handloom factories were widespread in the urban weaving complexes all over the country, but in Malabar and Sholapur, they represented the principal organization in weaving.

up cotton gins, sugar mills, and rice and oil mills. The other factor was a fall in the relative return on land from the interwar period, as agriculture became less profitable than before.

The Great Depression led to a reallocation of rural savings. Like elsewhere in the world, the depression of the 1930s brought in a crisis of inadequate liquidity, as real debt volumes increased and incomes fell. With the crash of agricultural prices, land lost its worth as collateral. Peasants were forced to liquidate gold and silver assets. Via banking, some of this rural capital moved into industry. These hypotheses are conjectural. But they are supported by the fact that the major expansion in small factories, at least in Tamil Nadu, occurred in the 1930s and the 1940s.

A further source of the growth of rural factories was the increased demand for their products. For example, the rice mills initially made 'parboiled' rice for export to South East Asia. Increasingly, local consumers began to replace the export market. Cheapness and better quality of the parboiled rice and consumption of rice by people who formerly ate coarser foodgrains were the major reasons. A similar set of circumstances encouraged growth in factories engaged in groundnut oil extraction and beedi-making.

***

Far from destroying handicrafts, free trade caused a differentiation among them. Globalization strengthened some actors and was adverse to others. In the process, the importance of commercial and industrial capital in the business and wage labour generally increased. The labour market emerged slowly, out of two traditional institutions, the family and master–apprenticeship. The decay in these institutions in the long run owed to many factors, such as migration, new entry in capital and labour, and a reduced role for craftsmanship. Children and women worked in small-scale industries in households and apprenticeships in earlier times. As the industries hired more workers from a casual labour market, adult males had a better chance of finding jobs.

Large-scale industry was a small activity in employment share by comparison. But it played a transformative role exceeding what its small share in employment suggests, as we see in Chapter 6.

6

Large-Scale Industry

Large-scale industry combined three things: employment of wage labour, use of machinery, and regulation by factory and company law. Between 1860 and 1940, employment in factories increased from less than 100,000 to two million. The share of factories in industrial employment of British India increased from almost zero in 1850 to 11 per cent in 1938, and in industrial income from 15 per cent in 1900 to 45 in 1947. The princely states saw a late start but rapid growth in the interwar years (Table 6.1).

The growth is impressive by any standard. But it had certain peculiar features. These industries mainly produced different kinds of textiles (cotton and jute being the most important), and processed agricultural commodities (rice mills, oil mills, sugar refining, and tobacco products, see Table 6.2). In short, they were intensive users of labour and natural resources, but not capital. Metals, machines, and chemicals—the capital-intensive industry—had a small share throughout. These industries were also geographically concentrated. Five cities—Bombay, Ahmedabad, Madras, Calcutta, and Kanpur—contained the bulk of factory employment. Most factory workers in these cities were migrants, and since migrants in India tend to be males, the labour force was predominantly male. Factory industrialization did not serve women workers well.

The growth of factories raises a few puzzling problems. If textile factories used less capital per worker than did metals or machines,

Table 6.1   Employment in factories, 1891–1938

	Total for British India	Percentage in British India of			Total for the princely states
		Men	Women	Children	
1891	316,815	80.2	13.8	6.0	n.a.
1901	468,956	79.5	14.6	5.9	n.a.
1921	1,266,395	79.8	14.8	5.4	129,968
1938	1,737,755	85.3	14.1	0.6	299,003

Source for Tables 6.1–6.4: India, *Statistical Abstracts for British India* (London: HMSO or Calcutta: Government Press, 1881–2 to 1890–1, 1898–9 to 1907–8, 1917–18 to 1926–7, 1930–1 to 1939–40).

Table 6.2   Industrial composition, 1921 (percentage of total employment)

	Share in large-scale industry	Share in industry
Textiles	41.6	25.7
Food, drink, tobacco	7.2	10.5
Hides and skins	0.9	2.0
Metals and machinery	4.6	11.4
Chemicals	2.6	3.7
Wood, stone, glass	7.1	10.1
Total (including others)	100.0	100.0

Source: India, *Statistical Abstracts for British India*, various years.

they still used a lot more capital than trading, which was the original business of most of the factory owners. Factories locked up capital for a longer time than did trade. Interest rates were high in India compared to Europe. Skilled managerial and technical labour was scarce in India. Why, then, did any large-scale industry emerge at all in India? How were these scarce resources obtained? A further question concerns the use of the company form in running factories.

A few people often connected by family and community ties established factories. Where capital and skills were scarce and accessible to a few people, we should expect such ties to persist. But management of companies with a network of family members created a problem of corporate governance, especially when public shareholding was involved. How was good governance achieved?

This chapter will show that the openness of the economy helped with access to knowhow and even capital. For example, profits from foreign trade created the purchasing power to buy machines. The use of trading profits and profits from financing trade confined entrepreneurship to the communities that engaged in trading and banking. India's links with Britain through trade and empire made it easy to hire foreigners to work these machines. India was also a major destination for British investment and industrial enterprise. Easy trading conditions made it unnecessary for Indians to produce machines, metals, and chemicals at home. So, the industry remained users of labour and natural resources. The five cities mentioned developed factories because these cities were transportation hubs, attracted migrants, had capital markets, and were sites of European settlement. They were well-connected through the railways with the regions where natural resources were available.

The governance issue is a little more complex. It may be that Indian companies never found a good solution to the governance issue. In any case, business organization mattered to shareholder interest depending on whether the company was controlled by professionals or family members, whether the corporate form would be used or not, and whether the use of management contracts (managing agency) made a difference to the operation of the company. Further, these choices varied by ethnicity and type of enterprise. It is, therefore, difficult to generalize on the subject, but certain causal links can be shown.

This chapter describes this industrialization and answers questions like who set up these factories, who worked in them, and how corporate governance was achieved. The chapter starts with a chronological account.

INDUSTRIALIZATION

1858–1918

Large-scale industry started before 1858 (Chapter 2) in isolated enterprises and steadily expanded from the 1860s. The railways and the telegraph system started in India in the 1850s. In 1869, the Suez Canal greatly reduced the shipping distance between Britain and India. These developments encouraged new forms of industrial enterprise. The principal industries in this period were cotton spinning and weaving and jute spinning and weaving, the former mainly based in Bombay and Ahmedabad and the latter in Calcutta.

The capital came from trading profits and foreign investment. Bombay and Calcutta benefited from the growth of India's trade with China after the Company's monopoly in China trade ended (1834–5). The American civil war (1861–5) cut off supplies of American cotton to Britain's textile industry. Indian cotton was suddenly in great demand. Profits of cotton trade found its way to a cotton mill industry in western India. The companies that formed did not all survive, but they popularized the notion of joint-stock companies.

World War I diverted the resources of the Western nations into producing war supplies. Britain's engagement in the war had contradictory effects on India. The demand for cotton and jute textiles increased, but machines, metals, and chemicals imported by Indian industry from Britain and Germany stopped. By the third or fourth year of the war, conditions were easier and exporting factories were making big profits.

1918–45

So far, industrialization had occurred without protective tariffs. Lancashire textile interests put pressure upon the Indian government to keep import duty low. The government did impose a nominal duty but neutralized it with excise duty on Indian cloth in the 1890s. Modern businesses included not just big factories but also trading firms, banks, and insurance companies. Because the group was diverse and all of them had connections with the world economy, protection was not the preferred option for all.

The war changed the government's attitude. Until then, the purchase of industrial goods for defence, railways, or administrative use was dependent on Britain. This dependence had created sudden shortages of these goods in India during the war. Many administrators now started supporting policies to develop India industrially, seeing how Indian resources had helped the war effort. That stance led to three commissions of enquiry. The Indian Industrial Commission (1916–18) was a fact-finding survey. But the other two—Fiscal Commission (1922) and Stores Purchase Committee (1920)—changed policy. One of these committees recommended protection to selected industries of domestic origin and another recommended that the government buy manufactured articles for its use from Indian sources as far as possible. Tariffs helped the budget when older sources of revenue were failing.

The political climate was also changing. Those industries that had made profits during the War were more demanding. Demand for tariffs joined with a demand for self-government. The decline in the influence of British manufacturing interests upon colonial policy enabled resisting their demands.

Between 1923 and 1939, 51 enquiries were made on the suitability of demand for tariffs. In 11 of these cases, tariffs were raised. These included salt, heavy chemicals, magnesium chloride, sericulture, plywood chests, gold thread, iron and steel, cotton textiles, sugar, paper and paper pulp, and matches. After that, more factories in sugar, iron and steel, cement, matches, paper, and woollen textiles came up, and the existing ones expanded.

The practical rule adopted for granting protection was called 'discriminating' protection, which meant that an application for protection needed to show that the applicant would be competitive shortly and not need protection after a few years. Nationalist historians have been critical of the discriminatory element in protectionism.[1]

---

[1] A.K. Bagchi, *Private Investment in India 1900–1939* (Cambridge: Cambridge University Press, 1972), 45; Rajat K. Ray, *Industrialization in*

To be fair to the Tariff Board, which considered the applications, this body was worried about low labour productivity in Indian manufacturing, often due to poor effort at training and skill-building within India.[2] In India, skilled labour was still scarce and frequently came from Britain, Germany, or the United States at a high cost. An Indianization of the supervisory staff did happen, but mainly in the cotton mills. Between the first origins of cotton mills in Bombay and 1925, the percentage of Europeans among the supervisory staff decreased from 100 per cent to less than 30. Other new industries (like steel) struggled to reduce its foreigner workforce.

By 1940, politicians, industrialists affiliated with the main political party, the Congress, and intellectuals campaigned for the removal of the discrimination clause. After that, protectionism became an entitlement for Indian capital and an instrument to serve the 'national interest'. Discriminatory protection ended up becoming indiscriminate protection.

Much of the industrial growth encouraged by protection occurred in cities other than the original five. The dispersal owed to the fact that the resources utilized in this phase, sugarcane or wool, for example, were available in distant regions. Besides, the reach of the railways and electricity had extended into the interior. Labour in the so-called 'up-country' was not unionized. New factories came up in or near cities such as Coimbatore and Jamshedpur.

Within older industries, such as the cotton and jute mills, and the older cities of Calcutta and Bombay, the situation was becoming more difficult. Japanese mills were selling a lot of cotton textiles in India. In steel, worldwide capacity building progressed faster than

---

India: Growth and Conflict in the Private Corporate Sector, 1914–47 (New York: Oxford University Press, 1979); Aditya Mukherjee, Imperialism, Nationalism and the Making of the Indian Capitalist Class (New Delhi: SAGE Publications, 2002), 191–5. One point of criticism was that the Tariff Board had too many technocrats and lacked members possessing a 'nationalist outlook'.

[2]   Tirthankar Roy, 'The Origins of Import Substituting Industrialization in India', Economic History of Developing Regions 32, no. 1 (2017): 71–95.

new demand, which placed a new firm, Tata Iron and Steel Company, in trouble. In jute, Indian capacity grew faster than world demand. Tariffs alone could not solve this problem. Some of the industries had to make innovations in technology and management.

Between 1925 and 1935, the world was in mild or deep depression. In steel, paper, sugar, and cement, Indian industry faced cheap imports and falling world prices. The Indian nationalists argued that the rupee was overvalued deliberately to ease foreign remittance and that the step hurt exports. The Great Depression (1929–30) began in the middle of these difficulties. The Depression hurt the businesses that were mainly selling abroad, such as jute. Other key Indian industries affected by excess capacity in the world were saved by tariff protection in the 1920s. Another factor that helped industry was wage cuts. But wage cuts came with a cost. It soured capital-labour relations in the old cities. Renegotiating wage and working conditions was becoming difficult and strongly resisted by workers in Bombay and Calcutta.

During World War II again, excess demand developed and prices soared. Again, supply bottlenecks developed. But Indian industry in 1939 was more diversified and better equipped to diversify than in 1914. If not so bad for the industrialists, this war was a more stressful time for workers than was the previous war. In the winter of 1942, with the Japanese occupation of Burma, India became the eastern front of the war. Unlike in 1914, British India, especially Bengal, was now a theatre of war. Anticipating a long engagement, large-scale requisition of rice began. Combined with harvest failures, the situation led to a large rise in the price of food in eastern India. Meeting the needs of its workforce became a serious challenge for the plantations and industry.

What were the major industries? Who set them up?

MAJOR INDUSTRIES

Cotton Mills

The first steam-powered factory making cotton yarn appeared near Calcutta in 1817 or 1818. This venture, like a few others in western and southern India, was set up by a European. But these firms did not succeed. In 1854, a Parsi merchant of Bombay, C.N. Davar, started the first successful cotton mill. The idea attracted other merchants of the city. Many of them were already engaged in cotton and textile trade. By 1865, there were 10 mills, the majority in Bombay. In the next few years, a boom and a crash shook up cotton export from western India. When the dust settled, a furious expansion of the mill industry began. By 1880, there were 58 mills with an employment of 40,000. Nearly 80 per cent of the workers were in Bombay and Ahmedabad. By 1914, the number of mills had risen to 271 and average daily employment to 260,000. The share of the two cities in employment fell to 60 per cent. Any small town that had a cotton market, a railway connection, a pool of migrant labour, and a handloom industry became an attractive location for a spinning mill. Using these strengths, Kanpur, Madurai, Coimbatore, Sholapur, Nagpur, and a cluster of cotton trading towns in the Deccan developed cotton mills.

Between 1870 and 1914, cotton mills were mainly selling yarn to handloom weavers in India and China. In both these markets, they successfully competed with British yarn in the coarser varieties. But they found it difficult to compete in the finer varieties. Later in this period, mills in Japan took over the China market. The loss of the China market and keener competition at home forced the mills of Bombay to make changes in the interwar period. They started weaving their yarn more than before and to spin and weave finer yarn. They tried to improve efficiency at the workplace and save on labour. For some mills that were already poorly managed, these changes were too little and came too late. The interwar period saw unemployment, strikes, demand for protective tariffs, intensification of nationalist sentiments among mill owners, and the beginning of bankruptcy in many of Bombay's cotton mills.

Jute Mills

Jute is a natural fibre grown mainly in southern West Bengal and Bangladesh. Jute is an excellent material for sacking cloth. The demand for sacks increased in the nineteenth century with growth in international commodity trade. Until the 1870s, Bengal raw jute was processed into sacking outside India, mainly in Dundee in Britain and somewhat later in Germany. But already by then, mechanized jute spinning and weaving had started near Calcutta. George Acland's mill of 1855 was the pioneer. In a short time, the Indian industry grew to become a virtual monopoly in the world. As in the cotton mills, the first 15 years of the industry faced unstable conditions. After 1870, expansion was rapid. Between 1869 and 1913, the number of mills increased from 5 to 64, and employment between 5,000 and 10,000 in 1869 to 215,000. Until World War I, Europeans owned and managed the industry.

The industry ran into rough weather in the interwar period. The world demand for sacking slowed down. The European owners and managers tried to form a cartel to cut production and raise prices. But now there were Indian jute mill owners who had earned a lot of money during World War I and recycled some of it into industry. They were out of the cartel. Therefore, collusion broke down.[3] Old firms failed to cooperate. The result was excess production, unstable profits, and increased competition. Eventually, the failure of the jute cartel invited the government of Bengal to impose production limits. But, as in Bombay, a large part of the industry was doomed already for having delayed technical improvements.

Other Industries

In the late nineteenth century, two large woollen mills started in Kanpur and Punjab, a match unit was set up in South India, a large paper mill started near Calcutta (Titagarh), and two leather manufacturing firms started in Kanpur. They were all European firms and dependent on government demand or demand from the European residents. Their demand being limited, there was little scope in these industries for more such firms.

---

[3] Bishnupriya Gupta, 'Why did Collusion Fail? The Indian Jute Industry in the Interwar Years,' *Business History* 47, no. 4 (2005): 532–52.

The most unusual enterprise in the twentieth century was the Tata Iron and Steel Company.[4] It began as a firm in 1907 and started production from 1911. Tata Steel owed its existence first of all to its founder J.N. Tata's persistence and vision. The firm of the Tatas was established in textiles and had a considerable brand name in Bombay. The Tatas were also the largest steel importer into India and knew the trade well enough to be confident of being able to produce steel at a lower cost. The firm followed almost 20 years of exploration and research into the supply of key raw materials in the region of India, where the factory finally came up. These raw materials were coal, iron, limestone, manganese, and water. Tata Steel, however, shared with the other large factories in this period their dependence on government demand.

The war gave a boost to steel, cotton, paper, and jute. The manufacture of Portland cement began. Tata Steel carried out its first major expansion between 1925 and 1935. Several new firms in cement manufacture began during 1920–35. Another large European firm joined the Titaghur paper mill. But all these industries faced falling prices from the late 1920s. They met this situation in different ways. In cement, smaller firms merged to create the Associated Cement Companies. In 1923, an influx of cheap Belgian steel pushed Tata Steel to near bankruptcy. Thanks to its valuable contribution during the War, Tata Steel had goodwill among the administrators and was protected from 1924. By 1937, Tata had weathered the long depression successfully.

The paper industry also received protection. But in this case, protective tariffs alone did not help, for India used raw materials such as *sabai* grass or straw that had become costly after Europe switched to the cheaper material, wood pulp. The Indian industry, therefore, had to shift to bamboo pulp. Factories shifted near sources of bamboo. Manufacturing of refined sugar received protection in response to a worldwide fall in cane prices that threatened to ruin Indian canegrowers unless a local sugar industry grew to use their product. A

---

[4] Vinay Bahl, 'The Emergence of Large-scale Steel Industry in India under British Colonial Rule, 1880–1907,' *IESHR* 31, no. 4 (1994): 413–60.

local industry did grow between 1919 and 1935, so rapidly that soon there was excess capacity. The older firms coped with excess capacity in the same way that jute mills hoped to deal with theirs. They formed cartels and sought government help to protect the cartel from the entry of new firms. They, however, succeeded in this venture to a limited extent.

Who were the factory workers?

LABOUR

Wages in India were low compared with the industrialized countries. But gathering a large number of workers in one worksite and making peasants and artisans adapt to the factory rhythm of work was not easy in the nineteenth century. Was the shift achieved using wage incentives, political intervention, or institutional changes?

The economic theory of labour supply predicts that labour supply increases with real wages. The economist W. Arthur Lewis suggested that in a traditional society with underemployed surplus labour, labour should be available for industrial work at steady and low wages for a long time, which should encourage factory-based industrialization.[5] Indian evidence shows that Lewis was right. But theory does not explain how labour moved from traditional to modern activities. They did not simply walk from the field to the factory expecting to get a job. Information about jobs and working conditions was scarce, and there were barriers to exit from the traditional society, such as caste-based occupational training.

Marxist historians suggest that a condition of excess or surplus labour emerged because of a prior dislocation. Friedrich Engels' history of the English working class showed that the Industrial Revolution destroyed the handicrafts.[6] Many people were distressed and had no choice but to work for wages. The British historian E.P.

[5] W.A. Lewis, 'Economic Development with Unlimited Supply of Labour', *Manchester School of Economic and Social Studies* 22, no. 2 (1954): 139–91.

[6] Friedrich Engels, *The Condition of the Working Class in England* (London: Penguin, 1987).

Thompson's work on the English working class was also a Marxist account; that is, it accepted that there were adverse conditions but suggested that the workers tried to change the situation.[7] Labour history scholarship in India initially followed the Marxist paradigm. New property rights in land, decline of the handicrafts, the high risks of grain exports, employer-friendly labour laws, and dishonest labour contractors pushed unemployed workers into the modern sector.

The story that large numbers were helpless victims of colonialism and globalization cannot be quite right. Those who came to work in the mills and plantations were predominantly men and not women. Were men more distressed than women? The peasants who came to work in the factories were usually the better-off landholding people, rather than the poor agricultural workers. If artisans were pushed by poverty into millwork, we would expect to see artisans in the factory to be the poorest of all workers. Skilled artisans like handloom weavers formed a labour aristocracy among the textile mill workers. They moved because their skills were valued, not because they had little option elsewhere.

There was a much simpler reason why Indian peasants took to factory work, which was the seasonality of agricultural work that left them unemployed for a large part of the year. The peasant family sent men to factories and kept women at home to do household work and mind the land. While the factory wage was low, combining agricultural work back home and factory work in the city could increase total earnings for a family with land. City work was not an alternative to rural work. The purpose of migration was not escaping distress, but to increase family incomes, reduce risks, and retain a hold in the rural economy.

Those who moved were mainly men. The practice of early marriage in India ensured that most women of working age were already married and had children to look after. They stayed home.[8] Some

---

[7] E.P. Thompson, *The Making of the English Working Class* (London: Penguin, 1980).

[8] Tirthankar Roy, *Rethinking Economic Change in India: Labour and Livelihood* (London: Routledge, 2005), Chapter 6.

of them did come to the cities and did join factory labour, but only when their husbands worked in another department of the same mill and neighbours and older siblings were available to look after young children. Some of them who did move to the cities tended to leave their jobs when more men came looking for jobs. In both cotton and jute mills, the percentage of women fell. Employment legislation made special provisions for women, such as maternity benefits and prohibition on night work, which discouraged employers from hiring women when men were available for the same work.[9] With such changes at the workplace, there was also a change in perceptions of women's work.[10] Women workers were meant to stay at home and look after the rural work of the family. With increasing withdrawal from paid work, women's work was devalued.

Factory wages did not stay low throughout. By the 1920s, average mill wages were considerably higher than wages everywhere else. The disparity was significant in the case of the pioneering mill towns. Around 1920, these towns attracted a large number of single male migrants who stood at the mill gates every morning seeking casual work when such work was becoming harder to come by. Population growth had increased labour supply, land surplus had run out, and these factors created a pool of surplus labour in the factory towns.

How did the potential migrants know where to go and how to find work? The labour contractor played an important role in informing and persuading the worker to move into the factory and by helping employers get many people in one place with some basic training in the tasks. Most large-scale enterprises in nineteenth-century India did not recruit workers directly but recruited through labour contractors. The employers left a great deal of supervision and training to these intermediaries. Against these services, the intermediaries received a crucial privilege: the freedom to hire and fire

[9] Rajnarayan Chandavarkar, *The Origins of Industrial Capitalism in India: Business Strategies and the Working Classes in Bombay, 1900–1940* (Cambridge: Cambridge University Press, 1994), 96.

[10] Samita Sen, *Women and Labour in Late Colonial India. The Bengal Jute Industry* (Cambridge: Cambridge University Press, 1999).

workers under them with only the minimum formal consent of the management.

The labour contractor was common in almost all societies that saw the emergence of factories. But whereas in England, United States of America, or Japan, the contractor disappeared as the employers took direct control of personnel management, in India, the contractor continued. In interwar Bombay, for example, the contractor remained powerful, whereas their authority also faced new challenges. Some managers would see the contractor as an obstacle to raising the output per worker. Skilled workers also resented their power.

Why did the contractor survive so long in the factories? One reason was the diversity of the workforce. The Indian factory workforce was the most ethnically diverse in the world. A group speaking one language and sharing one background usually monopolized one task. This type of division is called segmentation. Migrants of specific backgrounds moved into specific occupations.[11] Once a distinct ethnic group populated a certain division in the mill, subsequent recruits into that department tended to come from the same ethnic group. Some of the contractors were there simply because, as community elders, they wielded influence upon a group of workers with which they could communicate easily.

If these institutions solved the problem of labour supply, they may have created a problem of inefficiency. The economists Susan Wolcott and Gregory Clark draw attention to the low productivity of industrial labour in India.[12] The labour–machine ratio was higher in the cotton mills of Bombay than anywhere else in the world. Bombay had no problem competing with England or America because wage

[11] Arjan de Haan, 'Migration in Eastern India: A Segmented Labour Market', *IESHR* 32, no. 1 (1995): 51–93.

[12] S. Wolcott, 'The Perils of Lifetime Employment Systems: Productivity Advance in the Indian and Japanese Textile Industries, 1920–1938', *Journal of Economic History* 54, no. 2 (1994): 307–24; S. Wolcott and G. Clark, 'Why Nations Fail: Managerial Decisions and Performance in Indian Cotton Textiles, 1890–1938', *Journal of Economic History* 59, no. 2 (1999): 397–423.

levels were low. But when Japan emerged as a competitor, Bombay faced problems, because Japan had low wages and more efficient factories. The production of cloth per weaver was three and a half times higher in Japan and the difference in the spindle–worker ratio was almost as great.

The problem was present in all forms of industrial and agricultural work. In 1921–5, the average production per person of a coal mine in India was 40 per cent of that in the United States of America; the glass industry complained that workers as skilled as those of Belgium and central Europe were not available in India.[13] In sugar manufacture, India's main competitor was Java, where cane yield was three times more than in India. In shipping, the building of small steamers for inland navigation was cheaper in India because of the availability of Burma teak, but the shipping companies still preferred to import larger boats from England because of superior quality. In 1914–22, on average each employee of Tata Steel produced less than five tonnes of finished steel per year. The corresponding average for United States of America was 53 tonnes.

Why did these differences arise? There is not enough research work on the efficiency issue to answer the question. We do have some hypotheses about the cotton mill situation. Wolcott and Clark believe that Indians preferred to work to a lower level of effort. When the mills wanted them to work harder, the trade unions resisted.[14] Bishnupriya Gupta says that the managers failed to see that offering better wages could become an incentive for the workers to work harder.[15] I have suggested that mills relied too much on the labour contractor for training, but the contractors were after increasing their influence rather than improving efficiency and some of them were not very skilled themselves.[16]

[13] Roy, 'The Origins of Import Substituting Industrialization'.

[14] Wolcott, 'Perils of Lifetime Employment'.

[15] Bishnupriya Gupta, 'Work and Efficiency in Cotton Mills: Did the Indian Entrepreneur Fail?' (Working paper, University of Warwick, 2003).

[16] Tirthankar Roy, 'Labour Institutions, Japanese Competition, and the Crisis of Cotton Mills in Interwar Mumbai', EPW 43, no. 1 (2008): 37–45.

No matter the root, the efficiency issue caused the Indian nationalists discomfort. They demanded protection. But the tariff authority said that protection would shelter the inefficiency and the consumer would have to pay for that. As the nationalists gained in political power in the 1940s, the worry over efficiency died and protection became an entitlement for the indigenous industry.[17]

Who were the workers? Skilled workers in cotton, jute, steel, and other large-scale industries had a significant percentage of foreigners, followed closely by Parsis, and then Hindu upper and literate castes with high-school education. 'Skilled' in this context would mean workers with some formal training or education. All other workers, trained on the job, came from mainly the Konkan, the Deccan, and UP in the case of cotton mills and from north Bihar, eastern UP, and Orissa in the case of jute.[18] Poor agricultural conditions or low land–person ratio in these regions made these people willing to move.[19] However, as we have seen, migrants did not necessarily come from the poorest rural classes and many had land back in the villages they migrated from. The prospect of balancing idle and active labour time by peasant households contributed to migration potential.

Organized trade union movement began in the factory cities, especially Bombay in the 1920s. Why here and why so late? Bombay did see strikes before the mid-1920s, but these tended to be spontaneous, sporadic, and sudden. These strikes were in reaction to issues such as wages and working hours and ended as suddenly as they started. The first successful attempt at a large-scale trade union in Bombay was that of N.M. Joshi, who established the Bombay Textile Labour Union in 1926. In the next decade, eight other major unions

[17]   Roy, 'Origins of Import Substituting Industrialization'.

[18]   Ranajit Das Gupta, 'Factory Labour in Eastern India: Sources of Supply', *IESHR* 13, no. 3 (1976): 277–329; and Morris D. Morris, *The Emergence of an Industrial Labor force in India: A Study of the Bombay Cotton Mills, 1854–1947* (Berkeley and Los Angeles: University of California Press, 1965). See also 'Migration: Internal' in Ch. 11.

[19]   Lalita Chakravarty, 'Emergence of an Industrial Labour Force in a Dual Economy: British India, 1880–1920', *IESHR* 15, no. 3 (1978): 249–327.

started work, while a few older and small ones merged with the larger organizations or became defunct. The major issue in the 1920s was wage standardization across mills, a problem that reflected the hap-hazard way labour practices had developed in the city's textile mills. As the old textile factories fell in a crisis due to Japanese competi-tion and the employers tried to shed labour or extract more work from them, a series of strikes broke out and drew the government deeper into collective bargaining. A legacy of this involvement was the Bombay Industrial Relations Act of 1946, which recognized the Congress-affiliated Rashtriya Mill Mazdoor Sangh (RMMS) as the sole representative of textile workers in the city. During this episode, trade union membership increased from 100,000 in 1927 to 400,000 (or approximately a quarter of the factory workforce) in 1938.

If factory workers were unhappy about wages, were there grounds for their unhappiness? The supervisors and engineers in a factory could usually enjoy a comfortable lifestyle. But wages of ordinary workers were usually not sufficient to bring their families into the cities. Most earned an income too little or too insecure to think of growing roots in the city and giving up connections with the land. Some sources also found high levels of infant mortality and mor-bidity in the urban slums. The plague epidemic at the turn of the century exposed the poor living conditions in working-class neigh-bourhoods (see also Chapter 10). Based on these facts, historians have sometimes characterized factory workers in the big city as 'unfortunate human beings'.[20]

This is an unnecessarily gloomy description. Although the real wages of urban workers were low, to begin with, their wages were rising much faster than that of agricultural workers (Tables 6.3 and 4.8). Factory workers earned a wage two to three times that of agricultural workers in the interwar period. The city dwellers never suffered the threat of famine in the way the rural population did. Caste oppression and caste as a barrier to entry in new jobs were a weaker force in the cities. For individual workers, the opportunities for occupational and income mobility were greater in the cities than

[20] Dipesh Chakrabarty, *Rethinking Working-Class History: Bengal, 1890–1940* (Princeton: Princeton University Press, 1982), 11.

Table 6.3   Average real wage in large-scale industry, 1900–44 (annual average)

	Bombay cotton textile mills 1934 = 100	Ahmedabad cotton textile mills 1951 = 100	Calcutta jute mills 1951 = 100
1900–4	45.2	37.8	64.0
1910–14	51.6	39.0	57.0
1920–4	66.2	47.4	53.0
1930–4	109.4	88.0	61.8
1940–4	106.0	95.2	74.0

Sources: K. Mukerji, 'Trends in Real Wages in Cotton Textile Mills in Bombay City and Island, From 1900 to 1951', *Artha Vijnana* 1, no. 1 (1959): 82–95; K. Mukerji, 'Trends in Real Wages in Jute Textile Industry from 1900 to 1951', *Artha Vijnana* 2, no. 1 (1960): 57–69; K. Mukerji, 'Trends in Real Wages in Cotton Textile Industry in Ahmedabad from 1900 to 1951', *Artha Vijnana* 3, no. 2 (1961): 124–34.

in the villages. That such people struck work more often in the 1930s had nothing to do with their being unfortunate human beings. As Wolcott explained, Japanese competition threatened their habitual way of working.

Such was the story of the workers. What about capital and enterprise?

CAPITAL AND ENTERPRISE

Interest rates were very high in India. Banks and moneylenders did not lend for long-term investment. Although stock markets had begun before 1900, the amount invested in shares even by the end of the interwar period was too little. Ordinary people did not always trust the share market because there was too much insider trade and speculation. Radhe Shyam Rungta says that the share market was under the control of mainly Marwari brokers, which made for too much insider trading.[21] Whatever the problem, most investors could

[21] Radhe Shyam Rungta, *Rise of Business Corporations in India, 1851–1900* (Cambridge: Cambridge University Press, 1970), 211.

not rely on public subscription. How did the pioneers finance industrial investment?

The Indian pioneers came from communities that had specialized in trading and banking activities. Fixed capital in the large-scale industry came from the savings of the trading firm or borrowings from within a small set of people known to each other. European pioneers funded investment both from their profits as well as stocks floated in London and after 1900 in India too. Over time, the reputed firms, whether Indian or European, succeeded in raising money from the stock market. Big companies of Bombay and Ahmedabad were more successful in attracting deposits from indigenous bankers. Some cotton mills in the interior relied mainly on this mode of financing. The reliance on deposits of bankers, however, carried risks of a run on the company when the demand for money from commodity trade suddenly increased. Smaller firms used trading profits or borrowed from friends and relations to finance investment.

Who were these entrepreneurs? First, consider the foreign investors. The word 'multinational' today suggests a company with the head office in an industrialized country and subsidiaries in developing countries. Usually, the parent company has a technological lead in some field. Often, managers, rather than the shareholders, run such companies. Most foreign firms in colonial India were not like this. They were often trading firms, and not subsidiaries of a parent company, functioning as a partnership instead. Usually some of the partners were associated with another firm in London or Liverpool that took care of marketing and finance. Such firms, called 'free-standing companies' by Mira Wilkins, were common in the Asian port city.[22] It is from this pool that the first industrial ventures started.

For example, the Scottish firm of James Finlay began in 1765 as a cotton mill owner and textile trader in Scotland and continental Europe. In the 1830s, they started buying cotton from India and, in 1862, opened an office in Bombay. In the 1870s, they started jute

[22] Mira Wilkins, 'The Free-Standing Company, 1870–1914: An Important Type of British Foreign Direct Investment', EHR 41, no. 2 (1988): 259–82.

mills in Calcutta and, in the next decade, began selling Indian tea. By 1900, they owned the major part of the area under tea in the Anaimalai and the Nilgiri mountains. Their other ventures included a cotton mill in Bombay and a sugar refinery in UP.

Almost all the large British industrial firms in Calcutta had a beginning like this, though a few were set up by local merchants, officers, and artisans. The top firms included Andrew Yule (jute, tea, coal, paper, engineering), Bird and F.W. Heilgers (jute, coal, engineering, limestone), McLeod-Begg-Dunlop (jute, tea, railways), Jardine-Skinner and George Henderson (jute, tea, engineering), Octavius Steel (tea, electricity), Shaw Wallace (tea, coal), Gillanders-Arbuthnot (jute, tea, coal), Macneill-Barry (jute, coal, electricity), Martin-Burn (coal, wagons, dockyards, cement), Balmer-Lawrie (coal, paper, engineering), and Kilburn (tea, coal, engineering). Smaller groups included Kettlewell-Bullen, Mackinnon-Mackenzie, and Thomas Duff (all three in jute). Two other large houses, Williamson-Magor and Duncan Brothers, mainly owned tea estates.

Among the Indians, Parsi merchants and shipwrights of western India started the first factories, followed by traditional merchant communities such as the Khojas, Bhatias, Gujarati traders, Gujarati bankers, and Baghdadi Jews. Some of them, like prominent Parsi firms, had collaborated with the Europeans before. Others had their base in overland trade. The owners of the first cotton mills came from these communities, with a few from European trading houses dealing in cotton. The pioneering names among cotton millowners included Petit, Wadia, and Tata (Parsis); Currimbhoys (Khojas); Sassoons (Jews); Khatau, Gokuldas, Thakersey (Bhatias from Kutchch); and Greaves Cotton, W.H. Brady, and Killick Nixon (European houses). The origin of Ahmedabad's mill industry was more rooted in Hindu and Jain business. Among the prominent names, Sarabhai and Lalbhai were Jain traders already prominent as pedhis or banking firms. The combination of cotton textiles and cotton trade was an advantageous form of integration.

Industry in Calcutta, as we have seen, was mainly European-owned. But Indian traders based in Calcutta, chiefly the Marwaris, supplied European firms with raw materials. Throughout the eighteenth and the nineteenth century, the Marwaris had steadily dispersed from their original home in Rajasthan and resettled in new business towns as moneylenders and revenue farmers. From that base, they began to enter trade. The history of prominent Marwari houses such as Birla, Goenka, or Jalan suggests that their main interests about 1900 were in jute baling, mining, zamindari, and import agency. By the end of the interwar period, these firms had entered the jute industry and, on a smaller scale, sugar, paper, cement, construction, and share broking.

Their position as insiders in the stock market, and the small holdings of many of the British managing agents in the firms they controlled enabled the Indians to effect a series of takeovers in the 1950s and the 1960s. The British owners themselves found the changed political climate uncongenial. In the stock market manipulations, the Indians received implicit support from the ruling politicians. Several other firms, therefore, were voluntarily sold to Indians. Most of them were subsequently managed badly, owned by persons having little regard for efficiency, and were robbed of assets, though there were a few exceptions.

Unlike Bombay or Calcutta, Madras offered a narrower scope for collaboration between Indian and European capitalists. *Chettiars*, who were moneylenders, went overseas. Lower Burma became part of the British Empire in 1852. At that time, the economic potentials of the Irrawaddy delta were unutilized. A modified ryotwari enabled mortgaging landholdings. Credit fuelled export-oriented paddy cultivation until the boom ended in the Great Depression. Between 1880 and 1930, Chettiar firms met an increasing part of the credit demand of peasants, superseding Burmese firms. Their superior business organization, long apprenticeship, training in business ethics and techniques (such as a special accounting system), group solidarity, inter-firm lending, and informal sanctions to minimize default within the group were advantages. Chettiar enterprise in Burma, however, became caught up in an economic and political crisis in the 1930s, eventually forcing most firms to leave Burma. Profits in these foreign operations went into manufacturing.

In the interwar period, the Tamil Nadu region witnessed a vigorous growth of small-scale industry (Chapter 5). Two large-scale industrial complexes also came up around Coimbatore and Madras.

The main source of capital here was the savings of the rich cotton farmers-cum-traders. Cotton farming and trade played a pivotal role in early industrialization in all the regions of Tamil Nadu. In southern India, protectionism was a less important driver to industrial diversification. The locally rooted engineering industry also set South India on a different course from northern India. For example, R. and V. Seshasayee were Tamil Brahmins from Tiruchirappalli who ran an engineering repair shop during World War I, then diversified into a chemicals and engineering conglomerate.

MANAGEMENT

Most Indian firms managed their businesses by recruiting family members and relatives into the top management. Sometimes they also recruited more widely from the business community. A business community was any set of people bound by language, kinship ties, marriage, and shared economic interest. They used their social bonds to ensure that managers would be honest towards each other. If they were not, the truant members could be excommunicated or denied a good marriage or another job. Community was not the same thing as a Hindu caste. Non-Hindu groups in India also behaved in quite the same way as the Hindu ones in forming a bond based on kinship and marriage and used these to serve these business functions. The Parsis, the Bohras, the Jewish groups, and the Armenians were, socially speaking, as conservative as Hindu castes.

Most Parsi businesses in the nineteenth century recruited partners and managers from among other Parsis. *Shikarpuri* bankers and Chettiar bankers, likewise, displayed a strong preference for recruitment of agents exclusively from the same set. Unorthodox partnerships cutting across caste and community did occur. Bombay saw several such enterprises. Still, community-based collaboration was the more usual system in the mid-nineteenth century. It was because money and skills were both scarce resources, and people with money would not give it to a prospective mill owner unless they were sure of the reliability of the latter. And what better way to find out who was reliable except through one's relations?

But this propensity was changing. In the 1870s, legislation on contracts and negotiable instruments made a formal contract between two people as secure as an informal contract based on marriage ties, perhaps more secure. Inside some of the old communities, the Parsis being again an example, disputes between older and younger members were getting out of control. In the industrial era, a business reputation derived from how well particular companies performed and thus fixed upon successful entrepreneurs who ran these companies, rather than upon whole groups. Chambers of commerce were beginning to be more important than personal connections in lobbying and seeking cooperation.

In these ways, the community came under increasing pressure. It remained resilient for a long time, partly because the new environment created some kinds of risk for which community support was useful insurance and partly because laws on succession and inheritance of property respected the rights of the joint family (Chapter 2). In British Indian property law, the right of a joint family, consisting of the blood descendants of a male ancestor, over property held together, superseded the rights of the individuals within it. This form of property right, which the lawmakers had borrowed from Hindu and Islamic codebooks, helped business families because it enabled capital to stay undivided. At the same time, it increased disputes within the family between younger and older members over time. The more successful the business, the stronger would be the demand to divide property. The twentieth century saw an outburst of such demands among all traditional business families.

Even when families controlled companies, the same families also used some legally recognized business organizations like partnerships and managing agency. Until 1850, the partnership was the general form of ownership and management, which made raising finance and management difficult. The first Indian Companies Act of 1850 formally recognized limited liability. The period 1860–80 saw a boom in company formation and share markets. The Bombay stock exchange started in 1875 and began to attract small investors. In this situation, new paradigms in management started taking root. One such institution was the managing agency.

A managing agent was usually a partnership firm set up to manage other companies. The directors of the company asked the partnership firm to supply management service for a fee (and sometimes commission on sales) for a fixed term. The idea of a management contract had originated in the insurance business in the early nineteenth century. By the 1870s, it changed form and became established in large-scale industry, mining, and plantations.

Why did the managing agency become popular? It allowed companies to raise capital from the market, without exposing themselves to takeover risk, because management control was with the managing agency and protected by a contract. Further, a few firms would manage several businesses when managers were in short supply, and companies wanted to conserve managerial talent. A significant role for the agent was raising loans and deposits. Indian firms found it hard to meet their fixed and working capital requirements out of paid-up share capital and had to rely on loans and public deposits. Loans required a guarantor and deposits required the borrower to be a trusted and reputed name. The managing agents served these functions.

The managing agency worked very differently among Indians and Europeans. In most European businesses, the same family did not own both the managing agent and the managed company. The company had public shareholding and the agency was a partnership among people not related by blood or marriage. That was not the case with Indians. Most Indian agencies were family-owned and the companies they managed were majority-owned by the same family.

In both these cases, a corporate governance problem could arise; the problem would be serious with the second type of agency common among Indians. If a contractual fee secures the agent's income, why would the agent serve the interests of the shareholders? Among the European firms, the desire to protect their reputation kept this problem under control. Several of these managed a dozen or more companies each and their conduct was visible to the public. Among Indian firms, the problem was more serious. Families took decisions that were never recorded and never came to the public. Their control both over the agency and the managed company could mean that the majority shareholders could cheat the minority or public shareholders without facing any risk. For example, the agents speculated in commodity trade in goods and raw materials in which the company was interested. Such speculation was often against the company's interests.

The system became redundant in the mid-twentieth century. The board of directors could serve most functions of an agency. As management emerged as an independent profession, a market for managerial labour emerged and special institutions to supply management services became unnecessary. In 1970, the managing agency formally ended.

This discussion reminds us that the worlds of Indian business and foreign business were quite distinct. European firms were more global, dominant in overseas trade and oceanic shipping, and had easier access to joint-stock banks and the formal capital market. The Indians were dominant in overland commodity trade, produced and traded in handicrafts, used boats and carts for transportation, relied heavily on caste and community, dominated the markets in shares and bullion, and used indigenous bankers for remittance and capital. India was not exceptional in receiving foreign investment in the late nineteenth century. Many colonies did, in mines, plantations, and railways principally. India was exceptional in having a strong body of indigenous capitalists who carved their sphere of business alongside the colonial capitalists. The strength of indigenous capital made India unique among tropical colonies.

Why did these two worlds exist side by side? One answer is that they had distinct advantages, which made them specialize in different fields.[23] Each group could access a distinct kind of capital market, product market, and raw material market better than the other groups in the initial stages of development of factory industry. Europeans raised money from London; they bought shares in other European firms. These shareholders included former expatriates. Indians raised money from family and community resources.

[23] Morris D. Morris, 'South Asian Entrepreneurship and the Rashomon Effect, 1800–1947', Explorations in Economic History 16, no. 3 (1979): 341–61.

Europeans sold goods in export markets through a transportation and communication network centred in London. Indians sold goods in India and China. Europeans relied on indigenous agents for procurement of raw material. Indian industrialists had been raw material traders themselves, in cotton as well as jute.

The relative position of the two groups changed in the interwar period. World War I made many Indian firms very rich. The Great Depression hit the export-oriented foreign firms harder than it did the Indians. Indian industrialists were gaining political power at the same time.[24] The collapse of the world market during the Depression, the rise of nationalism, the development of formal and informal institutions, and the growth of a home market under tariff protection from the late 1920s led to a change in the comparative advantage of these fields. At the same time, political tendencies brought the Indians and the Europeans into conflict. In the jute industry, the mainly European cartel became weak because the Indian mill owners refused to cooperate with them. The Europeans' moves to seek government intervention in regulating the industry failed and made the antagonism worse. In tea, the cartel was more successful, but the non-cartelized Indian estates were growing rapidly.

Where did industrial technology come from and with what benefits and costs?

TECHNOLOGY

Technology in the factories came from Britain. In one view, the dependence on Britain was not good for India. The colonial state sponsored diffusion of those technologies—in such fields as railways and metallurgy—that would help British industry and, therefore, Indians learnt little from such inflow of knowledge.[25]

---

[24] B.R. Tomlinson, 'Colonial Firms and the Decline of Colonialism in Eastern India 1914–47', *MAS* 15, no. 3 (1981): 455–86.

[25] Daniel Headrick, *The Tools of Empire: Technology and European Imperialism in the Nineteenth Century* (New York: Oxford University Press, 1981), 205.

This overly pessimistic view does not explain technological choices and their consequences for the cotton mill industry, where choices were made not by the state but by the capitalists. The factory industry in textiles might not develop at all without the easy availability of British machines and engineers. The Indian technical personnel learnt the work and learnt how to repair and recondition machines quite successfully. The Empire enabled similar learning effects also in stationary steam engine, the telegraph, engineering education, and the railways.

***

India did not possess well-developed capital and labour markets in the nineteenth century. It did have cheap labour, cheap material, and community-bound entrepreneurial resources, but the capital was expensive, large-scale labour markets non-existent, transportation costs of material high, and the merchants did not understand machinery. Why, then, did India industrialize?

India's colonial connection was instrumental in overcoming these barriers to industrialization. The railways brought down carriage costs; British capitalists and shareholders invested in India; and Bombay's merchants found it easy to hire supervisors and buy machinery from Manchester with which they already had well-developed trading links. Not all industries had equal chances of overcoming the obstacles. The process favoured those industries, such as textiles, in which India had a resource cost advantage. In machinery and chemicals, domestic production would have needed much higher injections of capital and knowledge than was the case with the cotton mills. Capital and intermediate goods, therefore, were slow to develop.

In the prewar phase of growth, the colonial state hardly had a policy on industrialization, beyond keeping all markets open. The demand for protection, however, was growing from the 1920s, partly because the cotton mill owners found it hard to withstand Japanese competition without tariffs. Indian-origin industrialists thought protection was their entitlement as part of political freedom. In turn, the demand for protection covered up the fact that Indian productivity was low when compared with other emerging economies. There was, however, no serious discussion of this syndrome until recently, and soon after 1947, protection extended without regard for efficiency issues.

Factories were only one component of the modern sector. The next chapter discusses three other forms of the modern enterprise.

7

Plantations, Mines, Banking

In 1947, about 15 per cent of the workforce was engaged in activities outside manufacturing and agriculture, many of them in the three modern activities—plantations, mines, and banks. Like large-scale industry, these enterprises used new organizational forms, had global connections, and attracted investment from Europeans and Indians. Many business houses had investments spread over industry, mines, plantations, and banks. Like large-scale industry, mines and plantations processed natural resources available cheap in India. Like the former, these activities saw large rise in GDP and GDP per worker. This chapter is about these activities.

In 1921, plantations and mines together employed 1.1 million persons. The figure was less than 1 per cent of total employment, but one-third of employment in the modern sectors. Plantations employed 821,000 persons, 91 per cent in tea. Coffee and rubber employed another 7 per cent. Mines employed 268,000 persons, 68 per cent in coal alone. Modern banking was a small field in terms of employment, but it was crucial to the most important business of all—commodity trading. All three received significant investment by Europeans.

This chapter first covers tea and coffee, next coal, and lastly banking and insurance.

TEA AND COFFEE

When the East India Company lost its monopoly of China trade (1833), it turned to India for supplies of tea. Assam, which had become part of British India in 1825, had the ideal climate and topography for tea plantations. Efforts to develop plantations in Assam began. The first Indian tea was made in a government experimental farm and arrived in England in 1838. Encouraged by the reception, the Assam Company formed the following year, taking over the government's farms. Also in 1838, the government set up rules for leasing out land to plantation companies. The terms were liberal. The tea boom that came did not last long because labour was scarce, planters were inexperienced, transportation was poor, and the quality of tea bad. There were forests everywhere. Labour was not locally available.

In 1850, the main mode of transport between Assam and lower Bengal was country boats. The difficulty and uncertainty of the journey were so great that the journey between Calcutta and Gauhati took between two and a half months. 'In the rains', a historian of tea wrote, 'tea chests could be taken in canoes down the small streams flowing into the Brahmaputra, but in the cold weather these streams dried up and as bullock carts scarcely existed in Assam at that time, chests had to be carried by coolie or by elephant.'[1] A railway was necessary. Railway projects connected Calcutta and Chittagong with the tea districts of Bengal and Assam from the 1880s.

With these developments, the area under tea gardens expanded from 154,000 acres in 1880 to 337,000 acres in 1900. The number of workers increased from 184,000 to 665,000. Gardens came up in the Darjeeling hills and the Dooars region in North Bengal, and in the Surma valley in eastern Bengal. Nearly 75 per cent of tea land, however, was located in Assam. The share of Indian tea in Britain's market increased from 7 per cent in 1868 to 54 in 1896. The quality of tea improved, and the costs of production came down. Acreage

---

[1] Percival Griffiths, *The History of the Indian Tea Industry* (London: Weidenfield and Nicholson, 1967), 633–4.

expanded to 715,000 in 1921. No significant growth in acreage was possible after that time.

Between 1860 and 1900, tea plantations started in South India. Tea was growing in the Nilgiri hills. According to legend, Chinese prisoners stationed in the Nilgiris had helped planters manufacture tea. In the early years of Assam plantations, Chinese workers worked there. By 1900, cultivation started in the Wynaad (Wayanad) and the Kannan–Devan hills in North Travancore.

In the interwar years, the international tea trade cartel became powerful. The London-based Indian Tea Association started regulating the volume of production to keep prices high. The South Indian planters and the Dutch East Indies planters resisted them. World War II again was a period of growth in demand. But the 1940s also saw massive inflation in food prices. As tea employed many people, the gardens faced a problem of getting food for the labourers.

Tea sales took place in auctions at Calcutta and London. The participants in these auctions were the 'broker' firms who sampled, inspected, tasted, and valued tea from the plantations. They brought tea to the auctions and gave advances to the tea growers. There were a few broker firms in Calcutta. All were British concerns until Independence. Calcutta-based British managing agent firms controlled the majority of the estates and the largest of them. The major firms were Andrew Yule, McLeod, Begg-Dunlop (merged with McLeod in the interwar period), Jardine-Skinner, Octavius Steel, Williamson-Magor, Shaw Wallace, Gillanders-Arbuthnot, Davenport, and Duncan Brothers. James Finlay controlled almost the entire crop of the Kannan–Devan hills. Bengali capitalists entered the industry quite early (in the 1880s) but never dominated it. The majority of them owned small gardens in the Dooars.

Most Indian firms consisted of families rather than corporate firms. They did not have enough resources to invest in their estates and operated at the poorer quality range aimed at domestic consumers. In one view, their limited and low-level operation resulted from European dominance in the tea trade and regional politics.[2] The main

[2] Ranajit Das Gupta, *Economy, Society and Politics in Bengal: Jalpaiguri 1869–1947* (Delhi: Oxford University Press, 1992), 62–5.

barrier to entry into exports, however, was not the ethnic character of the tea cartel but the much higher capital and information necessary to succeed in exports. The capital was necessary in marketing and shipping and information needed about European markets. European firms had better access to capital, information, and an existing tea-marketing infrastructure in London's Mincing Lane.

About the middle of the nineteenth century, when plantations in Assam and Dooars began to develop, the regions were sparsely populated, had bad communications, and the local labour pool was either non-existent or insufficient. A class of contractors, called *arkatis*, travelled through lower Bengal and Bihar and delivered 'coolies' to the gardens. Some of the contractors were Europeans. Indenture contracts were written before the labourer came to the garden and could become familiar with the conditions.[3] The labourers understood little of the terms of the contract, which legally bound them to work in the plantations for a certain period. Until the railways opened, the journey to the plantations was hazardous and led to many deaths. Sanitary conditions at the transit points were poor. Not all the deaths, however, reflected the hardship of the journey. The migration was heavier during famines when immunity to epidemic diseases was generally low. The plantations offered poor quality of life. The newly cleared forests, in particular, exposed the migrants to malaria, known as the Assam fever. The work was heavy.

Workers often tried to run away, which gave rise to demands for strict laws against desertions. A law did become available in 1859. This was the Workmen's Breach of Contract Act, better known as the Act XIII of 1859, which made desertion a criminal offence. Employers could penalize and forcibly bring back the deserting worker. The use of criminal law to deal with desertion was controversial in its own time. The act was coercive.[4] But the workers were

---

[3] Formally, indenture was a contract to serve for a fixed term, usually several years. Informally, because workers were often non-literate and ill-informed, the contract could resemble slavery. Historical scholarship on South Asia debates its resemblance to slavery.

[4] See Rana P. Behal, *One Hundred Years of Servitude: Political Economy of Tea Plantations in Colonial Assam* (New Delhi: Tulika Books, 2014).

not ignorant of that fact and still wanted to come to work in the tea estates. The voluntary and incentivized nature of migration finds more recognition in recent studies on labour supply. For example, a paper investigating the effect of the act shows that labour supply varied with tea price, that is, rose when prices were high. But in areas covered by the act, supply response was weaker.[5]

An act passed in 1882 allowed free recruitment, that is, without contracts. In practice, most free labourers were also put on a contract after they reached Assam. The so-called free labourers did not often see the difference and the free recruiters did not try too hard to explain it to them.

In 1900, going to Assam, therefore, carried a negative image. But it is doubtful if the majority of the migrants were any longer forced or duped into going. Much migration to Assam was voluntary and induced by positive reports received from returnees. During famines and epidemics, Assam received a large number of migrants who expected that the estates would feed them and they did. Conditions of discipline in the plantations were harsh, but neither wage nor the quality of life was worse in the plantations compared to agricultural work in the source regions.

Social stresses, such as the difficulty of finding wives, added to the adverse image of plantation life. While a large number of women went to Assam, it was legally difficult for single women to migrate. Therefore, single women were scarce in the plantations. Around 1900, in the newer regions like the Surma Valley and in some of the older plantations in Upper Assam, a solution to these problems had been tried, namely, recruitment through garden sardars rather than by the outsider contractor. The sardar was a senior worker and supervisor. The planter gave him/her a paid vacation on the promise that he/she would bring friends and relatives to the garden. The sardar workers were cheaper and they came to the garden to stay there, for the sardars tended to bring whole families over to the plantations. The sardar also bore less of a search cost if indeed he/

    [5] Bishnupriya Gupta and Anand V. Swamy, 'Reputational Consequences of Labor Coercion: Evidence from Assam's Tea Plantations', *Journal of Development Economics* 127 (2017): 431–9.

she could persuade near relations to join the return party. Eventually, the *sardari* recruitment became legal and other systems illegal.

Wages of plantation workers were only slightly higher than the real income of agricultural labourers and usually less than those of factory or mine workers. Unlike these other workers, the plantation workers' earning capacity did not vary significantly by season. The working conditions improved after 1900. There was better medical care and sanitation. By the interwar period, abuses were the exception rather than the rule. Tea garden labour was now a settled population that had lost much of its attachment to its places of origin. In one account, no doubt one more sympathetic to the managers, relations at work were like a paternalistic hierarchy between the workers and the managers.[6] But laws to protect jobs and working conditions were slow to develop. These laws related to duration of contract, minimum wages, and execution of contracts after and not before the labourer came to the garden.

As in Assam or Dooars, workers in the South Indian plantations came from the plains. In the early years, hill ranges such as the Anaimalai were practically uninhabited and the workers carried many days' food with them when they came to work. However, unlike in eastern India, the South Indian labourers did not come from long distances. Many came from Mysore and Madras. Still, desertion was common and a more difficult problem because the breach of contract act did not extend to Mysore, a princely state. Ceylon plantations competed with Travancore and the Nilgiris for labour. The labour scarcity eased somewhat after the famine of 1876, which increased the flow of labour from the plains of Tamil Nadu towards the Nilgiri estates. Rising rent and stagnant wages in the agriculture of the plains increased the pressures to migrate to the plantation in the latter half of the century.[7]

Coffee plantations developed in the uplands of Mysore, Coorg, Travancore, and Wynaad, from the 1870s. Coffee may have been

[6] Griffiths, *The History of the Indian Tea Industry*, 345.

[7] Barbara Evans, 'From Agricultural Bondage to Plantation Contract: A Continuity of Experience in Southern India, 1860–1947', *South Asia: Journal of South Asian Studies* 13, no. 2 (1990): 45–63.

introduced to southern Mysore by an Arab pilgrim of the name Baba Budan in the seventeenth century or earlier. After the Anglo-Mysore wars, small settlements of Europeans developed in parts of the uplands. In this way, Mannantoddy, the only major town of Wynaad, became a home for a few European families. The European capitalists in Wynaad were mainly engaged in coffee at the end of the century. In Mysore, on the other hand, two-thirds of the area under cultivation belonged to Indian planters. About 1903, coffee engaged a little less than 100,000 workers (Figure 7.1).

Unlike in Assam, coffee workers did not have to travel very large distances. Still, labour supply was initially a problem, because it was seasonal and uncertain. In the mid-nineteenth century, nearly

Figure 7.1 Workers cleaning and sorting coffee, South India, 1890s. Although exports were large, growing Indian consumption in the cities sustained the markets for coffee and tea, especially coffee. The plantations were also a major employer in the princely states.

© Chronicle / Alamy Stock Photo

all workers were peasants in their villages or farm servants in paddy lands and returned to the village during harvests. The larger estates could not depend on such seasonal labour and moved towards indenture contracts and Tamil workers.

Initially, there were many obstacles to starting a coffee estate. Although connected by road to the ports of the Malabar coast, the uplands region was relatively isolated because of the difficulty faced by wheeled traffic on the 'ghat' roads. As late as 1865, coffee grown in Wynaad was transported to the ports using pack bullocks, large herds of which were brought in from Mysore during harvests. The transportation system improved somewhat in the latter decades of the nineteenth century. In 1881, the Mysore state reformed its mode of taxation of coffee, switching from an output tax to a land tax. The reform provided a major incentive to coffee estates to expand.

Despite their negative image as employers, there were many positive effects of the plantations. First, plantation labour paid better wages and more regular year-round wages; labourers received food security and medical care more than in agricultural villages. The nature of the work was similar; therefore, it was easier for agricultural labourers to join plantations, whereas the door to a factory job did not open to them. Second, the estates encouraged urbanization, transportation, schools, hospitals, and a local trade network that supplied material to the plantations and also facilitated marketing of rural produce. Third, they generated profits that flowed back into many mid-sized towns like Gauhati, Darjeeling, Siliguri, Dhubri, and Dibrugarh.

MINES

Modern economic growth was built upon fossil fuel. Coal was the main source of energy in the initial stages when steam engines dominated industrialization. India had substantial deposits of coal. But its wide usage had to await the growth of modern industry and transportation. The Company regime took some interest in developing the commercial extraction of coal. In the early nineteenth century, the main use of charcoal was in the smelting of iron by rural artisans.

For the same purpose, the ordnance factories needed coal in larger quantities. Such coal came from Britain, and sporadic attempts to use local coal did not satisfy the engineers. With the growth of steamships in Indian waters, the demand for local supplies strengthened. Calcutta's agency houses started small mining operations in western Bengal. The Carr Tagore Company (see Chapter 2) acquired the only major colliery, Raniganj, in the 1830s. It started enterprises that could use this coal. After Carr Tagore failed, the colliery passed on to European hands.

Several initiatives were taken during the late eighteenth century to commercially exploit the large coal reserves of eastern India, some sponsored or encouraged by the Company. These failed to produce a take-off until the mid-nineteenth century at least. The failure owed to three factors: inadequate mineralogical knowledge, inefficient transportation, and shortage of labour.[8] Rivers were not navigable throughout the year and road transport was costly. A sharp increase in coal output from the 1850s was possible because of new data collected by the Geological Survey of India, expansion of railway connection in the coal-bearing region, and greater circulation of labour in eastern Bengal and Chota Nagpur.

From the 1850s, the situation took a different turn. The railways connected Calcutta with the deposits in Raniganj in 1855. Barakar and Giridih became connected in the next 15 years and Jharia in 1893. By 1940, small railway lines connecting the mining towns with the main routes crisscrossed the Damodar river basin. Although smaller deposits emerged in central and southern India, the Damodar basin remained overwhelmingly important, with the result that almost the whole of India, excluding Bengal, had to bear high transportation costs of fuel. The cost was one factor encouraging the exploitation of hydroelectric power in western India.

While transportation of coal to distant users became progressively cheaper, further railway expansion itself turned into a major source of demand for coal. The jute mills of Calcutta were also a major user of

---

[8] Indrajit Ray, 'Dynamics of Bengal Coal Mining in the Nineteenth Century: Dissemination of Mineralogical Knowledge and Railway Networking', *IESHR* 52, no. 4 (2015): 463–99.

coal. At the end of World War I, the railways alone consumed about 30 per cent of the total Indian production of coal. Modern industry, plantations, and mining consumed 25–30 per cent. Shipping and the port trusts took 10–15 per cent, and small-scale industry and domestic users another 20–25 per cent. A substantial quantity was exported from India to Ceylon and South East Asia, replacing first British and later Japanese supplies.

The years between 1890 and 1919 saw a 'coal rush' in eastern India. Output increased from 0.3 million tonnes in 1860 (about double the volume of imports) to 2.2 million tonnes in 1890 to 22.6 in 1919 and 30 million tonnes in 1947. India was then a net exporter of coal. Table 7.1 presents some figures on the growth of production. The number of workers in the mines of Bengal increased from 25,000 to 175,000.

The mining business was profitable. In some years, it was exceptionally so. But the interwar period saw considerable fluctuations in prices and outputs. After 1920, exchange appreciation and a dull world market led to a fall in exports. The reputation abroad for the quality of Indian coal was not very good either. Conditions improved towards the end of the 1920s. But they turned adverse again during the Depression. In the early 1930s, many small collieries closed down, average dividends paid, and rates of profits dropped substantially. The Coal Mining Committee of 1936 was the response to these problems. World War II revived profitability.

Who invested in the coal rush of 1890–1919? As in all Calcutta-based modern enterprises, in coal mining, foreign firms and joint-stock companies were the main owners of capital in the prewar period. There was a close interlocking of jute and coal. The interlocking not only supplied the mines with a captive market but also supplied the mines with railway wagons for transportation to other users at a time when wagons were in short supply. The railways favoured the European firms with wagons. They did so ostensibly because their coal was of better quality but allegedly because of racial sympathies.[9]

[9] Ratna Ray and Rajat Ray, 'European Monopoly Corporations and Indian Entrepreneurship, 1913–1922. Early Politics of Coal in Eastern India', *EPW* 9, no. 21 (1974): M53–M55.

In 1914, 10 large European managing agencies based in Calcutta owned almost all of the capital of joint-stock companies interested in coal. European firms supplied possibly over 80 per cent of the output. The main consumers of this output were modern industry, shipping, and railways.

Small individually owned Indian firms were becoming important in the coal industry. Their share began rising from World War I. By 1947, they supplied about one-third of the total production. They mined low-quality coal from shallow pits, did not use much machinery, and mainly served the domestic users of coal and small-scale industries. Some of them owned zamindari estates. Zamindaris became involved in mining in varying degrees. The most well-known example perhaps is the Malias of Searsole near Raniganj. The prominent Indian colliers were Bengalis who were former employees or merchants of the European companies. The labour contractors in mining, again usually Bengalis, had also bought or started some collieries. An increasing proportion of coal mines changed hands in the interwar period as the Marwaris bought them from the Bengalis.

In 1914, the coal mining interests divided into two camps, the Europeans belonging to the Indian Mining Association affiliated to the Bengal Chamber of Commerce and the Indians organized under the Indian Mining Federation. The start of the latter association happened due to the railways' alleged preferential treatment of European colliers. These associations not only worked as cartels, but also as channels for information exchange. The Indian group tried to popularize the use of coal in industries where wood fuel was used. In the 1920s, both associations joined hands to resist labour militancy. Labour movements were causing the mining industry problems at a time when the market was beginning to experience depressed conditions.

The extraction technology stayed very basic. Coal was cut by hand, loaded by hand, hauled by hand, and, wherever possible, not extracted from great depths. The smaller the mine, the more primitive the technology. The largest of the European mines did use electricity and steam power for hauling coal, for pumping out water from the mines, and for lighting pits. But the majority did not. The Indian mine labourer's average output was less than half that of the British miner and one-fourth that of the Australian in the mid-1930s. Further, mines worked with little regard for conservation and safety. Underground fires, subsidence, and accidents were common.

The owners of the mine lands were the zamindars. They leased out land to the colliers and received a fixed rent. So they had no interest in productivity. Why did the colliers not invest more in improving the technology of mining? The low productivity was an adaptation to the low wages at which coal labour was available. The mines hired experienced and educated personnel only for their small managerial cadre. Labour contractors recruited the bulk of the coal labourers offering piece wages. With labour unrest rising from the 1920s, the mines did not want a permanent and skilled labour force. They made sure that their work practices were such as not to require a permanent labour force. The existence of a cheap and unskilled labour force on hire made mining costs unbeatably low. But it also led to neglect for mining technology and safety.

Among other mines, gold mines occurred in south-eastern Mysore. A European company leased these mines and started a township in Kolar. The first reports of profitable exploitation of gold here came in 1886. Within a few years, 'what was a desolate waste has thus become a great industrial town, employing nearly 10,000 labourers'.[10] The mines became a vital source of revenue for the Mysore state. Most workers were migrants of depressed castes, paid low wages, and usually of non-permanent status. The company's control over the judicial process influenced the workers' relationship with the employers. The work could lead to diseases and accidents. On the other hand, the enterprise generated considerable positive externalities. The image of plenitude and

[10] Mysore, *Mysore Gazetteer* (Mysore: Government Press, 1927), 2986. See also Janaki Nair, *Miners and Millhands. Work, Culture and Politics in Princely Mysore* (New Delhi: SAGE Publications, 1998), which is mainly a history of labour in the enterprise.

personal freedom that drew migrants to the mining town was well founded. Wages in the mines were higher than agricultural wages. Consumption was higher and more diverse. Social status was less oppressive, while entrepreneurial opportunities in the mining town were greater.

India was one of the major producers of mica in the world. The demand for mica increased worldwide along with the production of electrical and military aeronautics apparatus. The demand was not a steady one so that the prices and quantities fluctuated a great deal. Mica mines appeared in eastern India and the Nellore District of Madras. A study of mica in Nellore shows how mining could become lucrative, if a rather speculative venture. And yet it left rather little positive long-term effects on the local population or labour.[11]

Did mining help the development of the mining regions? Coal mining was a major source of income in Eastern India and a big field of Bengali investment. In the Damodar basin, the mines themselves were in rural or semi-rural areas. But these areas saw urbanization.

Table 7.1   Production of major minerals, 1891–1938

	1891	1921	1938–9
Coal (m tonne): Total	2.30	18.40	28.33[a]
Bengal, Bihar, Orissa	1.92	16.18	23.00[a]
Iron ore (m tonne): Total	0.02	0.94	2.74
Gold (m ounces): Total	n.a.	0.39	0.32
Mysore state	n.a.	0.38	0.32
Petroleum (m gallons):			
Total	8.47	305.68	322.66
Burma	8.47	296.09	251.33

Source: India, *Statistical Abstracts for British India* (London: HMSO or Calcutta: Government Press, 1881–82 to 1926–27, 1930–31 to 1939–40).
Note: Includes the Indian States.

[11] Keshabananda Das, 'Growth and Decline of Mica Mining Industry in Nellore, 1911–1950', *IESHR* 28, no. 4 (1991): 393–416.

Because these were homes of white-collar workers, small towns grew with modern services such as banks, hospitals, and schools. The region had a dense network of infrastructure, which made it suitable later for state-sponsored industrialization. But mines had a rather limited effect on the lives of the workers in the mines. There was little external pressure to make improvements in technology or offer labour better terms.

BANKS

Banking in colonial India came into two broad segments: informal and formal. The informal sector consisted of firms not legally recognized as either companies or banks. Formal or corporate banking in the colonial period had four types: exchange banks, Presidency banks, Indian joint-stock banks, and cooperative credit societies. Foreign-owned exchange banks were licensed to deal in foreign currency, so they financed foreign trade and remittance. The Presidency banks and private joint-stock banks handled domestic trade and remittance. Indian moneylenders, banking firms, and traders supplied the credit needs of peasants, landlords, and artisans. The borders between the segments were not clearly defined. The exchange banks deposited a part of their balances with the Presidency banks. The Presidency banks and Indian moneylenders often financed two stages of the same business. Cooperative credit societies started after the passing of the Cooperative Credit Societies Act of 1904, which exempted cooperative societies from the Indian Companies Act. Rural credit societies rapidly increased in number and deposits. But by 1947, this remained a tiny segment of banking and not an efficient source of rural finance either.

In the nineteenth and early twentieth century, many indigenous banking firms continued to do business in hundi, which functioned as trade bills or a banker's draft (see Chapter 2). The hundis came in a wide variety of contractual terms, dealing with the safe and honest delivery of the goods against which the bill was drawn. They had many names, a result of these contractual terms. Sometimes, the hundi bore the name of the community that floated it. Aside from hundis, throughout India, a great deal of the post-harvest crop movement was financed in the twentieth century utilizing inter-shroff short-term loans.[12] Traders borrowed from lenders who, in turn, borrowed from other lenders; the chain, at times, reached some of the large shroff houses whose bills were acceptable to the corporate banks. Large inter-shroff transactions, however, were strictly monitored through community channels.

But the dominance of the community distanced hundi from modern money markets.[13] Personal reputation mattered to the success of the hundi. Not everybody could enter the business as clients or as banking firms. The government was becoming more anxious about the personal nature of such transactions and the fact that the modern laws of contract did not cover them effectively. The government was also keen on taxing these contracts and succeeded partially using the Negotiable Instruments Act of 1881.[14]

A proper history of small-scale moneylending does not exist. This world changed a great deal between the late nineteenth century and the late twentieth. Moneylenders financed peasants and artisans, which the corporate banks never did. Many of the clients of the moneylenders were people in need of quick money and who could not give security. The strengths of moneylenders were their intimate knowledge of clients and absence of regulation, adding up to low transaction costs for customers. In a remote village, a moneylender could impose an effective monopoly. But the village moneylender, in lending to impoverished clients engaged in unstable livelihoods, also took unusual degrees of risk.

Coming to the corporate banks, let us first look at the exchange banks. The failure of the agency houses in Calcutta (Chapter 2) created a gap in financing foreign trade. Overcoming some resistance from the East India Company, foreign banks began to enter this field

[12] Shroff is a banker or money changer.

[13] 'The strong ties of caste and community tend ... to isolate the hundi market from the general modern market for short-term funds.' See S.K. Muranjan, *Modern Banking in India* (Bombay: Kamala, 1952), 146.

[14] Marina Martin, 'An Economic History of the Hundi 1858–1978' (PhD Diss., Department of Economic History, London School of Economics and Political Science, 2012).

from 1853. These banks formed in countries of origin. But they financed trade from and to India. Of the 17 exchange banks that remained at Independence, seven had their head offices in England, two each in the United States of America, Japan, and Pakistan, and the others were based in France, Holland, China, and Hong Kong. Four of these, including the Chartered Bank and Grindlays, had the bulk of their business in India. As a group, the exchange banks monopolized foreign trade financing. While the Indian private banks could in principle enter this market, they could not easily operate at the London end of the market. The majority of the clients of the exchange banks, on the other hand, for reasons of safety or easier communication, were foreigners themselves.

The three Presidency banks—the Bank of Bengal, Bank of Bombay, and Bank of Madras—were established between 1809 and 1843 with participation by the government in the capital and government control on management. Of these, the Bank of Bombay failed in 1868, shortly after the cotton boom of Bombay. But a bank of the same name was started again. These banks performed five key functions: They held the government's cash balances, issued (on a limited scale) and circulated currency notes, discounted bills and securities, advanced short-term working capital credit to private business, and accepted deposits from the public. Being partly the government's banker, the Presidency banks had to operate under restrictions. They could not deal in foreign exchange, which was considered a risky business. And, following Anglo-Saxon tradition, they did not supply long-term loans. They did, however, accept securities against advances and stimulate the capital market in this indirect way. In 1876, all three came under the Presidency Banks Act. In 1921, they were amalgamated to form the Imperial Bank of India. In 1947, the Imperial Bank was nationalized and renamed State Bank of India.

The main clients of the Presidency banks were businesses connected with European enterprise and that small segment of Indian enterprise that the Europeans understood or could easily communicate with. Thus, the largest of the shroffs, the indigenous bankers, were also clients of the Presidency banks. The Presidency banks were not easily persuaded to lend money to small- or medium-scale

Indian businesses. Increasingly in this period, joint-stock banks were started by Indians to meet that need.

The agency houses performed some banking services for the East India Company, private merchants, and the public. The 1830s and the 1840s commodity price crashes finished them off. A second banking boom occurred in Bombay in the 1860s, encouraged by cotton speculation. Again, most of the banks then started later went into liquidation. A third boom occurred with the spread of the spirit of swadeshi (nationalistic self-reliance) from 1906. The centre of this boom was Calcutta. But Indian banks elsewhere also profited from the nationalistic wave. In 1913–14, a few major bankruptcies led to a widespread crash of these banks. In the interwar period, the main episode of banking panic occurred in 1923.

In this awkward way, Indian joint-stock banks expanded and the habit of banking spread among urban households. Until the end of World War I, deposits held at the Presidency banks exceeded those held in the Indian joint-stock banks. After that, growth of deposits in Indian joint-stock banks was far more rapid, despite periodic panics. In 1947, the Indian banks together formed the largest segment in modern banking (Table 7.2).

Indian banks grew despite the risks because of the limited reach of the Presidency banks, the conservative policy of the latter, and

Table 7.2 Growth of deposits (in Rs billion)

	Imperial Bank	Exchange banks	Indian joint stock banks
1870	1.19	0.05	0.01
1880	1.14	0.34	0.06
1890	0.71	0.75	0.21
1900	1.57	1.05	0.81
1910	3.65	2.82	2.56
1920	8.70	7.48	7.11
1930	8.40	6.81	6.83
1939	7.88	7.51	9.81

Source: Reserve Bank of India, Banking and Monetary Statistics of India (Bombay: Reserve Bank of India Press, 1954).

the offer of high incentives by the Indian banks. The Presidency banks were slow to expand branches. They had almost no presence in smaller towns. Many such towns had considerable demand for credit due to agricultural trade. The Indian banks were a diverse group. At the top of the hierarchy were a set of relatively more sound and stable banks (mainly Allahabad Bank, Bank of Baroda, Bank of India, Punjab National Bank, and Central Bank of India). These were established in the larger towns and arose from existing business partnerships between large trading and industrial houses. All members of the set survive today as nationalized banks (two were recently merged with other banks). A group of Europeans started the Allahabad Bank in 1864. It functioned much like the other large Indian joint-stock banks. The Bank of Baroda was started in 1908 by the Maharaja of Baroda, Sayajirao Gaekwad, in close collaboration with the leading shroff houses of Baroda. The family of David Sassoon led the establishment of the Bank of India in 1906, with contributions to share capital from the leading Parsi, Gujarati, and Bohra houses of Bombay. The Central Bank was established in 1911 by a Parsi house and merged with the Tata banking business in the 1920s. A group of traditional business houses based in Lahore started the Punjab National Bank (1895), the only one of the set that claimed to be a nationalistic enterprise. To this list should be added the Canara Bank, set up by lawyers of the Goud Saraswat community, who had a tradition of community banking.[15]

All of these banks survived the panics. The ability of these banks to weather the risks of commerce owed to prudent management, the deep pockets of some of the main promoters, and a conservative investment profile. They held an unusually large proportion of assets in the form of government securities and functioned in this respect much like the Presidency banks. Further, almost all of these banks confined their operations to urban and larger clientele,

[15] The Central Bank of India, *Silver Jubilee Number* (Bombay, publisher unknown, 1935); Dwijendra Tripathi and Priti Misra, *Towards a New Frontier: History of the Bank of Baroda 1908–1983* (Delhi: Manohar, 1985); M.V. Kamath, *A Banking Odyssey: The Story of Canara Bank* (Delhi: Konark, 2006).

again like the Presidency banks. They had few branches and a few chosen clients.

On another end, lesser-known and informal firms sponsored many of the Indian banks. While they were less conservative about their clients, they had neither the brand name of the Presidency banks nor the image of high security that the government backing gave the latter. Therefore, they felt that they needed to offer high incentives to attract deposits and borrowers. Furthermore, the absence of an explicit regulatory system made them take undue risks. Insider lending to doubtful clients was common. 'Many of them avowedly exist to serve the interests of particular castes and communities.'[16] Loans made out to relations and kin had a high chance of turning bad because it was often difficult to punish or discipline relatives and friends. Thus, these banks suffered from under-capitalization, inexperience, insider lending, high chance of swindles, adverse selection, and the absence of a lender of last resort.

Many swadeshi or nationalistic banks started between 1906 and 1913. They had small paid-up capital, boards of directors predominated by lawyers, and management by persons without any experience or knowledge of banking. They secured deposits by offering high rates and lent on second-rate securities to risk-taking businesses. Unlike the Presidency banks, the swadeshi banks did not necessarily restrict themselves to working capital. While their reserves were small, the absence of a lender of last resort pushed even slightly troubled banks quickly into liquidation during episodes of panic. These dynamics of instability were in evidence on several occasions between 1913 and 1946.

The idea of a central bank had a long pre-history. Warren Hastings proposed it in 1773. The goals were to have a government's banker, develop a competitor for the shroffs, on whose help the Company still relied heavily, and resolve the chaos that arose from several currencies in circulation. A bank did materialize from this proposal. But despite making some profits in the few years when it had been at work, it was closed possibly due to conflicts within the Company.

[16] Muranjan, *Modern Banking*, 169.

Subsequently, the Presidency banks performed the role of a banker to the government.

There are four functions that a central bank is expected to perform: to be the banker to the government, banker to other banks, to regulate currency and money supply, and manage foreign exchange. The Presidency banks (and the Imperial Bank of India after 1921) served only the first of these. Also, they functioned as commercial banks. They did become bankers to other banks voluntarily. That is, they received deposits from other major banks, but not by force of law. Moreover, they were neither obliged nor expected to lend to other banks in times of crisis. The Presidency banks had little or no role in meeting the third and fourth objectives. Until the establishment of the Reserve Bank of India, the finance department of the government looked after the third objective.

In the 1860s, the proposal briefly revived. The then viceroy, John Lawrence, discarded it. His minute on the subject revealed that the government was not willing to accept the idea of a monetary authority independent of its influence. The proposal revived in the course of the 1898 currency reform committee. The Royal Commission on Indian Finance and Currency (1914) invited J.M. Keynes and Ernest Cable to write a proposal for a central bank. Keynes was known to be in favour of the idea. The government, however, remained inert and distracted by the war and the exchange controversy (Chapter 9). Besides, the idea of an independent monetary authority was still an anathema to many.

The idea finally came into its own at the 1926 currency commission and the 1931 Indian Central Banking Enquiry Committee. Reports of both committees officially endorsed it and recorded a strong recommendation for it from influential witnesses. One of them was Sir Montagu Norman, the then governor of the Bank of England. When the Reserve Bank finally started, one of its first tasks was to integrate what seemed to be a fragmented and chaotic banking system. This process could not happen suddenly, nor was it done completely. Rather, it was an attempt consisting of a series of steps, some of which were forced by circumstances such as further banking panics.

Despite the fluctuations and limited functions, banking did develop in India. Bank deposits as a proportion of GDP increased from less than 1 per cent in 1870 to 12 per cent in 1935. There is some sign that throughout colonial India, interest rates tended to fall during the time span covered by this book. The nominal Bank of Bengal bank rate was 7 per cent in 1857. The Imperial Bank of India's bank rate hovered between 5 and 6 per cent on average in the 1930s. The decline was a steady one and, excluding the price depression of the 1930s, would suggest a fall in real interest rates. The growth of formal banking, therefore, was a positive development. After Independence (1947), with the further growth of private corporate banks, the cost of short-term secured borrowing fell to 4–5 per cent (1950s).

There is little evidence, however, that the cost of long-term capital fell in response to these changes. Most ordinary loans advanced by bankers, whether formal or informal, were trade loans. Long-term capital remained expensive. Capital was always costly in India. In the tropical monsoon climate, agricultural operations were highly seasonal. Interest rates went up to extraordinarily high levels in a few months of the year. The attraction of making a quick buck by lending short term in the busy season was so great that little money was on offer to long-term borrowers. Stock markets, banks, and cooperatives eased the situation only slightly.[17]

Corporate banks were reluctant to lend to clients whom they did not know enough, which meant that many European banks did not easily do business with Indian clients. The banks insisted on good-quality securities, which none but the richest Indian firms could offer. The awkward relationship between European banks and Indian firms need not be seen in racial terms. The mainly European Bank of Bengal did a lot of business with Indians and discounted their bills. But it also discriminated between these bills on the degree of trust they could place on these. Such discrimination came from information asymmetry. Bankers did not know enough about their potential

[17] Tirthankar Roy, 'Monsoon and the Market for Money in Late Colonial India', *Enterprise and Society* 17, no. 2 (2016): 324–57.

clients. Asymmetric information was also present in the business of the exchange banks for the same reason. And in the business of the Indian joint-stock banks, preference for insider lending meant that clients who were not part of the inner circle of friends and relations had little chance of getting a good service.

Finally, a short description of the insurance business is in order.

INSURANCE

The history of the insurance business is significant for several reasons. It started early. The Calcutta agency houses introduced it in the late eighteenth century. They supplied mainly marine insurance. The Indian business enterprise of Calcutta was interested in insurance in this early phase. While the agency houses collapsed, the insurance business survived and continued to draw new entries. Insurance was also the originator of the managing agency system.

Commercial life insurance began in 1818 with the Oriental Life Assurance Co. of Calcutta (no relation of the company of the same name today). In 1823, the Bombay Life Assurance Company and, in 1829, the Madras Equitable Company formed. The idea of life insurance had come from London. In a country with low life expectancy, one would expect insurance to become instantly popular, if expensive. On the contrary, it remained confined mainly to the small resident European population. The reason was the absence of reliable mortality tables for Indians. It took nearly half a century more for Indian insurance providers to treat Indian lives as equivalent to the European ones. The Bombay Mutual Life Assurance Company was the pioneer in this respect.

From a small base, the total stock of policy values increased rapidly after the 1870s. Insurance was one business more or less unaffected by the Great Depression. Per capita policy value increased from about Rs 0.37 in 1901 to Rs 7.81 in 1941. But both coverage and average value were fractions of those of any developed country of that time. Other than its limited reach, a major problem of the business was the high mortality of companies rather than their clients. These problems were similar to those of the banking sector and were probably related.

***

The disapproving tone of the Marxist historians, who think that European capitalists in mines and plantations grew rich by brutally exploiting helpless Indian labourers, obscures both the entrepreneurship involved in these businesses as well as the many-sided experience of the labourers. These activities had significant positive spillovers. They generated incomes for themselves and the regional economies, contributed to the working of a modern global economy, and offered higher wage and food security to a million people directly employed by them. While migrant labour in plantations worked in a hierarchical environment, they came from backgrounds that had been usually more insecure and possibly more exploitative. These jobs hired many agricultural labourers, who faced little chance of finding a decent job anywhere.

Banking and insurance grew rapidly after 1870. This growth was not rooted in the old banking tradition. Rather, like mines, plantations, and a part of industry, it originated mainly in European enterprise and partly in Indian mercantile enterprise, both serving the massive rise in commodity trade from the nineteenth century. The growth occurred in a condition of pervasive capital scarcity, poor regulation, and opaque business communities. Inevitably, capital transacted in a manner that left much scope for secrecy and opportunism. While banks induced a fall in interest rates and a rise in deposit–income ratio, the scale of these changes was limited. A dualistic structure of banks, with good banks and good clients on one side and dubious banks and risky or unscrupulous clients on another, kept the risks of banking panics persistently high.

Chapters 4 to 7 have described production and occupations in which the role of infrastructure has been present throughout. Chapter 8 turns to this subject.

8

Infrastructure

At Independence in 1947, the visible legacy of colonial rule in South Asia was the modern infrastructure that the regime had left behind—the ports, canals, the telegraph, sanitation and medical care, urban waterworks, universities, postal system, courts of law, railways, meteorological office, statistical systems, and scientific research laboratories. All of it involved British knowhow, adapted to the Indian environment with Indian help, and much of it was built to assist governance. Once built, such assets did not serve only the empire but also helped private enterprise and ordinary people lead better lives. Railways brought down the very high trade costs of earlier times and helped trade, while also aiding famine relief and migration of people from the village to factories and plantations.

There was no one motivation that led to the creation of these assets. A development policy of which infrastructure was a part did not exist. Rather, military, commercial, and fiscal motivations all combined their influence on infrastructure investment. The absence of an explicit developmental goal imposed unevenness in the way these assets were created. There were huge regional inequalities in the supply of these goods. Princely states were in poorer, drier, and hillier areas than were most British Indian districts and lagged in railway construction. Nor was there one way of funding these assets. Private investors built the railways; the state guaranteed a return to capital. Canals and roads were a state investment. Administration differed too. Initially, the military departments built and managed some of these assets (Chapter 2). Over time, administrative departments took over the task. A division of labour evolved. The provinces looked after roads, schools, and healthcare; the federal government looked after the railways.

Despite this apparent disorder, a few principles stood out. One of these was that the state must invest in canal irrigation if it were to avoid the recurrent famines happening. This imperative came from prevailing climatic conditions, the notion that failure of rains for part of the year could create conditions that caused mass deaths. A second general principle concerned the railways. India was a composition of many types of geographies, and unless a railway system integrated these geographies, there was little hope for turning India into either a market for British goods or a supplier of food and material aboard. Trade was a priority for the empire.

In the interwar period, pushed by the nationalist movement and public opinion, the state adopted economic and social development as explicit goals. There was now more emphasis on schools and hospitals. However, this turn came at a time when the state was running out of money. In this time, some of the princely states forged ahead with schools and hospitals.

How did all such activity start?

THE IMPETUS

In the nineteenth century, the main focus of productive investment by the state was irrigation, railways, roads, and the telegraph. The pre-existing transport infrastructure of India was backward, given the size and geographical diversity of the land. For example, the road system that the Company had inherited was primitive. The problem of moving goods in bulk worried business interests and moving troops concerned the government. The knowledge and the capital to build railways or the telegraph were more cheaply available to India than other regions because Britain led in the technology and capital export. There was a growing view that the famines in the nineteenth century could be averted with more irrigation and more railways to distribute food from surplus to deficit regions.

The government, however, had limited financial capacity. It needed the intervention of a few people to turn infrastructure into a priority. One of these campaigners was Lord Dalhousie (James Broun-Ramsay), who in his dual capacity as the governor-general of India and governor of Bengal between 1848 and 1856 and from the belief that colonialism had a modernizing mission, was influential. A decade earlier, the British intellectual Thomas Macaulay had served Indian administration (1834–8) and set out a manifesto of Indian development, which made the case that Britain had a duty to impart useful knowledge to India. Dalhousie established the Public Works Department (1854) and initiated moves to set up a railway and a telegraph system. His successor Charles Canning (1856–62) had to pick up the bill but continued the drive. Charles Wood, who served as president of the Board of Control (1853–5) and as secretary of state (1859–66), simplified the administrative process in building infrastructure and created the Education Despatch, which set out the plan for grants-in-aid schools and three universities in India. The policy of state aid outlined in the document was to remain in force for the next several decades. Though subsequent developments belied Wood's hopes for primary education, a foundation for university education emerged.[1]

By the interwar period, the drive to create physical infrastructure had spent itself due to fiscal pressure, whereas popular demand for education increased. Irrigation was the original driver.

IRRIGATION

The Famine Commission enquiries from 1876 made it a canon that India, thanks to its tropical monsoon climate that made the region

---

[1] David J. Howlett, 'Ramsay, James Andrew Broun, first marquess of Dalhousie (1812–1860)', *Oxford Dictionary of National Biography*, 2004. Available at http://www.oxforddnb.com/index/101023088, accessed 12 May 2020; Thomas R. Metcalf, 'Canning, Charles John, Earl Canning (1812–1862)', *Oxford Dictionary of National Biography*, 2004. Available at http://www.oxforddnb.com/index/101004554, accessed; R.J. Moore, *Sir Charles Wood's Indian Policy 1853–66* (Manchester: Manchester University Press, 1966).

very hot and the rainy season very short, suffered from an acute seasonal scarcity of water, and that any serious effort to raise production and secure the welfare of the population would have to start with projects that delivered a reliable supply of water. In the end, the government could not do a lot in this direction, partly because of funds constraint and partly because its engineering knowledge was just enough to make use of rivers that had plentiful supply of water throughout the year and to draw canals out of these. The knowledge could not extend to providing water where water was absolutely scarce. Still, the effort was substantial. The acreage irrigated as percentage of cropped area increased from 5 or 6 per cent in the early nineteenth century to 22 per cent in 1938. Government canals irrigated about 60 per cent of the addition to irrigated area.

Continuing from where the story ended in Chapter 2, major new irrigation projects from the late nineteenth century were canals taken from Himalayan rivers (in Punjab, Sind, and UP), and weirs constructed on major rivers (South India). The Punjab canals spread water over formerly water-scarce territories, in contrast with canals in South India that mainly redistributed monsoon water and with canals in the UP that added surface water in a region well-endowed in groundwater. Among the largest projects undertaken were the Krishna and Godavari delta systems (1868) together serving close to a million hectares, the Western Jumna (Yamuna) Canal system (1892, half a million hectares), Sirhind canal (1882, one million hectares), Cauvery delta system (1889, 425,000 hectares), Upper and Lower Ganges canals (1854–78, 1.3 million hectares), and Sarda canal (1926, about half a million hectares). Smaller works that had considerable localized impact included the Sone canal (1879), the Nira valley system (1938), the Mettur project (1934), and the Upper Bari Doab canal (1879).

The Punjab canals led to the colonization of vast areas of wastes and pastures by migrant cultivators. Among the earliest canals constructed was the Bari Doab (1850–60). This canal irrigated the land between the rivers Beas and Ravi. The canal was meant to give employment to disbanded Sikh soldiers. Sirhind Canal (1869–87) was constructed on the left bank of the Sutlej, the headworks located at Ropar. The canal irrigated lands in Ferozepur and Ludhiana and the princely states of Jind, Patiala, and Nabha. The canal was a major source of prosperity for Ludhiana town. The Western Jumna Canal was a restored older work, which once irrigated lands around Karnal and Delhi. The Chenab Canal (operational in 1887) was constructed to irrigate the arid Barr region located in the Rechna Doab between the Chenab and Ravi Rivers. The Chenab Colony, among the most successful settlements, was formed out of the three adjacent districts of Gujranwala, Jhang, and Montgomery in 1892 and contained in 1901 a population of eight hundred thousand people. The canal irrigated an area of more than 20 million acres. The principal town in the Chenab colony was Lyallpur, named after Charles James Lyall, lieutenant-governor of Punjab in 1887–92 (see Chapter 4 on the canal colonies).

Under the Company, the engineering department of the army looked after canal construction. Canals were later handed over to the Public Works Department. For a few years after the Mutiny, the department was busy with reconstruction. A discussion soon started on its long-term goals. Irrigation was going to remain one of the goals. The first statement of an irrigation policy emerged through a series of official and semi-official writings. These made a distinction between those works built for purely administrative or famine relief purposes (later named 'protective' works) and those built to increase agricultural production (later called 'productive' works). The former class need not yield an income, though they might save the government money that would have to be spent on famine relief if a famine occurred. The latter class could be commercially profitable for the government. That irrigation works could be remunerative in both these senses, as money saved and money made, had already been demonstrated by several major works. For works that were too costly to be financed by the current revenue of the government, and which therefore needed raising loans in London, the projects must yield at least the interest on these loans.

What did this yield consist of? Irrigation can raise the productivity of land and, therefore, the income of the cultivators. The water that raised incomes was charged at a certain rate paid out of that income. This tax accrued to the Public Works Department and was a part of the rate of return on capital invested in irrigation projects. However, for such projects that had come up much before the department itself, no proper calculation of increased income or rate of return was possible. On the other hand, increased income from a plot of land also increased the rental value of that land. Land revenue was supposed to reflect the rental value. In areas not permanently settled, the government could realize this value. In ryotwari areas, irrigated land was charged higher land revenue. Again, no exact calculation was possible of how much the rental value of land would increase due to irrigation. Nevertheless, from time to time, land revenue on account of irrigation was estimated as the indirect return on irrigation projects.

The question of what monetary returns the irrigation schemes generated for the government was, thus, shrouded in speculation. The calculated rates of return varied widely between projects and regions. They also varied depending on whether the revenue generated and interest payments formed parts of the calculations. For the government to spend money on large projects with doubtful return was never a favourite option of those who decided Indian policy in London. In 1878, the 'Select Committee on East India—Public Works' stated that large-scale irrigation projects were, by and large, a failure both commercially and in preventing famines. Almost at the same time, the 1880 Famine Commission gave a more informed and balanced picture of irrigation projects. The commission concluded that irrigation projects were on balance profitable for the government, yielding about 6 per cent on capital, but only after the land revenue collected was considered.

Major works in Madras, on the Godavari and Cauvery deltas, yielded good returns. Works in Sind were also profitable. The overall return on works in North India was positive but not large. Ill-conceived projects in Bengal, Orissa, and Deccan yielded negative returns. Private companies first built some of these projects with the rates of return guaranteed by the government, similar to the agreement for railway construction. The government later purchased them at unjustifiably high prices. Generally, in irrigation policy, there was a powerful opinion against private enterprise. Involving the private sector in the water supply might complicate the question of property rights in water.

Partly at least, variability in the rate of return reflected the type of projects and, in turn, the topography of different regions. If the Company's works in southern India were generally well-paying, one of the biggest new projects taken up in northern India, the Ganges Canal, was running at a loss in the 1860s. The main reason behind this difference was the topography of Madras, which allowed the construction of simple, low-cost, low-height barrages on shallow riverbeds to irrigate large areas. The canals in such a system were suitable for navigation during lean seasons. In northern India, on the other hand, irrigation over a large area required extensive masonry work and many more bridges. And canal navigation was not a source of revenue as road traffic was already quite developed in the region.

The non-monetary returns of irrigation projects, such as famine relief or increased prosperity for cultivators, were also mixed. The canal-irrigated area as a percentage of cropped area was not too different between Madras and Punjab in 1900. Yet, Madras suffered far more from famines. Canals, as such, did not prevent water scarcity in the dry months if the region suffered from a general shortage of rain. In other words, the natural supply of water shaped the capacity of canals to prevent famines. In several parts of the canal-served agrarian countryside, there were dramatic improvements in the wealth and income of the people. But the human and economic costs of these extensive projects were also large. These costs occurred due to a persistent engineering defect, namely poor drainage of excess water. The consequences in North India were saline deposits in certain parts and an increase in malaria in others. The authorities knew that these costs were present but felt that the overall return justified them.

The net effect of canal irrigation, therefore, is controversial. Canals turned near-desert wastelands in Sind and Punjab into cultivable land, with huge benefits for the peasants and landlords in these regions. But these were initially water-scarce regions. The Ganges–Jamuna Doab in UP was different. It was a flat plain hemmed in by major rivers and had a high water table already exploited through wells. In one view, the environmental effects of canals in this region were generally bad. Canals blocked natural drainage routes and caused waterlogging. The excess saturation led to saline deposits,

called *reh*, which made large tracts less fertile and increased the incidence of malaria. The canals encouraged over-cropping and attracted
the formerly pastoral groups to cultivate. As a result, the quality of
livestock declined. Cash requirements to pay for the use of canals,
enhanced rentals, and changes in composition of crops contributed
to increasing rural inequality. While environmental distortions did
exist, the effects of canals on private profitability are another matter.
In another reading of the evidence, canals had significant benefits.
Canals enabled rise in yield per acre, reduced the impact of harvest
fluctuations, raised average living standards, and encouraged limited
industrialization, especially sugar refining.[2]

RAILWAYS

Until the mid-nineteenth century, the common systems of long-distance transport of cargo were pack animals and small sailing vessels
on navigable rivers. The semi-nomadic Banjaras drove large trains of
pack animals on roads that connected western and southern India
with eastern and northern India. In the Gangetic plains, the rivers
provided a major means of long-distance commodity trade. For
short-distance trade and travel, the common means of transportation were palanquins, small river-crafts, and bullock carts. The older
systems of long-distance trade required a lot of labour and time. The
railways destroyed them without much resistance. In contrast with
the railways, the government paid less attention to short-distance
travel, so that in that sphere, boats, carts, and palanquins survived
until well after 1947.

In the 1840s, there was a vigorous campaign for railways by
the City of London, which was the principal financier of railways
in Britain, and by business communities in London, Liverpool,
Calcutta, Bombay, and Madras. In 1849, the Cabinet, the Company,

[2] Elizabeth Whitcombe, 'Irrigation,' in *CEHI 2*, eds Dharma Kumar
and Meghnad Desai (Cambridge: Cambridge University Press, 1983),
677–736; and Ian Stone, *Canal Irrigation in British India* (Cambridge:
Cambridge University Press, 1984), Ch. 1.

and the promoters agreed to establish two experimental lines, one connecting Bombay with the Deccan cotton zones and the other connecting Calcutta with the Burdwan coalfields. From the beginning, two principles prevailed. First, the railways would be constructed by private enterprise on a 99-year lease, with the Government of India having the option to purchase the lines after 25 years. And second, the government, from its budget, would guarantee a 5 per cent return on capital where a company failed to earn a minimum of 5 per cent return. In exchange, the government exercised supervisory and advisory powers on railway development and administration. Once the contract had been agreed, railway development began in earnest, with capital raised in Britain. Between 1853 and 1870, more than 4,000 miles of lines opened; between 1870 and 1883, 6,000 more were added; between 1883 and 1925, 15,000 miles of railway track came up (Table 8.1).

The principle of railway construction went through four stages: 1849 to 1869 saw only private enterprise; 1870–80 saw the accent shifting towards state enterprise; from 1881 to 1924, recourse was again had to private enterprise in management with state ownership;

Table 8.1   Selected railway statistics, 1860–1940

	1860	1880	1900	1920	1940
Total route miles	838	8,995	23,627	35,406	41,852
Route miles per 000 sq miles	0.53	5.69	14.94	22.39	25.96
Route miles per m persons	3.4	35.0	82.9	115.9	107.0
Passengers carried (m)	n.a.	48	166	524	604
Goods carried (m net tonnes)	n.a.	n.a.	n.a.	86	129
Employment in railways	16,789	154,108	338,041	727,184	1,046,843

Source: M.D. Morris and C.B. Dudley, 'Selected Railway Statistics for the Indian Subcontinent (India, Pakistan and Bangladesh), 1853– 1946–47', *Artha Vijnana* 17, no. 3 (1975): 187–298.

and from 1924 onwards, the state assumed ownership as well as control.

By the end of the first stage, Calcutta, Bombay, Madras, and Delhi had become interconnected by the 'broad-gauge' system (the Indian broad-gauge was 5 feet 6 inches wide). While the growth of the railways in terms of lines, freight carried, and passengers carried was impressive, in 1870, none of the lines earned 5 per cent return, except the East Indian Railway running the profitable Calcutta–Delhi line. It seemed that the railway companies did not try hard enough to earn profits, given the guarantee clause. In the last quarter of the nineteenth century, the fiscal burden became too heavy to bear due to the depreciation of the rupee and the rise in interest rates on government borrowing abroad to pay for guarantees. There was a proposal to purchase the railways, but the secretary of state in London preferred instead to renegotiate terms with the private companies while agreeing to direct state investment in future railway construction. The first major metre-gauge lines (3.33 feet wide) were a product of direct state investment. Several of these were constructed as famine relief works. One of these famine lines in central India was absorbed into the main railway route between Calcutta and Bombay in the 1880s (Figure 8.1).The new state railway lines were well constructed and potentially more profitable, but these became a fiscal burden at a time when India faced a famine (1876–8). Between 1879, when the 25-year period of exclusive private ownership ended, and 1924, the ownership of the railway companies was in public hands. The government paid off or guaranteed return to the old shareholders. However, management remained in the hands of the old companies, with the condition that the managers would not be able to undertake capital expenditure without consent of the government.

This dualistic system led to the undercapitalization of the railways. At the same time, there were perennial problems of inefficiency generated by the guarantee clause. The companies, right from the early days, charged high rates for a small volume of traffic and never felt the need to enter into price competition. Consequently, a great deal of the potential benefits of the railways remained unutilized. There were other problems, like a shortage of wagons, and in turn, persistent uncertainty about shipment dates. With public opinion in

Figure 8.1 Construction of the Bengal–Nagpur railway, 1890. Both good news (growing grain exports) and bad (famines) induced the state to encourage railway expansion, in this case, in the vast and poorly linked Deccan Plateau.

© Southern Methodist University

Britain and India turning against private management, railways came under full government ownership and control in 1924. The network had, by then, become one of the world's largest, and yet it had also failed, to some extent, to fulfil its potential to serve as a truly mass transportation system, because its density was still small in relation to the enormous area served.

Between 1860 and 1940, total route miles had increased from 838 to 41,852. Route miles per 1000 square mile increased from 0.5 to 26; route miles per million persons increased from 3 to 107. Passengers carried by the railways increased from 48 million in 1880 to 604 million in 1940. The railways had revolutionized the mobility of people and goods in India (see Table 8.1 for more data).

Through the nineteenth century, the railways replaced many forms of indigenous bulk transport, chiefly boats and bullock trains. The triumph of the railways over pack bullocks and boats did not happen suddenly. The railways were not necessarily cheaper than the boats in regions where the two plied side by side on relatively shorter routes, though the railways always saved a huge amount of time. In the first few years of its operation in northern India, the railways met with stiff competition from the Ganges boat operators They cut rates, which, together with the railways' policy of charging high rates for freights, enabled the boatmen to continue. By the 1880s, however, the railways had won.

The economic effects of the railways came in two types. First, the railways stimulated a variety of activities and livelihoods. Railway construction worldwide stimulated the engineering industry, financial markets, and labour markets. In India, the first effect was relatively weak until World War I. Until then, nearly all of the railway material came from Britain. The government had built railway workshops for repair and production of parts. But they were not heavily used. Coal mining was perhaps the only major example of the backward linkage of the railways. After the War, a progressive Indianization began to occur. The role of the railways as a major source of demand for the basic metal industries increased after that. The effect on the capital market was small since the major part of the capital came from London. The labour market effect was of greater importance. By 1947, the Indian railways were the largest employer in the organized sector, a distinction maintained today. And the railways facilitated internal labour migration.

Second, the railways greatly reduced the average transportation cost measured in money and time (Table 8.2). Import and export trades in real terms increased enormously as a result of this reduction. Because these costs became a smaller part of the price, the supply of goods now responded to narrower differences between local and world prices than before. Raw cotton and hide and skin exports quickly expanded owing to this. The railways also facilitated the integration of markets, evident from declining regional variability in prices of foodgrains.

If the railways were so beneficial for the economy, it might come as a surprise that Indian nationalists relentlessly criticized the railways.

Table 8.2 Average transportation charges (per maund[3] mile)

	Carriage capacity	1840s and 1850s	1870s	1900s
Pack bullock	2 mds	2.5 pies	NA	NA
Two-bullock cart	20 mds	1.0 pies	NA	1.75 pies
Four-bullock cart	40 mds	0.8 pies	NA	1.25 pies
River boat	100–1000 mds			
(upstream)		0.4 pies	NA	NA
(downstream)		0.25 pies	0.15 pies	NA
Steamboat	NA	0.65 pies	0.24 pies	NA
Railway train	3500–7500 mds	NA	0.35 pies	0.18 pies

Source: I. Derbyshire, 'Economic Change and the Railways in Northern India, 1860–1914', *MAS* 21, no. 3 (1987): 521–45.
Note: md stands for maund (37 kg).

One point of controversy is the railway guarantee, which imposed a net payment burden on the budget and contributed to what the nationalists call drain of resources. By enabling grain exports, railways increased the risk and intensity of famines in India, whereas British capital in trade and railway construction gained, they said.[4] In the 1970s and 1980s, research done by economists rehabilitated

[3] British Indian official metrology adopted existing Indian measures, defining the units uniformly across regions. The standard measure of weight (outside South India) was the maund. One maund was divided into 40 seers, and one seer was divided into 80 *tolas*, each tola being 180 troy grains. Each seer was then equivalent to 2.057 lbs and one maund 37 kgs. The earlier definitions of maund were quite different. In the seventeenth century, the *man-i-Akbari* of northern India was again divided into 40 seers, but the seer of Akbar was of 30 *dams*, dam being the copper coin, and weighed less. In eighteenth-century Bengal, both the Akbari maund (25 kgs) and the colonial maund (37 kgs) were in usage.

[4] Bipan Chandra, *The Rise and Growth of Economic Nationalism in India* (New Delhi: People's Publishing House, 1966), 190–3.

the case for net benefits. One of these works showed that in the dry Deccan Plateau, railways played a role in the disappearance of famines in the twentieth century.[5] Another work estimated the social savings that followed from the massive fall in costs of trade and found this of significant order.[6] After that, research on these aspects became dormant, as a new wave in famine historiography seemed to support the nationalist cause that the railways served British capital and disserved Indian welfare.

Recently, railway scholarship has flourished again. Economists have unearthed new statistical data and used these innovatively to answer questions about structural change in the colonial economy. Did the major field of public-private partnership in British India, railways, succeed as a management model?[7] Did the railways mitigate famines and increase market efficiency?[8] Did the railways integrate markets?[9] This research answers all of these questions with

---

[5] M.B. McAlpin, 'Famines, Epidemics, and Population Growth: The Case of India', *Journal of Interdisciplinary History* 14, no. 2 (1983): 351–66; M.B. McAlpin, 'Dearth, Famine, and Risk: The Changing Impact of Crop Failure in Western India, 1870–1920', *Journal of Economic History* 39, no. 1 (1979): 143–57.

[6] John Hurd, 'Railways and the Expansion of Markets in India, 1861–1921', *Explorations in Economic History* 12, no. 3 (1975): 263–88.

[7] Dan Bogart and Latika Chaudhary, 'Railways in Colonial India: An Economic Achievement?', in *A New Economic History of Colonial India*, eds Latika Chaudhary, Bishnupriya Gupta, Tirthankar Roy, and Anand V. Swamy (Abingdon and London: Routledge, 2016), 140–60.

[8] D. Donaldson, 'Railroads of the Raj: Estimating the Impact of Transportation Infrastructure' (NBER Working Paper No. 16487, NBER, Cambridge Mass., 2010); Robin Burgess and Dave Donaldson, 'Can Openness Mitigate the Effects of Weather Shocks? Evidence from India's Famine Era', *American Economic Review* 100, no. 2 (2010): 449–53. See also citations in Chapter 10.

[9] T. Andrabi and M. Kuehlwein, 'Railways and Price Convergence in British India', *Journal of Economic History* 70, no. 2 (2010): 351–77; and Roman Studer, 'India and the Great Divergence: Assessing the Efficiency of Grain Markets in Eighteenth- and Nineteenth-Century India', *Journal of Economic History* 68, no. 2 (2008): 393–437.

a positive. It collectively suggests that the railways did indeed have significant beneficial effect on market exchange and welfare.

ROADS AND INLAND WATERWAYS

A systematic history of roads and road transport is missing. From the little research available on the nature of long-distance trade before the British came to India, it is fair to conclude that good and safe roads were a scarce resource in precolonial and early colonial India. At least partly, the poor condition of the roads reflected limited engineering capability in bridging the numerous rivers. The Company restored and constructed some major roads for military purposes. But regular allocation of funds for roads did not begin until the 1830s.

Early nineteenth-century examples of travel and cargo transport illustrate well the huge cost of road carriage. 'There were no metalled roads,' writes one historian of the overland grain trade in the western Gangetic plains, 'and the only carriers were the Banjaras. That the movements of grains so carried were small we can see by the very considerable difference in prices ruling in adjoining districts.'[10] During an 1804 famine in the Doab, wheat sold in Aligarh at three times the price prevailing in Bareilly, less than a hundred miles away, and yet the cost of transporting wheat from Bareilly was so great and the quantities so small that the starving population of Aligarh had to wait for grain carried upstream by the Ganges from places 600 miles away. In the western Deccan, road transport not only took a long time but also involved wastages. The transport from the fields to the port in Bombay, a distance of 300 miles, took two to three months to cover in bullock carts. The bullocks of one cart had their muzzles buried in the cargo of the cart in front, eating the cotton. The cargo was adulterated with dirt and other mixtures to make up for the wastages. In the central Indian uplands, especially the region between Mandla and Jabalpur, which was strategic for its location

[10] T. Morison, 'The Instability of Prices in India before 1861', *Journal of Royal Statistical Society* 65 (1902): 513–25.

in the middle of India, dense forests and the fear of tigers made it impossible to travel for all but the largest parties.

In some of these cases, the railways solved the problem. Investment in roads in general, however, continued to be a relatively low priority. Road length grew at a much slower pace than the railways. In 1931, the length of metalled roads as a ratio of the population (1000 persons) was as low as 0.4 miles. For comparison, the ratio was above one in much of contemporary developing Asia (1.5 in Ceylon and 2.2 in Malaya). If the public works in colonial India were biased in favour of the railways at the cost of roads, this bias derived from three things. First, road construction was considered too costly given the terrain, the rivers, and the high repair costs due to the monsoons. Secondly, roads brought the government no monetary return whereas the railways did.[11] The government did not seriously explore involving private enterprise in constructing a network of tolled roads. Third, the lobbies such as the Lancashire mills that pushed the government into investment in modern transportation wanted cheaper long-distance bulk carriage. Possibly, the priorities of public investment in transportation increased inequalities between long-distance and local trade. There was increasing inequality also between places located on the railways and those located at a distance from them because the road link between places located far away from the railways and the nearest station continued to be poor.

In northern and eastern India, the navigable rivers had always been the means of transportation of cargo. River traffic was cheaper than roads and carried larger volumes per head. But the role of rivers in long-distance trade was more or less confined to the Gangetic plains. The main traffic here connected Bengal with western and northern India via Mirzapur. Cargo went along the Ganges up to Mirzapur and then was carried overland more or less along the current Bombay-Agra railway line down south. This traffic was of great antiquity. It is known to have declined in the nineteenth century in competition with the railways.

[11] Vera Anstey, *The Economic Development of India*, 3rd ed. (London: Longmans Green, 1949), 129.

In one sphere, however, river transportation ruled unchallenged until 1947, and that was the traffic between Bengal and Assam. Steamboats on the Brahmaputra were the crucial means of transporting tea and garden workers. In the preceding century, railway links developed, but these remained 'feeders' to the river highway. It was only after the Partition in 1947 that a direct rail connection opened (the 'Assam link' in 1949) between Calcutta and Gauhati. Generally speaking, in eastern Bengal and Assam, a transportation system developed in which rail, road, and boats served each other rather than competing.

PORTS

The ports that carried the bulk of the foreign trade in the colonial period were new sites where railways and modern harbours converged, for example, Bombay, Madras, Calcutta, Karachi, and Rangoon. Each served as an export outlet for the products of a vast hinterland. The two western Indian ports enhanced their trade manifold with the American Civil War (1861–5) and the opening of the Suez Canal (1869). After that, Calcutta and Bombay also grew to become industrial centres. World War I, while upsetting private businesses through these ports, emphasized their military importance. The Bombay docks saw a modernization drive in the early interwar period.

These modern hubs of maritime trade did not begin with a well-developed infrastructure. Indeed, their nineteenth-century history demonstrates the great indifference of the local government, the public works, and even the merchant marine towards infrastructure. Even as maritime traffic in Calcutta increased fourfold between 1833 and 1863, the port lacked all-weather and deep-water docks with up-to-date systems of loading and discharging ships, that is, wharves, jetties, landing stages, and steam or hydraulic cranes. The look of the harbour had not changed since the eighteenth century. Much of the harder work was done manually with the help of low-wage workers. This state of things received a rude jolt in the devastating 1864 cyclone in Calcutta when ships were torn from their mooring and tossed around in the floodwaters like toys before their wrecks parked

in the heart of the European districts of the city. A few months after
the 1864 cyclone, the furious merchants of Calcutta issued a report
highly critical of the port, and serious efforts to build a modern dock
began only after this shock.[12]

POSTS AND TELEGRAPH

The foundations for a government postal system were in place
before 1858. But it became a widely used utility only in the late
nineteenth century. The process was led partly by the opening of
post offices in semi-rural areas. More than that factor, it was driven
by the demand for the services of the post office. Migration and
money orders, for example, were closely interdependent. In safety,
cost, and wide reach, nothing like the postal money order existed
in pre-British periods for the remittance of individual savings
within India. As a recent study of postal money orders has shown,
in the first decade of its operation (1880–90), the business grew
by almost 20 per cent per year and continued to grow at a brisk
rate. The post office was not altogether comfortable with having
to handle such large sums of money, but the service was just too
crucial for the enormous numbers that were leaving home for work
elsewhere. Money orders were a business for the post office. For
the majority of migrants, who were poor wage earners, they were
a 'lifeline'.[13]

Already in 1849, the Company had decided to construct a telegraph system along with the railways beside the railway lines. The
telegraph became an urgent necessity on account of tensions on
India's western frontier (the Afghan war) and the eastern frontier
(the impending war with Burma). The first line between Calcutta
and Diamond Harbour opened in 1851 and was immediately used

[12] Tirthankar Roy, 'State, Society and Market in the aftermath of
Natural Disasters in Colonial India: A Preliminary Exploration', *IESHR* 45,
no. 2 (2008): 261–94.

[13] Chinmay Tumbe, 'Towards Financial Inclusion: The Post Office
of India as a Financial Institution, 1880–2010', *IESHR* 52, no. 4 (2015):
409–37.

to send shipping news from the coasts to Calcutta. The major lines were completed before 1855. The remarkable speed owed to strategic needs and Lord Dalhousie's interest in the scheme.

The telegraph was a private enterprise in England and America and a state enterprise in continental Europe. In India, it turned out to be a state enterprise for military reasons, despite Dalhousie's general aversion to state monopolies. By 1857, the telegraph had shown itself to be an indispensable military tool in several conflicts, rebellions, and wars of annexation that distinguished Dalhousie's reign. Consequently, the mutineers saw it as a symbol of evil in 1857. With a vengeance, they destroyed telegraph establishments wherever they could and, to their detriment, never used it to communicate amongst themselves. As they began to retreat, the restored telegraph lines became powerful tools of combat in the hands of the government troops. With this lesson behind it, the beginning of Crown rule saw a massive expansion of the telegraph system both within the country and between India and Europe. From then onwards, the economic and private uses of the telegraphs began to overwhelm strategic needs, leading to rapid growth in the usage of the system (Table 8.3).

Table 8.3   Selected statistics of the posts and telegraph, 1858–1938

	1858	1891	1921	1938–9
1. Number of letters, newspapers, packets, parcels received (m)	n.a.	347	1422	1241
2. Inland money orders paid (Rs m)	n.a.	164	789	808
3. Paid telegraphic messages sent (value in Rs m)				
Government	0.20	1.45	2.97	1.63
Private	0.18	2.70	17.50	14.40
Foreign	–	1.54	5.87	3.85
Total	0.38	5.69	26.34	19.88

Source: India, *Statistical Abstracts for British India* (London: HMSO or Calcutta: Government Press, 1881–82 to 1926–27, 1930–31 to 1939–40).
Note: The telegraph data on the last column relate to 1936–7.

POWER

Electricity generation in colonial India saw significant private–public coexistence and cooperation. (After 1947, by contrast, the system was almost completely nationalized.) The first proposal for a private firm to produce electricity for Calcutta city came in 1891. In the next 10 years, legislation laid down the basic framework of regulation. Electricity was first introduced in 1897 by a small firm in the Darjeeling Municipality, utilizing a mountain stream. Two years later, the Calcutta Electric Supply Corporation Ltd started producing electricity with steam power. The gradual expansion of street lighting, factory lighting, electric tramways, and, finally, household connections changed the meaning of urban living and increased the inequality between the city and the countryside.[14]

Two other large hydroelectric projects came up before World War I: The Sivasamudram on the Cauvery erected by the Mysore government and the Khopoli plant of Tata Electric Power. The former supplied power to the Kolar gold mines and the latter to Bombay city. The report of the Indian Industrial Commission (1918) laid great emphasis on the need for organized exploitation of natural resources, including hydroelectric power. However, efforts in this direction had to wait until the mid-1920s, when the provinces recovered from the initial trauma of dyarchy—provinces had elected governments but limited autonomy—and pursued some of their now exclusive duties like electricity generation. In the interwar period, a large number of hydroelectric and thermal power units started, many of these in the territories of the princely states. In 1947, the installed capacity stood at 1.7 million kW.

LAW AND JUSTICE

Chapter 2 presents a general outline of the development of property and contract law. Whereas in both property law and commercial law, promotion of market exchange was a distant goal, in the

[14] Suvobrata Sarkar, 'Domesticating Electric Power: Growth of Industry, Utilities and Research in Colonial Calcutta', *IESHR* 52, no. 3 (2015): 357–89.

former sphere, a complicated legal system emerged that, in fact, obstructed transactions in assets like land. In commercial law, the state was more open to westernization. In the second half of the nineteenth century, legislation in these areas extended to companies, negotiable instruments, trusts, transfer of property, promissory notes, evidence, wills and probates, and specific relief, all of which were codified in one major thrust that took place between 1870 and 1890 and all of which drew upon English, rather than Indian, precedence. In agricultural land, a series of tenancy and debt laws restricted the mortgage market and obstructed land transfers. Property rights over land and other assets continued to be shaped by custom or the understanding of custom, which at times bogged the judiciary in conflicting interpretations and claims over what a valid custom was.

As Chapter 2 showed, the provincial judicature in the early nineteenth century consisted of a hierarchy of courts that practised a mixture of Indian and English law, whereas, in the Presidency towns, the Supreme Courts practised English law. From 1862, the tiered court system of the pre-Mutiny era ended and a unified system of courts emerged. The system of provincial and Presidency town courts merged. High courts were established in the three Presidency towns. Between 1886 and 1919, high courts appeared in Allahabad, Patna, and Lahore. The segmentation in judicature came to an end, and not surprisingly, segmentation in law between English and Indian traditions became exposed to keener criticism and more frequent disputation.

From the early days of the new regime, *vakils* were admitted into practice in the high courts, thus greatly enhancing the prestige of Indian lawyers.[15] The legal profession came into its own with this move. Legal practice from then onwards saw the entry of the best minds into the profession. Formal equality between Indian and European lawyers existed. Influential voices such as that of Justice

---

[15] A vakil was an attorney or agent. Before the British Indian courts, the vakil was usually an agent negotiating in business as well as political disputes that involved wealthy parties. In the courts system, the term referred to the lawyers.

E.J. Trevelyan helped achieve this equality. The Indian Bar Councils Act of 1926 created a system for regulating the conduct and quality of the legal agents. Legal education expanded in the last 30 years of colonial rule. Law students in universities numbered about 3,000 in 1911 and 9,000 in 1949. But the supply was insufficient. Pending cases piled up in the high courts. No wonder legal fees remained high and, with luminaries like Motilal Nehru, C.R. Das, or Pherozeshah Mehta, ran into hundreds of thousands of rupees per month.

Looking at the evolution as a whole, spanning both Company and Crown rule, we observe the creation of a system that at first tried and later slowly retreated from a dualist ideal where one set of laws would apply to the Europeans and another to the Indians. But problems remained or were created. Even as the imperial administration overall favoured westernization in law, the desire to preserve Indian custom for political reasons had many adherents. In Punjab, for example, there was a return to consolidation of custom. In land and property, the drive to preserve custom was stronger than in commercial law. That drive created new types of contest over what custom was and whether custom should prevail over equity. Above all, while the system improved and modernized its content, the growth of the judicial infrastructure was falling rapidly behind population growth, leading to a huge backlog of cases when India became independent.

EDUCATION

Continuing from Chapter 2, while the indigenous school education began to become extinct, the scale of the new state-sponsored system seemed to recruit relatively few students. Students of all levels as a proportion of total population increased from 1.3 per cent in 1891 to 3.7 per cent in 1931, whereas the proportion of persons of school-going age in total population was about 40 per cent in these dates. Forty per cent enrolment was a big improvement from the near-zero (Punjab), 8 (Bengal), 17 (Bombay), and 25 (Madras) that prevailed between 1825 and 1840 (see Chapter 2). But it was small relative to international standards. Only a fifth of the students who started school reached secondary levels.

Why was mass literacy so slow to develop in British India? One obvious constraint derived from the poverty of the state. The government did not have the money to build a mass education system that could accommodate 100 million children in 1931. Primary education was left to the local authorities and provinces, which were even more underfunded. Variable local taxable capacity made for significant regional inequality in the effort by public and local authorities to supply schools.[16] Western and southern India, in this way, ended up spending more money on education than did eastern India.

But public investment was not the only factor responsible. There were serious problems on the side of private funding. Individuals who had the resources to supply local schools were too slow or unwilling to shed the biases that had long confined education to only a few groups and the men within these groups. To expect the government to be an effective agent in mass literacy would mean not only a much larger scale of investment but also a battle against social prejudices and biases that derived from caste sentiments and the low status of women in society. The British Indian state had no stomach for such battles.

What exactly was the problem with private funding of schools? There were two problems. First, different castes and communities had different perceptions about useful knowledge. Some of them might supply schooling, but others would not find the contents useful. Literacy rates were above average for the upper-caste Hindus, principally, Brahmin, Kayasth, and corresponding groups, and among men than among women within these groups. Politically, these groups were not necessarily more powerful than, say, the peasants, to be able to manipulate entry into schools in their favour. They just sent their children to schools more keenly than did the others. These communities believed that education was valuable for them and knew why it was valuable. The historical pattern of

[16] Latika Chaudhary, 'Land Revenues, Schools and Literacy: A Historical Examination of Public and Private Funding of Education', *IESHR* 47, no. 2 (2010): 179–204.

demand for education at all levels was biased towards certain castes and communities because these people had an inherited association with literate services. Groups that had contact with commerce, state service, medicine, teaching, and priesthood in the pre-colonial times entered education, medicine, and public administration in the colonial times. These classes and castes eagerly used the new schools and colleges, while other classes and castes entered schools on a smaller scale and dropped out more readily.

The second problem was access. Where communities formally or informally controlled entry into schools—we should expect such control to be greater in privately owned schools—lower castes would not have access to almost any schooling. If such controls were not easy to exercise for some reason, say because the population is too mixed, private investment reduced. As Latika Chaudhary has shown in a series of works, ethnic diversity led to reduced incentive of moneyed people to invest in general schooling.[17]

Government schools provided a parallel institution where access was, in principle, much freer, though these too were not completely free from caste and gender biases. The problem was that the government effort was concentrated in the towns and the cities. Because of constraint of funds, the effort reached out to the countryside very thinly, if at all. The literate service castes were migrating to the towns and cities in large numbers. So, they faced a much better supply situation. The correlation between family history of literate services, preference for service professions, and, thus, preference for education was especially close in the three port cities—Madras, Bombay, and Calcutta.

The Parsi community displays the favourable combination especially well. They were mainly urban and part-commercial in the late nineteenth century. In 1931, the average literacy rate among the Parsi was 79 per cent (73 among Parsi women), whereas the general literacy rate was only 8.3 (2.3 for women). Among the Jains, again a commercial class, the literacy rate was 35 per cent (among men,

[17] Latika Chaudhary, 'Determinants of Primary Schooling in British India', *Journal of Economic History* 69, no. 1 (2009): 269–302.

11 among women). Tamil Brahmins in Madras city, though not commercial, had higher literacy.[18] Bengali upper castes in Calcutta similarly had higher literacy.

Groups like these used their privileged position in the towns and cities to advance from primary to secondary to college education. They formed a small proportion of the population, but that proportion had a high propensity to complete all stages of education. The castes that had formerly populated the literate professions, and who still had their eyes upon literate professions, commanded the money and the motivation (not to mention peer pressure) to complete primary school, secondary school, college, and university education. Those castes that wanted to join the literate professions found in the British Indian colleges and universities a particularly congenial environment, for the content of the education offered in these institutions was relatively international and suited the cosmopolitan cultures and professions of the three port cities.

These choices continued to play a role as late as the end of the twentieth century, when, for example, certain castes dominated recruitment into the newly growing software services profession. These were the same castes that had dominated the entry into formal primary and secondary education, and recruitment into literate professions, in the nineteenth century.

This pattern led to a strange mix of a low enrolment in primary schools and high enrolment in higher education, which was greater than in other countries at comparable levels of development. Enrolment in higher studies dropped away sharply in all countries, but dropped to a smaller extent in India, because many of the same people who entered primary schools stayed on in the system. The caste-based profession-oriented demand for education, therefore, imparted what appeared to be a bias for higher education. A paper comparing long-run trends in labour productivity in India and Britain observes that even as there was divergence in productivity

---

[18] See also C.J. Fuller and Haripriya Narasimhan, *Tamil Brahmans: The Making of a Middle-Class Caste* (Chicago: University of Chicago Press, 2014).

in agriculture and the absence of any trend in manufacturing, in the services, there was a convergence in productivity trends due to 'a long-standing bias towards secondary and higher education'.[19]

The beginnings of university education went back to the years immediately preceding the Indian Mutiny (1857). Prominent residents of Calcutta, both European and Bengali, had signed a petition to start a university in the city. However, financing such an enterprise did not command universal support. Nevertheless, a university governed in the same way as the University of London started in Calcutta in 1854. The next year, plans appeared for two more universities in Bombay and Madras. After 1857, institutionalization of higher and technical education proceeded faster, Indian exposure to Western science became systematic and wider and there was greater specialization, while institutions such as the Survey of India and the Geological Survey of India grew to be relatively large and autonomous bodies. In 1880, there were 83 colleges, including medical and engineering colleges, and 155 normal (teacher-training) and technical schools, with a combined student population of 14,000. More than a third of these were concentrated in Bengal.

The drive to start colleges and universities in India with public money and initiative was far in advance of what was later in evidence in colonial territories, whether British or other European powers. Yet, the development had two faces. The import of a British model of college and university education made their governance structure rather cumbersome. Within the university system, an excessive accent on literary education, the desire to emulate British precedence in all matters, poor development of laboratories, and administrative confusion limited the usefulness of the university as a vehicle for scientific research. On the more positive side, the supply of university-educated government officers was greatly facilitated, thus aiding the expansion of the bureaucracy and Indianizing it at the same time.

[19] Stephen Broadberry and Bishnupriya Gupta, 'The Historical Roots of India's Service-led Development: A Sectoral Analysis of Anglo-Indian Productivity Differences, 1870–2000', *Explorations in Economic History* 47, no. 3 (2009): 264–78.

More usefully, a part of the British tradition of scientific, engineering, and medical research was transplanted to India. There was agreement on a policy of transfer among influential Indians and professional bodies in Britain. When the Asiatic Society of Bengal urged the government to provide facilities for more teaching of the sciences, the *British Medical Journal* endorsed the demand. In scientific research, major developments occurred in the fields of geographical surveys, botany, geology, and meteorology. Medical research, too, had many landmarks. Yet, whenever applied research tried to exceed its boundaries and venture into pure science, funding tended to become scarce, and publicists and officers expressed the idea that pure sciences should be left to British institutions.[20]

HEALTHCARE

The mortality rate was high in India before British rule. It began to come down significantly after 1920 (Chapter 10). Three types of government initiatives contributed to this decline. These were sanitation, medical care, and famine prevention. The first two initiatives began in the barracks.[21] The stress on sanitary reforms had a great deal to do with the exceptionally high death rates in the army. There was a growing sense that communicable diseases such as cholera, smallpox, or plague thrived on poor water supply, contaminated food, poor drainage, poor sewage, and crowded living conditions. Army death rates dropped dramatically in the last quarter of the century with reforms in these aspects.

The Indian Medical Service (IMS) had begun as early as in 1764. It recruited health professionals using a competitive examination, which Indians could take from 1853. The IMS was, at first, meant to look after the troops. But its duties gradually widened. Government hospitals expanded rapidly from the third quarter of the nineteenth century. Dispensaries also increased. At first, mainly the Europeans

[20] Deepak Kumar, *Science and the Raj, 1857–1905* (Delhi: Oxford University Press, 1995).

[21] India, *The Report of the Royal Commission on the Sanitary State of the Indian Army* (London: HMSO, 1863).

and Anglo-Indians used these institutions, which were concentrated in the towns. Indians rarely came to these places for treatment. For the upper castes, they carried the image of being impure places. The upper castes also had access to the more effective forms of traditional systems of medicine. When Indians did begin to come to government hospitals, a large proportion was of lower castes. Gradually, however, prejudices against government hospitals began to weaken. One factor in this change of attitude was the latter's success in surgery.

From the 1860s (after the Royal Commission on Sanitation submitted a report in 1863), sanitary reforms began to touch the civilian population and local governments. Large municipal corporations built hospitals staffed with European health officers. Municipalities paid more attention to pure water supply and proper sewage. Public health offices became effective in dealing with major outbreaks of communicable diseases, of which three were especially virulent— malaria, plague, and smallpox. Great epidemics, such as the plague epidemic that raged between 1896 and 1920, saw some early and a rather drastic implementation of the new ideas of how to decontaminate affected habitats.

Until the middle of the interwar period, these measures made little difference to the aggregate death rates. After that, a steady decline in death rates began to occur. The exact causes of the decline are not clear. Sanitation and medical care had limited reach. Still, these limited measures did contribute to the rarity of epidemics after 1920. The other factor behind the decline in death rates was the low frequency and severity of famines in the twentieth century (Chapter 10).

***

Although the outcome of a disjointed set of efforts, the assets created during the British rule helped the nation-state after 1947 in pursuing its development goals. Infrastructure was almost completely nationalized, except for a few electricity companies. Electricity generation, distribution, road construction and maintenance, education, and healthcare became (or remained) responsibilities of the states. The accent on large canal projects continued, partly to resettle refugees from Pakistan. Irrigation and electricity joined together in the hydro-electric projects, of which there were many examples between 1950 and 1970.

One factor behind the uneven nature of spending on infrastructure before 1947 was the limited financial capacity of the state. Government investment was a declining proportion of national income in the twentieth century. The difficulty of raising taxes imposed a long-term constraint on the budget. These hints at a constraint lead us to take a closer look at how the government worked.

9

How the Government Worked

Wat makes a colonial government colonial? The simple answer
is that it is a government with several decision-making centres.
After Pitt's India Act of 1784, a three-headed government came into
being. The India Office in London managed the currency and raised
loans from the banking district of London. The governor-general or
viceroy collected the Indian taxes and decided how to spend it. The
viceroy decided policy in consultation with a council consisting of
members who specialized in law, military affairs, and public works.
The third head of the government was in the provinces where the
local government raised some local taxes and spent this money and
what it received from the centre on roads, schools, and hospitals.

These three levels did not work in concert. Their priorities were
different. Trade, exchange, and defence were of foremost importance to London. The Government of India, on the other hand, was
relatively more concerned with internal peace and law. Local issues
of a developmental or welfare nature engaged the provinces most
directly, but the provinces were financially the weakest link in the
system. If and when British and Indian interests seemed to conflict,
these three levels at times took different views.

What difference did divided heads of government make? It made
innovation difficult. Innovation was badly needed because the revenues, which initially came mainly from land taxes, were small given
the generally poor yield of land. Newer and more modern taxes were

slow to develop. The economy was dependent on public debt. But here, the government was in trouble again. For raising more debt in London would mean a higher payment by the Indian government abroad on account of debt service. This payment the Indian nationalists called drain and did not like. Therefore, the government remained small. Revenue to national income ratio was a low 3–5 per cent throughout.

Indirectly, the fact that the government had nothing quite like an economic policy or a policy to develop India left it unmotivated to raise incomes. Its main concern was to keep trade and factor markets open.

TRADE POLICY

Until World War I, trade between India and Britain was effectively free of tariffs. Many colonial administrators believed in the benefits of free trade. British manufactures needed to seek markets all over the world, and many British trading firms were setting up bases in India. The Lancashire mill owners were a powerful lobby in British politics. This lobby resisted attempts to impose or increase an import duty, for textiles formed the main import by India from Britain and India bought 30 per cent of British textile export in 1865. On the issue of customs duty, the Indian government, which wanted to explore all sources of tax, and the British exporters influencing the India Office in London did not see eye to eye. Until World War I, therefore, rates of import duty on textiles were low. Such duties were removed and reimposed from time to time and partly offset by excise on competing goods produced by the mills in Bombay and Ahmedabad.

During the war, India's contribution to the war effort was critical for London. After the war, the government of India's point of view on taxation could not be ignored. Tariffs were a convenient way to raise revenues at a time of scarcity of money. Indian sentiments in favour of industrialization were growing. And the influence of British business on the imperial policy was in decline. Japan had emerged as a competitor of Britain in Asian markets. These circumstances weakened the resistance to customs tariffs. There was steady and significant increase in average tariff rates after 1920.

Tariffs were one part of trade policy; controlling the value of the currency was another. The government's control on the Indian exchange rate continued to be controversial, a subject taken up further on.

THE FISCAL SYSTEM

The British Empire in India was a poor state. Tax per head in British India was among the smallest not only in the world but also within the imperial domain.[1] The state earned too little money because it relied on the land tax and land yielded little. This dependence on an archaic tax was reducing over time but not quickly enough. British India was not a weak state. It spent enough to maintain a large army. By this means, British India kept the princely states pacified and the internal and external borders open to trade, migration, and investment. In this latter role, the power of the State was an instrument to forge close interdependence within India, and between India and the world economy. But the State never had much money left over to spend on public goods or agricultural development.

At any time in the nineteenth century, the principal tax was the land revenue. Fragmentary data show that land revenue accounted for 80–95 per cent of total revenue in 1809–10 in the provinces (Chapter 2).[2] In 1858–9, land tax yielded about half of total revenues. Provincial statistics show quite a large variation in the pattern, predictably, with the Permanent Settlement areas showing the least dependence on land revenue (Table 9.1). Next in importance were two commodity taxes of a rather special nature—one of those imposed on the export of opium and the other on the sale of salt. Together, the taxes on these two items accounted for 24 per cent of

[1] Ewout Frankema, 'Raising Revenue in the British Empire, 1870–1940: How Extractive were Colonial Taxes?', *Journal of Global History* 5, no. 3 (2010): 447–77.

[2] Colonel W. H. Sykes, 'The Past, Present, and Prospective Financial Conditions of British India', *Journal of Royal Statistical Society* 22, no. 4 (1859): 455–80.

Table 9.1 Composition of government revenue and expenditure, 1858, 1900, and the 1920s

	1858–9 (revenue) 1900–1 (expenditure)	1920–30 (average annual)
Per cent of total revenue		
Customs	8	26
Land revenue	50	20
Salt and opium	24	neg.
Excise	4	17
Income tax	0.3	10
Per cent of total expenditure		
Defence	22	34
Administration	24	11
Debt service	4	9
Public works	17	7
Education	2	6
Health	2	3

Sources: For 1858–9 and 1900–1, see Dharma Kumar, 'The Fiscal System', in *CEHI* 2, eds Dharma Kumar and Meghnad Desai (Cambridge: Cambridge University Press, 1983), 905–44, Tables 12.4 and 12.8; 1920–30 calculated in Tirthankar Roy, 'The Role of the State in Initiating Development: A Study of Interwar South and Southeast Asia', *IESHR* 33, no. 4 (1996): 373–401.

revenues in 1858–9. A more modern type of tax, such as income tax, customs, and excise, accounted for a small proportion of revenue (12 per cent in 1858–9). The tax system as a whole, therefore, was regressive and income-inelastic. A tax on salt fell in equal extent on the rich and the poor, for both consumed the same quantity. The limited reach of the income tax left many prosperous people out of the tax net. Land tax was a tax on asset and did not change with income. Thus, even as the economy expanded, the revenue did not grow automatically.

After World War I, the pattern of taxation changed. The importance of land tax had decreased to about 20 per cent of revenue in the 1920s. Land tax as a proportion of the value of agricultural production declined from possibly 10 per cent of net output in the middle or early nineteenth century to less than 5 in the 1930s. The opium tax became negligible and salt tax was a smaller source than before. On the other hand, income tax, customs, and excise had expanded their combined share to over 50 per cent. A sustained campaign by associations of landlords against taxation was one factor behind the fall in the importance of land tax. Tax in the permanent settlement areas was a fixed nominal amount, and the government's attempts to change the system on financial grounds failed. Land tax in the ryotwari areas fell upon the peasants, whom administrators often considered to be the most reliable political ally. After the Mutiny (1857), there was little appetite for taxing the farmers more.

On the other hand, scarcity of money forced the government to experiment with customs and income tax from the mid-nineteenth century. In this effort, the government could score some success only in the interwar period. Like customs, income tax again was the scene of a battle, if a more subdued one. The government did not have the machinery to implement a tax on self-employed people. The groups more easily targeted and assessed were those closest to the government. These were the landlords, the government employees, and owners of industrial firms, many of whom were Europeans. Some of these groups resisted being taxed. Over time, the groups expanded, diversified, and their resistance to taxation weakened.

The government's limited revenue went to fund defence, civil administration, and debt service. Some of these expenditures were made in sterling and went out of the country. For example, interest payment on loans raised to finance construction of railways and irrigation works, pensions paid to retired officers, and purchase of stores were payments in sterling.

These payments, Indian nationalists argued, reduced the capacity of the domestic economy to generate savings and investment, an argument that became known as the drain theory (Chapter 3). In principle, if taxes funded such payments, domestic consumption or saving could fall. If the government's savings funded such payments, public investment could fall. If foreign loans funded such payments, debt service would rise. All three methods were used to meet these charges. None of the adverse effects would follow if these charges corresponded to factor services that increased national income. The potential adverse effects, in other words, depended on the value delivered against these charges. The drain theorists did not measure such value and ignored the issue.

But the issue remained. For example, when the Indian government paid a higher salary to a European for work that an Indian could do for less, there was a potential reduction of national income; but when the government paid a high salary to a European engineer or a university professor who had technical skills not available in India, the expenditure generated national income. These two things were mixed up in the budget and in the minds of the proponents of drain (see also Chapter 3).

It is nevertheless clear that the poverty of the government hurt investment. Not more than 25 per cent of total expenditure consisted of investment, that is, went to the construction and repair of national assets (Table 9.2). If we consider only net investment, that is, creation of new assets, the percentage was smaller. Depreciation accounted for about one-third of gross investment in the prewar period and over half of gross investment in the middle of the 1930s. The percentage of investment in expenditure fell quickly towards the end of the interwar period, as debt service and administrative commitments took increasing priority over investment. The major sectors that saw capital expenditure were irrigation, roads, railways, and telegraphs. Increasingly from the interwar period, investments under these heads went into depreciation rather than new assets.

Table 9.2   Gross public investment as a proportion of public expenditure, 1898–1938 (percentage)

	Investment/expenditure ratio
1898–9 to 1913–14	23.5
1919–20 to 1929–30	23.4
1930–1 to 1937–8	15.7

Source: M.J.K. Thavaraj, 'Capital Formation in the Public Sector in India: A Historical Study, 1898–1938,' in *Papers on National Income and Allied Topics*, ed. V.K.R.V. Rao (Delhi: Allied Publishers, 1962).

In the twentieth century, the demand for welfare expenditure gained strength. The demand arose from the realization that education was a means of social advancement that the colonial rulers neglected. Partly, it was a result of political decentralization after 1919, whereby provincial budgets, responsible for education and health, became more exposed to local political pressures. High levels of illiteracy and mortality showed that being a colony of Britain for over half a century had done little to enable India to approach British standards of social development. The slight rise in the proportion of public spending on education and health in the interwar period reflects an attempt to redress this neglect of social infrastructure. The attempt, however, was a limited one, given the government's poverty and other expenditure commitments.

In the prewar period, public savings financed investment. Of the average gross investment, 90 per cent came out of the government's surplus of revenue over current expenditure. But in the interwar period, the percentage dropped to 65. The net increase in liability to meet public investment rose from an average of 10 per cent of investment in the prewar period to 35.

A big puzzle of the story is that the British Indian government had access to the cheapest and most developed money market in the world, that British Indian debt was rated high in this market, and yet, the government seemed reluctant to raise debt and use it to expand its developmental activities. Debt-GDP ratio was low and rose up to a point and then did not rise any further (Table 9.3). In sources on public finance, a clear explanation of why the government was so cautious about raising money in London when it was easy to do so cannot be found. A recent paper suggests that the fear of the nationalists who attacked interest on public debt as the most onerous type of drain might be the answer.[3]

Where do the provinces fit in? During the Company's rule, the finances of the three major presidencies were more or less autonomous. But there was a tendency to centralize control over finances.

[3] Tirthankar Roy, 'State Capacity and the Economic History of Colonial India', *Australian Economic History Review* 59, no. 1 (2018): 80–102.

Table 9.3   Public debt and debt–GDP ratio

	Debt in million Rs	National income in million Rs	Debt–GDP ratio
1900	3.4	12.7	26.5
1910	4.5	18.0	24.9
1920	7.6	33.3	22.8
1930	10.1	25.9	39.0
1938	9.5	23.5	40.6

Source: State debt figures from Neil Charlesworth, 'The Problem of Government Finance in British India: Taxation, Borrowing and the Allocation of Resources in the Interwar Period', *MAS* 19, no. 3 (1985): 521–48; national income from S. Sivasubramonian, *National Income of India in the Twentieth Century* (Delhi: Oxford University Press, 2000).

By 1882, the basic structure of financial federalism was well established. The centre was responsible for certain heads of revenue and certain types of expenditure. The provinces were responsible for some others. A few other taxes were divided up between the centre and the provinces. Customs, salt tax, opium tax, and railway income were the main revenues raised by the centre. The provinces had full control over receipts of provincial administrative departments such as law and justice or education. Land revenue and excise were divided up. Only the centre could borrow. As for expenditure, the centre looked after defence whereas the provinces were in charge of local administration, education, and health.

The system generated political tensions. The basic grievance of the provinces was that they had too many inflexible sources of revenue and yet were responsible for expenditures that had to expand with the growth of population and income. There were great inequalities between the provinces in per capita tax burden and per capita expenditure. Provinces with Permanent Settlement raised less revenue on average and spent less. Provinces such as Bombay or Madras raised more on average and spent more. The settlement pattern, however, was only one determinant of these inequalities. There were possibly others, which remain obscure.

The Government of India Acts of 1919 and 1935 and the legislative assemblies created after the 1919 act restructured federal finance and exposed it to pressure from elected representatives. The divided heads of revenue were abolished. Land revenue was given over to the provinces. The centre took the income tax. The central budget now had to be balanced by contributions made to the provinces, which added another bone of contention. These changes did little to meet the grievance of the provinces. The 1935 Act went a little further in giving a larger share to the provinces. Although the reform did increase the provincial share of revenue (Table 9.4), the scale of the change was too small to satisfy the provinces. The idea of a five-yearly finance commission to review the structure of federal finance, an institution that continues today, was another result of this Act.

The government balanced its budget. That is, it balanced current revenue with current expenditure. Famines, wars, and depressions upset the balance. The wars fought by the Company and the uprising of 1857 left a large burden of debt. The famines of 1876 and 1896 added to debt. These debts were paid back from current revenues without serious problems. The large increases in military expenditure during World War I not only forced the government to borrow but since the London market was no longer easy to borrow from, the government was forced to turn towards Indian sources.

The Great Depression changed the situation. Political unrest and weak exports reduced confidence abroad in Indian securities. The government could, in theory, devalue the rupee and stimulate the economy. But such a step would have increased the value of India's

Table 9.4   Shares of the centre and the provinces in gross public investment, 1920–37 (percentage)

	Centre	Provinces	Total (including municipalities and local governments)
1920–1 to 1929–30	56	35	100
1930–1 to 1937–8	46	39	100

Source: Thavaraj, 'Capital Formation in the Public Sector in India'.

net government remittance abroad. Fearing that India would fail to meet this commitment, authorities in London prevailed on India not to devalue but to cut expenditure instead. The resultant massive contraction in government expenditure intensified the effects of the depression.

With World War II, India again faced a deficit situation. The government had to spend much larger sums and proportions of the budget on defence, not only on its behalf but also on behalf of Britain's war efforts on promise of repayment from Britain later. While taxes and borrowings increased, these were insufficient to cover the deficit. India now had a central bank and enjoyed more monetary autonomy than before. Britain borrowed from India, and the securities went into the reserve. Consequently, the money supply increased. The nominal demand for goods expanded, but the supply of essential goods, including grain, was diverted to the war effort. The net effects were inflation, erosion of real incomes, and a fall in the burden of private debt. For some reasons that are not totally clear, the effect was severe in Bengal and much less noticeable in every other province. During the Bengal famine of 1943, some half a million people died of starvation and disease. The last days of the war saw government control over supplies of essential commodities. The food rations were the precursor to the public distribution system with which independent India has been so familiar.

The end of the war also saw a steady liquidation of India's accumulated foreign debt. This balance was a result of Britain's obligations to India on account of the war. India, thus, entered Independence with a large credit balance in sterling.

THE MONETARY SYSTEM

The larger aim of monetary policy was to stabilize economic transactions between Britain and India. In turn, this larger aim contained three specific aims—to make private transactions free of exchange risks, to provide the government some stability in its calculation of the remittances to be paid, and to restrain India's import of gold. Exchange rate was important because an appreciation hurt commercial interests exporting from India, and depreciation made it difficult for the budget to meet its sterling obligations. The Indians' love affair with gold worried the monetary authorities. India played a counter-cyclical role in the world economy. This role was mediated by the desire of Indians for gold and silver. In a world characterized by fixed exchange rates and gold as a main item of reserves, economic growth in India led to Indians buying a lot of gold at the expense of monetary gold elsewhere. This the authorities worried about.

These aims and anxieties caused little political controversy until World War I when the British economy was growing and India's trade and industry benefited from the connection with Britain. But the environment changed after that. The monetary policy of British India became a source of controversy in the interwar period because the objective of protecting the budgetary obligations, it was argued, prevailed over the objective of helping private commerce. The issue was whether the Government in India was allowed by London to pursue a stabilization policy independent of British economic interests. Gold too became controversial in the 1930s, for a different reason. To understand these developments better, we need to take a close look at the exchange system.

Silver, as Chapter 2 shows, was widely accepted in India as a means of payment. With the currency reforms of 1835 (Chapter 2), a modified silver standard emerged. In other words, silver became an accepted means to settle the balance of trade. A promise to mint coins on the presentation of silver bullion supported the silver rupee. There were two ways that money could be transferred between India and the rest of the world. The India Office sold council bills in London at an announced exchange rate, which the exchange banks purchased, sent to India, redeemed at the treasury, and financed trade demands for money. The receipts in London were used to meet the home charges. Alternatively, traders could buy silver in London, ship it to India, and have these minted into silver coins for a fee.

In the last quarter of the nineteenth century, an excess supply of silver in the world led to a fall in silver prices, which made the second mode of payment the more profitable. The council bill system came under threat unless the government devalued the rupee. Depreciation did occur, but at considerable cost to the budget. On the recommendations of a committee of enquiry headed by Farrer

Herschell, the lord chancellor, free coinage of silver ended in 1893. The next few years saw shipping of silver bullion for payment, and yet, the rupee did appreciate somewhat. In 1898, on the recommendation of another committee under the direction of Henry Fowler, a gold exchange standard was introduced.

In the gold exchange standard, the rupee was convertible against sterling and not against gold, at a ratio of 16d (pence) per rupee, or Rs 15 for a pound sterling. These years witnessed an animated discussion within India and in London on the merits of a full gold standard for India. The desire for a gold standard was strong in India, and the view that the gold exchange standard was adequate for India was just as strong in London. At stake was the autonomy of Indian monetary policy. For many contemporaries, the gold standard represented the freedom for India to settle her obligations directly using flows of metals. World War I shelved these debates.

To support the exchange, the India Office sold council bills in weekly auctions at the Bank of England. Until 1905, the volume of these sales was limited to the home charges. The limit ended after that, and the sale of these bills effectively became a strategy to stabilize the exchange by preventing free movement of metals for settlement of balance of trade. An official gold standard reserve began, based at the India Office in 1902. The reserve consisted mainly of British government securities, treasury bills, exchequer bonds, and consols, in turn contributing to keeping interest rates low in Britain. The India Office also used the gold standard reserve of India in the call money market, leading to a closer alliance between the India Office and the City of London or the financial hub of the western world. The only occasion in the prewar period when the government needed to draw on the currency reserve occurred in 1907 when a trade deficit threatened a depreciation of the rupee. On this occasion, the government also used the reverse council bills, a counterpart instrument that facilitated the supply of sterling.

The gold exchange standard faced its first big crisis towards the end of World War I. The first years of the war saw a loss of confidence in the rupee due to inflation in silver prices. From 1916 to 1917, the inflation made it likely that silver rupee coins would disappear from circulation. An appreciation of the rupee was inevitable.

Between 1917 and 1919, the rupee floated. By December 1919, the rupee had appreciated by 75 per cent. A committee of enquiry was established to study the situation; it recommended an exchange rate at two shillings, provoking a strong minority report from the Indian member who advocated a return to the prewar ratio. Silver prices, however, eventually stabilized, and confidence in paper currency returned in the next two years, with the result that early in the 1920s, the rupee depreciated somewhat. In 1925, another committee of enquiry endorsed the then prevailing ratio, 18d, to be the basis for a return to a modified gold exchange standard. From 1926 on, the rupee was again closely controlled to remain near 18d, the rate that was to prevail for the next several decades.

A very different political world was now unfolding rapidly in India. From the early twentieth century, as Chapter 1 shows, a criticism of the government's preference for keeping India open to the world economy was gaining in popularity. These views did not influence the nationalist movement too deeply until the 1920s. From the 1920s, intellectuals and economists joined the mainstream of the Indian nationalist movement with a sustained attack on colonial monetary policy.

If world trade had grown and the sterling had been a strong currency, few Indians would have wanted an end to the principles that governed Britain's management of Indian monetary system. But World War I damaged the international gold standard and sterling's position as a leading currency. In the emerging political environment of the 1920s, Indian commercial and political opinion united in the belief that the rupee was overvalued at 18d. The demand for a full gold standard and autonomy with regard to the exchange rate was growing again and now allied itself with economic nationalism.

The conduct of Indian monetary policy during the Great Depression, which seemed to serve British interests at the expense of Indian ones, worsened the controversy.

DEPRESSION AND MONETARY POLICY

The beginning of a fall in world commodity prices in the second half of the 1920s turned the terms of trade adverse for India and weakened the balance of payments. Further, the fear that the rupee might devalue eroded confidence in the rupee. Official and non-official opinion in India favoured depreciation of the rupee. But depreciation was not acceptable to London for fear that the increased burden of the home charges might lead the Government of India to default on its external obligations. Neither of the two options usually available to the India Office in dealing with a financial crisis—fresh borrowings in London or drawing on the reserves—seemed practicable in the prevailing economic and political climate. The options available to the monetary authorities in India were even more limited and inflexible. A postponement of India's sterling obligations was discussed but did not materialize.

Eventually, on London's insistence, the Government of India carried out monetary contraction, in the hope that this would reduce prices and raise demand for Indian goods. The goal was not easily attainable, for the demand depression was not specific to India but a global phenomenon. The contraction, therefore, had to be a deep and a sustained one. Furthermore, as the contraction continued and the less it seemed to work, the harder it became to return to devaluation, for the expected devaluation would have to be larger than before, causing larger-than-before adjustments in the budget. The Government of India feared that the resultant decline in prices would raise real interest rates and rents and would cause hardship. These fears proved correct. The financial situation did cause widespread transfer of assets from debtors to creditors in rural India and led to rural unrest over rent and debt.

Interestingly, national income data does not suggest that India was deeply affected by the Depression, at least not as much as other tropical primary product–exporting countries. After all, the trade sector was smaller in India than many other tropical export economies (exports were 7–9 per cent of NDP in 1929), the share of net private foreign investment in national income was less than 1 per cent, agriculture mainly served the domestic market, and industry received protective tariffs in the 1920s. The effect of the Depression on the financial system was subdued, because most banks lent only short-term in commodity trade, whereas long-term investment came from own savings or the informal sector. Other historians disagree that the Depression was a benign event. Underneath the tranquil picture presented by national income statistics, there did occur an upheaval, caused by three circumstances: conflict between debtors and creditors, contradictory interests of exporters and domestic market suppliers, and above all, contradiction between British and Indian stabilization and the long-term economic interests of the two countries.[4]

One major mechanism helping such transfer was the sale of gold jewellery. Rural assets held in the form of gold and silver began to be liquidated. At the same time, the British government's decision to leave the gold standard in 1931 depreciated the pound and, with it, the rupee, against gold. These circumstances led to a rise in the price of gold in terms of rupees. Based on an 18d rupee, the price of gold was lower in India than in the international market, causing a great quantity of this gold to be sold abroad. In the next five years, these gold exports reflated the Indian economy, restored the balance of payments, and provided the Government of India with enough remittance to meet its sterling obligations. Nevertheless, these exports were widely seen as a sign of distress and a lost opportunity to build a currency reserve for India, and thus left Britain–India relations much impaired.

The establishment of the Reserve Bank of India in 1935 was the first step in the dissociation of monetary policy from balance of payments. By then, the nationalists had changed their demand from monetary autonomy to full political independence. The change rested on an argument that the economic legacies of colonial rule had been damaging overall. Economic nationalism refers to the argument and the sentiment around it.

ECONOMIC NATIONALISM

The 1920s saw the articulation of two types of criticism of the monetary regime that fed into the sentiment that historians often call

[4] See discussion and citations in Dietmar Rothermund, *The Global Impact of the Great Depression, 1929–1939* (London: Routledge, 1996).

economic nationalism. The phrase means the claim that a nation needs to be in control of its economy and sometimes regulate it with a heavy hand to assert its independence.

Business persons and nationalist politicians alleged that the rupee tended to be systematically overvalued to subsidize government charges in sterling. Such a bias effectively taxed exporters, even though it might encourage private investment in the shape of imported capital goods. The main evidence for inadequate supply of rupees was a steady decline in price level in the second half of the 1920s. Officials in charge of operating the system disputed the meaning of this evidence. A second criticism found expression in contemporary scholarly views on India but took shape more explicitly in later research. India, like the rest of the interwar world, had a fixed or closely controlled exchange regime. However, while the world retreated from fixed exchange rates during the Depression, in India, monetary policy remained overly rigid because of its status as a colony.

During and after World War I, Britain was faced with trade and liquidity problems at home and feared that the Indian gold appetite might upset Britain's own post-war adjustment process. Under these fears, the British authorities tried to restrain expansionary tendencies in India. In short, adjustment in a beleaguered Britain hurt economic expansion in India. The classic example of the divergence of interests was the Great Depression.

These specific criticisms of monetary policy joined a wider criticism of the open economy that Britain had imposed on India for so long. Demand for tariffs grew (Chapter 3). Antipathy towards foreign capital was rising. Britain, it was said, was not only dealing with its short-term crisis using India but had used India all along to grow rich.

***

The nationalists accused the British government of ruling India to serve British interests. The proposition was correct. The British government did have British economic interests in mind while ruling India. But British interests and Indian interests did not necessarily conflict. In the golden age of globalization, roughly 1860–1914, the government tried to keep conditions of trade as stable as possible and this would have helped many businesses with a stake in the world economy. Conditions, however, changed in the late 1920s. Fewer Indians had a stake in a collapsing world economy, and the government's attempts to force a customs union on India angered them. Late in the interwar period, British interests and Indian interests were not compatible anymore.

The long-term failure of the state did not, however, rest on whose interests the state was serving; it rested rather on the weak capacity to make investments and, in turn, on the methods adopted to manage the economic system. The most serious weakness of the method was the divided responsibility between London and India, a situation that forced both parties to be conservative and risk-averse. The state was poor, thanks to its dependence on agrarian taxes. It stayed poor because of its cautious approach to debt, commodity, and direct taxes. It became bankrupt because, in the strained conditions of the Depression, British investors lost interest in Indian securities. The only long-term solution to this syndrome was to integrate monetary management and fiscal management, ending London's authority on the former, a move that happened too close to World War II to be immediately effective.

If the government was an area of significant inertia, it had a mixed role in the population transition, the subject of the next chapter.

10

Population

India's population, long stagnant or growing only at a slow pace, began to grow rapidly from the 1920s. Given the large initial size of the population, demographic change in this region was a turning point in world population history. What had changed to produce this turn? What effects did demographic transition impart upon the labour force? The present chapter considers the demographic transition with attention paid to the causes of population growth and to famines and epidemics.

POPULATION

General Trends

Three things influence population growth: the economic rationality of having large or small families; the social–cultural contexts influencing preferences for large or small families; and healthcare systems and nutritional status, which shape human ability to control or cope with biological processes. The different paces at which these factors change lead to periods of high or low population growth.

The 'demographic transition' theory sets out these relationships.[1] In pre-modern times, death rates were high, owing to diseases and

---

[1] See F.W. Notestein, 'Population: The Long View', in *Food for the World*, ed. T.W. Schultz (Chicago: University of Chicago Press, 1945).

famines. It was a rational choice to sustain high birth rates. The net growth of population was small. Religion, moral codes, and custom approved of high fertility. From the nineteenth century, death rates started to fall because of improved healthcare and nutrition. But religion, morality, and customs had a life of their own and did not weaken quickly. As mortality began to fall, fertility remained high and the world saw high population growth. Eventually, the economic costs of having large families would become excessive. More women working for wages meant more women regarding the time spent on children as lost wages. Skills became more complex and were learnt in the university rather than at home. Costlier education meant more parents valued the cost of raising children. Eventually, societies experienced a fall in fertility and the rate of population growth.

In most developing countries, the demographic transition started later than in Europe but was speedier. The decline of mortality was relatively quick, showing the actions of basic technologies contributing to disease and epidemic control. But fertility stayed high, because in agricultural societies, labour was highly valued. Besides, in India, early marriage restricted women's participation in wage work and education.

When and why did the transition happen? The systematic census began in India from 1881. Officers of the East India Company realized the administrative need for population data but did not always have the means to carry out large-scale surveys. For the pre-1881 period, and especially for the pre-British period, officials, statisticians, and historians made estimates of the population using different assumptions. Some of these estimates assumed that wars and political instability in the eighteenth century depressed population growth. Yet, with a few exceptions, politics was probably never more than a minor source of mortality at any time in India's history. The main influences were disease, epidemics, famines, inadequate nutrition, and poor hygiene. We do not know enough to suggest patterns of dynamics in these variables over centuries. One study uses an acceptable method and suggests a small positive growth rate of population in 1801–71.[2]

[2] P.C. Mahalanobis and D. Bhattacharya, 'Growth of Population in India and Pakistan, 1801–1961', *Artha Vijnana* 18, no. 1 (1976): 1–10.

For 1881–1941, we have more reliable data, which show three things. First, the population growth rate was small (on average about 0.4) between 1881 and 1921. Second, the growth rate increased from 1921–31 (Table 10.1). And third, there were fluctuations in 1872–1921. The 1876–7 famine and the influenza epidemic of 1918–19 caused unusual mortality immediately before a census count so that both 1872–81 and 1911–21 censuses show near-zero growth. But the intervening censuses show somewhat higher rates growth.

There were differences between major regions. One source of difference was the uneven impact of famines. The worst famines in the colonial period occurred in dry-land southern and western India. Western India experienced a less than average population growth

Table 10.1 Population of colonial India and the Indian Union, 1881–1951

	British India and the states excluding Burma		Present territory of India		
	Total (millions)	Average annual growth rate (%)	Total (millions)	Average annual growth rate (%)	Number of persons added every 10 years (millions)
1881	257	–	–	–	–
1891	282	0.9	–	–	–
1901	285	0.1	239	–	–
1911	303	0.6	252	0.6	13
1921	306	0.1	251	0.0	–1
1931	338	1.0	279	1.1	28
1941	389	1.4	319	1.4	40
1951	–	–	361	1.3	42

Source: Leela Visaria and Pravin Visaria, 'Population (1757–1947)' in *CEHI 2*, eds Dharma Kumar and Meghnad Desai, (Cambridge: Cambridge University Press, 1983), 463–532.

rate and great fluctuations. Again, famines partly explain the pattern. The worst of these episodes occurred in 1896. Northern India also experienced slow growth. Parts of this region were susceptible to scarcity, if not famines. The Gangetic delta offered more secure lives, thanks to more secure agriculture.

Because the fertility rate was relatively high and stable, the age composition of the population remained stable. Children (0–14 years) formed 35–40 per cent of the total population. The elderly (60 years or above) formed 4–5 per cent. Persons of working age (15–59) formed 66–67 per cent.

One peculiar feature of the Indian population was a lopsided gender ratio. There were about 1030–70 males per 1000 females. In North India, there was an excess of males, and in South India, there was an excess of females. Three hypotheses have been offered to explain the excess of males in the north: systematic under-enumeration of females, systematic under-reporting of female births, and greater risks of death for women both at birth and at the time of child-bearing. The third kind of risk arose from social biases against the girl child. They arose more specifically from such practices as early marriage of girls. Table 10.3 shows that the average age at the time of marriage was higher in South India. The sex composition varied by region because of practices like female infanticide among some communities, and the neglect of female infants and children varied too.

Why did mortality decline?

The Fall in Death Rates

Table 10.2 shows the general tendencies in death and birth rates. The mortality rate, initially high by world standards, declined steadily and quickly from 1921. Mortality was high, mainly owing to famines. The disappearance of famines after 1900 was one major factor in the fall in death rates.

Along with famines and diseases, high maternal and infant mortality contributed to high death rates. Infant mortality per 1000 live births was above 200 in 1901. It came down to 180 by 1931 and to 116 in 1951 in the Indian Union. The 1931 level did not compare too

Table 10.2   Crude death and birth rates, 1881–1951

	Death rate (deaths per 1000 persons)	Birth rate (births per 1000 persons)
1881–91	40–2	47–9
1891–1901	38–50	46–51
1901–11	41–4	44–8
1911–21	42–50	45–9
1921–31	33–8	42–8
1931–41	30–2	43–5
1941–51	25	40–2

Source: See Visaria and Visaria, 'Population', for these estimates.
Notes: The figures for death rate and birth rate show the range of different estimates.

badly with the poorer countries in South America or even Europe and was somewhat above the rates in British Malaya. But it was still among the world's highest. High infant mortality came from the poor health of the mothers, in turn, a result of child marriage, frequency of motherhood, primitive obstetrics, and unsanitary conditions. Very few women in India worked in the cities, where the quality of medical care was better than in the village. Even when they did, they did not necessarily live healthier lives. An enquiry in Bombay found that women mill workers did not have fewer children than in the rural areas and had less rest during and after pregnancy than in the rural areas.[3] As the average age at marriage started to increase, if very slowly, the effect of this bad tradition became weaker (Table 10.3).

India, as a whole, practised child marriage, but there were regional variations. The age at marriage was the lowest in eastern India (Greater Bengal, eastern UP, but not Assam) and parts of central India. Age of consent laws existed in British India, but few respected the law until the enactment of the Child Marriage Restraint Act of 1929. This act made the marriage of women below the age of 14 punishable, if not invalid. The act was no more than a piece of paper for a long time after it became law. Marriages occurred in public

---

[3] India, *Census of India 1931*, Vol. 1, Part I, Report, (Delhi, 1931), 92–3.

Table 10.3 Mean age at female marriage

	1901	1931	1961
Eastern India excluding Assam	11	11	15
Assam	15	14	19
North India excluding Punjab	13	12	14
Punjab	15	15	17
Maharashtra and Andhra Pradesh	12	11	15
Tamil Nadu and Karnataka	15	15	17
Kerala	18	17	20
India	13	13	16

Source: Kakoli Banerjee, 'Marriage Change in Rural India, 1921–1981', *The History of the Family* 3, no. 1 (1998): 63–94.

places in open defiance. Different religious communities had different views on it. In western India, marriages could be held a few miles away from the village, inside the territory of a native state where British laws did not apply. Nevertheless, the act and the few actual convictions under it had a mild deterrent effect after 1930.

In world history debates, there are two positions on mortality decline. The first emphasizes public health measures that led to better treatment of communicable diseases, such as malaria eradication, immunization, improved sanitation, and antibiotics. A second view says that these measures were not very popular before mortality began to decline, and therefore, improvement in nutrition and better resistance to diseases should be the reason. The fall in India did not happen due to medical intervention alone or due to nutrition, but due to speedier distribution of food in times of temporary but acute shortage. If famines were the main cause of mass death in India, the disappearance of famines should explain the fall in death rate. Long-distance private trade in grain expanded. As the railways grew in density and reach, grain could move into scarcity areas much faster than before in response to higher prices of grain.

The role of medical intervention was not negligible, however. Control of epidemics, some of which returned during famines, was a significant factor behind the fall in deaths. Three diseases—cholera, plague, and malaria—took a heavy toll of life in the late nineteenth and the early twentieth century. Famines were rare in the city, but diseases were not. Urbanization induced the spread of diseases. The crowded and unsanitary living conditions of the city were a new phenomenon in colonial India. Army barracks were particularly susceptible to epidemic attacks.

The IMS was always short of people, money for research, and the ability to campaign among vulnerable people. Its poor capacity to deal with epidemics and famines was exposed time and again. But it did not stop its employees from doing research on their own time and using government laboratories for the purpose. This freedom was used much in the same way in which Company doctors had researched Indian diseases in earlier times. It was experimental and exploratory in nature. But around 1900, thanks to better scientific knowledge and better instruments, the research began to produce some remarkable successes.

Ronald Ross' work on the malaria parasite (1897) was an example. Between 1882 and 1927, 'fever', the generic term for malaria, accounted for about two-thirds of all deaths. Malaria had a close association with agricultural expansion because new cultivation zones often had pools of dammed up water. As a better understanding of causation emerged, the frequency of deaths from the disease fell (Figure 10.1). The growing world trade in the cinchona plant also helped, even though attempts to acclimatize the plant in India in the 1880s failed.

Cholera was common in the army barracks, religious fairs, marketplaces, and towns. Until the 1870s, doctors and sanitary commissioners disagreed on whether the disease was airborne or waterborne. By the 1890s, there was agreement on the causes and cholera mortality started to fall rapidly thereafter. The first breakthrough with leprosy was achieved in the 1880s with the finding that the disease spread through contact, which led to the creation of leprosy asylums. By 1910, knowledge on the disease had improved and shown that bad nutrition and sanitation had more to do with its spread than casual contact. The number of people who suffered started to fall rapidly thereafter.

From its first major appearance in Bombay in 1896 to 1938 when plague almost disappeared, the disease claimed twelve million lives. The plague bacilli were native to the Himalayan foothills and the Western Ghats in Mysore. A combination of circumstances— crowding and malnutrition— made it travel fast in these years. Both cholera and malaria had an association with famines and scarcity, but the plague did not. All three hurt the poor more than the rich. Plague also affected certain professions, for example, grain dealers, who were more exposed to infected rats. When it first occurred as a pandemic in colonial India, the official response was to segregate infected persons, often by force. How the disease carried and the role of rodents was poorly understood. And therefore, these efforts failed to check deaths in the crowded slums of Bombay, even as these generated hostility to the health officer and public hospitals. The unpopular steps like compulsory segregation and evacuation no longer seemed necessary, as the cause of the disease was revealed in research carried out in Bombay. Thus, a more effective response took shape.

The cities enabled public health officers to observe how epidemics touched some settlements and spared others, even when these were located side by side. That knowledge of the distribution of epidemics was crucial to understanding the role of sanitation practices. For example, in the 1890s, the Plague Research Committee made the important claim that the plague bacillus spread through human excrement, again showing how poor sanitation in the city slums made some of these diseases impossible to control.

Smallpox was a worldwide killer in the eighteenth and nineteenth centuries, and India was no exception. Although the smallpox vaccine had been discovered in 1796, throughout the nineteenth century, its diffusion was rather slow. Hospital records show that in 1852, the smallpox fatality rate (deaths per affected population) was as high as 42 per cent in Calcutta. Fatality rates, however, dropped to less than 25 in rural areas. 'After a long and bitter fire-fighting operation, lasting most of the nineteenth century, smallpox was, like a fire, controlled but not extinguished'.[4]

[4] J. Banthia and T. Dyson, 'Smallpox in Nineteenth Century India', *Population and Development Review* 25, no. 4 (1999): 649–80.

Persistence of High Birth Rate

What about fertility rates? The smaller the chance of survival of children, the more would parents want many children and large families. This simple reason—that is, the fierce desire for children to keep the family line from going extinct—may explain why, historically, birth rates in India were high. The birth rates did not attain the biological maximum but matched the high death rate. There were social measures to ensure a high birth rate. The most effective was to get women married early, although locally, several social practices worked in the opposite way, such as female infanticide in North India and prohibition on widow remarriage among the Hindus. These measures came from male-child preference and worries over division of property.

Why did fertility remain high even after mortality began to fall? Early marriage reflected a strong cultural value. It restrained the participation of women in commercial work and led to low levels of female literacy (practically zero literacy before 1901). It was associated with a social attitude that did not see women as productive workers, and therefore, did not see them as legitimate claimants to property. Women themselves did not value their time spent at home in economic terms. These bad values did not die easily.

Migration

After the death and birth rates, the third influence on population is international migration. International migration increased in the nineteenth century, and many people who moved were Indians. But international migration was not a significant influence on population growth rates. In 1881–91, for example, net emigration from India was about 700,000, a mere 0.3 per cent of the 1881 population. In the next decade, the percentage was a little higher, but it declined after that.

Its scale was still large. Organized emigration began in the 1830s when recruiting agents contracted with potential workers and arranged to send them abroad. During 1830–70, Madras and Calcutta were the main ports of embarkation. The destinations were the British colonies in South East Asia, Mauritius, Burma, the Pacific, and the West Indies. The Madras port sent several hundred thousand

Tamils to Ceylon and Burma, and many others to Mauritius, South Africa, and the West Indies. The French ports in South India were other points of embarkation. Overseas migrants, like migrants to the Assam plantations, came from certain regions, perhaps the most important was Chota Nagpur. 'Hill coolies', the phrase used in early nineteenth-century official documents, referred to a group of people who lived on the margins of the forests and were already familiar to the indigo planters of Bihar as reliable wage workers. At a time when wage workers were not easy to find, their reputation travelled to the European shippers of indentured labour in Calcutta and onwards to the sugarcane planters in Mauritius and the Caribbean.

Emigration increased during famines. The decade of the 1830s, which saw the Guntur famine and a massive cyclonic storm followed

Figure 10.1   A team of men dusting both banks of a small stream with insecticide to prevent malaria, c. 1929.

by inundation, was disastrous for agriculture in the Andhra coast and pushed many people out of their homes and towards the Madras port. Still, employers found it difficult to employ enough people and had to hire contractors and agents who would find and persuade potential migrants. The contractors sometimes exploited these people. Some historians call the employment of migrant workers in tropical colonies slavery in another name.[5] Calling it slavery is an exaggeration. Coercion and fraud were less common than believed; most went willingly and earned a wage higher than that back home. After completing a five-year indenture, returnees brought with them comfortable sums of money and it was their campaign that induced others to join them on the return journey.[6]

Table 10.4   Major channels of internal migration, 1901–31

East India	Bihar and UP to Assam plantations
	Bengal (mainly Mymensingh District) to Assam, peasants migrated in search of land for resettlement
	Bengal to Burma, to work as labour and in the tertiary sector
	UP to Bengal, to work in industry, mines, and the tertiary sector
Central India	UP to central India, to work in mills
	Chhattisgarh to Berar, to work as agricultural and mill labour
	Hyderabad to Berar, mill labour
South India	Madras (Tamil Nadu) to Mysore, labour in mines, and into the tertiary sector
	Madras to Burma, labour and the tertiary sector
North and Western India	Within Punjab, east to west, peasants and pastoralists resettled as peasants in the canal areas
	Rajputana to Punjab, trade
	Rajputana to Bombay, trade

Source: Census of India, Vol. I, Parts 1–2, 1901–31.

[5] Hugh Tinker, A New System of Slavery (London: Oxford University Press, 1994).

[6] Marina Carter, Servants, Sirdars and Settlers: Indians in Mauritius, 1834–1874 (New York: Oxford University Press, 1995).

Internal migration did not affect population growth but had many similarities with international migration. Persons who declared themselves as 'immigrants' or born in another place formed about 1.8 per cent of the total population of India in 1901 and 3 per cent in 1931. In absolute terms, there had been an increase of about five million persons who had moved long distances. The percentages varied between regions. For example, 12–15 per cent of Assam's population were immigrants in 1901–31. Like the emigrants abroad, the vast majority of migrants moved into specific occupations and areas of opportunities that had colonial origin, for example, plantations, large-scale industry, and service in Burma. As Table 10.4 shows, there were many channels of internal migration, and finding one set of causes explaining all is difficult (see also Map 10.1).

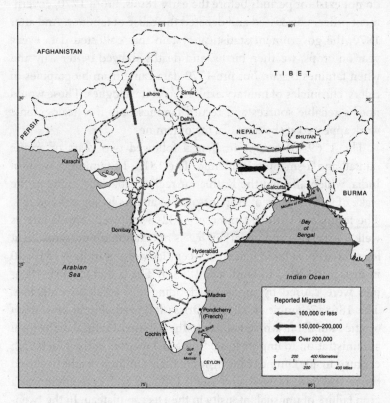

Map 10.1.   Major channels of internal migration

Source: Author

Famines have figured in discussions on death rate and disease. Why did these happen? Why did they become rare after 1900?

FAMINES

While medical intervention brought down mortality among all sections of the population exposed to the common pathogen, the end of famine brought down mortality among the rural poor of vulnerable regions. What are famines and why did they happen?

Famines, defined as episodes of acute starvation on a large scale, were a frequent occurrence in India until the early twentieth century. However, it is impossible to construct any sensible history of the frequency or intensity of famines in the long run. The required sources do not exist for periods before the early 1800s. From 1770, government officers discussed and debated the cause of famines. And after 1870, the government statistical system that collected data every year on crops, weather, births, and deaths showed better why and when famines began. But pre-1770 data came from biographies of rulers, chronicles of military exploits, and travelogues. These would not be reliable sources and record famines only if a hagiographic work appeared at the time of a major famine.

The 1769–70 famine in Bengal followed two years of erratic rainfall and a smallpox epidemic. The 1812–13 famine in western India, which affected the Kathiawar region especially, came in the wake of several years of crop loss due to attacks by locusts and rats. The legendary Guntur famine of 1832–3 followed crop failure as well as excessive and uncertain levels of taxation on peasants. In at least three episodes in nineteenth-century western India—1819–20 in Broach, 1820–2 in Sind, and 1853 in Thana and Colaba—famines were caused by monsoon flooding and resultant crop loss. The 1865–7 famine in coastal Orissa followed several seasons of erratic rainfall but worsened due to the persistent refusal of the local administration to import food. In the last quarter of the nineteenth century, major famines causing more than a million deaths occurred thrice: 1876–8, 1896–7, and 1899–1900. In each case, there was a crop failure of unusual intensity in the Deccan plateau. In the twentieth century, major famines were fewer. In 1907–8, the state relief machinery effectively dealt with extensive crop failure and epidemic threats. Food procurement for World War II, combined with crop failure, caused the harshest famine of the twentieth century, the 1943 Bengal famine.

Famines meant a sharp and sudden rise in food prices. Such a development could have different effects on different classes of people. For example, when food prices rose, farmers purchased less cloth, which meant that artisans had less money to buy food. Peasants usually had some storage of grain. The labourers, like the artisans, had no grain storage. The 1876 famine drove large numbers of rural labourers and handloom weavers of South India to enlist for emigration to British tropical colonies abroad. The 1896 and 1899 famines again encouraged migration. Famines also affected land transfers between the poor and the richer peasants, but these effects are not well-researched.

Practically every known famine in nineteenth-century India started because of failure of the monsoon rains, usually successive failure of rains. In the 1876–8 and 1896–8 Madras and Bombay famines, the first few months after a harvest failure saw a rise in food prices and rise in deaths. Deaths were more common among men who left home in search of work, among the children and the elderly, and among lower-caste people. Almost always, crop failure drove people to change diets and forage for food in the forests and commons. In the first few months of starvation, people would consume fodder and seeds, so that livestock mortality increased. Towards the end of a famine, epidemic diseases claimed lives. Sustained malnutrition reduced biological resistance to smallpox, plague, cholera, pneumonia, and diarrhea and made the population susceptible to malarial death. The chances of contamination of common pools of water was high during famines.

Why did famines occur? A big debate in Indian history concerns why famines happened. Few have offered a theory that explains both the occurrence of famines and the disappearance of famines.

In colonial times, there was a view that famines were natural disasters. The economist Thomas Malthus said that too many people trying to compete for limited food could lead to famines. In the presence of overpopulation, a mild crop failure could have devastating consequences. Malthus' influence upon officers in India was strong.

But the reports on the nineteenth-century famines did not endorse the Malthusian theory of the famine. The reports of the Indian Famine Commission (1880, 1898, 1901, and the Famine Enquiry Commission Report of 1945), the Report of the Indian Irrigation Commission (1901–8), and Famine Codes (1880, and provincial codes to follow) did not think famines happened because of overpopulation, but because of a risky agrarian environment. In a tropical region, water was a scarcer resource than land. When monsoon rain was the main source of water, a big risk attached to the supply of water. Not all regions were equally affected, of course. But those 'poor in soil, their rain-fall precarious, little ... artificial irrigation [were] severely affected whenever drought visited'.[7]

This theory is the ecological account of famines. When it first developed, it disputed an assumption that since famines represented Malthusian checks, human or state intervention could not or should not try to solve the problem.[8] Others believed that state relief would make many people, who were not too distressed, seek relief.[9] The ecological theory changed both attitudes. It led to the formation of an emergency response or a relief system and justification for government investment in irrigation canals. The ecological theory, however, cannot explain why famines disappeared after 1900. Geography did not change in 1900. Whereas more canals were built in response to the ecological theory of famines, these canals came up in the water-rich areas rather than water-poor ones, which needed them the most to avoid famines. What other explanations exist?

[7] India, *Report of the Indian Famine Commission. Part I: Famine Relief* (London: HMSO, 1880), 5.

[8] S. Ambirajan, 'Malthusian Population Theory and Indian Famine Policy in the Nineteenth Century', *Population Studies* 30, no. 1 (1976): 5–14.

[9] David Hall-Matthews, 'The Historical Roots of Famine Relief Paradigms,' in *A World Without Famine? New Approaches to Aid and Development*, eds Helen O'Neill and John Toye (Basingstoke and London: Macmillan, 1998), 107–21.

The Indian nationalists believed that free trade caused famines. Shortly after the famine of 1896–8, some Indian bureaucrats and nationalist writers, such as K.L. Datta and R.C. Dutt, suggested that the export of foodgrains from India had reduced domestic food availability during periods of bad harvest and thus increased the intensity of famines.[10] Sections of the bureaucracy held that on the contrary, trade stabilized consumption, for exports increased when domestic prices were low and good harvests had created a surplus over consumption needs, while exports fell when prices were high. Statistical tests prove that the mechanism did work this way.[11]

Michelle McAlpin examined the long-term impact of markets on famines. For the Bombay Presidency, McAlpin showed that markets and railways improved food distribution so much that the incidence and impact of famines came down. In the Indo-Gangetic basin and coastal Andhra, irrigation development helped mitigation of famines. The effect followed not only from local increases in production but also from easier movement of crops, which the railways made possible. Recent research on food markets and famines supports McAlpin's thesis that the railways led to better and faster distribution of food, leading to reduction in famine.[12] Similarly, information about local agricultural conditions was limited and travelled slowly, which affected the quality and speed of response to famines in the nineteenth century. After 1890, crop output and weather reporting systems improved greatly, making relief response much quicker than before.[13]

[10] B.M. Bhatia, *Famines in India* (Bombay: Asia Publishing House, 1963), 14–21.

[11] Martin Ravallion, 'Trade and Stabilization: Another Look at British India's Controversial Foodgrain Exports', *Explorations in Economic History* 24, no. 4 (1987): 354–70.

[12] D. Donaldson, 'Railroads of the Raj: Estimating the Impact of Transportation Infrastructure' (NBER Working Paper No. 16487, NBER, Cambridge Mass., 2010); Robin Burgess and Dave Donaldson, 'Can Openness Mitigate the Effects of Weather Shocks? Evidence from India's Famine Era', *American Economic Review* 100, no. 2 (2010): 449–53.

[13] Tirthankar Roy, *Natural Disasters and Indian History* (New Delhi: Oxford University Press, 2012).

The Bengal Famine of 1943 was an exception to the monsoon-induced famines described above. Food price rose in 1943 in Bengal because of the War and government purchase of rice on a large scale. This one example has led to a surprisingly high degree of theoretical dispute about why famines occurred, mainly because Amartya Sen has used it to make a bigger point about famines. Sen says that famines could happen without a crop shortfall. The price of food could rise because the government bought up food to feed soldiers engaged in a war, encouraging speculation by grain traders.[14] This argument has little relevance for the nineteenth-century famines in the Deccan. But does it explain the Bengal famine? Historians disagree on whether it does or not. Scholars who have reexamined the evidence believe that there was a harvest failure before the famine and that the role of speculation was exaggerated. Because of political rivalries within the elected legislature in Bengal province, there was a lot of misinformation and lack of information about just how bad the situation was, which reduced the effectiveness of the response.

Returning to the nineteenth-century dryland famines, the ecological theory of famines supported the case for government relief to provide food to the needy. In the early nineteenth century, the East India Company left famine relief to the native princes. In precolonial India, the prospect of famines had encouraged the construction of state granaries to be used for relief purposes. Common measures to prevent the occurrence of famines included irrigation tanks and canals. On a more limited scale, private and temple charity was also at work. However, both the granaries and the private systems were localized whereas starvation was widespread.

In the second and the third quarters of the nineteenth century, administrators advocated irrigation works and restoration of disused tanks as insurance against future famines. A clear policy in this regard did not take shape until 1880. There was resistance within the administration to expenditure on irrigation, which, it was felt,

---

[14] A. Sen, *Poverty and Famines: An Essay on Entitlement and Deprivation* (Oxford: Oxford University Press, 1983).

brought uncertain returns. The state agency in relief, it was sometimes argued, interfered with the agency of the market in bringing
food to the needy. The ferocity of the 1876 famine reduced these
resistances.

Between 1876 and 1896, a relief infrastructure was set up in
British India. The main element of the policy was relief camps
where starving persons could receive food in exchange for labour
at public works projects, such as the construction of railways or
irrigation canals. A famine insurance fund was started in 1881, out
of which relief-related expenditures should come. The relief camp
was not unknown in 1876, but its effectiveness during that episode
was in serious dispute. Its scale was small, the labour requirement
was hard to enforce due to a shortage of supervisors, and entry
was based on the degree of distress, which was hard to define and
subject to abuse. By the end of the century, the relief camp was a
well-established institution in Madras and Bombay Presidencies
and could mobilize thousands of labourers for construction works.
The Famine Commission of 1881 outlined the relief policy, and
the provincial Famine Codes wrote down detailed instructions for
the local administration to follow. If the relief camp was efficient in
mobilizing labour, it was not very effective in averting large-scale
mortality. Many seekers of relief, such as the artisans, could not offer
the kind of labour the camps wanted and paid for. Some did not want
to eat the same food as others did due to caste prejudices. Women
often avoided the camps. The Famine Codes became progressively
lengthier to accommodate this heterogeneity.

***

Population history in British India is a story, simultaneously of transformation and inertia. Population growth began to accelerate due to
a decline in mortality rates. The decline reflected new standards of
health and sanitation and the disappearance of famines after 1900.
This latter development reflected India's newly acquired ability to
adapt to its climatic conditions. On the other hand, birth rates, infant
mortality, and adverse sex ratio of women changed little, and wom-
en's access to industry and service jobs fell. In short, there was little

improvement in women's status in society and in the low value they commanded as commercial workers.

Natural resources figured prominently in the previous chapter. It is appropriate to discuss the natural environment more generally, which the next chapter will do.

11

The Economy and the Environment

In the last 20 years, research on environmental history in colonial India has advanced. Much of this scholarship does not address economic history issues and is concerned with forests. Still, it has important lessons for economic history. This chapter draws out some of these lessons. Despite the availability of many surveys and reflective essays on the field, a review dedicated to the environment–economy interaction does not yet exist.[1]

It is first necessary to answer two larger questions. Why should economic historians be interested in environmental history? How are the two fields of research related? The natural environment shapes long-term economic change in several ways, via the quality or quantity of resources of potential economic value, via climatic conditions that shape moisture or seasonal variations in agricultural conditions, and via risks of disasters. These geographical conditions

---

[1] For recent surveys, see Michael Mann, 'Environmental History and Historiography on South Asia: Context and some Recent Publications,' *South Asia Chronicle* 3 (2013): 324–57; and introduction to Deepak Kumar, Vineeta Damodaran, and Rohan D'Souza, eds, *The British Empire and the Natural World: Environmental Encounters in South Asia* (New Delhi: Oxford University Press, 2011).

are of a lasting nature. They become active drivers of economic change when private enterprise and public policy become interested in the resources and try to mitigate the risks, and when knowledge and information-gathering on these conditions for scientific or commercial purposes start to speed up. The speeding up did happen in the colonial times. The actions of these forces can be studied by distinguishing between three main fields of action—agriculture, forests and commons, and cities and public health. Figure 11.1 shows the relationship in a schematic way.

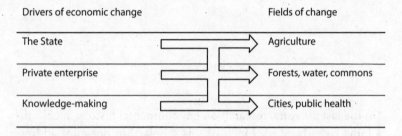

Figure 11.1   Environment and economy interactions

Source: Author

The chapter has three main sections, each section dealing with one of these drivers.

ACTIONS OF THE STATE

Property Right in Land and Changing Land Use Patterns

The colonial rulers defined private property in land differently from previous regimes. They defined it as an ownership right rather than as a right to use the produce of land. But access to village grazing land, currently unused land or the category official statistics called 'waste' land, and forests required setting out rules of use rather than of ownership, and this task was left incomplete.

A variety of consequences followed from the anomaly. Peasants grabbing village commons was not uncommon. But more commonly, a sharp division came into being between nomads, pastoralists, and

forest-dependent peoples who *used* resources and the peasants, planters, and landlords who *owned* resources. The legal regime favoured
the landholders. Regulation and property rights imposed pressures
upon the former groups to become peasants, usually as tenants and
labourers. In turn, the redefinition of land right as a proprietary right
sharpened the distinction between cultivated land, forests, pastures,
village commons, and plantations. These categories had been more
mixed up in earlier times.

The combined process of displacement on one side and intensive
use of land on another encouraged large-scale migration. Peasants
migrated towards land-abundant regions. Migrant labourers populated the plantation zones. The so-called wastes were converted into
arable land on a large scale. And village commons were converted
into private lands. Although migration flows formed a small proportion of the population stock, migration could still have a huge impact
in certain regions. For example, Assam, since the late nineteenth
century, witnessed both peasant migration and worker migration
into the plantation zones on a very large scale and became *the* settler
economy within colonial India.[2]

Table 4.2 sums up the official statistical data on land use. Common
lands were the extent of forests and uncultivated wastes available for
cultivation. Wastes not so available usually represented areas for resi-
dential purposes and water bodies. These data suggests a slight fall in
the area under uncultivated wastes available for cultivation between
1890 and 1939, increase in the area under cultivation including current fallows, and increase in the area under forests. However, this
data is not wholly reliable. The area under forests is not the area
under actual forests but the area under the forest department.

Nevertheless, even these data suggests one indisputable fact. Since
no significant change in the total area occurred after 1921, the per

[2] On the history of these migrations and how these resettlements
changed the society and the economy of Assam, see Sanghamitra Misra,
*Becoming a Borderland: The Politics of Space and Identity in Colonial
Northeastern India* (Abingdon: Routledge, 2011); Jayeeta Sharma, *Empire's
Garden: Assam and the Making of India* (Durham: Duke University Press,
2011).

capita availability of the commons had begun to shrink. If we ignore official statistics, the total area under wastes and forests (except in Burma) is likely to have fallen in the latter part of the British period.

A study of long-term patterns of land use provides a firmer basis for such a conclusion.[3] The study covers Bihar, Punjab, and Haryana between 1850 and 1970. The commonly held view that there was deforestation is confirmed. In Bihar, forest cover declined by 30 per cent between 1890 and 1970. However, forests retracted not due to conversion of forests into arable land, which changed little in extent, but due to degradation of forests into scrubland, attributed to the demand for timber and demographic pressure. In Punjab and Haryana in the same period, arable land expansion occurred at the cost of all forms of woods and grasslands. In this region, the proportion of land area under forest was much smaller than in Bihar. The declining proportion of grass and scrublands showed that significant expansion of arable land had taken place on the fringes of deserts. 'Decade by decade,' the paper concludes, 'depletion and land conversion have proceeded hand in hand. Vegetation cover moved down the scale of abundance: from forest to woodland; from woodland to scrub; from scrub to grasslands; from grasslands to barren areas. Simultaneously, cultivated lands have made large absolute and relative gains' (p. 724).

A part of the process was the conversion of commons adjacent to the village. What were these lands? In about 1850, most lands which lay outside the arable cultivated zone in or near villages and not used for habitation fell into three broad classes: forests and woods, areas described as grasslands or scrubs, and village grazing lands or village commons. A range of rules and conventions governed access to and use of these lands. Forests and commons located in estates where a ruler could effectively claim ownership or taxation rights were private resources. Forests inside zamindari estates were of this kind. Otherwise, forests and commons could be either open access or under collective rights of varying degrees of formality.

---

[3] J.F. Richards, J.R. Hagen, and E.S. Haynes, 'Changing Land Use in Bihar, Punjab and Haryana 1850–1970', *MAS* 19, no. 3 (1985): 699–732.

In the pre-British period, the right to the use of uncultivated common land within easy access to the village tended to be decided jointly by dominant peasant families and clans. Where the areas were large and the population that used the commons not settled near these lands, the rights tended to be periodically negotiable with the local rulers. An example was the nomadic pastoralist communities that traversed the scrubs and savanna in North and South India. Locally, collective bodies such as village communities sometimes negotiated these rights. In the nineteenth century, the commons within easy access of the village began to disappear, or access to the commons became increasingly difficult. Pastures likewise began to become increasingly inaccessible, affecting the pastoralist communities.

These processes related to 'sedentarization' and 'peasantization' of the communities who earlier depended on the commons. They settled as farmers, which is what the government also wanted. Several factors led to this change. First, the British redefined their political relationship with pastoralist communities and often imposed new taxes on them. In regions located near areas of conflict such as Punjab, some pastoralist communities who were not believed to be sufficiently loyal fell a victim of these conflicts. Second, various forms of joint rights on the use of the commons were either not understood or ignored. These were replaced by private property, encouraging the dominant cultivators to try to enclose and subdivide common lands wherever they could. In Bengal, the zamindars imposed restrictions on the use of forests within their domains, which was one of the grievances that led to the Santal Rebellion in western Bengal in 1855. Third, large canal irrigation systems crisscrossed and broke up grazing grounds and converted some of them into cultivable land. Fourth, population growth led to encroachment on forests and grazing grounds.

Restrained access to the forests and enclosures for private or collective use had several economic effects. Regional studies hint at the disappearance of occupations, insufficient subsistence, and problems for agriculture. Also, with the bureaucratization of forest management, tensions developed between the government and the forest dwellers over such issues as abuses of power by petty officials, loss of rights of collection of forest products, and collective responsibility for damage.[4]

Punjab is a well-researched study of these processes.[5] In Punjab, initially, 'unclaimed' wastes were abundant both outside village areas and within them under the joint management of village proprietary bodies. The region had abundant, if poor-quality, land and natural conditions that led to a large pastoralist population. These people migrated along traditional routes that intersected the open grasslands. The revenue policy wanted to maximize revenue per unit of land. The policy forced the authorities to try to bring village wastes under cultivation or reserve these for the use of the cultivators and to reserve the 'open wastes' outside the village areas for the government. Accordingly, village boundaries were demarcated and access to the open wastes prohibited. Some of these vast open wastes were later used to resettle cultivators in the canal colonies. The village wastes were divided among proprietors according to their ancestral shares, and the pastoralists could not use these.

The pastoralist population faced a lack of access to both their traditional routes and old grazing grounds. A few continued within the new regime. But large numbers settled down as peasants and as small-scale traders. Many turned to wage labour. The wastes declined in scale. The length of the fallow period fell. And there was a disturbance of the balance between cultivation and livestock breeding, which may have intensified the effect of famines in some areas. Customary laws on the use of the commons were not ignored. But these laws were so badly misinterpreted that traditional authority declined anyhow.

[4] Richard Tucker, 'Forest Management and Imperial Politics: Thana District, Bombay, 1823–1887', *IESHR* 16, no. 3 (1979): 273–300.

[5] Minoti Chakravarty-Kaul, *Common Lands and Customary Law. Institutional Change in North India over the Past Two Centuries* (Delhi: Oxford University Press, 1996); Neeladri Bhattacharya, 'Pastoralists in a Colonial World,' in *Nature, Culture, Imperialism. Essays on the Environmental History of South Asia*, eds David Arnold and Ramachandra Guha (Delhi: Oxford University Press, 1995), 49–85.

At the same time, the economic environment was changing. Canals increased the productivity of land. The railways extended markets. Public works were major consumers of the produce of the waste land, from timber to rubble. Population growth and migration reduced the supply of cultivable land. The commons were either reserved or turned into farms. Within the village, the decline of traditional authority and increasing competition for land led to partition and enclosure of the village commons, as well as to 'free-riding' or overuse of the commons that remained.

Regulation on Forests

The first Forests Act appeared in 1865. The authorities decided that the precolonial system was for the ruler of the land to exercise absolute ownership right to the commons. In effect, the state asserted property rights over the forests. There then followed a combination of destruction and conservation. In the early nineteenth century, forests under British supervision were destroyed for reasons of defence. This factor was active in the eastern part of the Ganges–Jumna interfluvial tract or submontane north Bihar.[6] The exploding demand for railway sleepers, wood fuel for railway locomotives, and timber for shipbuilding led to the destruction of trees in large numbers.[7] In several parts of India, the destruction upset the pattern of vegetation and wildlife. At the same time, reservation was also used to regulate commercial exploitation and conservation.

What was all this a change from? What rights were there before? Who were the people who gained or lost in the process, and how similar or different were their situation before the change? Conceptual frameworks developed in the 1980s, especially through the work of Madhav Gadgil and Ramachandra Guha, proposed two ideas:

[6] M. Mann, 'Ecological Change in North India: Deforestation and Agrarian Distress in the Ganga-Jamna Doab 1800–1850', *Environment and History* 1, no. 2 (1995): 201–20.

[7] P. Das, 'Colonialism and the Environment in India: Railways and Deforestation in 19th Century Punjab', *Journal of Asian and African Studies* 46, no. 1 (2011): 38–53.

that collective bodies such as village communities negotiated right of access and that designated castes specialized in the maintenance of forest resources, before colonialism.[8] For some, specialization in resource use made them take care of the resource responsibly. The forests of the western Himalayas were earlier used by a large migratory pastoralist population as well as by the peasants who lived on small plots of hillside lands between the forests. As the elevation increased, agriculture alone became insufficient to sustain a living and had to be combined with animal husbandry, mining, trade, and extraction of diverse resources from the forests. The idea of some precolonial equilibrium brings into sharp relief the disruption caused by the colonial rights regime that weakened the community by empowering owners of the land, weakened traditional conservation practices by reserving forests for the use of the state, and, in both these ways, destroyed an indigenous moral economy about responsible use of nature.

The notion of a precolonial equilibrium is controversial. It is not clear how far the village community or traditional communities were pre-existing or recreated by the colonial state while trying to define customary property rights.[9] Sumit Guha, among others, disputes the notion of a precolonial equilibrium marked by a separation between agriculture and forest dependency into distinct fields of specialization.[10] Forests, instead, were tied to the agrarian landscape through a set of dynamic relationships. People combined livelihoods and identities, and peasants used forests as a resource as well

[8] Ramachandra Guha, *The Unquiet Woods: Ecological Change and Peasant Resistance in the Himalaya* (New Delhi: Oxford University Press, 1989); Madhav Gadgil and Ramachandra Guha, *This Fissured Land: An Ecological History of India* (Berkeley and Los Angeles: University of California Press, 1992).

[9] Chetan Singh, *Natural Premises. Ecology and Peasant Life in the Western Himalaya 1800–1950* (Delhi: Oxford University Press, 1998); R. Grove, V. Damodaran, and S. Sangwan, 'Introduction' to *Nature and the Orient* (New Delhi: Oxford University Press, 1989).

[10] Sumit Guha, *Environment and Ethnicity in India 1200–1991* (Cambridge: Cambridge University Press, 2006).

as a political domain. In many regions, dominant peasant clans had superior rights to the forests and retained these rights in the colonial regime. Sustained criticism of the concept of the forest dweller as a relic from times before agricultural civilization, or attempts to 'essentialize' the original dweller as 'tribe,' has also helped blur the boundary.[11] Present-day scholarship on nomadism confirms that agrarian and nomadic environments can coexist and exchange people between them.[12]

In the nineteenth century, the demand for railway sleepers, fuel for railway locomotives, and timber for shipbuilding enormously increased the use of forest resources. Private contractors took forest patches on lease and cut down trees in large numbers. In several parts of India, the destruction upset the pattern of vegetation and wildlife. However, the lobby for conservation was growing in influence. In 1864, the establishment of the Forest Department and the Indian Forest Act the next year were the first steps towards formal legal restraints on access to forest resources. A more comprehensive and powerful act came up in 1878.

Research on the history of colonial forestry has investigated the roots of state control and ownership of Indian forests through these laws. Commercial over-exploitation was one motivation. A better assessment of the commercial value of forests, in which non-timber resources such as medicinal plants figured in an increasingly important way, also strengthened conservationism. The economic motive was only one of several independent roots of forest policy. Another imperative was the will to govern by taking control of a collective resource. The representation of nature as a wild space occupied by tribes located on the margins of settled agricultural society encouraged the integration of such spaces with new laws.[13]

[11] S. Das Gupta, *Adivasis and the Raj: Socio-economic Transition of the Hos, 1820–1932* (Hyderabad: Orient BlackSwan, 2011).

[12] P. Robbins, 'Nomadization in Rajasthan, India: Migration, Institutions, and Economy', *Human Ecology* 26, no. 1 (1998): 87–112.

[13] K. Sivaramakrishnan, *Modern Forests: Statemaking and Environmental Change in Colonial Eastern India* (Stanford: Stanford University Press, 1999).

The years between the first two forest acts saw a debate on the nature of rights and privileges, ancient laws, and adaptations needed therein, which could be the basis for practical forest policy. The 1878 act classified forests into three types: 'reserved' forests that were to be under state ownership and control, in exclusion of all or nearly all private rights; 'protected' forests again in state control but not in exclusion of existing rights of usage; and 'village forests' under the management of the village. Understandably, the most commercially valuable forests were reserved. However, protected forests were also progressively reclassified as reserves over time, which shows up in land use statistics as a rise in the extent of forest area (Table 4.2).

The legislation had three significant effects. First, the net income of the forest department increased. While conservation did reduce the scale of exploitation, new uses for forest resources, such as an urban market in furniture, were created, and the state now collected rent from such uses. Second, the scale of destruction did fall, even though World War I saw a sudden revival of timber extraction. And third, customary rights to access were curbed. This move affected the hunter-gatherers as well as groups who lived on forest resources. In at least one sphere, the new laws showed up to be iniquitous: While the small-scale hunting of the forest-dependent peoples was outlawed or curbed, state officers embarked on large-scale hunting of big and small 'game'.

How did the livelihoods of people who lived in or near forests change?

Forest-Dependent Peoples

The economic history of forest dwellers and indigenous peoples whom official sources called 'tribes' revolves around two big changes—erosion of land rights and migration. The tribes were part forest-dependent because the lands that they tilled did not provide sufficient sustenance. Nor did most such lands provide a taxable surplus. The forest-dependent communities tended to be taxed only nominally, often taxed by the plough rather than land area, and the burden of taxation fell upon communities rather than individuals. This situation made the property rights of the forest-dependent peoples different in nature from those that existed in the plains and fertile river valleys.

Progressively in the nineteenth century, the livelihoods of the forest-dependent people were affected. The first Indian Forest Act formally closed access to the forests. Forest administrators developed a deep interest in the widespread practice of shifting cultivation and a generally negative attitudes towards the practice. Similarly, forest conservation affected hunter-gatherer communities and artisanal groups like ironworkers who gathered raw materials from the forests.[14] People affected by these changes were forced to emerge from the forests and move to the croplands of the plains where long-settled farming communities held property rights. Further, the communities that had practised more settled agriculture near or inside the forested zone tended to lose control over property. Outsiders and adventurers from the plains, who secured property in such land by paying money to the zamindar, reduced the indigenous farmers to tenant status.

A third factor acted upon the indigenous people in a rather more positive way. The forest-dependent peoples had always been relatively mobile and available for wage labour in the plains. The poor soil and water scarcity of the uplands made eking out a living there difficult even in the best of conditions and made them willing to move. From the nineteenth century, the opportunity of moving away en masse grew as demand for indentured workers increased manifold (see Chapter 10). The availability of this outlet saw vast numbers leave the uplands for work elsewhere.

The most studied example of the transformation is Chota Nagpur.[15] Forests surrounded the Chota Nagpur plateau before

[14] Ramachandra Guha and Madhav Gadgil, 'State Forestry and Social Conflict in British India', *Past and Present* 123, no. 1 (1989): 141–77.

[15] J. Hoffmann, 'Principles of Succession and Inheritance among the Mundas', *The Journal of the Bihar and Orissa Research Society* 1 (1915): 5–19; Sarat Chandra Roy, *The Mundas and their Country* (Ranchi: Crown, 2004) original 1912; P.P. Mohapatra, 'Class Conflict and Agrarian Regimes in Chota Nagpur, 1860–1950', *IESHR* 28, no. 1 (1991): 1–42; B.B. Chaudhuri, *Peasant History in Late-precolonial and Colonial India* (Delhi:

British rule extended to the region. It had virtually no roads suitable for wheeled traffic and, therefore, little long-distance trade. The major rivers in the region were not navigable in the dry seasons, were dangerous in monsoon, and had no known bridges before the railways of the late nineteenth century. Although well endowed with minerals and iron ore, the local iron industry was practised on a small scale mainly for a local clientele. The population groups living in this zone—the *Munda, Oraon, Kherias, Hos, Birhors,* and *Bhumijs*—cultivated land in the river valleys but usually without irrigation. The laterite soil and undulating topography made even the best crop a paltry one. Land did not produce much more than a precarious subsistence in these areas.

When Eastern India became a Mughal province, there was not much interest in imposing the authority of the provincial capital in the uplands. The local chieftains did try to install a form of *jagirdari,* and in some areas, these attempts saw limited urbanization.[16] By and large, however, the attempt was a limited one, and neither the chieftains nor the imperial administration tried too hard to extract taxes from the uplands. A quit-rent from the villages was all that was collected. As a result of the isolation of the state from the peasants, an indigenous property right evolved in these regions. Labour, not land, was the more critical resource for the peasant and the state.

Pearson Longman, 2008), 716–19; J.C. Jha, *The Kol Insurrection of Chota-Nagpur* (Calcutta: Thacker Spink, 1964).

[16] In North India, the precolonial term 'jagir' referred to an assignment of a part of the revenues of the state to a superior officer. One standard reason for the award of a jagir was the military one; the revenues were to be used for the maintenance of troops under a commander, who held the assignment. Further qualifications specified whether or not the assignment was perpetual, hereditary, unconditional, or conditional upon the performance of a specific service. In theory, most jagirs reverted to the king upon an end of the service. The award of a jagir was implemented by the *nazim,* or the viceroy of the province, who also supervised the reversion of the jagir to the king. The jagir system fell into disuse after the seventeenth century as most revenue grants to commanders and warlords became effectively hereditary.

Property rights rested on groups of people and was contingent on work. Village heads represented an authority over people and were free to allocate land amongst the residents of the village.

This situation continued for some time after the Company assumed power in eastern India. However, the Permanent Settlement (1793) initiated a process of change by converting the old estates into zamindari property and by imposing greater demands upon the zamindars. An asymmetry in rights came up in the uplands; the state recognized the private proprietary right of the chieftains, who paid the taxes. But the state had no means of defending or defining the village-based right to the cultivation of the indigenous people. Thus, when the chieftains farmed out taxation rights to a large number of intermediaries, and the latter tried to squeeze new taxes from the indigenous people, the police and the courts could only defend the former and not the latter. The Kol insurrection of 1831 was a violent reaction against the collapse of the upland order. The Santal Rebellion of 1855 had similar origins (Figure 11.2). Although the property rights regime recognized customary rights after that, already the indigenous people had begun leaving the uplands in large numbers. From the 1930s, a steady flow of emigrants began towards tea plantations in the north-east, Mauritius, and the Caribbean.

In the drier uplands, famines affected the population already suffering from weak access to the commons. When famine conditions struck central India, the tribal groups suffered because of a double squeeze.[17] From a long time past, when communities found themselves short of food, they went in search of food in the forests and common lands. These communities knew wild grass, fruits, leaves, and barks that were edible and they survived on these things for quite some time. It was often by observing these 'wanderings' that government officers in the eighteenth century sensed a famine had

[17] D.E.U. Baker, 'Towards an Understanding of Famine: Northern Madhya Pradesh 1891–1901,' in *India's Colonial Encounter: Essays in Memory of Eric Stokes*, eds M. Hasan and N. Gupta (Delhi: Manohar, 1993); see also V. Damodaran, 'Famine in a Forest Tract: Ecological Change and the Causes of the 1897 Famine in Chota Nagpur, Northern India,' *Environment and History* 1, no. 2 (1995): 129–58, for a similar story.

Figure 11.2 Santal village, c. 1890. The Santal Rebellion of 1855 generated an interest in the experience of the indigenous peoples of eastern India, especially how their lives changed after the Permanent Settlement and forest laws.

© Alamy Stock Photos

begun. The tribal groups knew more about such matters than the peasants, but their knowledge was useless, given that the government had closed access to the forests. Since the tribal groups lived partly in forests, partly outside, partly in the hills, and partly in the plains, conventional relief camps could not reach out to them effectively.

As in land, in water too, state intervention initially took the form of legislation.

Intervention in Water

As Chapter 2 has shown, flood control and the construction of embankments formed a priority for the colonial state from early on, partly because the rule began in the Bengal delta where monsoon floods were a regular occurrence. Further, the unpredictable rivers of the delta posed a tax problem for the government. Revenues came from the land, which was supposedly a fixed resource, but in practice, shifts in rivers could create new land and erase old ones at surprisingly high frequency.[18] Controlling this process would require strong embankments. But embankment construction and flood control required collective action, which the zamindars were not able or willing to offer.

These were problems of the deltaic lands, which were not ordinarily water-scarce. In the semi-arid landscape of northern, western, and southern India, the problem was of a different kind—an absolute or seasonal scarcity of water. Access to water was usually limited and expensive. That the state could help cultivation above all by redistributing water was received wisdom. The Company's engineers did not have to try too hard to persuade their bosses to consider canal and dam construction. From the 1870s, famine commissions added an urgency to this policy, projecting irrigation as the only preventive measure the state could undertake against famines in the drylands.

In the end, the canal projects that the state did embark on remained geographically confined to the western part of the Indo-Gangetic basin and, on a more limited scale, deltas of Godavari and Krishna in south-eastern India. Canals redistributed surface water from perennial rivers. The redistribution was possible at all with the Himalayan snowmelt rivers and in the deltas of rainfed rivers. But since they operated in technically water-rich areas, occasionally they also had adverse environmental consequences. In western UP, canals interfered with natural drainage, caused salination of soil, waterlogging, and malaria epidemic (Chapter 4).

Partly inspired by these assessments of the colonial water projects, historians at times treat these projects less as an economic benefit and more as a symbol of power and authority. They offer two stories. First, the colonial revenue policy and property right

[18] One study of the Kosi basin in Bihar suggests that the state, in its drive to collect more revenue, ignored and failed to address problems like these. Christopher V. Hill, 'Water and Power: Riparian Legislation and Agrarian Control in Colonial Bengal', *Environmental History Review* 14, no. 4 (1990): 1–20.

regime weakened and eventually destroyed local small-scale systems of irrigation that relied on community management.[19] Thus, before new hydraulic knowledge established itself as the best option, old local knowledge had to retreat and be forgotten. The second thesis is related to the first one. Colonial hydrology, then, was not the best option, but it appeared as the superior technology because it represented the authority of the state.[20] Technology and power, control over water, and control over people, thus, reinforced one another.[21]

These stylized models of transition that discuss irrigation as a power game contain elements of truth. For example, many local systems of water recycling did disappear. But there are two problems with these models. First, they exaggerate the capacity of local systems and underestimate peasants' choices. Like the story of forest management, they hint at a golden age of community control that may never have existed. Second, they exaggerate colonial power. Colonial hydrology had limited reach. The proportion of irrigated land was about one-fifth overall at the end of colonial rule and considerably smaller in the water-scarce Deccan Plateau. The state never delivered results in the arid lands and uplands, where famines usually started. The famines themselves underscored the failure and the limits of colonial science in the matter of water. The problem of water distribution in these lands was far too big for the engineers to solve. Colonial hydrology symbolized state power in some regions; it symbolized a weak state elsewhere.

Land and water issues concerned mainly the countryside and resource use for living. Cities raised a different set of issues, that of disease, congestion, pollution, and the quality of life.

[19] Nirmal Sengupta, 'The Indigenous Irrigation Organisation in South Bihar', *IESHR* 17, no. 2 (1980): 157–87.

[20] David Gilmartin, 'Water and Waste: Nature, Productivity and Colonialism in the Indus Basin', *EPW* 38, no. 48 (2003): 5057–65. See also the survey by Rohan D'Souza, 'Water in British India: The Making of a "Colonial Hydrology"', *History Compass* 4, no.4 (2006): 621–8.

[21] D'Souza, 'Water in British India: The Making of a "Colonial Hydrology"'.

Cities, Public Health

European expansion in the New World destroyed native ecosystems and populations through new diseases, plants, and animals, enabling the creation of neo-Europes in these regions. In the Old World of Asia, the impact was of a different order from that of the 'Columbian exchange'. The existence of developed agricultural civilizations, dense settlements, and, therefore, greater disease resistance enabled these populations to withstand the disease organisms that came with the Europeans. Indeed, tropical Asia had more to offer by way of disease organisms. The demographic balance of payments was against the Europeans in this case. Cities, however, were remarkably unhealthy spaces initially.

The Company's rule over India began with the administration of three port cities. When the rule became secure in the nineteenth century, and earlier in Calcutta, these cities experienced large-scale migration and a population explosion. Water supply, sanitation, public health, and settlement patterns came under immense pressure. An 1840s survey of vital statistics in Calcutta reveals the appalling conditions of health in the city.[22] Crude death rates among the English population was 35 per 1000; among the Armenians and other Europeans 40–60, and among the Portuguese 125. The high figure for the Portuguese reflected the fact that more Portuguese settlers lived with children. Infant mortality, likewise, explained much of the difference between the Hindus (65) and the Muslims (28). More Muslims than Hindus in the city were single males. These figures were influenced by 'the great inundation' of the city in 1833, which affected the slums that housed the poorer Europeans and Indians. Calcutta was among the wealthiest cities in the nineteenth century, and yet, Muddoosoodeen Gupto, a doctor of the city, '[did] not see in the town of Calcutta any children that are in perfect health'.[23] Conditions could not be very different in Bombay and Madras.

[22] Cuthbert Finch, 'Vital Statistics of Calcutta', *Journal of the Statistical Society of London* 13, no. 2 (1850): 168–82.

[23] Finch, 'Vital Statistics of Calcutta.'

The presence of wealthy merchants and a powerful state did not automatically translate into efficient civic management. As Mariam Dossal's work on Bombay shows, the attempt to use wealth and power to improve public health and urban public goods often faced obstacles.[24] Merchants were reluctant to fund public projects, and the imperial administration had different priorities. Nevertheless, professionals such as the civil engineer Henry Conybeare, whose 1852 report on sanitary conditions in Bombay influenced the decision to construct large-scale water supply and urban improvement projects, did make a difference[25] Over time, sanitation, disease control, and centralized supply of water became interconnected goals. And yet, as John Broich has shown, urban water schemes faced resistance from locals when these involved closing of wells and even failed because the local geography did not always suit piped water projects.[26] By the early twentieth century, industrialization and the burning of coal and wood created a new problem in the cities, air pollution, which drove the city administration to create regulations that had consequences for the economy of ordinary households.[27]

The long-term effect of the disjointed efforts to control epidemics and improve life expectancy was nevertheless a positive one. Dryland famines disappeared after 1900, thanks more to the railways and water projects. Urban sanitation improved. Epidemics came under control. Infant mortality implied in the 1850 report on Calcutta city was around 250 per 1000. It was about 200 in 1900.

[24] Mariam Dossal, *Imperial Designs and Indian Realities: The Planning of Bombay City 1845–1875* (Bombay: Oxford University Press, 1991).

[25] See Mariam Dossal, 'Henry Conybeare and the Politics of Centralised Water Supply in Mid-nineteenth Century Bombay', *IESHR* 25, no. 1 (1988): 79–96.

[26] John Broich, 'Engineering the Empire: British Water Supply Systems and Colonial Societies, 1850–1900', *Journal of British Studies* 46, no. 2 (2007): 346–65.

[27] M.R. Anderson, 'The Conquest of Smoke: Legislation and Pollution in Colonial Calcutta,' in *Nature, Culture, Imperialism: Essays on the Environmental History of South Asia*, eds D. Arnold and R. Guha (New Delhi: Oxford University Press, 1995), 293–335.

From 1921, the rate began to fall rapidly, in all regions, reaching 146 in 1947. Science, the state, and taxpayers' money did confer a great benefit upon the Indian population, longer life. Paradoxically, the demographic transition imposed pressure on limited land and water.

Compared with the sphere of state intervention, the other spheres where capitalist enterprise and scientific research acted as drivers in long-term economic change can be discussed quickly, partly because many of the relevant themes under these two headings also involved the agency of the state and have been touched on already, and partly, these themes appear in other chapters.

PRIVATE ENTERPRISE

Commercial exploitation of resources looms large in the story of the forests. For example, the growth of railways and the construction industry raised the value of timber and forest resources, which encouraged further regulation as well as the controlled exploitation of forest resources. Alarmed by these tendencies and informed by ideas that linked forests and climate, the state also introduced conservation measures. However, forests were not the main field of interaction between commerce and natural resources. It was land, trade, and manufacturing.

Global economic expansion and the global shift in terms of trade in favour of agriculture (Chapter 3) encouraged expansion in cultivation. The agricultural expansion was a combined story of commercialization, industrialization, and banking growth. During the colonial era, a pattern of economic change emerged in which land, trade, finance, and manufacturing became interdependent parts of a single system. Natural resource was the fuel that ran the system. Agriculture was the main livelihood and it expanded by bringing in new land under cultivation. Trade was the most important occupation outside agriculture, but it was dependent on trading in agricultural commodities. Modern and traditional industry processed natural fibres mainly and, therefore, gained from the domestic production of fibres. Growth of trade enabled merchants to make enough money to invest in modern industry. Labour and capital markets also adapted to this interdependence. Natural resources were key to the possibility of such interdependent change.

Geography not only enabled but also constrained the process. The tropical monsoon climate created high seasonal variations in agricultural activity. A short busy season around the harvest saw volume of trade rise quickly, and interest rates shoot up, wages and employment rise, and demand for money explode. During a long slack season, interest rates fell, workers were idle, and trade subdued. Seasonality shaped labour and capital markets in important ways. For example, most of the wage workers in the modern factories came from villages where they went back during harvests. The employers resented their continuing ties with the village, but this was an effect of the environment rather than a culturally conditioned choice. Similarly, the very high busy season interest rates made the short-term money market so attractive for most moneylenders and bankers that they preferred to keep money idle for much the year instead of lending it in the long-term market or to industries.[28] Industries were starved of capital.

Agricultural growth, in turn, put pressure on the environment. In the first half of the nineteenth century, the expansion of cultivation made some types of fuels such as straw or charcoal gathered from the commons more expensive, which hurt certain traditional industries. Salt production in Bengal is one example of this effect.[29] Several attempts to start iron smelting on a large scale by European artisans failed to make profits, among other reasons, because of charcoal shortages (Chapter 2). More generally, agricultural growth led to deforestation, changes in river morphology, imposed pressure on soil quality, and on the commons, as the previous section has discussed (see also Chapter 4). Canals occasionally had adverse effects on the environment (see earlier discussion).

[28] Tirthankar Roy, 'Monsoon and the Market for Money in Late Colonial India', *Enterprise and Society* 17, no. 2 (2016): 324–57.

[29] Sayako Kanda, 'Environmental Changes, the Emergence of a Fuel Market, and the Working Conditions of Salt Makers in Bengal, c. 1780–1845', *International Review of Social History* 55(Supplement) (2010): 123–51.

Railway construction began as a private enterprise in India, encouraged by state-guaranteed profits. Although defence was one of the original aims behind state sponsorship, the railways mainly facilitated commodity trade. In turn, the railway construction boom in the late nineteenth century led to deforestation and extraction of timber, especially in the foothills of the Himalayas.[30]

Agricultural expansion intensified competition for land and water. In land, rising rents (see Chapter 4) reflected the scarcity value and competition for land. In irrigation water, where the supply was limited and confined to specific sources, there were conflicts over distribution. With canals and tanks, 'head-reach' and 'tail-end' farmers faced different supply situations and levels of water security during scarcities. The inequality, if not redressed by collective action or state intervention, would induce one group of farmers to overuse water and switch to water-intensive crops, and another group to seek alternative sources and other livelihoods.[31]

While resource-intensive economic change did unleash disruptions, these consequences influenced a growing idea of preservation and environmentalism.

THE STUDY OF NATURE

The tropics challenged European notions of nature. The Indian climate, the geology, the quality of land, and the germs that caused diseases were very different from those regions that the Europeans had left behind. The numerous attempts that followed from the late eighteenth century to gather data and discuss these in an emerging Indo-European public sphere, in such platforms as the Asiatic Society, for example, can be seen alternatively as helping efficient exploitation of resources or helping 'environmentalism'. Broadly, environmentalism is the idea that the state should manage the environment to protect

[30] Das, 'Colonialism and the Environment in India.'

[31] For a discussion on distributional conflicts, and a case study, see Velayutham Saravanan, 'Technological Transformation and Water Conflicts in the Bhavani River Basin of Tamil Nadu, 1930-1970', *Environment and History* 7, no. 3 (2001): 289–334.

it from disruptive human action.[32] Behind the latter notion, there was another developing idea that human welfare depended on sustaining the environment. Studies of environmentalism find Richard Grove's work, which shows how European thinking on nature was influenced by meeting non-European environments, useful.[33] The birth of scientific forestry is traced to ideas called 'desiccationist', held together by the belief that there was a link between tree cover and soil erosion and drought.[34] Later studies on scientific forestry also emphasize the training of the participants and the intellectual exchanges they took part in.[35]

All this is not to suggest that environmentalist notions did not exist in indigenous societies before, but they did not form part of public intellectual discourse, and one with political effect, to the extent the colonial-era environmentalism did. The anxiety that human action could, in fact, damage nature was a modern one and reinforced by deforestation and agricultural intensification in colonial regions. Nevertheless, the application of management ideas derived from environmentalist impulses often came in conflict with existing practices, resistance by locals who lost access to resources, and simple impracticality, friction that Guha demonstrates well.[36] And there were many disagreements and differences within environmentalism.

The systematic study of nature was a nineteenth-century Indo-European enterprise. By systematic study, I mean an attempt to construct theoretical models of climate, geology, and ecology from raw data and recognizing feedbacks between the theoretical enterprise

[32] On environmentalism, see Gregory A. Barton, *Empire Forestry and the Origins of Environmentalism* (Cambridge: Cambridge University Press, 2002).

[33] Richard Grove, *Green Imperialism: Colonial Expansion, Tropical Island Edens and the Origins of Environmentalism, 1600-1860* (Cambridge: Cambridge University Press, 1995).

[34] Grove, *Green Imperialism*.

[35] S. Ravi Rajan, *Modernizing Nature: Forestry and Imperial Eco-development 1800-1950* (Oxford: Oxford University Press, 2006).

[36] Ramachandra Guha, 'Scientific Forestry and Social Change in Uttarakhand', *EPW* 20, no. 45/47 (1985): 1939–52.

and the data-gathering one. Researches like these delivered a significant result in the field of epidemic control (Chapter 10). The systematic study of nature, in this sense, had significant implications for material life, livelihoods, and economic history.

In public health and epidemic control, research and observation led to measures that contributed to the demographic transition. South Asia faces a significantly above-average risk of occurrence of natural disasters like earthquakes and coastal storms. These events interested the amateur geologists, ship captains, port assessors, and weather scientists from the early nineteenth century, because they were often directly affected by such events. Well before the state had created institutions where geographical research would take place, research papers began to be published, often using limited quantities of data on the nature of these events. Every earthquake confronted the nineteenth-century geologist in India with a set of 'baffling phenomena'. While meeting these challenges, geologists enriched the understanding of Himalayan plate tectonics. The great Bay of Bengal storms of the nineteenth century led to the formation of a theory of cyclones in the region. Initially, the data gathered to study these phenomena were random. But in the long run, the scientific enterprise led to the creation of a meteorological department and targeted geographical information systems that could predict the occurrence of major climatic events.[37]

***

Economic change in colonial India was natural resource-intensive. Colonialism and globalization changed the intensity and pattern of the use of natural resources. The specific forces included state intervention acting via legislation and investment in infrastructure, industrialization, and agricultural expansion, and the emergence of a systematic study of nature.

What were the effects? These changes put enormous pressure on land, forests, and the livelihoods of groups that depended on

[37] See on this subject, Tirthankar Roy, *Natural Disasters and Indian History* (Delhi: Oxford University Press, 2012).

common resources. Over the entire period, land use changed, and forests retreated or degraded. On the other hand, these changes also delivered unprecedented agricultural expansion, resource-driven industrialization, and commodity trade, and perhaps the greatest benefit of all, a steady decline in mortality from 1900. The speed of these processes varied regionally. Agricultural growth, supported by state intervention in water, was deeper in the Indo-Gangetic basin and the deltas than in the arid interior, where colonial hydrology was no match for the natural environment.

So far, princely states have stayed in the background. The next chapter brings these territories to the centre stage.

12

The Princely States

The princely states were the kingdoms that British India did not annex to itself. The states were allies of the British, and those in northern India had demonstrated their loyalty during the great Mutiny (1857). After this event, the Crown took over in British India and announced a stop to further conquest. Thereafter, the states lived under an agreement with British India; two points of the agreement were that they would keep trade open and would not raise an army. A British resident stationed in or near the capital city of a state observed the regime and, in some cases (like Mysore), took a part in running it. The states ruled over 40–45 per cent of the area of India and 25 per cent of the population (Map 1.1).

How did colonialism shape their economies? Did freedom make them more welfare-minded governments than British India? This is a difficult question to answer because the states were very diverse, and we do not know enough about them to say just how diverse they were. Indeed, being free may have made them more dissimilar than similar. With 560-odd states in existence, the smallest being of 7 square miles and the largest 83,000, to claim that freedom made these similar in capacity or intent is doubtful. I will use averages, mainly to illustrate if their geographical situation made a difference. Much of the scholarship on princely states exist as case studies. These studies caution against generalizing about their history because we do not know anything about most of them. These studies, however, do offer

302   ECONOMIC HISTORY OF INDIA

some generalizations. I will return to these generalizations, but first, it is useful to have a general idea about what kind of territories the chapter is going to discuss.

WHO WERE THE STATES?

There were about 560 of these states. Probably the smallest state was Naigawan in the Gangetic plains. At seven square miles, it was little more than a village. In fact, well over half the states, almost all of them in the formerly Maratha-ruled western India, were not much more than a cluster of villages each. At the other end, there were the six larger states: Hyderabad, Mysore, Travancore–Cochin (two similar states joined together in 1949), Baroda, Indore, and Gwalior. At 83,000 square miles, Hyderabad was larger than most British Indian provinces. In the north-western frontier regions and eastern and northern Burma, large territories were governed by tribal councils. These territories, though clubbed with the princely states, were not governed by hereditary princes.[1]

These states were distinct from British India by being independently ruled. But in financial capacity, most of them were weaker than a British Indian district, even the larger of the landlord estates. The so-called king of Darbhanga, for example, commanded a territory of 2,500 square kilometres and revenue that far exceeded that of most of the states. But the king was not an independent prince, only a zamindar created by the Permanent Settlement.

In matters of administration, most states maintained their bond with tradition. They were ruled by a coterie of palace insiders, drew their main income from directly owned land or Khalsa land, and spent most of their money on maintaining the palace.[2] The economy

[1] For a descriptive history, see W. Lee-Warner, *The Native States of India*, (London: Macmillan Publishers, 1910). See Barbara Ramusack, *The Indian Princes and their States*, (Cambridge: Cambridge University Press, 2008), for an analytical history.

[2] The Arabic word *khalsa* or the Hindi word *khalisa* means pure; in Mughal India, the word sometimes referred to land on which the sovereign had right over.

was agricultural in most states and left on its own. Where feudal lords held land, a large part of the revenue and military force was beyond the control of the palace. So was the system of law and justice. But things were changing between 1860 and 1940, in at least three ways. In varying degrees, all states took part in these three processes.

First, there was increasing acceptance of the idea of bureaucratic rule. Formally, the government remained a despotism. But in practice, several states left governance to bureaucrats headed by a chief minister and even experimented with representative government. Second, they tried to centralize their authority. Again, their capacity to do so varied. In those states where feudal landlords retained their hereditary rights and power, the states could do little to increase their revenue. No state carried out thoroughgoing land reform. But they passed laws, experimented with alternative sources of revenue, and discussed a state-directed economic development of their domains more readily. Third, the nationalist wave in the late interwar years stressed the need for governments to spend more on public goods and industrialization; the states were influenced by that wave.

So much for governance and ideology. What about economic change?

ECONOMIC HISTORY: HOW DIFFERENT WERE THE STATES FROM BRITISH INDIA?

In the absence of more specific data, it seems fair to say that most states in the late nineteenth century understood by economic prosperity a concept very similar to how British India saw economic development—the growth of commerce and cultivation. Railways and irrigation were the key instruments to achieve these aims. But promoting trade, building railways, and supplying irrigation water to cultivators were all challenges more difficult to meet in the states. This was so because most of them were small in size, situated in hilly land, dry and landlocked, and without perennial rivers. When possible, they built railways and joined them with the network of lines that connected the port cities of British India.

The nineteenth-century globalization, together with initial differences in geographical endowments, favoured British India more than the princely states. This globalization relied on the ports for export, the deltas and the Indo-Gangetic basin for production of the commodities that went into trade, and foreign money raised by debt and investment to fund railways and irrigation. In all three respects, British India was better endowed than were the states. These conditions, therefore, led to increasing inequality between British India and the princely states. Table 12.1 gives us a snapshot of how much the states fell behind. At the same time, most states emulated that model, with more limited resources, rather than pursuing a radically different pathway.

Table 12.1   British India and the states, 1905

		British Indian districts (201)	Princely states (198)
1	Population, average per unit	968,764	318,865
2	Area, average per unit (square miles)	3891	3171
3	Population density	425	199
4	Cultivated area/total area (per cent)	52	20
5	Rainfall, annual (inches)	60	42
6	Total revenue per capita (Rs)	2.05	4.34
7	Total revenue per square mile (Rs)	425	386
8	Land revenue per square mile of cultivated area (Rs)	1060	899
9	Proportion of non-agricultural to total revenue (per cent)	36	47
10	Roads (miles of paved road per 1000 square miles)	49.3	14.6
11	Railways (miles per 1000 square miles)	6.5	6.0
12	Size of the largest town as a ratio of population, per cent (size shown in bracket)	4 (38,634)	4 (13,334)
13	Literacy rate	4.3	3.5

Source: India, *The Imperial Gazetteer of India*, vols 1–31 (Oxford: Clarendon Press, 1908). The figures are population-weighted or area-weighted averages as appropriate.

John Hurd II processed census data to show that in the early twentieth century, the states lagged behind British India on three benchmarks: proportion of employment outside agriculture, the rate of migration, and urbanization. He attributed their poorer record on non-agricultural activity to the refusal of British India to guarantee princely state loans (which reduced capital expenditure) and the feudal structure of the states. Excessive influence of landlords reduced the freedom of the kings.[3]

Employment and urbanization are indirect and unreliable measures of economic change. We need more direct measures of comparison. In national income trends, the states did not show a distinct pattern of change from British India. I base this conclusion on the data for Figure 1.1 (Chapter 1), which includes the princely states. Going by this data set, the states took part in business growth, mortality decline, and a stagnant rural sector. Income for the states, however, are of worse quality than population numbers.

Another useful source allows us to compare the states and British India, only for one year (1908), but in great detail. The 25-volume *Imperial Gazetteer of India* collected a lot of information on regions. The Imperial Gazetteer did not set out to collect statistical information. But it used a uniform questionnaire in its descriptions of territorial units so that it is possible to pick from the descriptions numbers relating to the area, population, revenue, rainfall, cultivated and irrigated areas, roads and railways, literacy, and the size of the largest town. From this source, partial or full details are available for 430 districts of British India and 130 princely states, covering 97 per cent of the population and 93 per cent of land area.[4]

The source reveals a few small differences in the conditions of the two types of territory. British India had a higher population density (rows 1–3 of Table 12.1) because it ruled over the coasts,

[3] John Hurd II, 'Some Economic Characteristics of the Princely States of India, 1901–1931' (PhD thesis, University of Pennsylvania, 1969). These hypotheses were re-examined by others with different data and results.

[4] More on the data, Tirthankar Roy, 'Geography or Politics? Regional Inequality in Colonial India', *European Review of Economic History* 18, no. 3 (2014): 306–23. The raw data set is available on request from the author.

the deltas, and the Indo-Gangetic basin, the most fertile and populated regions. The Company state in India began in the deltas and the coasts because it had been set up by the maritime merchants who had operated in the deltas and the coasts. These zones also had higher agricultural yield and richer states. On the other hand, a large part of the arid lands, deserts, forests, and dry uplands of the Deccan Plateau fell within the domain of the princely states (see rows 4 and 5 in Table 12.1).

This basic geographical difference led to a few other differences. One of these was in fiscal capacity (rows 6–8 of Table 12.1). Revenue in all cases came mainly (60–80 per cent) from land; agriculture formed the principal livelihood. Given that the major part of the revenue came from land, an appropriate measure of the productive capacity of a region should be land revenue per cultivated area. The governments of the princely states were on average poorer if we measure revenue per acre. But given the higher population density in British India, revenue per head was smaller there. Also, princely states were relatively more dependent on non-land taxes (row 9 of Table 12.1), because they needed to compensate for their lower land tax.

Using this measure (tax per mile), we can test if British India and the princely states became more unequal over time or not because revenue per mile data is available also from an 1853 report.[5] A comparison of the two data sets suggests increasing regional inequality between 1853 and 1908. There was almost certainly a fall in inequality between 1908 and 1950, which we know because the statistical measure of regional inequality within the Indian Union reported immediately after Independence in 1947 was significantly lower than what the 1908 gazetteer data would reveal to us. I will return to the rise and fall of regional inequality a little later.

The differences in geography and fiscal capacity translated into differences in infrastructure. There were few all-weather roads in the territory of the states (row 10, Table 12.1). In the heyday of railway expansion in India (1870–1920), the states built their own railways. Most served passenger traffic. In western India (such as Saurashtra

---

[5] Anon., *The Native States of India* (Pamphlet) (London, 1853).

in Gujarat), the states were so many and each so small that the state railways were built in small uncoordinated segments that did not feed effectively into the long-distance routes running through British India (row 11, Table 12.1). Not surprisingly, the scale of urban settlements was smaller on average within the princely states (row 12, Table 12.1). Because urbanization was limited, investment in schools was also limited, though, in respect of literacy (row 13, Table 12.1), princely states and British India were roughly similar.

The biggest cities in this time were the port cities. The four major ports, Bombay, Calcutta, Madras, and Karachi, were all located in British India. Among the larger princely states, only Travancore–Cochin had a long seafront. The economy of the two states was also more export-oriented, a fact helped by a rich maritime tradition. Of the other major states, Baroda was well connected by rail with the Bombay port. But nearly all the others were landlocked and had no comparable history of long-distance commerce by sea.

Now consider some other differences between the two territories that Table 12.1 does not report on. Foreign investment inflow was significantly less in the states, with a few exceptions. The largest states (Mysore, Travancore, and Hyderabad) received more foreign investment in mining, railways, and trade. In Hyderabad, the railways and the colliery received foreign capital. In Mysore, the Kolar goldfields, the single largest modern enterprise in the state, were foreign-owned. In Travancore and Cochin, plantations had a significant foreign presence.

Except for these few cases, little foreign investment entered businesses in the princely states, compared with British India. Industries were set up mainly by indigenous land-owning groups, such as the *Kanbis* in Baroda or the Syrian Christian community of Travancore–Cochin. In Indore and Gwalior, enterprise and capital in the textile industry mainly came from North Indian merchant communities like the Marwaris.

As in British India, in the princely states, the prospects of trade and industry depended on the availability of local natural resources and access to a seafront. The industrial composition was similar. Thus, in Gwalior, Indore, Baroda, Hyderabad, Travancore, Cochin, and Mysore, cotton textiles dominated large-scale industry until the 1920s, when some diversification happened. Coal mining, tobacco manufacturing, and cement were important in Hyderabad and gold mining, steel, sandalwood oil, and soap factories in Mysore. Around 1880, a company formed to exploit the coal reserves in the south-eastern Hyderabad state, discovered in 1872. A railway connected the mining village with the main lines. By 1920, a township of several thousand people had developed in the area known as Singareni mining complex. In Travancore and Cochin, the major forms of modern enterprise were plantations of tea, rubber, and coffee, and agricultural processing industries such as coir and cashew.

To sum up the discussion so far, all available data show that the states were not radically different from British India, but that with their poorer access to capital, markets, ports, and transport networks, they were less well placed than some regions in British India to gain from the economic globalization process.

What about their governments? Were they radically different from the government of British India? The revenue data in Table 12.1 showed that on average, the states earned about the same kind of money as did British India. What about expenditures?

GOVERNMENTS: STRUCTURE AND ECONOMIC POLICY

In terms of revenues, both territories mainly relied on land taxes. At least, they did in the nineteenth century. Both zones understood well the dangers posed by over-reliance on the land tax, especially in times of famine when the land tax fell and the state needed money for famine relief. The governments of both the states and British India tried to diversify the tax base and raise more money in the interwar period. In this effort, British India was more successful because it had bigger ports and could raise customs revenue. S. Sivasubramonian's national income calculations show that in 1921–41, real income per person generated by the government more than doubled in British India and nearly doubled in the states. In both, the dependence on land tax was reduced and that of commodity taxes and state royalties or excise increased.

There was one difference between British India and the states that mattered crucially to funding capital expenditure. Few princely states borrowed from the market, whereas the Government of India did on a large scale to fund capital expenditure. The states were not encouraged to raise foreign sovereign debt, whereas British India could. British India feared that it might need to guarantee loans raised in London on behalf of states that did not have the capacity to take large foreign loans. Most states could not approach the London money market on their own anyway. In running the financial system and the fiscal system, the British Indian government and British businesses in Asia enjoyed greater access to the London money market than did their counterparts in the princely states. The Government of India security was a major financial instrument in London. Foreign capitalists in the late nineteenth century sold shares in London. Railway companies in the mid-nineteenth century raised capital in London. Balancing these inflows, there were also vast outflows of factor payments, debt service, and government remittances. This outflow the nationalists called drain, as we have seen. The princely states did not see such outflow. By its reluctance to sponsor the states' public debt, British India sheltered them from the so-called drain.

If the lack of access to foreign debt market was bad news for them, the princely states got a huge gift from British India in return. In British India, the major expenditure was the maintenance of an army. In effect, the army guaranteed peace also in the princely states, for by the terms of their agreement, British India would come to the aid of a princely state if one of them was attacked by another. The princely states needed to keep small armies to maintain peace on their borders, an implicit subsidy delivered by British India (see also Figure 12.1).

What, then, did they spend their money on? As far as we can see from the accounts of a few large states, the biggest item of expenditure was an item called 'palace expenses', that is, the upkeep and maintenance of the royal household. We can safely assume that for most smaller states where business conditions were not great, this one item would almost exhaust the budget. Indeed, together with administration, including police and justice, palace expenses took away a large proportion of the expenditure. For example, in Mysore during 1905 and 1910, these heads accounted for over half of public expenditure.

Figure 12.1   Maharana and the British agent at the hunt, c. 1878

Note: With British India taking over their defence duties and not much money or territory to command, many princes and their British political agents had time to kill.

© Alamy Stock Photos

There were, however, a few quite exceptional cases. These exceptional cases also became more active in the early twentieth century. Invariably, these states controlled larger territories than average, which translated into bigger-than-average scale of government income. In some cases, the economic structure was such as to permit a state income per head of population larger than that in British India.

THE FOUR EXCEPTIONS: TRAVANCORE, BARODA, MYSORE, AND HYDERABAD

Hyderabad and Mysore were large enough to generate sufficient revenues and undertake ambitious developmental projects. In Mysore, the share of income from excise, forest royalties, state railways, and royalties from the Kolar gold mines increased substantially between 1880 and 1910. Forest income was also crucial in some of the sub-Himalayan states. Mysore also had plantation land and developed rice-based economies on the south-western coast, where a banking hub emerged on the back of commodity trading. Baroda, linked with Bombay and Ahmedabad by train, shared in the textile-based industrialization that was in full swing in these cities. The businesses of Baroda maintained a good relationship with the court. The state could rely on the bankers to raise money. The Bank of Baroda was a product of such collaboration. Three of these states, Mysore, Baroda, and Travancore, where some of these strategies succeeded more than their neighbours, are often marked out from the rest and called the 'progressive' states.[6] Their progressive credential may be overrated. They had a larger revenue capacity to undertake projects. Most states were too small to do that.

Travancore scored a significant success in raising revenue from non-land sources. To see this, compare Travancore's finances with those of its neighbouring Indian province, Madras, around 1901–4.[7]

Revenue/head, Madras: Rs 1.24
Revenue/head, Travancore: Rs 2.71
Revenue/square mile, Madras: Rs 340
Revenue/square mile, Travancore: Rs 1516

[6] See Ramusack, *The Indian Princes and their States.*
[7] I draw the data from V. Nagam Aiya, *Travancore State Manual* (Trivandrum: Travancore Government Press, 1906), 645 and *Statistical Abstracts for British India* (Calcutta: Government Press, 1901–4).

Travancore had greater financial resources because it had a different economic structure from neighbouring Madras. Travancore was relatively well watered and had land suitable for plantations. The state earned an income from the assessment of plantation land, lands growing tree crops, from pepper monopoly, and was not too dependent on taxes that were taken from the peasants. The revenue was more stable because Travancore did not suffer from famines.

What difference did earning power mean? In the interwar period, the concept of development changed. Nationalist criticism that the colonial state had neglected industrialization and welfare and the example of Soviet socialism made state leadership in industry and education more of a priority than it had been before. Both British India and the states tried to deliver more on these heads. The larger states could spend more. British India, with its military expenditure commitment, had a smaller capacity to spend on other heads. At this point, there may have been a divergence between British India and the states, on expenditure on non-defence public goods per head, but that conjecture remains a conjecture until more revenue and expenditure data become available.

The larger states did not all go in the same direction. The Travancore state focused on education. Travancore did not need to spend money on canals. It was already a well-watered region and had a different crop regime from North India. It spent money on education instead. In the 1850s, when the education drive began, the state relied on the partnership of the Christian missions. Later, it took on some of the financial burdens upon itself. In this way, a combination of Christianity and greater state capacity led to a literacy drive that made this region way more educated than the rest of India at the time of Independence.[8]

In Mysore, Hyderabad, and Travancore, the government played or wanted to play an active role in initiating industrialization. In Mysore, discussions about state aid to industry turned into a debate between two approaches, one focused on adapting traditional industry to modern markets and consumption patterns, and another on capital and

---

[8] Robin Jefferey, ed., *People, Princes and Paramount Power: Society and Politics in the Indian Princely States* (Delhi: Oxford University Press, 1978).

intermediate goods under state sponsorship. The second approach, identified with the Mysore prime minister (Diwan) M. Visvesvaraya, won the debate. In the early twentieth century, a gold field, cigarette factories, textile mills, and a steel factory were started in the public and the private sectors. Mysore's terrain and the many rivers had alerted the policymakers to hydroelectric potentials. Bangalore was possibly the first major town to be illuminated by electricity. Hyderabad confined itself to industrial development under the leadership of the local landed and trading communities. But even here, the state gave direct and indirect encouragement to industrialization.

In Punjab, where new irrigation canals were opening, the princely states wanted to share in the gains by sharing some of the expenses. British India could build more large-scale canal projects than could the princely states, because the former controlled larger territories, had more peasants living in them, and expected the peasants to pay a fee. But where possible, states took part in canal projects. The co-funded Sirhind canal on the Sutlej, for example, irrigated lands in Ferozepur and Ludhiana Districts of British Punjab and lands in the princely states of Jind, Patiala, and Nabha.

Some princely states compensated for the limitations of their financial system by sponsoring banks. The Bank of Baroda was started in 1908 by the Maharaja of Baroda, Sayajirao Gaekwad, in collaboration with the leading shroff houses of Baroda. Hyderabad pioneered the concept of state-backed investment banking, which was used by governments in post-Independence India.

Although smaller than their counterparts in British India, the capitals of almost all princely states, small or large, saw new schools, colleges, and, in some cases, universities appear in the early twentieth century. There was a similar clustering of schools and hospitals in the British Indian district towns too, but the development in the states usually received personal attention by the ruling elites in contrast with the situation in British Indian districts.

DID INDEPENDENCE MATTER?

Did independence make the states ideologically more driven or motivated to play a developmental role? A recent scholarship suggests that this was the case and that independence did make the states more development-minded, more inclined to spend on public goods, whereas the weight of colonialism made the British Indian provinces less willing or able to spend on infrastructure and welfare.[9] The argument is not wholly persuasive. It overlooks state capacity. Their independence from British India notwithstanding, the princely states' capacity to design an autonomous development policy was constrained. There were three types of constraints.

One of these was colonial interference, such as the embargo imposed on raising loans in London. Individual projects designed in the states invited colonial interference, sometimes to the detriment of the project and the states concerned.[10] Such interferences did happen, though any claim that the states could do much better without British India poking its nose is far-fetched. Most states were simply not creditworthy. Further, colonial interference was not uniformly bad for them. The British Indian Army subsidized the states' military expenditure. If British India interfered in the states' affairs, sometimes against their interest, there was also the occasional collaboration. The Sirhind canal in the north and the administration of Mysore are examples of such collaboration. So, colonialism was not universally a constraint on the capacity of the princely states.

The second type of constraint was internal. A feudalistic political structure, where much wealth and power rested with the landlords, made the kings weaker and left them less room to design and fund developmental projects.[11] Confirming this link in a different way, in Baroda, a deficiency of landlords made the court freer to act. Overall, the evidence to support or dispute this hypothesis is anecdotal.

A third constraint arose from geography. The states were too resource-constrained to play the globalization game. The predominance of arid, upland, landlocked, and forest zones in their domain

[9] Lakshmi Iyer, 'Direct versus Indirect Colonial Rule in India: Long-term Consequences', *Review of Economics and Statistics* 92, no. 4 (2010): 693–712.

[10] See discussion in Ramusack, *The Indian Princes and their States*, 186–204.

[11] Hurd, 'Economic Characteristics'.

made them less able to promote trade by building railways and ports. They, on average, earned less money per square mile than British India. Even though they earned more money per head, most of the states were simply too small to make use of the economies of scale that large-scale projects would deliver. For example, the railways they built were too small and too few.

The exceptions to this rule were the so-called progressive states— Mysore, Baroda, Travancore, and to a lesser extent, Hyderabad. These states thought about big projects and about the state's role in shaping development. Baroda set up banks, Travancore invested in education, Hyderabad constructed railways, and Mysore went for industrialization and electricity. These states are called progressive to imply that they were more enlightened and more developmental, a propensity that must have come from their independence.

This is a wrong reading of the situation. Whether these states were more enlightened or not is irrelevant. They thought in developmental terms because they could. Compared with the other states, these four had the advantage of scale. They earned enough money and commanded big enough territories to undertake projects that involved economies of scale, like dams, railway, power stations, banks, and roads. It was their size that made them think differently. Economic structure mattered too. For example, the chance to collect more money in South India from mines and plantations was an advantage. These were cheaper taxes to collect than a tax on peasants. In 1905, the revenue per head of Mysore, Travancore, and Baroda was double that of British India, and the revenue per square mile was three times that of British India.

***

The message of this chapter is that the princely states were not strikingly different from British India in the nineteenth century. Both zones understood by economic progress the same thing—the growth of commerce aided by railways and canals. Princely states were constrained by geography, state capacity, lack of access to big capital markets, and small scale of units, to play that game as much as did British India. Whether they were independent or dependent had little relevance to how they defined progress or what they did to achieve progress.

The interwar years saw a convergence. In both zones, progress now meant state-aided industrialization and welfare. A few large states were more able to do this than was British India, where the globalization-led change was coming under stress and the still heavy burden of military expenditure left little money to spare.

13

Indian Economy after Independence

At independence from British colonial rule (1947), the economy of India presented a paradoxical mix. Some of the cities were among the most industrialized in the tropical world and possessed large seaports, railway hubs, universities, hospitals, banks, and multinational companies. Many of these institutions had been set up by Indian entrepreneurs who profited from India's trade with the British Empire. On the other hand, most of the population lived in villages and cultivated land. If the village was in an arid or upland district, the land produced too little even for a comfortable subsistence. Wedded to the idea of a small government, the colonial rulers never seriously considered a policy to develop these regions. Between 1900 and 1947, this world was in a crisis because the open land frontier had disappeared and population growth accelerated during these years.

In the backdrop of increasing inequality, a nationalist narrative of underdevelopment emerged, which blamed poverty on colonialism and globalization and advocated a bigger state, public control of productive assets, and a retreat from the world economy. Later, the Marxists added force to this statist way of thinking by holding private capital responsible for India's poverty and underdevelopment. Faith in openness as an agent of development or faith in economic integration with the world economy—the only significant element in the colonial economic policy—was in retreat.

For 40 years after Independence, the Indian union tried a strategy of development that reflected such thinking. The democratic political system was robust enough to give the state credibility as an active agent of change. The result was that trade and foreign investment fell, the size of the government increased from about 3 per cent of GDP in 1931 to 22 in 1981, and a new regime of industrialization financed by taxes and foreign aid, rather than profits, began. In the 1980s, after a series of macroeconomic crises, the strategy was partially given up. The economy opened to trade and private capital inflow again. Almost immediately, GDP growth rate jumped, led by massive rise in manufacturing and services exports.

The revival of private enterprise strengthened a pro-market counter-narrative on development, one which made continued market reform the priority of development strategy. The counter-narrative is far from the political mainstream. Although faith in openness as an agent of development was back again, it was qualified and restrained by xenophobic nationalism. The sentiment against big capital, and support for some version of a nationalistic pathway, remain entrenched. India's development discourse is a contested field.

An overview of the political economy of independent India, such as this chapter will present, cannot settle ideological battles. It should still answer three broader questions. First, why was there a turnaround in the pace of economic change? The average income in India was 30 per cent of the world average in 1950 and fell to 20 per cent in 1980. After 1980, there was a turnaround, and by 2017, the Indian average income exceeded 40 per cent of the world average. The first of the three questions is: Why did Indian economic growth display this pattern of a divergence followed by a convergence? Did the pattern reflect shifts in ideology or the context in which ideas of development took shape?

The turnaround of the last quarter century, some critics say, was 'an uncertain glory', for the country's record in poverty eradication, education, and healthcare provision was less than impressive.[1] In

---

[1] Jean Drèze and Amartya Sen, *An Uncertain Glory: India and its Contradictions* (Princeton and Oxford: Princeton University Press, 2013).

some respects, the colonial pattern of economic change had been improved upon, and in some other respects, the improvement was not significant at all. Others suggest that the economic resurgence failed to create enough jobs and that the impulse was confined to specific regions and livelihoods. The second question is: Why did improvements in the quality of life lag achievements in income creation? And if the quality of life did fail to improve enough, then a third question follows: Why did the democratic political system survive at all if it failed to distribute the benefits from economic growth?

The first part of the survey will offer a chronological history, and the second part return to these three questions.

THE CHRONOLOGY OF TRANSITION 1950–2015

The Partition

In 1947, British colonial rule in South Asia ended and the region saw the creation of several independent nations, principally India, Pakistan, and Ceylon (Sri Lanka). The map of the region was redrawn in 1971 with the birth of Bangladesh.

The Partition of India was a traumatic episode. It involved the largest forced migration the world had seen, affecting possibly a million people. On the Bengal frontier, it generated a dislocation that continued on a milder scale for many years. Those who moved included many merchants, artisans, and peasants. Some had lost their lands, assets, and customers and had to change occupations. The trauma was heightened by the fact that the new borders had been drawn in a hurry, without regard to patterns of settlement, trade routes, and natural borders such as rivers and hills.

In comparison with the Partition, another managed territorial restructuring, the incorporation of the princely states (kingdoms not colonized by British India) into the new democratic nation state was handled with greater firmness and planning, though few among the rulers of the larger princely states happily cooperated with the project.

When the dust settled and the immediate economic and human trauma subsided, the new government began to design strategies of economic development.

A New Economic Policy

British colonialism had generated inequality. It stimulated business, including trade and industrialization, in and around the port cities. But barring a few exceptions like the canal-watered Punjab province, the rule made little difference to the countryside. Most villages in the vast land were trapped in a low-productivity agricultural production system and had few schools, hospitals, or police and law courts within easy access.

The independent state had a big task ahead of itself, transforming the economic system quickly to make it beneficial for the poor. In performing this task, four colonial-era institutions were to come in handy. These were the bureaucracy, army, an elected legislature, and the central bank. In themselves, these institutions would not amount to much. But they allowed for a continued influence of bureaucratic, professional, and intellectual classes on economic and developmental administration, which made for reasonably effective implementation of policy. Outside the state apparatus, colonial-era firms and Indian business communities dominated commerce and industry, and a section of this set influenced economic policy.

The state reduced the challenge of economic transformation to one main programme—rapid industrialization. Already before Independence, intellectuals close to the main political party, the National Congress, and business leaders had expressed a desire for industrialization with socialistic central planning. Despite some disagreement among them, these publicists agreed on one thing, the need to restrain foreign trade and implement protection as a favour to Indian producers. The Bombay Plan document (1944), prepared by seven leading industrialists and publicists, saw the main form of government regulation to come in the shape of protective tariffs. It proposed a broadly deregulated domestic economy but allowed scope for public investment in industries of strategic importance.

There was another strand within the Congress, the one inspired by the nationalist leader M.K. Gandhi, that considered rural regeneration and self-sufficiency to be the main goal of development.

Internal debates on policy leading up to the First Five-Year Plan in 1950 saw repeated conflicts and compromise between these two visions—socialist industrialization and regeneration of the village.

The design of the industrial policy that took shape in the mid-1950s had much in common with what many other developing economies of the time tried to do and one element of distinctness. The key common element was protectionist industrialization or import-substituting industrialization, as it became known. With the world economy in disarray after the Great Depression and the Second World War, faith in international trade and cross-border investment as instruments of development was at its lowest ebb. Influenced by a business lobby that hoped to gain the most from protection, the politicians had grown allergic to openness. The nineteenth-century European examples of protected industrialization, the infant industry ideology, and the example of managed industrialization in the Union of Soviet Socialist Republics (USSR) gave support to the self-reliant protectionist industrialization strategy that most developing countries then wanted.

But the Indian story also had a distinct element. The Indian leaders decided that capital-intensive industry—metals, chemicals, and machines—should take priority over traditional sectors like textiles, minerals, or tea. Protectionist industrialization meant, for India, building capability in an area where there was little inhouse expertise and which were too expensive for the domestic capital market to finance. Therefore, the Indian pathway came to depend on the state. The state could recycle taxpayer's money into priority projects. Eventually, it would do much more—also license private investment, license foreign exchange usage, and control and own almost the entire banking system. Domestic production of capital-intensive goods in a capital-scarce economy required average tariffs to be raised to levels much higher than otherwise necessary. With private imports to become very expensive, the government became the principal approved channel for the import of essential raw materials, food, and technology. To reduce the fiscal burden, exchange rates were fixed and overvalued. All of these elements did not appear at one time, but most of them were in place soon after 1956 and consolidated further between 1965 and 1980.

Between 1950 and 1955, the implementing agencies came into being, and regulatory laws were passed. The Industrial Policy Resolutions of 1948 and 1956 set out the goals of policy, and the Industries (Development and Regulation) Act of 1951 created the instruments of implementation. The tools designed to manage a desired pattern of investment were tariffs, industrial licensing, and public investment. Less noticed at the time, a further set of regulations set out the state's commitment to labour. The Industrial Disputes Act (1947) made it difficult for an employer to retrench workers in a factory and created a role for the government in collective bargaining and dispute settlement. The principle of job protection was subsumed under the pursuit of 'social justice'. While it was in some way a reward to the politically affiliated trade unions for their contribution to the nationalist movement, it was also consistent with the new ideology of industrialization. The state gave employers protection from imports and, in exchange, made them accept laws that gave workers protection from unemployment.

The strategy could not succeed without heavy dependence on cheap foreign resources, like aid, because a lot of the technology in the capital goods industries had to come from abroad. In this way, foreign aid and relations with the donor countries became essential components of the pursuit of economic development. The form of international economic relations shifted from partnerships between private businesses to intergovernmental negotiations on projects and from trade agreements to aid negotiations.

Compared with the colonial times, when 70–80 per cent of aggregate investment had occurred in the private sector, in 1950–64, the government and the private sector shared investment about equally. The private share fell further thereafter, to revive after the mid-1980s.

Performance in 1950–65

In the first 15 years after this policy started, GDP growth was much higher than in the preceding decades. The main growth sectors were oil, gas, steel, heavy machinery, railways, and power. The state led the investment and expansion in these areas. The private sector diversified marginally into industrial machinery and machine tools.

A churning in private investment, however, had begun. The traditional industries, textiles, mining, finance, and plantations did not do badly, but they started to retreat relatively. These businesses were not strong candidates to bid for finance and investment licenses, because the government had its eyes elsewhere. High tariffs and exchange manipulation were hurting the exporters. Several formerly exporting industries reoriented towards the domestic market. In tea, the export-production ratio declined. Investment fell, and therefore, quality improvements suffered. In textiles, India retreated from the world market from the 1950s. A textile policy designed in 1950 and in force until 1985 sheltered the handloom technology of cloth production from competition by saddling the factories with numerous restrictions. In steel, protection, discouragement to exports, and public sector dominance led to a pattern of growth that neither met demand nor utilized the resource advantage that India possessed.

Although the overwhelming priority was industrialization, the countryside did receive attention. Soon after Independence, the government embarked on a series of river-valley irrigation schemes, the most important of which was constructed on the Sutlej River. The project, Bhakra–Nangal, followed the colonial pattern of canal development. The concentration of investment in Punjab reflected a political priority, to resettle a large number of refugees on land as most of them had been farmers earlier.

In the rest of India, the focus of rural development policy was land reform and collective use of resources via cooperatives and community development. The two significant aims of land reforms were the elimination of 'intermediary interests' like the zamindars or the non-cultivating landlords and the imposition of a ceiling on maximum holding. The expected outcome was that peasants who were not mere tenants but owners of assets would have the incentive to work hard and improve both their own conditions and that of the land. The redistribution worked in this way. The portion of a landed estate that exceeded the ceiling fell in a potential surplus, available for redistribution to small owners and the landless.

Estimates of the surplus potentially available exceeded the surplus available for distribution, which again was higher than the land distributed. These anomalies revealed the political and legal capacity of the owners to hold onto their property. Redistribution of land happened with notable success in very few states. West Bengal, where the communist movement was growing in strength, was one where it did happen. The immigrants from the then East Pakistan formed a promising recruiting ground for the Communist Party of India, especially because the ruling Congress was often used as a lobbying platform by the older residents to block the immigrants from claiming state resources. The resultant consolidation of local power under a communist flag ensured that the landed interests were not too successful in concealing their excess holdings.

In the mid-1960s, a terrible harvest failure threw the whole development project in disarray. Production of grain fell by 10–20 per cent in the 1965–6 season. A war with Pakistan, high levels of foreign debt service, and food imports quickly drained foreign reserves, forcing India to seek more Western aid. Even as these external and internal shocks forced a temporary freeze upon state planning, a new government came to power in Delhi, following the death of the first prime minister Jawaharlal Nehru.

Crises, Contradiction, and Critique: 1965–85

The 1960s ended with the consolidation of power for Indira Gandhi. The famine had underscored the dismal state of the rural poor who had voted her to power. It was her turn to do them a favour. One outcome of her *garibi hatao* (remove poverty) campaign was an extension of roads, schools, bank branches, and electricity connection to the villages. A second and very big plank of her back-to-the-village posture was the Green Revolution. Administrative energy in the 1960s was redirected to implementing a new agricultural technology consisting of high-yielding varieties of wheat that came from the Americas and the application of chemical fertilizers to which these seeds, more than the traditional seeds, were responsive. The success of any new package of fertilizers and high-yield seeds was, however, restricted to regions that could access water at relatively low cost. Therefore, the sharp increase in productivity that did emerge from the policy remained confined to a few regions.

As for industry and finance, Gandhi proved to be a much harder socialist than her father Nehru. A tighter industrial licensing policy was introduced in 1970. Firms and business houses possessing assets amounting to more than a stipulated level had to register themselves with the newly created Monopolies and Restrictive Trade Practices Commission and seek approvals for expansion or diversification. Approvals were never easily granted. Non-registration invited penalties. Regulatory controls were tightened and the dominance of the state in investment much enhanced. In 1969, leading private banks were nationalized. Insurance companies followed suit in 1972. Public development banks were established to supply long-term loans to industry, whereas the nationalized banks were pushed towards providing direct and indirect support to rural lending.

The root of the back-to-the-village movement in Indira Gandhi's time was a crisis in the village itself. The 1966 harvest failure exposed the neglect of production conditions in agriculture in the previous 15 years. With the memory of a terrible famine in 1943 still fresh, the fear of famine was ever-present. A second drought in 1972 revived these fears, even though on this occasion, food imports stayed in check. The sense of insecurity about food supplies led to two long-term patterns of change—the Green Revolution mentioned before and the public distribution of food (more on this later).

The root of the tightening socialistic controls over private capital in industry is less obvious. The first few years of protectionist industrialization saw the emergence of a few business groups with semi-monopoly positions in certain capital goods industries. This was causing worry, to Gandhi especially because she suspected that these lobbies did not support her leadership, but also to many economists and leftist politicians. Gandhi's ideological proximity to the USSR was another factor driving her towards a bigger state and a weaker private sector.

In the 1960s, a schism had begun to appear in the pattern of industrial development assistance from foreign donors. In March 1965, three-quarters of cheap loans from the USSR flowed into the public sector, whereas three-quarters of cheap loans from the United States of America for industrial development flowed into the private sector. In key industries such as oil refinery and steel, the government had found partnerships with Western firms and governments difficult to sustain. In the 1950s, negotiations with the oil multinationals on profit margins and exploration rights repeatedly broke down. The significant new factor in the world oil industry in the 1950s was the emergence of USSR as a source of supply. India welcomed this development. Soviet aid began to enter from the late 1950s into refinery projects. India, by then, was dependent on Russian oil. Simultaneously, restrictions on refinery expansion were imposed on private companies.

Against the backdrop of growing friendship with the USSR, the West's support for Indian industrial policy became hesitant. American dithering on a large steel project, Bokaro, exposed uneasiness in the United States of America over becoming an indirect agent in India's quest for socialism. The decision exposed cleavage within American diplomatic policy circles about cooperation with New Delhi on Indian terms. Again, as Bokaro showed, the presence of the USSR as a willing partner saved India from softening its stance on public ownership.

By the mid-1960s, the USSR had quietly entrenched itself as the leading partner in India's quest for industrialization (Figure 13.1). Frictions apart, economic choices did not mar the Western foreign policy stance towards India until Nehru's death in 1964. The political situation after that forced a sharper polarization of interests.

Between 1965 and 1971, the years when India and Pakistan fought two wars, South Asia emerged as a theatre of the cold war. After the 1965 war with Pakistan, America insisted on tying aid to some diplomatic commitment or initiative on Kashmir. India's stand on the Kashmir issue did not respond to these demands. A turning point in Indo-US relations had been reached, which showed up in the increasing dependence of India on Soviet arms.

In the first half of the 1960s, Sino-Indian and Sino-Soviet conflicts had brought Indian and Soviet military interests in the region directly in line. After the Indo-Pakistan war of 1965, which Pakistan fought with American and Chinese weapons, India's dependence on Soviet arms deepened. In the end, the USSR gained the most, politically, from following a pro-India stance in the South Asian stage. The commitment survived the death of two Indian prime

Figure 13.1   Soviet experts in Bhilai Steel plant, 1962. A Soviet engineer in Bhilai with one hand outstretched pointing at the socialist future.

© Alamy Stock Photos

ministers in quick succession and the removal of the pro-India Nikita Khrushchev. After the Indo-Pakistan conflict of 1971 and the Indo-Soviet arms treaty of the same year, the foreign policy stance of the United States, under Richard Nixon's administration, turned firmly against India.

India's trade regime was nearly collapsing in these years. The balance of payments was forever under pressure. And yet, the so-called rupee trade arrangement that evolved out of the new warmth with the USSR made it possible to import oil without a collapse of the foreign exchange reserves. Under this arrangement, India had the option of repayment with Indian goods rather than convertible currencies. Although the USSR was never the largest trade partner, India's economists saw the barter trade as an instrument with which too much Western pressure could be resisted. Dependence on the USSR increased, and by the end of the 1960s, a quarter of India's exports went into servicing debts to the USSR.

While the political situation pushed India towards Soviet friendship, the economy showed signs of strain. After the 1965 harvest failure, the Aid-India Consortium (started in 1958) extended aid on condition that India devalued its currency. And the United States of America, in repeated negotiations, insisted that India refrain from criticizing its foreign policy in South East Asia. Devaluation was adopted (1966), the imperative having come from the Western aid-givers. This condition raised a political controversy in the Indian Parliament and media. Public representation of foreign aid had become sensitive for the Indian leaders. The sentiment was revealed during the bilateral meetings discussing food aid from the United States of America. When asked by the US secretary of state what questions she expected to face in Parliament on famine relief, the new prime minister of India answered, 'Have I sold the country?'[2]

Besides tacit Soviet support for socialism in India, in regulating private capital with a heavier hand, Gandhi also aimed to take some wind off the sail of a growing communist movement at home. In the countryside, the food crisis of the mid-1960s had created an explosive situation. In the cities, the left-leaning economist was more vocal than ever before. Since foreign aid was a route through which foreign capital entered India, and aid represented a dependence on foreign know-how and money, it was never totally acceptable to the economists. Hidden strings, it was believed, made aid an instrument in the service of foreign capital. In the 1970s, Maoist groups grew in influence in some regions. Maoist critiques of Indian policy placed the United States of America, the USSR, private capital, and military aid all in one basket.

Partly in deference to the anti-multinational and anti-American political mood, the general stance of the Parliament towards foreign investment was hostile and hardened further in the 1970s. In 1973, the Foreign Exchange Regulation Act was enacted, restricting the repatriation of private income. International firms were disallowed majority share ownership. Some of the largest multinationals left

[2] United States, 'Foreign Relations of the United States 1964–1968', Volume XXV (South Asia). Available at https://history.state.gov/historicaldocuments/frus1964-68v25, accessed 12 May 2020.

India in this interregnum, whereas those that remained almost stopped making new investments in India.

The outcome of these regulations was an investment depression between 1965 and 1975. In the older industries like textiles, bankruptcy was beginning to spread. Many troubled private firms were nationalized to protect jobs, putting further pressure on a strained budget. Unable to retrench or redeploy labour, the employers became reliant on casual labour, which carried an aura of illegality and exploitation. Trade unions, in their turn, were a field of a contest between regional political parties and local leaders, many of whom tried to break the monopoly of recognized unions. These new dynamics engendered some of the largest and most violent industrial disputes, such as the Bombay Textile Strike (1982–3). Tariffs rose to extraordinarily high levels. If oil is excluded, India was trading a lot less than ever before. Since exports did not pay for foreign loans and foreign investment was negligible, the major part of new foreign aid went into paying older debt rather than investment. While growth rates decelerated, an increase in population growth rate depressed GDP growth per head.

Growth rates in manufacturing had been above 7 per cent per year between 1956 and 1966 and dropped to 4–5 per cent in 1966–75. Inside academia, opinion was divided on the origins of the industrial stagnation. The Marxists proposed that unbridled capitalism had given rise to inequality and 'under-consumption'. According to an emerging neoliberal school, excessive government investment in projects that yielded low private and social returns was responsible.

Indeed, the extreme form of import protection practised in India, with average tariff rates nearing 100 per cent, hurt export. Whereas freer trade in the colonial period had given domestic industry access to new technologies and helped them learn, restricted trade made learning difficult and reduced competitiveness. Inefficiency spilt over. For example, the high cost of locally produced machines raised the cost of goods made by using those machines. Potentially exportable labour-intensive manufactures, like textiles and clothing, could not buy technology abroad and modernize. The quality of light manufactures and consumer goods, despite a robust historical legacy, was poor by world standards and the producers of these goods faced bankruptcy.

Manufacturing income showed signs of recovery in the late 1970s. The exact reasons for the almost invisible turnaround remain unclear. The failure of some of the industry-wide strikes had reduced the scale of industrial disputes, which may have benefited the employers. But it also made them wary of hiring. There was little improvement in industrial employment. In the 1980s, organized manufacturing saw 'jobless growth'. Even as production and investment in manufacturing picked up, employment growth was near-zero.

Despite a Green Revolution, rural poverty had remained high in the 1970s and real wages in agriculture hardly moved. For much of India, canals were not a viable technological option to make water available to farmers. Landholdings were too small for the adoption of some labour-saving technologies associated with the new agricultural strategy. The appeal of land reform, therefore, remained strong. When the Communist Party of India (Marxist) formed a government in West Bengal in 1977, it quickly set in motion laws to secure the rights of more than a million tenants, a move that saw nearly 8 per cent of operated area vested in state and redistributed to new titleholders.

With poverty still extensive, the government intervened in the distribution of food. Although in its original aim the public distribution system was meant to serve poor consumers when food prices increased, as the Green Revolution took root, an additional aim was to stabilize and shore up post-harvest prices when the harvest was good, in deference to powerful farm lobbies. Special-price shops then sold this food to card-holders at a subsidized rate. While pursuing two objectives, helping the farmers and helping the poor, the government ended up paying a substantial subsidy from the budget.

A wind of change had begun blowing in the first half of the 1980s, when Indira Gandhi was still the prime minister. Several business-friendly and export-friendly measures were taken in the early 1980s in the last years of her life. The anti-monopoly provisions were relaxed, the exchange rate was allowed gradually to recover parity with the market rate, and hostility towards foreign investment was reduced. The moribund Indian automobile had become a symbol of the failure of the industrialization policy. Preparations were now made for Maruti, the iconic new generation car, to be made by a joint venture between the state and the Suzuki Motor Corporation of Japan. There was no full-scale reform yet. But the wind was gathering strength.

And yet, when economic growth did recover, the state was not the active agent, but just a lucky beneficiary of an emerging globalization in labour services, which the Indians readily embraced.

Transition: 1986–2010

In the 1980s, three positive developments happened. First, the flow of remittances from migrant workers in the Persian Gulf states from the mid-1970s had eased the balance of payments and made the politicians more willing to take a chance with little reforms here and there. Second, there was a mini Green Revolution in some of the most deprived areas of the country that did not have canal water. And third, the government was beginning to encourage technology import in the private sector, under the leadership of Rajiv Gandhi, the prime minister.

By 1985, the USSR was in the throes of its collapse. The collapse of the rupee trade meant that any subsequent investment strategy that relied on imported technology would have to be financed with exchange earning by the private sector. The remittances came as a solution. In the 1990s, tariffs were sharply reduced across the board, exchange rates liberalized, industrial regulation eased, and state investment rolled back. Budgetary support for many government enterprises was reduced. In the second half of the 1990s, the reforms extended to financial deregulation, privatization of government firms, removing price controls, privatization of the services provided by the utilities, and industrial relations. Long-standing restrictions on foreign private investment were eased early in the 1990s.

The reforms encouraged investment and GDP growth rate, despite a recession in the late 1990s induced by the Asian crisis and domestic political uncertainty. When combined with a deceleration in population growth rates, the effect upon GDP growth per head was larger than before. The GDP growth was remarkable for another reason. In the 1990s, it had owed to a revival of labour-intensive manufactured goods exports, like textiles. But in the 2000s, it was sustained by unprecedented growth rates in the skilled services export, like software.

A permanent legacy of Indira Gandhi's back-to-the-village movement was the subsidized provision of inputs like credit, electricity, and fertilizer. Between 1970 and 1995, the percentage of villages receiving power increased from 34 to 90. The extension of electricity encouraged the use of electric pumps to distribute water. The dominant mode of irrigation development, therefore, changed in the 1980s from canals to tube wells and pumps. The trend induced a second Green Revolution, now in the poorer peasant economies of the east, like West Bengal and Bihar. Viable rice seeds, which became available from this time, consolidated the second revolution in the paddy-growing areas.

The combined effect of the two waves of agricultural transformation was nothing less than revolutionary. Agricultural production and income increased between 2 and 4 per cent per year between the 1970s and the 1990s. The spectre of famines and import dependence disappeared. Average rural incomes increased. The percentage of the rural population living below the officially set poverty line had hovered in the range 50–65 in 1950–70; the first Green Revolution set off a slowly declining trend, bringing the ratio to about a third at the end of the 1980s, from which level it declined further in the 2000s.

Sometime in the mid-1990s, diminishing returns in agriculture kicked in. In parts of eastern India where farmers had recklessly exploited groundwater resources, the water table fell and incidences of arsenic poisoning increased. As the water table dropped and electricity supply became unreliable, farmers in some regions started shifting back to a mainly rainfed agricultural regime. Through distorted prices, chemical fertilizers had been allowed to replace organic manures almost completely, imposing ecological stress. With the land being of greater value than ever before, competition and bargaining between rival claimants for farmland, which included farmers, urban developers, and industrial interests, threatened to become politically explosive.

Further, both the first and the second green revolutions succeeded in regions where alluvial soil, surface water, and groundwater
permitted water harvesting and where complementary investment
in rural roads and electricity was possible. It was a great deal weaker
in regions where well irrigation remained costly even with state aid
(regions within arid peninsular India) and where the state failed to
invest in complementary infrastructure (Bihar, for example).

There was other bad news for farmers. Haunted by the spectre
of famines, the government did not encourage the export of grains.
Exports constituted not more than 15–18 per cent of agricultural
output. The restrictions deprived the farmers of the chance to make
good use of world market booms and further depressed private
investment in agriculture without subsidization. Until 1995, the
export of agricultural goods was prohibited. If not in the foodgrains,
in a few areas, a limited change did happen, however. In the Uruguay
Round Agreement on Agriculture, tariffs in the developed markets
were reduced by 35–45 per cent on fruits and vegetables, flowers, and other agricultural products. Following this development,
farmers and orchard owners in India began diversifying into non-
traditional, high-value-added products such as fruits and flowers.
Floriculture emerged as a money-spinner in Southern India. Other
success stories included basmati rice and soybeans.

The great paradox of post-reform India was that manufacturing
never regained momentum. In the 1990s, large-scale industry displayed a mix of bankruptcy and growth. There was sharper inter-firm
polarization, as new entrants had better access to foreign capital,
technology, and flexible labour markets, whereas many incumbents
had to adapt to increased foreign competition while still burdened
with large labour overhead and poor machinery. Openness drove
many weak and overcapitalized firms to the wall. Important industry
sectors to decline were cotton spinning and weaving in mills, jute
spinning and weaving in mills, and synthetic textiles. A few groups
within machinery and metallurgy declined too, chiefly ferrous
metals.

The revival of manufactured exports came mainly from small
firms, but the general picture of small firms was not very bright either,
since many of them faced difficulty raising money for investment in

a high-cost capital market. Across small and large firms, deregulation of import offered a few firms—better managed, more creditworthy, and already technologically advanced—the chance to globalize with success.

If not manufacturing, service exports did surprisingly well. Many global firms entered India, and several emerged from within India; almost all were engaged in the knowledge-intensive sectors. To some extent, the emergence reflected the legacy of globalization in the colonial times, and to some extent, it reflected capability created in the previous decades. In pharmaceuticals, implicit protection in the old regime, in the shape of process patents, had fostered indigenous research and development. After the reforms, this nurturing enabled several firms to emerge from the experience with superior research capability. The accent on higher and technical education in Nehru–Gandhi's times and Rajiv Gandhi's positive views on computers had helped build capability in information technology.

The knowledge industry, in turn, reshaped the concept of entrepreneurship in India. It heralded an end of the community-bound entrepreneurship that had been the standard of big business since its inception in the nineteenth century. New trends in entrepreneurship matured. One of these was the rise of the engineer-entrepreneur.

Critics of the reforms argued that wages and employment growth decelerated in the 1990s. In the same way that reforms affected the firms, openness after many years of closure can produce mixed effects on labour. In some sectors facing obsolescence, there would be more unemployment, and elsewhere, employment would grow. Employment growth rate, in fact, rose in large-scale industry. But neither the employers nor the workers, nor the economists, seemed happy about the fact.

The pro-reform economist believed that labour laws were still too rigid. For the employers, the fundamental contradiction in the economic reform process was that it had reduced protection but not changed labour laws. The quid pro quo between the state, employers, and the unions, started in Nehru's times, had collapsed. The employers now wanted de-protection of jobs. The organized trade unions felt that since the reforms made it possible for new firms to bypass rigid labour laws, any move towards a formal reform of the laws would be unfair. On the local level, labour institutions did change. There was more use of contractual labour. The political stance of some state governments was pro-employer. New policy instruments, such as special economic zones, played a role in pursuing the agenda. So did a series of pro-employer court judgments against the application of the old labour laws. Still, little formal relaxation was on offer.

New industries and firms, thus, spawned a different set of bargaining institutions, and a different profile of labour. In few firms that started after 1992 was there a presence of the national trade unions, even any trade union at all. Knowledge-based industries, such as pharmaceuticals or software, did not involve a large shop-floor workforce

Table 13.1 Average annual growth rates of GDP by sector of origin, 1865–2018

	GDP at factor cost, constant prices				Population	GDP per head
	Primary sector	Secondary sector	Tertiary sector	Total		
1865–1910	1.1			1.5	0.5	1.0
1910–40	0.0	2.3	2.2	1.1	1.1	0.0
1950–64	3.0	6.8	3.8	4.1	1.9	2.1
1965–85	2.5	4.3	4.4	3.6	2.3	1.4
1986–2010	3.4	7.0	8.0	6.5	1.7	4.6
2011–18	2.7	5.6	8.6	6.6	1.3	5.2

Sources: For Indian Union data, annual growth rate series available from Government of India, *Economic Survey* (New Delhi: Ministry of Finance, various years), are used to construct the table. Available at https://www.indiabudget.gov.in/economicsurvey/allpes.php (accessed 12 May 2020). For British India, see Table 1.2 of this book. a. 1900–46. British Indian growth rates are point-to-point exponential rates. The prewar data is indicative.

Notes: Indian Union from 1950, British India for periods before. The primary sector consists of agriculture, forestry, and fishing; secondary sector of manufacturing, mining, electricity, gas, and construction; and the tertiary sector of trade, hotels and transportation, financial and business services, administration, and defence. Where growth rates are available by sub-group, simple averages of growth rates by sub-group is taken.

Table 13.2   Investment ratio and size of government (proportion of GDP, percentages), 1900–2016

	Gross investment			Government expenditure
	Government	Private	Total	
1900–13	2.2	4.7	6.9	
1913–39	2.0	7.3	9.3	5.2
1950–64	5.3	6.1	11.4	12.9
1965–85	7.5	4.6	12.1	16.4
1986–2007	7.5	16.5	24.0	11.7
2008–16	7.5	24.3	31.8	14.9

Sources: For the Indian Union, see India, *The Imperial Gazetteer of India*, vols. 1–31 (Oxford, 1908). On British Indian data, see Table 3.16. a. Government revenue in National Income, 1920–30.
Note: Indian Union from 1950, British India for periods before.

Table 13.3   Size of the external sector (proportion of current GDP, percentages)

	Merchandise trade (export plus import)	Net foreign aid	Net foreign direct investment	Net invisibles
1910–14	20.0	0.0	0.0–1.0	−3.0
1956	13.6	0.6	0.0	1.2
1960	9.1	2.3	0.0	0.5
1970	7.0	1.0	0.0	−0.3
1980	14.4	1.3	0.0	2.9
1990	14.6	0.8	0.0	−0.1
2000	22.8	0.1	1.0	2.6
2006	33.4	0.0	1.6	5.6
2016	32.3	0.4	1.5	N.A.

Source: See under Table 13.1. a. 1920–30 (see Chapter 3).
Note: Indian Union from 1950, British India for periods before.

and, thus, did not fit the traditional model of labour organization and action. Many firms in cotton yarn and food processing had started in semi-rural areas, outside older labour agglomerations. In the export processing zones, labour was markedly out of the sphere of influence of protective unions and politicians. In the export processing zones, again, a larger component of the workers were women, a trend that some authors attribute to the employers' desire for a relatively vulnerable and non-unionized workforce.

Tables 13.1–13.3 show with numbers the transitions discussed in the previous section. With this overview behind us, let me now return to the three questions that the chapter had started from.

INTERPRETATIONS AND DEBATES

Why the Reform Happened?

Why was there relatively weak growth before 1980 and a reversal after? Why did India embark on economic reforms?

India's economists in the 1950s believed in their capacity to transform the country. In 1992, an economist-turned-politician Manmohan Singh strengthened liberal reforms. If we follow this pattern, we might think that changes in belief alone led to India's transition from one regime to another. Politicians and economists believed in socialism to begin with, then discovered they went too far socializing the system, that private enterprise had been squeezed too hard, and made amends. They believed in self-reliance to start with, shunned the world market in the first 30 years, and seeing that this was a little crazy and unfair on foreign investors, returned to openness after that.

These statements wrongly imply that politicians and economists had the power to generate growth or to stop and start private investment. In fact, that power was constrained throughout. The reforms came when the constraints had eased somewhat. To that easing, no credit is due to the politicians and economists who, in the 1970s, had no clue as to how it was easing.

The real story was this. Indian development was funded by the taxpayer's money, whether in Nehru–Gandhi era or Singh era. It was socialist in this sense throughout its post-colonial history. And it was an expensive process. The heavy budget commitments also posed a risk of inflation. A similar risk appeared from the balance of payments side. In the 1970s, the budget and the balance of payments was going haywire. After that decade, the state managed to reduce both risks because of fortuitous improvement in the balance of payments. This backdrop of improvement, not scripted by the economists, enabled the formal reforms.

In the Nehru era, and especially under Indira Gandhi, the state was recycling taxes both to industrialization and to agriculture, taking on a massive budgetary burden upon itself. The agriculture burden was still modest in the 1960s, but it was starting to grow. Budget deficit was chronic and threatened inflation often. A great deal of electoral politics and political instability before the 1980s had owed to inflation. To this source of risk, another risk was added, thanks to retreat from the world economy. That was the balance of payments risk. The closure of the economy meant that there was too little foreign investment coming in and too little export effort because the flow of technology had slowed. In turn, the balance of payments became weak and vulnerable to external shocks. For, even as the spending commitment in foreign money had increased substantially, the economy's capacity to earn foreign money had fallen.

The turnaround at first came from a more comfortable balance of payments condition. The government had no role in making it happen. The millions of Indian labourers who went to the Persian Gulf to work in the wake of the successive oil price hikes made the balance of payments solvent again. The reduced risks imparted stability to the economy and permitted the government to relax its trade and exchange policy. In the 1990s and beyond, exports and foreign investment picked up, and India has not since seen a severe threat of a balance of payments problem.

These conditions enabled a retraction of state commitment from industrialization. The precondition was a revival of private investment. As private investment looked up in the 1980s, the textile policy that restrained investment in the cotton textile industry was reformed. Anti-monopoly laws were still in place but rarely applied. While private investment thus revived, the government stepped back from its commitments in the manufacturing industry.

The 2000s could very well see crisis developing from agriculture. The spectre of a slowdown in agriculture has been present since the second Green Revolution tapered off. As we enter the 2000s, we find an Indian state that had reduced its budgetary commitment to industry and increased its fiscal commitment to agriculture. This balancing act would be unsustainable without giving over investment to the private sector.

To sum up, the relative slowdown and revival had little to do with the downfall of socialist ideology and the emergence of capitalism. It had a lot to do with luck and the adjustment of the government's commitment.

Why did India's reforms happen? A strand in the scholarship on India's political economy would say that the politicians re-embraced capitalism because socialism had failed to deliver equity. This leads us to the issue of social development.

Why a Poor Record of Human Development?

Jean Drèze and Amartya Sen in *An Uncertain Glory* showed how inequality remained entrenched despite recent economic growth. Well into the 2000s, India stood badly on the benchmark called multidimensional development indicators relative to the poorer nations of the world, large emerging economies, and even South Asian neighbours like Bangladesh and Sri Lanka. Corruption was rife. Privileged affluent consumers extracted more from the state, leaving little for the poor. The poor were deprived of access to the essential public services, and worryingly, the affluent classes shaped the public discourse on development. By saying this, Drèze and Sen criticized the economic liberal lobby that wanted more capitalism unrestrained by state regulation.

Throughout the colonial and the postcolonial times, primary education had been neglected in India. There was more private money in higher and technical education, which did not suffer as much. The government also wanted engineers for its own industries and sponsored technical education. Private effort and capital on public welfare and public goods remained generally exclusive and sectarian in Indian society. The result was a slower change in measures of 'human development' during a time when plans for rapid economic development were put into effect.

That some form of government failure did afflict the record cannot be denied. Was it a failure of ideology, however? Many of the vital public goods in India are the responsibilities of the states (provinces). Except for some of the southern states, most states in India had an indifferent record of supplying public goods and services. Since the reforms began, mobile capital and skilled labour readily migrated to the business-friendly states. Some states lost taxable money in the process.

There was also a political shift that made some states less able to rise to the challenge. In the first half of the 1990s, the fabric of federalism, so far held together by dominant governments at the centre, became strained as a coalition of regional parties called the shots in the new regime. At the same time, almost every measure of the soundness of the state governments showed downward drift. The major part of the state's tax income derived from the sales taxes, which were often waived in a competitive bid to attract industry. The power of states to borrow was limited and was curbed in the early 1990s. In some ways, then, the states became more dependent than before upon central assistance. The division of assistance was based upon distributional rules that gave higher weight to poverty and levels of backwardness, in effect discriminating against fiscal and economic health. Some of the industrially endowed states paid the price for the reckless nationalization of bankrupt enterprises and expansion in public undertakings that they had indulged in the 1970s. The rate of return on investment in state-owned businesses was low.

To this burden were added waived farm income taxes and lost taxes from alcohol in states that prohibited its consumption. As new enterprise formation picked up in the 1990s, the fiscal weakness of the state also owed to the choices made by new firms about industrial location. The uneven response of the states to the challenges of institutional reforms, it is believed, made business more selective about location. Given that changes in labour regulation were highly variable regionally, private capital migrated, where it could, to pro-employer states.

The intense focus in Nehru's years upon industrialization and in Gandhi's time upon rural infrastructure and agricultural subsidies had left in neglect roads, railways, ports, electricity, telecommunication, financial services, schools, and hospitals. Much of this infrastructure was a responsibility of the states who found themselves bankrupt, at least partly owing to the fiscal burden that rural development and providing security to rural incomes imposed on them.

If indeed the performance on delivery of welfare was so uneven, why did the democratic political setup survive? Why did people vote at all?

Why did Democracy Survive?

In the 1970s and 1980s, political scientists asked why democracy survived at all when the civic culture was weak, the middle class small, ethnic and regional differences marked, and traditional loyalties and patronage strong. If indeed the poor were short-changed systematically, the question is even more relevant. Why did people vote at all in elections?

Some of the more well-known hypotheses about the robustness of Indian democracy suggest that it survived because it refused to be captured by the elite. Contrary to what Drèze and Sen claim, despite inequality, the control on public goods and services was broadly democratic. There were abuses, but as exceptions than the rule. As several commentators on Indian politics say, the poor voting in elections point at 'the marginality of class politics', which helps to explain 'centrism' in state policy, constitutional and political arrangements that allowed sharing of political power, the capacity to give political voice to the marginalized, and a combination of factors from the institutionalization of civil liberty to the ability to accommodate pluralism[3]. In short, the ideas that the state is weak, that it works only for sectional interests, that it cannot deliver a pro-poor policy for these reasons, and that therefore the state gave up on socialistic ideals and invited markets back in, are simplistic.

[3] On centrism and marginality of class politics, see Lloyd and Susanne Rudolph, *In Pursuit of Lakshmi: The Political Economy of the Indian State* (Chicago: University of Chicago Press, 1987) 1–23.

***

The chapter has reviewed economic change and the political context for economic change in the Indian Union from 1947 to 2015 and, using the overview, answered three broader questions. First, it asked why there was a turnaround in the pace of economic change around 1980. The answer is, the economy returned to openness and reliance on private investment from a strategy that had reduced their role before. Why was there such a shift? The chapter suggests that the shift owed less to ideological changes and more to an unintended return to globalization in the labour market that eased a formal return to globalization. Second, some critics of recent economic growth in the region consider that improvements in the quality of life lagged achievements in income creation after the turnaround. Why was that the case? The chapter suggests that along with a legacy of neglect, the rapid decline in regional finances contributed to the failure. And if the quality of life did fail to improve enough, then a third question follows, why did the democratic political system survive at all if it failed to distribute the benefits from economic growth? The chapter draws on recent debates on the question to suggest that the failure tends to be exaggerated.

To end the book, it will be useful to return to the questions I started with in Chapter 1 and repeat what evidence-based scholarship suggest should be the answers.

14

Conclusion

The book began by first exploring macroeconomic data and then asking seven questions based on the data. Answering these questions should give us a good understanding of the sources and patterns of economic change in India in the colonial period.

The first of the seven questions concerns the growth process. It builds on the evidence that national income in industry and services grew much faster than in agriculture. Why did colonialism and globalization generate inequality? In British India, the two forces were not really independent, because the state was keen to keep markets open and exposed to trade, migration, and cross-border investment. The answer outlined in Chapters 3–8 is that the root of the uneven growth was in agriculture, which faced limited access to water unless the state stepped in. Where this constraint eased off and land was not already scarce, farmers experienced improvement in levels of living. The rest of the economy gained from openness in a variety of ways.

Inequality between agriculture and other activities need not cause inequality between persons, if workers could freely move from the stagnant to the growing activities. Employment and wage data suggest that such movements occurred on a limited scale. Why were so few poor people able to move to better jobs? We cannot be sure where the limits came from: caste as a barrier to occupational choices, poor state efforts on education, limited access to training, low female age at marriage that ruled out shifts of occupation for most rural women, or technological change in the growing activities.

With so many people living off poor-quality land, population growth would add to the stress the agricultural stagnation might cause. Why did the population begin to grow at a faster pace from the 1910s? The story of mortality decline told in Chapter 10 hinges on epidemic control and the retreat of famines. The colonial government was an agent in making these things possible, if indirectly via investment in the railways and fostering research on tropical diseases.

Where the government was needed to play a more direct and a more developmental role, in education, healthcare, and agricultural development, it failed to deliver significant results. Chapters 8 and 9 suggest that it failed to deliver because its capacity was too small. Why was the government so small? In the mid-nineteenth century, the answer would be obvious: It relied too much on a tax from land, in a region where land produced little output. With that constraint in place, the colonial state succeeded in raising more than its predecessors by recasting the relationship between the peasants and the state. But these steps had reached their limits by 1870. Since then, fiscal policy was a project to raise revenue and public debt, a project that was held back by the fact that the monetary and the fiscal systems were split between London and India, leaving both branches of the government too conservative.

The previous paragraph begs in the assumption that the British Indian state was willing to spend on public goods but did not have the capacity to do that. An indirect test of the assumption could come from how the princely states behaved in this respect. If they were much more proactive in spending on public goods, we should reject the assumption and conclude that colonialism created a state that was able but unwilling to commit to the welfare of the people. What was the performance record of the princely states? Chapter 12 shows that by most benchmarks of economic performance, the princely states were more similar than different from British India. There were a few exceptions to the rule, but these exceptions did have higher capacity to invest. In short, until better and more data on the states become available, the available evidence confirms that capacity ruled over political will to limit the role of the state in both British India and the princely territories.

Resource-driven economic change was bound to impact the environment. A state so dependent on taxes from resource use would inevitably take steps to make resource use easier than before. How did the state and the markets impact the environment? Chapter 11 shows that the state played an ambiguous role, both encouraging exploitation and conserving natural resources. Historians explain the conservationist impulse in different ways. But the chapter also shows that the state was not the main agent impacting the environment; private enterprise and knowledge and information-gathering, not always state-led or state-sponsored, played a significant part too.

When British rule in India ended, the politicians who framed India's development policy deliberately tried to reduce the role of openness in the economy and increase the role of the state manifold and in many ways, from regulation of labour and capital to direct industrial investment to the nationalization of the financial system. Many economists now would think that the recipe did not work or at best worked for some time before running out of steam. What went right and what went wrong with the development effort of the state after colonialism ended? Chapter 13 says that the retreat from openness hurt the global businesses that had developed during the colonial era, leaving the economy exposed to balance of payments crises, whereas the move towards industrialization via public spending wasted taxpayers' money and entailed a neglect of human development. Amidst this negative picture, the success of the Green Revolution stands out as a symbol of the productive use of the taxpayers' money. India's reforms in the 1990s brought the country back to openness, globalization, and private investment, while leaving it to confront the huge environmental costs of the successive waves of the Green Revolution.

No doubt, future research will reshuffle this set of seven questions through which I have outlined the economic history of colonial and postcolonial India and dispute the answers I offer to some of them. If such research also uses or makes available new evidence, there will be real progress in the field.

Primary Sources

A great many source materials are now available online. Some are available in password-protected sites and others can be downloaded for free. This section lists a few of these, for the benefit of the curious student and for the teacher wishing to use some of these documents to design exercises.

CHAPTER 2. TRANSITION TO COLONIALISM 1707–1857

Ghulam Husain Khan, *The Siyar-ul-Mutakherin* (trans. John Briggs), London: John Murray, 1832. Available at https://archive.org/details/siyarulmutakheri00ghulrich, accessed 11 November 2017.

British Parliamentary Papers, *The Fifth Report from the Select Committee of the House of Commons on the Affairs of the East India Company*, Volume 1, Madras: Higginbotham, 1866. Available at https://archive.org/stream/in.ernet.dli.2015.282118/2015.282118.The-Fifth#page/n0/mode/2up, accessed 11 November 2017.

Henry Thomas Colebrooke, *Remarks on the Husbandry and Internal Commerce of Bengal*, Calcutta, 1804. Available at https://archive.org/details/remarksonhusban01colegoog, accessed 11 November 2017.

CHAPTER 4. AGRICULTURE

British Parliamentary Papers, *Report of the Indian Famine Commission. Part II. Measures of Protection and Prevention* (London: House of Commons,

1880) (available through vendors of Parliamentary Papers, such as ProQuest).

British Parliamentary Papers, *Copy of Mr Robertson's Report of his Tour in Coimbatore*, London: House of Commons, 1878 (available through vendors of Parliamentary Papers, such as ProQuest).

John Forbes Watson, *Report on Indian Wheat* (London: George Edward Eyre and William Spottiswoode, 1879) (freely downloadable from Google Books, requires account).

S.S. Thorburn, *Musalmans and Moneylenders in the Punjab* (London: William Blackwood, 1886). Available at https://archive.org/details/cu31924013743848, accessed 11 November 2017.

CHAPTER 5. SMALL-SCALE INDUSTRY

Government of India, *Report of the Fact-Finding Committee on Handlooms and Mills* (Delhi: Government Press, 1942) (available through Gokhale Institute of Politics and Economics library website, http://dspace.gipe.ac.in/xmlui/handle/10973/24184).

CHAPTER 6. LARGE-SCALE INDUSTRY

British Parliamentary Papers, *Copy of Report of Indian Factories Commission* (London: House of Commons, 1891) (available through vendors of Parliamentary Papers, such as ProQuest).

S.M. Rutnagur, *Bombay Industries: The Cotton Mills*, vols 1–2 (Bombay: Textile Journal, 1927) (available through Gokhale Institute of Politics and Economics library website in http://hdl.handle.net/10973/28929 and http://dspace.gipe.ac.in/xmlui/handle/10973/25131).

CHAPTER 7. PLANTATIONS, MINES, BANKING

British Parliamentary Papers, *Copy of Doctor McClelland's Report on Coal-Fields of India* (London: House of Commons, 1863) (available through vendors of Parliamentary Papers, such as ProQuest).

CHAPTER 8. INFRASTRUCTURE

Indian Tarriff Board, Government of India, *Report of the Indian Tariff Board on the Iron and Steel Industry* (Delhi: Government Press, 1934) (available through Gokhale Institute of Politics and Economics library website http://hdl.handle.net/10973/18339).

CHAPTER 9. HOW THE GOVERNMENT WORKED

Indian Fiscal Commission, *Report of the Indian Fiscal* Commission (London: HMSO, 1921–2) (available through Gokhale Institute of Politics and Economics library website, http://dspace.gipe.ac.in/xmlui/handle/10973/21777).

India Office (Great Britain), *Report of the Committee on Indian Railway Finance and Administration* (available through Gokhale Institute of Politics and Economics library website, http://dspace.gipe.ac.in/xmlui/handle/10973/21512).

CHAPTER 10. POPULATION

British Parliamentary Papers, *Copy of Mr Geoghegan's Report on Cooly Emigration from India* (London: House of Commons, 1874) (available through vendors of Parliamentary Papers, such as ProQuest).

'Reports on Plague Investigations in India (prepared by the Advisory Committee Appointed by the Secretary of State for India, the Royal Society, and the Lister Institute)', *The Journal of Hygiene* 7, no.6 (1907): 693–985.

Government of India, *Report of the Indian Famine Commission, 1898* (Simla: Government Press, 1898) (available through Gokhale Institute of Politics and Economics library website, http://dspace.gipe.ac.in/xmlui/handle/10973/38204).

CHAPTER 11. THE ECONOMY AND THE ENVIRONMENT

British Parliamentary Papers, *Papers relating to Measures for introducing Cultivation of Tea Plant in British Possessions in India* (London: House of Commons, 1839) (available through vendors of Parliamentary Papers, such as ProQuest).

Report of the Proceedings of the Forest Conference held at Simla, October 1875, eds D. Brandis and A Smythies (Calcutta: Government Press). Available at https://ia801601.us.archive.org/10/items/in.ernet.dli.

2015.34807/2015.34807.Report-Of-The-Proceedings-Of-The-Forest-Conference-Held-At-Simla.pdf

W. Schlich, *Review of the Forest Administration in British India for the year, 1882–1883* (Simla: Government Central Branch Press, 1883) (semi-annual publication, this volume is available through Gokhale Institute of Politics and Economics library website, http://hdl.handle.net/10973/40133).

Further Readings

CHAPTER 1

Amiya Kumar Bagchi, *Colonialism and Indian Economy* (Delhi: Oxford University Press, 2010); Irfan Habib, 'Colonialization of the Indian Economy, 1757–1900', *Social Scientist* 3, no.8 (1975): 23–53; Latika Chaudhary, Bishnupriya Gupta, Tirthankar Roy, and Anand Swamy, 'Introduction', in *A New Economic History of Colonial India*, eds Latika Chaudhary, Bishnupriya Gupta, Tirthankar Roy, and Anand Swamy (Abingdon and New York: Routledge, 2016), 1–14; Morris D. Morris, 'Towards a Reinterpretation of Nineteenth Century Indian Economic History', *Journal of Economic History* 23, no.4 (1963): 606–18; Tirthankar Roy, *How British Rule Changed India's Economy: The Paradox of the Raj* (London: Palgrave, 2019).

CHAPTER 2

General Works

Tirthankar Roy, *An Economic History of Early Modern India* (London and Abingdon: Routledge, 2013).

Indian Ocean Trade

Ashin Das Gupta, *The World of the Indian Ocean Merchant* (Delhi: Oxford University Press, 2003); Giorgio Riello and Tirthankar Roy, 'Introduction', in *How India Clothed the World*, eds. Giorgio Riello and Tirthankar Roy (Leiden: Brill, 2010), 1–30; Kenneth McPherson, *The Indian Ocean: A History of People and the Sea* (New York: Oxford University Press, 1998); K.N. Chaudhuri, *Trade and Civilization in the Indian Ocean: An Economic History from the Rise of Islam to 1750* (Cambridge: Cambridge University Press, 1985); M.N. Pearson, *The Indian Ocean* (London: Routledge, 2003); M.N. Pearson, *The New Cambridge History of India: The Portuguese in India* (Cambridge: Cambridge University Press, 1987); Om Prakash, *European Commercial Enterprise in Pre-Colonial India: The New Cambridge History of India* (Cambridge: Cambridge University Press, 1998); Sanjay Subrahmanyam, *The Portuguese Empire in Asia, 1500–1700: A Political and Economic History* (London and New York: Longman, 1993); Tirthankar Roy, 'The Indian Ocean Trade, 1500–1800', in *India in the World Economy from Antiquity to the Present* (Cambridge: Cambridge University Press, 2012), 78–122.

Land and Agriculture

There are four articles on agrarian relations in Dharma Kumar (ed.), *CEHI*, Vol. 2 (Cambridge: Cambridge University Press, 1983). See Eric Stokes, 'Northern and Central India', in *CEHI 2*, 36–85; B. Chaudhuri, 'Eastern India', in *CEHI 2*, 86–176; H. Fukazawa, 'Western India', in *CEHI 2*, 177–206; and Dharma Kumar, 'South India', in *CEHI 2*, 207–41. Also see Ira Klein, 'Utilitarianism and Agrarian Progress in Western India', *EHR* 18, no.3 (1965): 576–97; M.B. McAlpin, 'Economic Policy and the True Believer: The Use of Ricardian Rent Theory in the Bombay Presidency', *Journal of Economic History* 44, no.2 (1984): 421–7; Neeladri Bhattacharya, 'Colonial State and Agrarian Policy', 113–23, and Burton Stein, 'Introduction', 1–32, both in *The Making of Agrarian Policy in British India 1770–1900*, ed. B. Stein (Delhi:

Oxford University Press, 1992); Neeraj Hatekar, 'Pringle's Ricardian Experiment in the Nineteenth Century Deccan Countryside', *IESHR* 33, no.4 (1996): 437–57.

Industry and Services

The five articles on regional economy in *CEHI 2*, by Tom G. Kessinger, 'North India', 242–70; S. Bhattacharya and B. Chaudhuri, 'Eastern India', 270–332; V.D. Divekar, 'Western India', 332–51; and Dharma Kumar, 'South India', 352–75, contain some discussion on banking and finance; Indrajit Ray, *Bengal Industries and the British Industrial Revolution (1757–1857)* (London: Routledge, 2011); In *Entrepreneurship and Industry in India, 1800–1947*, ed. Rajat Ray (Delhi: Oxford University Press, 1992), 18–30; Tirthankar Roy, 'Trade, Migration, and Investment 1800–1850,' in Roy, *India in the World Economy*, 123–57.

Mutiny and Its Aftermath

Tirthankar Roy, 'The Mutiny and the Merchants,' *The Historical Journal* 59, no.2 (2016): 393–416.

CHAPTER 3

Income and Wage Data

K. Mukerji, 'Trends in Real Wages in Cotton Textile Industry in Ahmedabad from 1900 to 1951,' *Artha Vijnana* 3, no.2 (1961): 124–34; Mukerji, 'Trends in Real Wages in Cotton Textile Mills in Bombay City and Island, From 1900 to 1951,' *Artha Vijnana* 1, no.1 (1959): 82–95; Mukerji, 'Trends in Real Wages in Jute Textile Industry from 1900 to 1951,' *Artha Vijnana* 2, no.1 (1960): 57–69; S. Sivasubramonian, *The National Income of India in the Twentieth Century* (Delhi: Oxford University Press, 2000).

Labour Force

Alice Thorner, 'Women's Work in Colonial India', School of Oriental and African Studies, London, 1984; Alice Thorner, 'The Secular

Trend in the Indian Economy, 1881–1951', *EPW* 14, no.28–30 (1962): 1156–65; Daniel Thorner, '"De-industrialization" in India, 1881–1931', in *Land and Labour in India*, eds Daniel and Alice Thorner (New York: Asia Publishing House, 1962); Dharma Kumar, 'The Forgotten Sector: Services in Madras Presidency in the First Half of the Nineteenth Century', *IESHR* 24, no.4 (1987): 367–93; J. Krishnamurty, 'Occupational Structure', *CEHI* 2, 533–50. Tirthankar Roy, *Rethinking Economic Change in India: Labour and Livelihood* (London and Abingdon: Routledge, 2005).

Trade, Balance of Payments, Public Finance

A.K. Banerji, *Aspects of Indo-British Economic Relations, 1858–1898* (Bombay: Oxford University Press, 1982); Banerji, *India's Balance of Payments* (Bombay: Asia 1962); B.R. Tomlinson, *The Political Economy of the Raj 1914–47* (London and Basingstoke: Macmillan, 1979); Colin Simmons, 'The Great Depression and Indian industry: Changing Interpretations and Changing Perceptions', *MAS* 21, no.3 (1987): 585–623; Dietmar Rothermund, *India in the Great Depression, 1929–39* (Delhi: Manohar, 1992); Rothermund, *The Global Impact of the Great Depression, 1929–1939* (London: Routledge, 1996); G. Balachandran, *John Bullion's Empire: Britain's Gold Problem and India between the Wars* (Richmond: Curzon Press, 1996); K.N. Chaudhuri, 'Foreign Trade and Balance of Payments' in *CEHI* 2, 804–75; Neil Charlesworth, 'The Peasant and the Depression: The Case of the Bombay Presidency, India', in *The Economies of Africa and Asia in the Interwar Depression*, ed. Ian Brown (London: Routledge, 1989); Tirthankar Roy, 'State Capacity and the Economic History of Colonial India', *Australian EHR* 59, no.1 (2019): 80–116.

CHAPTER 4

Surveys

B.B. Chaudhuri, 'Peasant Response to the Market', in *Peasant History of Late Pre-Colonial and Colonial India* (New Delhi: Centre for Studies in Civilisations and Pearson Longman, 2008), 403–510;

'Introduction', in *Agricultural Production and Indian History*, ed. David Ludden (Delhi: Oxford University Press, 1994), 1–23; K.N. Raj, N. Bhattacharya, S. Guha, and S. Padhi (eds), 'Introduction', in *Essays on the Commercialization of Indian Agriculture* (Delhi: Oxford University Press, 1985); Latika Chaudhary, Bishnupriya Gupta, Tirthankar Roy, and Anand Swamy, 'Agriculture n Colonial India', in *A New Economic History of Colonial India*, ed. Latika Chaudhary, Bishnupriya Gupta,Tirthankar Roy, and Anand Swamy, 100–16; Sabyasachi Bhattacharya, Sumit Guha, Raman Mahadevan, Sakti Padhi, D. Rajasekhar, and G. N. Rao (eds), 'Introduction', in *The South Indian Economy. Agrarian Change, Industrial Structure, and State Policy c.1914–1947* (Delhi: Oxford University Press, 1991); Sugata Bose (ed.), 'Introduction', in *Credit, Markets and the Agrarian Economy* (Delhi: Oxford University Press, 1994).

Regional Histories of Production and Demand Conditions

Crispin Bates, 'The Nature of Social Change in Rural Gujarat: The Kheda District 1818–1918', *MAS* 15, no.4 (1981): 771–821; Donald W. Attwood, *Raising Cane. The Political Economy of Sugar in Western India* (Delhi: Oxford University Press, 1993), Chapters 2–7; Himadri Banerjee, *Agrarian Society of the Punjab 1849–1901* (Delhi: Manohar, 1982); Ian Derbyshire 'Economic Change and the Railways in North India, 1860–1914', *MAS* 21, no.3 (1987): 521–45; Ian Stone, *Canal Irrigation in British India* (Cambridge: Cambridge University Press, 1984), Chapter 8, 278–346; Ian Talbot, *Punjab and the Raj* (Delhi: Manohar Publishers, 1988); Imran Ali, 'Malign Growth? Agricultural Colonization and the Roots of Backwardness in the Punjab', *Past and Present* 114, no.1 (1987): 110–32; Indu Agnihotri, 'Ecology, Land Use and Colonisation: The Canal Colonies of Punjab', *IESHR* 33, no.1 (1996): 59–68; M.B. McAlpin, *Subject to Famine. Food Crises and Economic Change in Western India, 1860-1920* (Princeton: Princeton University Press, 1983) Chapter 7; Neil Charlesworth, *Peasants and Imperial Rule: Agriculture and Agrarian Society in the Bombay Presidency 1850–1935* (Cambridge: Cambridge University Press, 2002); Sumit Guha, *The Agrarian Economy of the Bombay-Deccan 1818–1941* (Delhi: Oxford University Press, 1985).

Amalendu Guha, 'A Big Push without a Take-off: A Case Study of Assam 1871–1901', *IESHR* 5, no.3 (1968): 199–221; Guha, 'Assamese Agrarian Societies in the Late Nineteenth Century: Roots, Structures and Trends', *IESHR* 17, no.1 (1980): 35–94; A. Satyanarayana, 'Expansion of Commodity Production and Agrarian Market', in Ludden, *Agricultural Production and Indian History*, 182–238; B.B. Chaudhuri, 'Growth of Commercial Agriculture in Bengal—1859–1885' in Ludden, *Agricultural Production and Indian History*, 145–81; C.J. Baker, *An Indian Rural Economy, 1880–1955: The Tamilnad Countryside* (Delhi: Oxford University Press, 1984), Chapter 3; David Gilmartin, 'Scientific Empire and Imperial Science: Colonialism and Irrigation Technology in the Indus Basin', *JAS* 53, no.4 (1994): 1127–49; David Ludden, *Peasant History in South India* (Princeton: Princeton University Press, 1985), Chapter 5, 130–63; D.E.U. Baker, *Colonialism in an Indian Hinterland. The Central provinces 1820–1920* (Delhi: Oxford University Press, 1993), 107–235; G.N. Rao, 'Transition from Subsistence to Commercial Agriculture: A Study of Krishna District of Andhra 1850-1900', *EPW* 20, no.25–6 (1985): A60–A69; Haruka Yanagisawa, *A Century of Change: Caste and Irrigated Lands in Tamil Nadu 1860s–1970s* (Delhi: Manohar, 1996); J. Pouchepadass, *Land, Power and Market. A Bihar District under Colonial Rule, 1860–1947* (New Delhi: SAGE Publications, 2000); Laxman Satya, *Cotton and Famine in Berar, 1850–1900* (Delhi: Manohar, 1997); M.S.S. Pandian, *The Political Economy of Agrarian Change: Nanchilnadu 1880–1939* (New Delhi: SAGE Publications, 1990).

N. Benjamin, 'The Trade of the Central Provinces of India (1861–1880)', *IESHR* 15, no.4 (1978): 505–15; Peter Harnetty, 'Crop Trends in the Central Provinces of India, 1861–1921', *MAS* 11, no.3 (1977): 341–77; P.P. Mohapatra. 1990. 'Aspects of Agrarian Economy of Chotanagpur 1880-1950', PhD dissertation, Jawaharlal Nehru University, New Delhi, India; R.D. Choksey and K.S. Sastry, *The Story of Sind* (Pune: Dastane, 1983).

Land and Credit Markets

B.B. Chaudhuri, 'Control over Land and Credit', in Chaudhuri, *Peasant History*, 511–78; Jacques Pouchepadass, 'Land, Power and

Market: The Rise of the Land Market in Gangetic India', in *Rural India: Land, Power and Society under British Rule*, ed. Peter Robb (Delhi: Oxford University Press, 1992), 78–108; Latika Chaudhary and Anand Swamy, 'Protecting the Borrower: An Experiment in Colonial India,' *Explorations in Economic History* 65, no.3 (2017): 36–54; Chaudhary and Swami, 'A Policy of Credit Disruption: The Punjab Land Alienation Act of 1900,' *EHR* 73, no.1 (2020): 134–58; M.A. Reddy, *Lands and Tenants in South India: A Study of Nellore District, 1850–1990* (Delhi: Oxford University Press, 1996); Nariaki Nakazato, 'Regional Pattern of Land Transfer in Late Colonial Bengal', in *Local Agrarian Societies in Colonial India. Japanese Perspectives*, eds Peter Robb, Kaoru Sugihara, Haruka Yanagisawa (Richmond: Curzon Press, 1996), 250–79; Sumit Guha, 'Agricultural Rents in India c. 1900–1960', in *India's Colonial Encounter: Essays in Memory of Eric Stokes*, eds M. Hasan and N. Gupta (Delhi: Manohar, 1993); Guha, 'The Land Market in Upland Maharashtra 1820–1960', *IESHR* 24, no.2–3 (1987): 117–44, 291–322.

Rural Labour

Tirthankar Roy, 'Growth of a Labour Market in the Twentieth Century', in *A New Economic History of Colonial India*, eds Chaudhary, Gupta, Roy, and Swamy, 179–94; Utsa Patnaik, 'On the Evolution of the Class of Agricultural Labourers in India', *Social Scientist* 11, no.1 (1985): 3–24.

CHAPTER 5

Douglas E. Haynes, *Small Town Capitalism in Western India: Artisans, Merchants, and the Making of the Informal Economy, 1870–1960* (Cambridge: Cambridge University Press, 2012); Haruka Yanagisawa, 'The Growth of Rural Industries in Tamilnadu and their Domestic Markets, 1900–1950', in *History and Society in South India*, eds T. Mizushima and H. Yanagisawa (Tokyo: Tokyo University of Foreign Studies, 1996); Tirthankar Roy, *Traditional Industry in the Economy of Colonial India* (Cambridge: Cambridge University Press, 1999).

Roy, *Crafts and Capitalism: Handloom Weaving in India* (London and New Delhi: Routledge, 2019).

CHAPTER 6

Surveys

Bishnupriya Gupta and Tirthankar Roy, 'From Artisanal Production to Machine Tools: Industrialization in India in the Long Run', in *The Spread of Modern Industry to the Periphery since 1871*, eds K.H.O'Rourke and J.G. Williamson (Oxford: Oxford University Press, 2017), 229–55; Gupta, 'The Rise of Modern Industry in Colonial India', in *A New Economic History of Colonial India*, eds Chaudhary, Gupta, Roy, and Swamy, 67–83; Morris D. Morris, 'The Growth of Large-scale Industry to 1947', in *CEHI* 2, 551–676; Rajat K. Ray, 'Introduction', in *Entrepreneurship and Industry in India, 1800–1947*, ed. Ray.

Cotton Textile Industry

Rajnarayan Chandavarkar, *The Origins of Industrial Capitalism in India* (Cambridge: Cambridge University Press, 1994), Chapters 1, 6.

Institutions and Organization

B.B. Kling, 'The Origin of the Managing Agency in India', *JAS* 26, no.1 (1966): 37–47; Maria Misra, *Business, Race and Politics in British India, c.1850–1960* (Oxford: Clarendon Press, 1999), 17–65; Tirthankar Roy and Anand V. Swamy, *Law and the Economy in Colonial India* (Chicago: University of Chicago Press, 2016); R.S. Rungta, *Rise of Business Corporations in India, 1851–1900* (Cambridge: Cambridge University Press, 1970), Chapter 11, 203–18.

Business History

Dwijendra Tripathi, *The Oxford History of Indian Business* (Delhi: Oxford University Press, 2004); Medha Kudaisya (ed.), *The*

Oxford India Anthology of Business History (New Delhi: Oxford University Press, 2011); Rajat K. Ray (ed.), *Entrepreneurship and Industry in India, 1800–1947* (Delhi: Oxford University Press, 1994); Tirthankar Roy, *A Business History of India: Enterprise and the Emergence of Capitalism since 1700* (Cambridge: Cambridge University Press, 2018).

Technology

Tirthankar Roy, 'Technology in Colonial India,' *Technology and Culture*, 2020.

CHAPTER 7

General Works on Plantations

Percival Griffiths, *The History of the Indian Tea Industry* (London: Weidenfeld and Nicholson, 1967); S.G. Speer, *UPASI 1893–1953*, Coonoor, no date; Ranajit Das Gupta, *Economy, Society and Politics in Bengal: Jalpaiguri 1869–1947* (Delhi: Oxford University Press, 1992), Chapter 4; Tharian George and P.K. Michael Tharakan, 'A Traditional Economy: The Case of Tea Plantations in Penetration of Capital into Kerala,' *Studies in History* 2, no.2 (1986): 199–229; Virginius Xaxa, 'Colonial Capitalism and Underdevelopment in North Bengal,' *EPW* 20, no.39 (1985): 1659–65.

Labour

Bishnupriya Gupta and Anand V. Swamy, 'Reputational Consequences of Labor Coercion: Evidence from Assam's Tea Plantations,' *Journal of Development Economics* 127, no. C (2017): 131–9; C.P. Simmons, 'Recruiting and Organizing an Industrial Labour Force in Colonial India: The Case of the Coal Mining Industry, c. 1880–1939', *IESHR* 13, no.4 (1976): 455–85; Dilip Simeon, *The Politics of Labour Under Late Colonialism. Workers, Unions and the State in Chota Nagpur 1928–1939* (Delhi: Manohar, 1995), 16–18, 23–30, 149–58; Ranajit Das Gupta, 'From Peasants and Tribesmen to Plantation Workers—Colonial Capitalism, Reproduction of Labour Power and Proletarianisation in North East India: 1850s–1947', *EPW* 21, no.4 (1986): PE2–PE10; Rana P. Behal, *One Hundred Years of Servitude: Political Economy of Tea Plantations in Colonial Assam* (New Delhi: Tulika Books, 2014); Ravi Raman, *Global Capital and Peripheral Labour: The History and Political Economy of Plantation Workers in India* (London and New York: Routledge, 2010).

Capital

A.K. Bagchi, *The Evolution of the State Bank of India*, Volume 2 (New Delhi: Sage Publications, 1997), 66–72; C.P. Simmons, 'Indigenous Enterprise in the Indian Coal Mining Industry, c. 1835–1939', *IESHR* 13, no.2 (1976): 189–218; D. Rothermund (ed.), *Urban Growth and Rural Stagnation. Studies in the Economy of an Indian Coalfield and its Rural Hinterland* (Delhi: Manohar, 1980); G.R. Desai, *Life Insurance Business in India* (Delhi: Macmillan, 1973); Henner Papendieck, 'British Managing Agencies in the Indian Coalfield', in *Zaminders, Mines, and Peasants: Studies in the History of an Indian Coalfield*, eds D. Rothermund and D.C. Wadhwa (Delhi: Manohar, 1978); R.S. Rungta, *The Rise of Business Corporations in India, 1851–1900* (Cambridge: Cambridge University Press, 1970), 203–19; Tirthankar Roy, 'Monsoon and the Market for Money in Late Colonial India,' *Enterprise and Society* 17, no.2 (2016): 324–57.

CHAPTER 8

Irrigation

Elizabeth Whitcombe, 'Irrigation' in *CEHI* 2, 677–736; Ian Stone, *Canal Irrigation in British India* (Cambridge: Cambridge University Press, 1984), Chapter 1, 1–12, Chapters 2, 13–67, and Chapter 8, 278–347; Imran Ali, 'Malign Growth?: Agricultural Colonization and Roots of Backwardness in the Punjab', *Past and Present* 114, no.1 (1987): 110–32.

Railways, Telegraph, Law, Education, Healthcare, Institutions

Arun Kumar, *Medicine and the Raj: British Medical Policy in India, 1835–1911* (New Delhi: SAGE Publications, 1998); Dan Bogart and Latika Chaudhary, 'Railways in Colonial India: An Economic Achievement?', in *A New Economic History of Colonial India*, eds Chaudhary, Gupta, Roy, and Swamy, 140–60; Ian Derbyshire, 'The Building of India's Railways: The Application of Western Technology in the Colonial Periphery 1850–1920', in *Technology and the Raj: Western Technology and Technical Transfers to India, 1700–1947*, eds Roy MacLeod and Deepak Kumar (New Delhi: SAGE Publications, 1995); John Hurd, 'Railways' in *CEHI 2*, 737–61; Lakshmi Iyer, 'The Long-run Consequences of Colonial Institutions', in *New Economic History*, eds Chaudhary, Gupta, Roy, and Swamy, 117–39; Latika Chaudhary, 'Caste, Colonialism, and Schooling: Education in British India', in *New Economic History*, eds Chaudhary, Gupta, Roy, and Swamy, 161–78; Saroj Ghosh, 'Commercial Needs and Military Necessities: The Telegraph in India' in *Technology and the Raj*, eds MacLeod and Kumar; Roy and Swamy, *Law and the Economy in Colonial India*.

CHAPTER 9

Fiscal System and Policy

Dharma Kumar, 'The Fiscal System', in *CEHI 2*, 905–44; M.J.K. Thavaraj, 'Capital Formation in the Public Sector in India: A Historical Study, 1898–1938', in *Papers on National Income and Allied Topics*, ed. V.K.R.V. Rao (Delhi: Allied Publishers, 1962); P.J. Thomas, *The Growth of Federal Finance in India* (London: Humphrey Milford, 1939).

Monetary System and Policy

G. Balachandran, 'Colonial India and the World Economy, c. 1850–1940', in *A New Economic History of Colonial India*, eds Chaudhary,

Gupta, Roy, and Swamy, 84–99. See M. De Cecco, *Money and Empire: The International Gold Standard* (Oxford: Blackwell, 1974), on pre-war years; Tomlinson, *The Political Economy of the Raj: 1914–47*.

Ideological and Political Roots of Policy

Sabyasachi Bhattacharya, *The Financial Foundations of the British Raj: Ideas and Interests in the Reconstruction of Indian Public Finance, 1858–1872* (Simla: Indian Institute of Advanced Study, 1971); S. Ambirajan, *Classical Political Economy and British Policy in India* (Cambridge: Cambridge University Press, 1978), Chapter 1. See also the Table 3, p. 269, for an overview of government intervention.

The State and Economic Growth

Roy, 'State Capacity and the Economic History of Colonial India', *Australian Economic History Review* 59, no.1 (2018): 80–102; Roy, 'Why was British India a Limited State?' in *Fiscal Capacity and the Colonial State in Asia and Africa 1850–1960*, eds Anne Booth and Ewout Frankema (Cambridge: Cambridge University Press, 2019), 77–109.

CHAPTER 10

Population

Ira Klein, 'Population Growth and Mortality in British India, Part I: The Climacteric of Death', *IESHR* 26, no.4 (1989): 387–403; Klein, 'Population Growth and Mortality in British India, Part II: The Demographic Revolution', *IESHR* 27, no.1 (1990): 33–63; Leela Visaria and Pravin Visaria, 'Population (1757–1947)', in *CEHI 2*, 463–532; P.C. Mahalanobis and D. Bhattacharya, 'Growth of Population in India and Pakistan, 1801–1961', *Artha Vijnana* 18, no.1 (1976): 1–10; Sumit Guha, 'Mortality Decline in Early Twentieth Century India: A Preliminary Enquiry', *IESHR* 28, no.4 (1991): 371–91.

Tim Dyson, *A Population History of India: From the First Modern People to the Present Day* (Oxford: Oxford University Press, 2018).

Famine

A.K. Sen, *Poverty and Famines: An Essay on Entitlement and Deprivation* (Oxford: Oxford University Press, 1983); David Hall-Matthews, 'The Historical Roots of Famine Relief Paradigms,' in *A World Without Famine?*, eds Helen O'Neill and John Toye (Basingstoke and London: Macmillan, 1998); Ira Klein, 'When the Rains Failed: Famine, Relief, and Mortality in British India', *IESHR* 21, no.2 (1984): 185–214; M.B. McAlpin, *Subject to Famine: Food Crisis and Economic Change in Western India, 1860–1920* (Princeton: Princeton University Press, 1983); Tim Dyson, 'On the Demography of South Asian Famines', *Population Studies* 45, no.1–2 (1991): 5–25, 279–97; Tirthankar Roy, 'Indian Famines: 'Natural' or 'Man-made'?' in *In Quest of the Historian's Craft: Essays in Honour of Prof. B.B. Chaudhuri*, eds Sanjukta Das Gupta and Arun Bandopadhyay (New Delhi: Manohar, 2017), 75–103.

CHAPTER 11

Christopher Hill, *South Asia: An Environmental History* (Oxford: Oxford University Press, 2008); D. Arnold and R. Guha (eds), *Nature, Culture, Imperialism: Essays on the Environmental History of South Asia* (New Delhi: Oxford University Press, 1995); D. Kumar, V. Damodaran, and R. D'Souza (eds), *The British Empire and the Natural World: Environmental Encounters in South Asia* (New Delhi: Oxford University Press, 2011); M. Rangarajan and K. Sivaramakrishnan (eds), *Shifting Ground: People, Animals, and Mobility in India's Environmental History* (New Delhi: Oxford University Press, 2014); R. Grove, V. Damodaran, and S. Sangwan (eds), *Nature and the Orient* (New Delhi: Oxford University Press, 1998); Tirthankar Roy, 'Land Quality, Carrying Capacity and Sustainable Agricultural Change in Twentieth Century India,' in *Economic Development and Environmental History in the Anthropocene*, ed. Gareth Austin (London: Bloomsbury, 2017), 159–78.

CHAPTER 12

Bjørn Hettne, *The Political Economy of Indirect Rule: Mysore 1881–1947* (London and Malmö: Curzon Press, 1978), Part III; C.V. Subba Rao, 'Role of the State in Industrialization: The Case of Hyderabad', in *The South Indian Economy*, eds Bhattacharya et al.; Lakshmi Iyer, 'Direct versus Indirect Colonial Rule in India: Long-term Consequences,' *Review of Economics and Statistics* 92, no.4 (2010): 693–713; Raman Mahadevan, 'Industrial Entrepreneurship in Princely Travancore: 1930–47,' in *The South Indian Economy*, eds S. Bhattacharya et al.; T.M. Thomas Isaac and P.K. Michael Tharakan, 'An Enquiry into the Historical Roots of Industrial Backwardness of Kerala—A Study of the Travancore Region', Centre for Development Studies, Trivandrum, Working Paper No. 215.

CHAPTER 13

Abhijit Banerjee and Rohini Somanathan, 'The Political Economy of Public Goods: Some Evidence from India', *Journal of Development Economics* 82, no.3 (2007): 287–314; Ashok Gulati and S. Narayanan, *The Subsidy Syndrome in Indian Agriculture* (Delhi: Oxford University Press, 2003); Atul Kohli, *The State and Poverty in India. The Politics of Reform* (Cambridge: Cambridge University Press, 1987); Ian Talbot and Gurharpal Singh, *The Partition of India* (Cambridge: Cambridge University Press, 2009); Jean Drèze and Amartya Sen, *An Uncertain Glory: India and its Contradictions* (Princeton and Oxford: Princeton University Press, 2013); Lloyd J. Rudolph and Susanne H. Rudolph, *In Pursuit of Lakshmi. The Political Economy of the Indian State* (Chicago: Chicago University Press, 1987); Maitreesh Ghatak and Sanchari Roy, 'Land Reform and Agricultural Productivity in India: A review of the evidence. *Oxford Review of Economic Policy* 23, no.2 (2007): 251–69.

Michael Aldous and Tirthankar Roy, 'Reassessing FERA: Examining British Firms' Strategic Responses to "Indianisation",' *Business History* early-view on journal website; Philippe Aghion, Robin Burgess, Stephen J. Redding and Fabrizio Zilibotti, 'The Unequal Effects of Liberalization: Evidence from Dismantling the

License Raj in India', *American Economic Review* 98, no.4 (2008): 1397–412; Ramachandra Guha, *India after Gandhi: The History of the World's Largest Democracy* (London: MacMillan, 2007); Tirthankar Roy, *The Economy of South Asia – From 1950 to the Present* (Basingstoke: Palgrave, 2017).

Index

Act XIII of 1859 192
Adam, William 61
agency houses 43, 203, 210. *See
   also* Calcutta Agency House
   banking services of 205
   and Indian partners 50
   opium trade of 50
agriculture 6–7, 9–10, 66–9, 72–6,
   85–6, 88–9, 97–102, 127–8,
   130–1, 147–8, 172, 193–4, 278,
   284, 338–9, 343
   commercialization of 105
   depression and 39, 105
   development of 67, 90, 243, 344
      growth of 7, 21, 76, 98, 109,
         146, 296, 300, 306
   income from 7, 66, 74, 81
   measuring change in 99–102
   monsoon 122, 128
   private investment in 333
   processing industries 308
   production 69, 111, 216, 244,
      332, 354
   productivity in 9, 41, 99

regions of 15, 109–17
slowdown in 69, 76, 83
underinvestment in 134
Ahmedabad 112, 161, 164, 168,
   179, 242, 311, 352
   mill industry 180
Aid-India Consortium 328
Allahabad Bank 206
American Civil War (1861–5) 46,
   106, 164, 228
Andrew Yule 180, 191
Anti-monopoly laws 338
apprenticeship system 156
Arkwright, Richard 45
artisans 50, 52–4, 59, 80–2, 138,
   144–6, 150–7, 171–2, 196,
   202–3, 271, 275
Arthur Lewis, W. 171
Assam Company 190
Aurangzeb 19;
   death of 46
Awadh 2, 19, 31, 64

Bagchi, A.K. 52, 144, 359

Baghdadi Jews 180
balance of payments 96–7, 254–5, 293, 327, 331, 337–8, 345, 353
Balmer-Lawrie 180
bankers 20, 23, 30, 32, 40, 47–8, 57, 64, 81, 208–9
    Gujarati 180
    indigenous 179, 185, 204
banking system 47–51, 92, 160, 163, 189–211, 321, 347, 352
banks 51, 76, 86, 89, 95, 189, 202–11, 315, 317, 324
    Bank of Baroda 206, 267, 311, 313
    Bank of Bengal 204
    Bank of Bombay 204
    Bank of England 208, 252
    Bank of India 206
    Bank of Madras 204
    Canara Bank 206
    Central Bank of India 206–8, 250, 320
    corporate 203, 209
    Indian 91, 205–7
    liquidation of 205
    Punjab National Bank 206
    State Bank of India 204, 359
    Union Bank 51
Baroda 206, 302, 307, 311–15
Battle of Plassey 2, 27
Begg-Dunlop 191
Bengal 233;
    famine in 9, 250, 271, 274
    rice 107–8
    sicca rupee 57
    silver rupee 56
    zamindars of 133
Bentinck, William 61
Bhatias 48, 180

Bhilai steel plant 327
bhomias 22
Bird and F.W. Heilgers 180
Birla 181
blue mutiny 43
Board of Control 34–5, 55, 214
Bohra House 206
Bokaro steel project 326
Bombay 54–5, 112–13, 118, 158, 164, 166–70, 174–6, 179–82, 204–6, 219, 221, 228, 264–5, 293–4, 353;
    port 307
Bombay Industrial Relations Act of 1946 177
Bombay Life Assurance Company 210
Bombay Mutual Life Assurance Company 210
Bombay Plan document 320
Bombay Textile Labour Union 176
Bombay Textile Strike 329
borrowers 207, 209
borrowings 90–1, 136, 179, 250
    peasant 126. See also credit; lending
British, Britain 31, 34, 44, 55, 80, 90
    imports from 79
    and India 4, 32
    Indian cotton in 45–6
    military power 55
    trade with 12
British Colonial Rule 3, 14, 16, 38, 47, 56, 64–5, 128
    independence from 317
    and poverty 12
    in South Asia 319
British Crown 2, 78

British East India Company 2, 20.
  See also East India Company
British Empire 4, 32, 65, 78, 317, 362
  Lower Burma as part of 181
  Opium and 44
British India 2, 34–5, 243, 301–9,
  311–16, 319, 343–4, 349, 351,
  354, 357, 359–62
  agricultural productivity in 9
  healthcare and education in 9
  population history in 275
  and princely territories 345
  provinces of 84, 302, 314
  taxes in 90
  territory of 31
Broich, John 294
brokers 50, 59
business 92. *See also* capitalism,
  capitalists, merchants
  Indo-European 53
  large-scale 59
  organization 28, 163. *See also*
    managing agency
business community. *See*
  communities

Cable, Ernest 208
Calcutta 30, 43–4, 54, 60–1, 158,
  164, 166–7, 169, 180–1, 190,
  221, 229–30, 235–7, 265–7
  auction of tea at 191
  maritime traffic in 228
  as wealthiest city 293
Calcutta agency Houses 210
Calcutta Electric Supply
  Corporation Ltd 231
canals 58, 100, 104, 110–13, 212,
  219, 272, 274, 291, 296–7, 312,
  315, 330, 332

construction of 45, 57, 216
Ganges 215, 218
irrigation 110–11, 113, 213, 218
Punjab 215, 320
Sirhind 215, 314
Sone 215
and wells 103
Western Jumna 216
Canning, Charles 214
capital 11–12, 94–6, 148–50,
  156–7, 160–4, 178–82, 184–5,
  192, 198–9, 211–13, 216–17,
  220, 295–6, 307–8, 313, 358–9
  fixed 179
  and intermediate goods 187,
    312
  long-term 97, 209
  in opium 45
capital market 88, 185, 204, 223,
  334
  domestic 321
capital-intensive: goods 321
  industry 161, 321
capitalism 11–13, 151, 329, 339,
  357–8
  poverty and 12
capitalists 12, 149–50, 157
  British 187
cargo 28, 219, 226
  transportation of 227
Carr Tagore Company, The 51, 197
cash crops 114, 124, 128
caste system 7, 15–16, 59, 61–2,
  121–3, 127, 132, 182, 185,
  234–6
  oppression in 131, 177
Chambers of commerce 183
Charter Act of 1813 41
Chaudhuri, B.B. 135

Chettiar: bankers 182
    enterprise 181
Child Marriage Restraint Act of
    1929 262
China 11, 13, 25, 27, 43–4, 79
    trade 41, 164, 190
Christian missions 312
Clark, Gregory 174–5
cloths, machine-made 51
coal reserves 197, 308. *See also*
    mining
coast-to-coast shipping 46
Cochin 307–8
Colonial India 15, 76, 81–2, 92,
    227, 231, 264–5, 277, 279, 350,
    352–4, 356–8, 360
    banking in 202
    Economic change in 66
    historians of 58
    hydrology 292, 300
    national income for 5
colonialism 1–4, 6, 9–10, 13–15,
    55, 57, 61, 63, 98–9, 101, 153–
    6, 214–15, 314, 343–6, 355
    capitalism and 12
    inequality and 7
colonialism and globalization 1–5,
    7, 9–10, 14–15, 172, 299, 317,
    343
    poverty and 12–13
commerce 49, 65, 68, 199, 206,
    235, 295, 303, 315, 346
commercial law 58–9, 232–3
commercialization 98–9, 104–9,
    115–17, 123–4, 127–34, 136,
    138, 295
commodities 1, 4, 257, 304
    agricultural 76, 104–5, 295
    Bengal rice 107–8

cement 165, 167, 170, 180–1, 308
cloths 27, 42, 46–7, 51–2
coal 170, 175, 180, 189, 196–9,
    294
coffee 189, 194–6, 308
cotton 42, 45–7, 78, 104–6,
    111–14, 117, 124, 158, 161,
    164, 166, 168, 170, 173,
    179–80
cotton textiles 15, 26–7, 42, 51,
    78, 152, 165–6, 180, 307
gold 25, 88, 97, 200, 250–3, 255
iron 15, 53, 151–2, 165, 170,
    196, 347
overseas demand 75
rice 26–7, 100, 106–8, 112, 114,
    116, 118, 136–7, 140, 158,
    160–1, 167, 332–3
rubber 189, 308;
salt 23, 42, 46, 51, 54, 115
saltpetre 23, 42
silk 23, 33, 42, 50, 117, 139,
    147–8
silver 26–8, 44, 75, 85–6, 88, 92,
    251–2, 255
steel 15, 152, 165–7, 170, 176,
    308, 322–3, 325
sugar 23, 42, 50, 161, 165, 167,
    181, 219, 354
tea 44, 51, 78, 97, 108, 180, 186,
    189–91, 308, 321, 323
tobacco 42
trade 51, 80, 179, 185, 211, 254,
    300
wheat 75, 100, 105–6, 111,
    117–18, 124, 158, 226, 324
Communist Party of India 324
Communist Party of India
    (Marxist) 330

communities 46, 48–51, 56, 149, 157, 179, 234–5, 261, 263, 286, 289
 Chettiars 49, 181
 Hindu and Muslim trading 49
 Kanbi Patidars 132
 Marwaris 48–9, 180, 199, 307
 Parsis 50–1, 176, 180, 182–3, 235
 of traders 48–9, 313
 village 284
conservationism 285
consumers 139–40, 145, 151, 154, 157, 160, 191, 199, 283, 330, 339
consumption 1, 5, 23, 76, 160, 201, 273, 340
 urban 76
continental monarchies 25
Conybeare, Henry 294
coolies 190, 192. See also workers
cooperative credit societies 202
Cooperative Credit Societies Act of 1904 202
corruption 60, 339
cotton 46, 164
 cultivation 45, 112, 118
 demand for 164
 export 45–6, 106, 168
 from Gujarat 45
 handloom weaving 139
 Indian 45–6, 106, 164
 mills 45, 106, 141, 147, 166–9, 176, 179–80, 187, 347
 textiles 15, 26–7, 42, 51, 78, 152, 165–6, 180, 307. See also under commodities
council bill system 251
courts of law 5, 126, 212, 320

Cowasjee, Rustomjee 51
credit 119, 123–7, 132–3, 181, 202, 206, 332, 337, 354–5
 for industry and services 89
cultivation 39, 41, 110, 112, 131, 133, 137, 191, 279, 282, 289, 291, 295–6
 of cash crops 111
 cost of 38
 expansion of 21, 35, 75
 of grains and oilseeds 111
 of indigo 42
cultivators 34, 40. See also peasants
 ryotwari and 37
 taxation on 21
 types of 21
currencies 57
 introduction of 56
 reforms 251
Currimbhoys 180

da Gama, Vasco 25
Dale, Stephen 48
Dalhousie, Lord 214
Das, C.R. 233
Datta, K.L. 273
Davar, C.N. 168
Davenport 191
death rates 238–9, 258–9, 261
 in English population 293
debt 92, 94, 242, 245–6
 market, access to foreign 309. See also credit; financial services; lending
Deccan Agriculturists Relief Act (1879) 125
Deccan Plateau 18–19, 103–4, 112–14, 151, 270, 306
deindustrialization 51, 53, 144–5

Delhi 19, 22, 24, 48, 57, 216, 221, 238, 347, 350–60, 363
delta 26, 58, 291, 300, 306
    Cauvery 215
    Krishna and Godavari 215
depreciation 86, 221, 246, 250–2, 254
depression 76, 87–8, 96–7, 105, 133, 148, 167, 186, 198, 249–50, 253–7
devaluation 39, 57, 75, 98, 173, 251, 254, 328
development policy 212
diversification 79, 307, 325
doctrine of lapse 31, 64
Dossal, Mariam 294
drain theory 94–6, 245
Drèze, Jean 339
Duff, Alexander 62
Duncan, Andrew 53
Duncan Brothers 180, 191
Dutch East India Company (Vereenigde Oost-Indische Compagnie) 26. See also East India Company
Dutt, R.C. 12–13, 273

East India Company 35, 53, 190, 203, 205, 259, 274, 346;
    bankers and 48
    and rise of State 29–34
East Indian Railway 221. See also railways
economic: development 303, 319, 322
    history, theories of 11–14
    nationalism 253, 255–6
    policy 242, 308–11, 318, 351, 363

prosperity 303
    system 94, 257, 320
economic change 14, 80, 85, 278, 295, 303, 305, 342–3, 345, 354, 362
    colonial pattern of 319
economic conditions 19
    in mid 1700s 17–29
economic growth 6, 10, 12, 15, 61, 67, 73, 75, 77, 83, 318–19, 339, 342
economies 2, 10, 14, 28, 51, 78, 153, 188, 255, 301, 315, 317–41, 350, 353
    eighteenth-century 16
    plantations and rice-based 311
    stagnation of 6–7
economists 14, 69, 102, 115, 133, 224–5, 325, 327–8, 334, 337–8, 345
education 7, 9, 49, 55, 63, 67, 233–9, 247–8, 312, 315, 318, 343–4;
    colleges in India 61
    in English 62
    indigenous 61–2
    in schools 16, 62–3, 196, 202, 213, 234–5, 241, 307, 313, 320, 324
    technical 237, 334, 339
    universities 16, 51, 95, 212, 214, 233, 236–7, 313, 317
electricity 150, 166, 180, 240, 313, 315, 332–3, 341
    connection 324
    generation 231, 239
emigration 266–7, 271
employment 70, 131, 144, 157, 160, 168–9, 189, 296, 305

in commercial firms 62
growth of 68, 334
industrial 141, 147, 156, 161,
    330
Engels, Friedrich 171
entrepreneurship 141, 163, 179,
    183, 211, 334, 352, 357–8, 363
    community-bound resources
    187
environmentalism 10, 297–8
epidemics 193, 239, 258–9, 263–5,
    294
European companies 199–200. *See
    also* Dutch East India Company;
    East India Company
exchange banks 202
Expenditure, public 90–2, 94,
    245–6, 248, 250, 308–9, 312
exploitation 12, 14, 116, 126, 197,
    286, 329, 345
export 42, 45–6, 75–6, 78, 96, 99,
    105, 113–14, 118, 153–4, 160,
    186, 242–3, 329–30, 332–3,
    336–8
    of cotton 106
    of cotton textiles 27
    paddy cultivation for 181
export markets 99, 106, 114, 160
    Europeans in 186
    of hide in Kanpur 154
extraction technology 199. *See also*
    mining

factories 23, 53, 73, 148, 150, 154,
    157–8, 160–3, 165, 170, 172–4,
    177, 186, 188, 322–3;
    rural 160
famine 8–9, 132–3, 192–4, 213,
    224–5, 249, 258–61, 263–5,

270–5, 289, 291–2, 324–5,
    332–3, 354–5, 362;
    1804 226
    in Bengal 9, 250, 271, 274
    rice 107–8
    dryland 294
    insurance fund 275
    Malthusian theory of 272
    relief 216, 218, 308, 328
    relief camps 275, 290
Famine Codes 272, 275
Famine Commission 214, 217,
    272, 275, 291
farmers 105, 112, 118, 135–6, 138,
    271, 281, 323, 330, 332–3, 343.
    See also peasants
federalism 213, 340
feudalistic structure 314
    feudal lords in 64, 303
finance commission 249
financial: federalism 248
    instrument 309
    resources 22, 312
    services 69, 341
    system 27, 46, 114, 243–50,
        254, 309, 313, 344–5, 360
financiers 50, 219. *See also*
    moneylenders
Finlay, James 179
Fiscal Commission 165
Five-Year Plan 321
flood control 63, 290–1
floriculture 333
food: to card-holders 330. *See also*
    public distribution of food
    crisis 328
    processing 143, 336
foodgrain 23, 46–7, 78
    production of 117, 148

foreign aid 96, 318, 322, 328–9
Foreign Exchange Regulation Act 328
forests 115, 117, 151–2, 267, 271, 277–81, 287, 289–90, 295, 299–300, 306
    dependent peoples 279, 286–90
    regulation on 283–6
Forests Act 1865 283
Fowler, Henry 252
fraud 51, 268
free trade 146, 160, 242, 273
French East India Company 30

Gaekwad, Sayajirao 206, 313
Gandhi, Indira 324–5, 328, 330, 332, 338, 364
Gandhi, M.K. 320
Gandhi, Rajiv 331, 334
gender 61–2
    inequality 15
gentrification 22
geographical regions 17
George Acland's mill 169
Gillanders-Arbuthnot 180, 191
globalization 6, 9–10, 12–16, 153, 299, 303–4, 308, 314, 316–17, 331, 334, 342–3, 345
    Colonialism and 4
    inequality and 7
Gobindchand 50
Goenka 181
Gokuldas 180
gold exchange standard 252
Goldsmid, H.E. 39
Government Lands (Punjab) Act 1912 110
Great Depression 78, 85, 87, 91, 96, 105, 181, 186, 249, 253, 256, 353. See also depression

Greaves Cotton 180
Green Revolution 10, 99, 114, 138, 324–5, 330–2, 339, 345
gross domestic product (GDP) 9, 67, 80, 189, 209
    growth of 318, 322, 329, 331
groundwater resources 332. See also canals
Guha, Amalendu 144
Guha, Ramachandra 283, 364
Gujarati House 206
Gujarati maritime merchants 28
Gupta, Bishnupriya 175, 350, 354, 357–8
Gupto, Muddoosoodeen 293
Gwalior 24, 302, 307

hajj 24
Hamilton, Francis Buchanan 62
handicrafts 12, 121–2, 139–40, 151, 158, 160, 171–2, 185. See also artisans
    transition in 144–6
handloom 156, 347
    industries 150, 168
    towns 150
    weaving 52, 140, 146–51, 157, 168, 172, 271. See also power looms
Hargreaves, James 45
harvest failure 18, 126, 137, 167, 271, 274, 325, 328
Haryana 111, 280
Hastings, Warren 58, 61, 207
    legal system during 60
healthcare 9, 67, 213, 238–9, 318, 344, 360
Heath, Josiah Marshall 53
Herschell, Farrer 252
Heston, Alan 5

History of British India 35
human development 339–41, 345
hundis 48, 202–3
Hurd II, John 305
Hyderabad 19, 302, 307, 311–13,
    315, 363
    industrial development of 313
    manufacturing in 308
    Nizams of 31
hydro-electric projects 240

immigrants 117, 269, 324
Imperial Bank of India (renamed).
    See State Bank of India
Imperial Gazetteer of India 305
Imperial Preference treaty (1921)
    80
imports 27–8, 42, 53, 75, 78–9,
    139, 152, 175, 198, 223, 321–2
    of cloth and yarn 51
income 7, 9, 54, 56, 68, 70, 81, 85,
    88, 132–3, 216, 218, 242, 244,
    311–12
    components of 6
    creation 319, 342
    trade and 42
income tax 244–5, 249. *See also*
    taxation
independence of India 212,
    313–15
Indian Bar Councils Act of 1926
    233
Indian Central Banking Enquiry
    Committee 208
Indian Companies Act 202
Indian Forest Act 285, 287
Indian Industrial Commission 165,
    231
Indian Medical Service (IMS) 238
Indian Mining Association 199

Indian Mining Federation 199
Indian nationalists 94–5, 134, 144,
    167, 223, 242, 245, 273
Indian Ocean Trade 24, 28, 34
Indian Tea Association 191
Indo-Gangetic basin 18, 20–1, 24,
    103, 291, 300, 306
Indo-Pakistan conflict 1971 326–7
Indore 302, 307
Indo-Soviet arms treaty 327
Indo-US relations 326
industrial: development 313
    disputes 329–30
    diversification 182
    enterprise 163–4
    organization 143–4
    policy 321–2, 325–6
    revolution 13, 15, 52, 75, 105,
        145, 171
    and transportation revolution 2
Industrial Disputes Act (1947) 322
industrialists 16, 89, 166–7
industrialization 54, 72, 144–6,
    161, 163–4, 187, 294–5,
    299–300, 311–13, 315–16, 318,
    320–3, 325–6, 338, 340
    factory-based 171
    import-substituting 321
    labour-intensive 145
    pattern of 141–4
    protectionist 321, 325
Industries (Development and
    Regulation) Act of 1951 322
industry 24, 51–2, 65, 139–41,
    143–5, 151–8, 160–1, 163–5,
    169, 169–71, 186–7, 307, 312,
    320, 339–40, 352–3, 358
    cheap imports and 167
    large-scale 80, 140–3, 158,
        160–2, 164, 171, 176, 179,

184, 189, 333–4. *See also*
　small-scale industry
loans from USA for 325
modern 95, 140, 196, 198–9,
　295, 357
and services 6–7, 66, 69–70, 76,
　82, 85, 89, 97, 343
types of 140–1
urban 23, 122
inequality 7, 9, 14–16, 67, 69,
　80–1, 85, 133, 140, 149, 339,
　341, 343
international 14
and poverty 81–3
regional 83–5, 99, 212, 306
infant mortality 177, 261, 275,
　293–4
infrastructure 4, 9, 16, 89–90,
　211–12, 214, 239–40, 299, 306,
　341, 347
judicial 60, 233
revolution 110, 117
transport 213
inland waterways 226–8
institutions 4, 9, 11, 54, 58, 156,
　160, 236–7, 239, 357, 360
after independence 317
reforms 40–1, 340
insurance 50, 119, 183–4, 189, 210,
　210–11, 274
interest rates 89, 124, 162, 178,
　209, 211, 221, 252, 296
investment 84, 92, 94, 124, 136–7,
　243, 245–7, 304, 325, 329–30,
　339–40
British 163
cross-border 321, 343
direct 89, 97
finance 179

foreign private 86, 331
industrial 76, 80, 179
infrastructure 212
in irrigation 57, 67, 75, 90
in land 136–7
licenses 323
private 4, 90, 235, 256, 321,
　323, 337–8, 342, 345
productive 88, 213
public 63, 91, 227, 234, 245,
　247, 320, 322
in public goods 55
in Punjab 323
in railways 344
in roads 227
savings and 85–9
by *zamindars* 41
iron: consumption of 152
import of 53
iron and steel industry 15, 53,
　151–3, 347
irrigation 55, 57, 91, 95, 102, 117–
　18, 124, 213–19, 240, 288, 292,
　303–4, 359. *See also* agriculture;
　canals; cultivation
modes of 103
projects 110, 216–18, 245
systems 22, 75, 90, 281

Jagatseth 49–50
Jain traders 180. *See also* marwaris
Jalan 181
James Finlay 179, 191
Japan 25, 79, 90;
　mills of 166
Jardine-Skinner 180, 191
joint-stock banks 185, 202, 205–6,
　210. *See also* banks
Joshi, N.M. 176

Kanpur 154, 161, 168–9
Karachi 228, 307
Karkhanas. See factories
Kashmir 3, 107, 326
Kettlewell-Bullen 180
Keynes, J.M. 208
Khan, Nizam Ali 31
Khatau 180
Khatris 48
Khojas 48, 180
Khrushchev, Nikita 327
Kilburn 180
Killick Nixon 180
K.L. Datta committee 130
knowledge industry 334
Kolar gold mines 231, 311
Komatis 49
Krishnamurty, J. 70

labour 3, 118–19, 121, 128, 144–5,
    148, 160–1, 171–8, 190–4, 197,
    200–2, 275, 334–5, 337–8, 353,
    358
    agricultural 81, 97, 105, 110,
        122–3, 130–1, 138, 154, 194,
        196, 211
    contractors 173–5, 199–200
    demand for 82
    division of 24, 79, 149, 154, 213
    factory 154
    farm 118. *See also* labour, rural
    landless 81, 131
    low productivity of 166
    market 72, 82, 123, 160, 223,
        342, 356
    migrant 4, 168, 211, 279
    mobility 8–9
    productivity of 68
    rural 89, 271

    skilled 90, 94–5, 149, 152, 166,
        340
    supply 82–3, 171, 174, 193, 195
    surplus 156, 171, 173
    tea prices and supply of 193
    unrest 200
land: cultivable 218, 281, 283. *See
    also* cultivation
    market 119–20, 356
    patterns of use 278–83, 300
    property and revenue 20–3
    property rights in 34–5, 121
    redistribution of 324
    reform 303, 323, 330, 363
land reform. *See* land
land tax 20–1, 34, 90, 134, 196,
    241, 243–5, 308
    reforming of 33
landlords 17, 19, 21–2, 30, 33–5,
    38, 40, 81, 135, 245, 303, 305,
    314. *See also* income tax;
    taxation
    property rights to 84
    tax-collecting 36
Law, Prawnkissen 51
law and justice 55, 65, 231–3, 248,
    303
Lawrence, John 208
leather manufacturing 140, 154
lending 47, 51, 127, 178, 203–4,
    208–9, 296
    insider 207, 210. *See also* credit
Levi, Scott 49
literacy 61, 305, 307. *See also*
    education; Mass education
livelihoods 19, 69, 72, 99, 114, 223,
    286–7, 297, 299, 319, 353;
    agriculture as principal 306
livestock 219, 271, 282

loans 50, 88–9, 91, 124, 126, 157,
    184, 207, 216, 245
    cheap 325
Lohanas 48

Macaulay, Thomas 63, 214
Mackinnon-Mackenzie 180
Macneill-Barry 180
Madras 30, 54–5, 57, 123, 181,
    217–19, 221, 228, 233, 235,
    237, 307, 311
    gold pagoda of 57
Madras Equitable Company 210
malaria 218–19, 239, 264–5, 267
    as Assam fever 192
Malthus, Thomas 271–2
manufacturing 47, 69, 75,
    170, 181, 189, 237, 295,
    318, 329–30, 333–4. See
    also leather manufacturing,
    industrialization
    income 330
    British 242
    as labour-intensive 329
    in Mysore 308
Marathas 2, 19–21, 30–1, 55, 64,
    132, 302
    raids by 31
    ruled western India 302
maritime trade 19, 24, 48–9, 65,
    228. See also trade
markets 4–5, 11, 26, 41, 112–13,
    123–4, 133–4, 146–7, 152,
    157–8, 184–5, 204, 273, 308–9,
    353–6
Markovits, Claude 49
Martin-Burn 180
Maruti cars with Suzuki Motor
    Corporation 331

Marwari merchants 44, 117. See
    also under communities
Marx, Karl 11–12
Marxists 12–13, 171–2, 211, 317,
    329
Mass education 61, 234. See also
    education
Mayor's Courts 60
McAlpin, Michelle 273, 351, 354,
    362
McLeod-Begg-Dunlop 180, 191
medical care 194, 196, 212, 238–9,
    262–3, 270. See also healthcare
Mehta, Pherozeshah 233
merchant profit 150
merchants 16–17, 20, 22, 24, 26,
    34, 40–1, 44, 47, 49, 62, 64–5,
    148, 150
    and bankers 20, 30, 32, 40,
    47–51, 64
    hide 154
    Parsi 168, 180
middle class 81
migrant: labour 4, 121, 146, 168,
    211, 279
    peasants 21
    workers 268
migrants 122–3, 156, 161, 173–4,
    176, 192–3, 201, 229, 267, 269
    of depressed castes 200
migration 123–4, 131, 156, 160,
    172, 176, 192–3, 266–9, 279,
    283, 286
    internal 118, 269
    international 266, 269
    into textile towns 148–9
military expenditure 90, 95, 249,
    314, 316
Mill, James 35

mills 106, 116–17, 123, 140–1,
    146–8, 150, 157–8, 160–1, 166,
    168–9, 171–7, 179–80, 333. *See
    also* factories
    jute mills 116, 166, 168–9, 171,
        173, 197
    spinning 146, 148, 168
mining 68, 128, 131, 181, 184–5,
    189, 197–201, 211, 284, 315,
    323;
    coal 50, 198, 201, 220, 223, 307.
        See also coal reserves
    and European companies 200
    foreign investment in 307
    gold 308
    labourers in 200
    mica 201
mirasdars 22, 37
monetary: policy 250–1, 253–6
    system 250–3
moneylenders/moneylending 48,
    76, 81, 89, 116, 124–7, 133–4,
    178, 181, 202–3, 296
    Indian 202
    Marwari 125
    in small-scale 203
    village 88–9
Morris, Morris D. 144
mortgage 88, 120, 124–6, 135–6,
    232. *See also* moneylenders/
    moneylending
Mughal Empire 2, 9, 17, 19, 25–6,
    65
    as agrarian empire 34
    collapse of 24
    disintegration of 32
    fall of 19–20, 65
    fiscal system of 46
Mukherjee, Moni 5

Mutiny 2, 64–5, 125–6, 216, 245,
    301
Mysore 2, 31, 194–6, 265, 301–2,
    307–9, 311–15, 363
    Kolar goldfields in 307
    plantation in 311

Nader Shah 19
Naigawan 302
Naoroji, Dadabhai 12–13, 94
Napoleonic wars 41–2, 46
national income 5–7, 41–2, 67–70,
    78, 86, 88, 91–2, 97, 240, 246,
    254
    agriculture and 7
    export and 28
    industry and services 7
    statistics of 6, 67, 255
nationalism 14, 186
nationalization 345
natural resources 4, 13, 161, 163.
    See also under resources
nature, study of 297–9. *See*
    environmentalism
Negotiable Instruments Act of
    1881 203
Nehru, Jawaharlal 324–5
Nehru, Motilal 233
New Economic Policy 320–2
Nixon, Richard 327
nomadism 285. *See also*
    communities, pastoralists
non-agricultural activities 76–83
non-land sources 311
Norman, Montagu Sir 208

Octavius Steel 180, 191
opium trade 23, 42–5, 47, 50, 54,
    106, 243

Opium War of 1839–40, 44
Oriental Life Assurance Co,
    Calcutta 210

Parachas 48
Parsi businesses 182, 206
Partition of India 228, 283, 319,
    363
pastoralists 39, 278, 281–2
peasants 21, 36, 38–40, 43, 75–6,
    80–1, 84–5, 88–9, 110, 115–17,
    119–20, 124–6, 132–6, 270–1,
    278–9, 284, 288, 312–13,
    353–4, 358–9
    earnings of 127–31
    holdings of 136
    Jats 132
    part-time 23
    property rights of 23, 34
pedhis (banking firms) 48, 180
per capita expenditure 248
Permanent Settlement 35–6, 40–1,
    248, 289, 302
    or Zamindari Tenure 35–6
Persian-Arabic codebooks 58
Petit 180
Pitt's India Act, 1784 33, 241
plague epidemic 177, 239
plantation 43, 117, 123, 128, 167,
    172, 184–5, 189, 191–4, 196,
    198, 211–12, 312, 315
    in Anaimalai 180, 194
    in Assam 116, 190–2, 267
    coffee 194–5
    in Dooars 191–2, 194
    free recruitment in 193
    land 311–12
    in South India 194
    in Travancore and Cochin 307

political economy 35, 132, 318,
    339, 353, 359, 361, 363
political system,
    democratic 318–19, 342
population 258–66
    European 54, 210
    growth of 6, 8–9, 67–8, 130,
        258–60, 266, 269, 275, 281,
        283, 329, 331, 361
port/ports 24, 30–1, 77–8, 116–
    17, 119, 151, 153, 158, 196,
    226, 228–9, 304, 308
    cities 15–16, 24, 41, 49, 54, 64,
        83, 85, 89, 235–6, 293
    trusts 198
Portland cement 170
Portuguese, arrival of 25–6
postal system 55, 212
posts and telegraph 229–30
potters 153–5
poverty 1–2, 9, 12, 80–2, 97, 99,
    246–7, 317–18, 330, 332, 340
    eradication 318, 324
    inequality and 81–3
power looms 41, 147, 150, 158. See
    also handloom
Presidency banks 202, 204–8. See
    also banks
prices 42–3, 75, 88, 105–6,
    113–14, 125, 130, 135–6, 167,
    169–70, 223, 251–4, 271, 273,
    330
    agricultural 75, 105
    and tea trade 191. See also K.L.
        Datta committee
princely states 37, 84, 90, 101,
    161, 201, 213, 216, 231, 243,
    301–16, 319
Principles of Political Economy 35

Pringle, Robert 38
printing technology 63
private: enterprise 89, 92, 95, 212,
    217, 220, 227, 230, 278, 295–7,
    337
    investment 4, 90, 235, 256, 321,
        323, 337–8, 342, 345
    property 5, 16, 35, 119, 278,
        281, 289
privatization 331
product, domestic 3
production 1, 5, 41, 43, 45, 100,
    102, 151–2, 156–7, 190–1, 198,
    201, 211
    conditions 102–4, 325
    of grain 324
    pre-factory systems of 156
property rights 21, 23, 34–5,
    37, 40, 119, 121, 124, 133,
    283–4, 286–7, 289, 291. See also
    institutions
    in land 278–83
    reforms of 37, 40, 65
    system of 21, 35
    in water 217
protectionism 165–6, 182
proto-industrialization 145
public: health 278, 293–4, 299
    investment 63, 91, 227, 234,
        245, 247, 320, 322
    savings 247
    works 123, 131, 153, 217,
        227–8, 241, 283
public distribution of food 325
public goods 41, 55, 84, 89, 243,
    303, 312, 314, 339–41, 344,
    363
    education as 61
    State and 54–64, 89

State investment in 89
    supply of 84
Public Works Department 214, 216
public-private partnership 225, 231
Punjab 46, 48, 103–4, 106, 109–
    11, 115, 118, 125–8, 132, 158,
    215–16, 218, 233, 280–2, 354
    irrigation in 313
Punjab Land Alienation Act
    (1900–1) 125
purchasing power 146–7, 163

quality of life 193, 292, 319, 342

railways 77, 95, 104, 111–13, 115–
    19, 123–4, 138, 152, 163–6,
    185–7, 197–9, 212–14, 219–29,
    245–6, 273, 294–5, 303, 305–7,
    315, 360
    companies 95, 221, 309
    construction 45–6, 91, 212,
        217, 220–1, 223–4, 275, 297
    foreign investment in 307
    income 248
    investment in 344
    materials 152, 223
    of States 307, 311
    undercapitalization of 221
'raiyati' rights 120
Raniganj 197, 199
Rashtriya Mill Mazdoor Sangh
    (RMMS) 177
redistribution: of canal waters 291
    of land 323
reforms 33–4, 57, 196, 238, 249,
    331, 334, 337–40, 363
    of currencies 251
    in taxation 31. See also
        Institutional Reforms; see

also under land; land tax;
    property rights
remittance 50, 185, 202, 229, 250,
    255, 331
    government 92
    private 92
rent 35–6, 40–1, 75. *See also*
    tenancy
Report of the Indian Irrigation
    Commission 272
Reserve Bank of India 208, 255
resources 21–2, 25, 28–9, 33, 94–5,
    133, 135, 157, 161–6, 185, 187,
    276–80, 284–6, 295–300, 322–4
    endowments 61, 83, 115, 136–8
    financial 22, 67
    forest 285–7, 295, 312
    ground 332
    land as 21
    natural 4, 13, 143–4, 161, 163,
        189, 231, 276, 295–6, 299,
        307, 345
Restrictive Trade Practices
    Commission 325
revenue 23, 28, 37–8, 54, 217–18,
    241–2, 244–5, 247–9, 302–3,
    305–6, 308, 311–12, 315
    farming 36, 47
    payments 57
    system 21
Ricardo, David 35, 39
rivers 44, 46, 103, 110, 114–16,
    215–16, 218–19, 226–7, 288,
    290–1, 313, 319. *See also*
    resources, natural
roads 91, 95, 99, 196, 212–13,
    218–19, 226–8, 241, 246,
    305–6, 315
    investment in 227

Robb, Peter 131
Ross, Ronald 264
Royal Charters 26, 30, 32, 60
royalties 308, 311
Rungta, Radhe Shyam 178
rupee 57, 91
    devaluation of 75
    sicca as 57
    silver as 56
    trade arrangement 327
rural: assets 125, 255
    credit business 127
    credit societies 202
    development policy 323
    industry 23
    population 128, 138, 177, 332
ryotwari 37–41, 119, 132, 217, 245
    agricultural depression in 39

salt, monopoly on 54
salt tax 245, 248. *See also under*
    taxation
sanitation 194, 212, 238–9, 264,
    275, 293–4
Santal Rebellion 281, 289–90
sardari recruitment 194
Sassoons 180
savings 12, 67, 86, 88–9, 94, 179,
    182, 229, 245, 254
    and investment 85–9
scholarship 10, 56, 139, 145, 277,
    301, 313, 339
scientific forestry 298
seaboard 2, 15, 17–19, 25–6, 83, 115
Seal, Motilal 51
Select Committee on East India—
    Public Works 217
Sen, Amartya 274, 339, 363
serfdom 122, 131

Seshasayee, R. 182
Seshasayee, V. 182
settlement patterns 115, 248, 293, 319
Shah, Mohammad 19
share markets. *See* stock markets
shareholders. *See* stock markets
Shaw Wallace 180, 191
Shikarpuri bankers 182
shipbuilding 24, 49–50, 152, 283, 285
Shipping 198
shroffs 204, 207
silver rupee 57, 251
Sind 48, 103, 215, 217, 218, 270
Singh, Manmohan 337
Sino-Indian conflicts 326
Sivasubramonian, S. 5, 100, 141, 308, 352
    national income calculations of 308
skilled labour 200
services 95
small-scale industry 69, 80, 139–41, 143, 151, 155, 157–8, 181, 198–9
    modern 139–40, 158
Smith, Adam 11
socialism 326, 328, 337, 339
South Asia 1–2, 117, 153, 212, 299, 319, 326, 362, 364
    industrialization and poverty in 1
South Indian planters 191
Soviet arms 326
special economic zones 335
stagnation 2, 82
    institutional explanations for 133–6

starvation 250, 271, 274. *See also* famine
statistical systems 212, 270
sterling 44, 90–1
Stern, Philip 32
stock markets 178–9, 181, 183, 209
    Rungta on 178
    shareholders of 22, 38, 179, 184–5, 187
Stores Purchase Committee 165
strikes 44, 168, 176–7, 330. *See also* labour unrest
Subarna Baniks 49, 51
Suez Canal 78, 164, 228
Surat 28, 50, 149, 157
surface water 103, 215, 333
surplus 323
    and consumption 273
    and distribution 323
    of food 213
    of land 66, 104

Tagore, Dwarkanath 50
Tariff Board 166
tariffs 41, 78, 92, 165, 167, 187, 242–3, 322, 329, 331, 333
    protection from 167, 186
Tata, J.N. 170
Tata banking business 206
Tata Iron and Steel Company 167, 170, 175
Tatas 170, 180
taxation 21–2, 33, 35–6, 38–9, 41, 67, 90, 92, 133–4, 242–5, 248, 250, 286, 289, 344–5
    collection of 124
    farming 20, 47
    gathering procedures 20
    landlords for 34–6

on opium 245, 248
problem with river delta 291
reforms in 39
ryotwari 38
on salt 245, 248
rights 2, 20, 34, 280, 289
tax-free grants 21
tea plantations 190–1, 289, 308, 359
tea trade, international 191
tea-marketing infrastructure,
    London 192
technologies 23, 28, 140, 146–7,
    156, 199, 202, 186–7, 259,
    321–2, 329, 333, 338, 358, 360
    labour-intensive 140
    labour-saving 330
telegraph 5, 55, 107, 138, 158, 187,
    212–13, 229–30, 246, 360. See
    also post and telegraph
tenancy 36, 40, 120–1, 130, 133, 232
    and debt laws 65, 232
textiles 23–4, 27, 42, 45, 48, 158,
    161, 187, 242, 321, 323, 329,
    332. See also under commodities
    export market 42
    foreign 50
    of India 24, 27, 41
    job loss in Bengal 52
    jute 97, 164
    production 46, 143, 149, 151
    Tata 170
Thakersey 180
Third Anglo-Maratha War of 1818
    20
Third Battle of Panipat 20
Thomas Duff 180
Thompson, E.P. 171–2
Thorner, Alice 70
Thorner, Daniel 70, 72

Titaghur paper mill 170
trade 12, 15–17, 23–8, 41–8, 50–1,
    54, 69, 75–8, 105–6, 111–13,
    115–16, 156–7, 251–3, 295–6,
    303–4, 318, 351–3
    Arabian Sea 24, 45, 49
    Bay of Bengal 49
    Bengal-China 44
    caravan 24
    cotton 136, 164, 180
    domestic 46–7, 202
    and empire 32–3, 317
    export market of hide 154
    financing foreign 202
    foreign 2, 24–5, 41–6, 78, 104,
        139, 146, 163, 203, 228, 320
    foreign investment in 307
    Indo-European 49, 59
    intra-Asian 79
    long-distance 15, 113, 150, 154,
        219, 226–7
    openness to 92–4
    overland 18, 24, 44, 48, 180
    policy 242–3
    routes 78, 319
    textiles 168
trade unions 175–6, 329, 335
traders 24, 28, 33, 48, 50, 65, 81,
    157, 202–3, 251
    Dutch 26
    English 26
    European private 33
    Gujarati 180
    private 30, 43–4
    profits among 77, 80, 85, 163–4,
        179
transportation 46, 53, 66, 69, 105,
    111, 113, 115, 185–6, 190,
    196–8, 219, 226–7

Travancore 194, 307–8, 311–13, 315
   financial resources and 312
Travancore-Cochin 302, 307
Trawdi Shri Krishna Arjunji Nathji,
   Surat 50
treasury 19, 22, 251
Treaty of Nanking (1842) 44
Trevelyan, E.J. 233
tribal: councils 302
   groups 289–90.
Twomey, Michael 52, 144

underdevelopment 12, 317, 358
unemployment 51, 70, 146, 168,
   322, 334
   in industry and services 70
   seasonal 128
Union Bank, collapse of 51. *See also*
   under Banks
Union of Soviet Socialist Republics
   (USSR) 321, 325–8, 331
United Company of Merchants
   of England Trading to the East
   Indies. *See* East India Company
United States of America 79, 97,
   174–5, 204, 325–6, 328
urbanization 117, 201, 264, 305,
   307
Uruguay Round Agreement on
   Agriculture 333

village landlords 21, 33
'village republics' 22, 38
Visvesvaraya, M. 313

Wadia 180
wages 81–2, 130–1, 136, 167, 171,
   173–7, 193, 196, 200–1, 259,
   268

factory 172–3
labour by 80, 121, 140, 160–1,
   282, 287
rates of 123, 128
real 81, 127–8, 130, 147, 153,
   171, 177, 330, 352
standardization of 177
War of the Austrian Succession 30
warlords 19, 21, 33–5
waste land 278, 283
water supply 137, 217, 239, 272, 293
weavers 50, 52, 59, 140, 147–50,
   156, 168, 172, 271
   Silk 157
Weber, Max 11
welfare 9–10, 225–6, 241, 247,
   298, 301, 312, 314, 316, 341,
   344
   expenditure 247
   intervention 290–2, 300
   private capital on public 339.
   See also public goods
Western firms and governments,
   partnership with 326
W.H. Brady 180
wheat-exporting 118. *See also under*
   commodities
Wilkins, Mira 179
Williamson-Magor 180, 191
Wingate, George 39
Wingate–Goldsmid settlement 39
Wolcott, Susan 174–5
women: in industry and services
   72–3. *See also* gender.
   participation in industrial work
      72, 143
   in work participation 148
   workers 122, 146, 148, 161,
      173, 352

wood fuel 53, 151–2, 199, 283
workers 6–7, 141–3, 147, 149,
    160–1, 167–8, 171–8, 189–90,
    192, 194–6, 198, 200, 202, 334,
    337. *See also* labour
    agricultural 122–3, 130, 177
    Azamgarh 123
    coffee 195
    earnings of 127–31
    factory 81, 161, 171, 177
    in Gulf migrant as 331
    leather 153–5
    plantation 194, 359
Workmen's Breach of Contract Act.
    See Act XIII of 1859
world economy 4, 78, 105, 243,
    251, 253, 257, 317–18, 321,
    351–2, 360
    Britain and 4
    expansion of 75
    India and 2, 10, 78

world markets 98, 104, 186, 323, 337
    collapese of 133
World War I 68, 79
World War II 9, 321
    food procurement for 271
World Wars 79–80, 164, 167, 169,
    182, 186, 198–9, 228, 231, 242,
    244, 249–53, 256–7

Yang, Anand 47

zamindari 38, 41, 51, 181, 199
    estates 36, 40–1, 49, 51, 64, 120,
    199, 280
    regions 132
    sponsorship 62
    tenure 35–9
zamindars 21–2, 35–8, 40–1, 81,
    84, 120, 132, 281, 287, 289, 291
    mine lands of 200
    taxation target and 35